(Continued from front flap)

which have been of significant importance in the long-range professional development of clinical psychology. Among them are The Psychological Clinic, The Institute for Juvenile Research, The Training School at Vineland, Worcester State Hospital, The Menninger Foundation, and Wichita Guidance Center. The second section presents the role of the clinical psychologist as he operates in some of the large-scale programs in government agencies—the Veterans Administration, the Armed Services, the Public Health Service. The third section is composed of a series of descriptions of the role and function of clinical psychologists in such additional settings as the Psychiatric Clinic, a Psychological Service Center, Private Clinical Practice, a Clinic for Alcoholics, a Student Counseling Bureau, Industrial Employee Counseling; Centers dealing primarily with antisocial behavior, such as the municipal and juvenile court, training schools for delinquents, and the prison; as well as Centers dealing with educative, remedial and rehabilitative problems. Each chapter has a bibliography, and there is an extensive index.

This book is offered not only to the clinical psychologist who, busy in his own particular setting, may be unaware of how much is being done in other settings: it is offered also to psychologists in other applied and academic fields as well as to psychiatrists, social workers, anthropologists and sociologists who, despite working so closely with the clinical psychologist, often have only a vague idea of what constitutes a clinical psychologist.

SURVEY OF CLINICAL PRACTICE
IN PSYCHOLOGY

Survey of
CLINICAL PRACTICE IN PSYCHOLOGY

EDITED BY

ELI A. RUBINSTEIN, Ph.D.

Assistant Chief Clinical Psychologist, Mental Hygiene Clinic, Veterans Benefits Office, Veterans Administration, Washington, D.C.; Clinical Associate, Catholic University of America, Washington, D.C.

AND

MAURICE LORR, Ph.D.

Chief, Neuropsychiatric Research Unit, Veterans Benefits Office, Veterans Administration, Washington, D.C.; Lecturer and Research Consultant, Catholic University of America, Washington, D.C.

Foreword by Laurance F. Shaffer

INTERNATIONAL UNIVERSITIES PRESS, INC.

NEW YORK

TABLE OF CONTENTS

Part III.

REPRESENTATIVE AGENCIES AND SETTINGS MORE RECENTLY INCLUDING CLINICAL PSYCHOLOGISTS AMONG THEIR PROFESSIONAL STAFF

A. Centers Concerned Primarily with Mental Health Problems

B. Centers Dealing Primarily with Antisocial Behavior

C. Centers Concerned Primarily with Educative, Remedial, and Rehabilitative Problems

FOREWORD

LAURANCE F. SHAFFER

Clinical psychologists are busy and versatile people, as the chapters of this volume clearly show. Even experienced members of the profession find it difficult to secure a comprehensive view of all the duties that clinical psychologists perform, the many places in which they work, and the wide range of human problems with which they try to cope. No one person could prepare so informative and so provocative a survey as have the authors of these twenty-seven chapters, each writing as a first-hand participant in a distinctive specialty.

Within the apparent diversity of clinical psychology, considerable unity can be discovered. The characteristic responsibilities of clinical psychologists are similar whether they work in universities, the community, hospitals, schools, prisons, or industries. Their duties also cut across the varied kinds of persons and problems with which they deal—whether school child or neurotic adult, psychotic patient or delinquent juvenile, mental defective or unhappy senescent. With all these persons, psychologists first try to achieve an understanding based on the hypotheses of their science and the techniques of their profession. Then they apply their understandings so as to help the people help themselves. The basis of this common ground is that people are people. The major concerns of clinical psychologists are to understand them and to help them—no matter whether these activities are labeled "diagnosis" and "therapy," or called by other less pretentious names.

Clinical psychology also has historical unity; it is no johnny-come-lately among the professions. From forty to sixty years ago, as the growth of psychology began to catch up with human needs, applications were established independently and almost concurrently in a university clinic, a clinic for delinquents, a school for the feeble-minded, and a state mental hospital. Clinical psychology did not originate in one kind of setting and slowly spread to the others. Its multiple roots are of long standing. In its several places of origin the essential processes of psychology were what they are today, the assessment and remedy of human troubles, together with research to increase the breadth of understanding and the value of techniques.

Psychology has grown not so much by the invention of new basic functions as by the extension and development of the fundamental ones. In the diagnostic area, methods for assessing and describing broader aspects of personality are supplementing the older techniques for testing intelligence and school achievement. Some progress has been made in developing ways to help people. A generation ago, the seriously disturbed were only "cared for." They were "treated" hardly at all, by psychology or by any other profession. It is no wonder, then, that the earlier psychologists in mental hospitals engaged only in diagnosis and research, for treatment was almost nonexistent. The less severe problems were formerly treated with advice, teaching, and manipulation. The backward child was tutored or placed in a special class, the delinquent was moved to a foster home, and the anxious parent was given intellectual instruction on child rearing. The concept of working *with* a client to help him discover solutions to his problems, in place of working *on* him, has developed slowly but continuously.

This volume's survey of contemporary clinical psychology shows that the profession's evolution, while well under way, is still in an early stage. Its progress from the beginnings in the eighteen-nineties up to the present time is probably only a small fraction of its ultimate potentiality. In spite of six decades of experience we have only begun to know how to predict human behavior by methods of clinical assessment, or to help persons realize themselves through therapeutic efforts.

One result of the present gap between psychology's aspirations and its achievements is that many psychologists are conflicted. They are highly motivated to help people, they are under pressure to complete cases quickly because of the high ratio of patients or clients to trained workers, and they are not too sure of their methods and tools. Quite a few of the chapter authors complain, with justification, that they work under the burden of haste with makeshift, abbreviated methods which do not permit them to give the quality of service to which they aspire.

Another conflict voiced by many is that the heavy load of service robs time and energy from research. Except in universities, in large Federal agencies, and in a few other well-favored programs, psychologists have a hard time reconciling their need to help people with their equally urgent need to improve their insights and techniques by experimental development. Not only is the urgency of research acknowledged by all, but several contributors stress the value of integrating research and service. Fruitful hypotheses spring from the perplexities met while giving services, and the end results of research need to be tested for their practicability in use as well as for their broader validity.

The chapters show that clinical psychology has always had intimate relations with other professions, mainly with medicine and social work.

The issues arising from interprofessional relations have been met in the past, are very much with us in the present, and probably will remain in the indefinite future. They will never be solved once and for all. It is no surprise, however, to find that almost all contributors report good interprofessional relations in their own experiences. When sincere and well-qualified professional people work together toward common objectives, they generally acquire mutual respect. Intimacy and respect generate warm personal feelings which transcend professional labels and titles. Conflicts, in contrast, are nurtured in isolation and thrive on lack of contact and communication. By showing so many instances of professions working together harmoniously, this volume makes some contribution toward interprofessional understanding.

The future of clinical psychology seems bright if psychologists retain a high regard for human welfare, and also a constructive dissatisfaction with their modest though worth-while present accomplishments. Psychologists are wanted. Individual people and social institutions are expressing a demand for psychological services that the profession cannot now meet. The problem of the immediate future is to keep a balance between the direct services which give such prompt gratification, and the more remote but potentially greater rewards for increasing the value of all services through research.

PREFACE

Psychology is today in a period of very active professional growth, in which psychological skills and techniques are being applied to a widening variety of problems. A large share of this growth has been taking place in the specialty known as *Clinical Psychology,* and a considerable body of literature has accumulated on various technical and theoretical developments in this field. Much has been written on projective techniques, diagnostic test development, the process of psychotherapy, and research in personality dynamics. However, comparatively few attempts have been made to provide a comprehensive description of the function and role of the clinical psychologist himself. This book makes such an attempt.

There is, unfortunately, no simple or completely adequate way to provide such a survey or description of the field. We cannot, in the flux of diverse activity today, write a job description that would fit, either durably or well, the work of the majority of psychologists in the clinical area. Nor is there, at this time, any one skill or service around which revolves the rest of professional functioning. Indeed, there is no ready answer to the seemingly clear question, "What is a clinical psychologist?" And yet, as clinical psychology becomes more widely practiced, that question is being asked with increasing frequency by professional colleagues and interested laymen and, even, by the clinical psychologist himself.

The complexity involved in attempting a description of clinical psychology is due, in an important measure, to the character of psychology itself and the nature of its functioning. Psychology rarely functions alone. In an official statement by the American Psychological Association on psychology and its relationship with other professions, this point is made clear. (It should be emphasized here that clinical psychology is an integral part of the whole of psychology and not a separate professional entity.)

American psychology, because of its very nature, is involved in intricate relations with many other scientific and professional fields. Historically rooted in both philosophy and the natural sciences, some of the content of psychology overlaps that of other academic disciplines. Much of the application of psychology occurs in settings where older, more established professions are already on the scene; in other words, the psychologist applies his own techniques and insights to problems of long-standing concern to ministers, lawyers, social workers, educators, administrators, politicians, physicians, engineers, or other professional people.[1]

Because clinical psychology does operate, with other professions, in a realm of overlapping and interdependent activities it has long been concerned about its professional identity. Among the earliest attempts to fix the position of clinical psychology in the professional world were individual formulations of a definition of the field. Louttit, in 1939, collected some 40 definitions of clinical psychology and divided them into four categories. The first and largest group described clinical psychology as a study of the behavior of the individual. The second group of definitions centered around the psychometric or testing function of the psychologist. As Louttit indicated, this is a limited and unsatisfactory definition but is often the conception held by members of allied professions. The third type of definition restricted clinical psychology to the study of the subnormal or abnormal. The fourth grouping rather completely ignored clinical psychology as an offshoot of psychology and merely considered it an alternate name for a medical specialty. A survey of the literature revealed no such latter definition offered after 1925, which would seem to eliminate at least one complexity of identification by establishing, for psychology, undisputed claim to the name.

However, for professions as well as people, owning a name precedes a long and sometimes painfully slow period of extensive growth and character formation. For clinical psychology, and for the entire professional development in psychology, this painfully slow period lasted almost up to World War II. All during the twenties and thirties various professional organizations, mainly local and state, were concerned with identifying and promoting the practice of psychology. However, no single group spoke for all of professional psychology. The American Psychological Association, which would have been the obvious representative body, had, ever since its founding in 1892, restricted itself to being a scientific society. Some attempts were made, especially after World War I, to make professional issues a concern of the American Psychological Association, but each attempt was eventually abandoned. The first effective nationwide endeavor at establishing a professional organization in psychology was made in 1937, when the American Association for Applied Psychology was formed. This association was organized from previously existing groups, two of the most important being the Association of Consulting Psychologists, and the Section on Clinical Psychology of the American Psychological Association. The general proposals of this organization included consideration of the professional development of applied psychology, of which clinical psychology was an important part.

[1] *Psychology and its relations with other professions.* Washington, D. C.: American Psychological Association, 1954, p. 1.

Very soon the Association became concerned with problems of training, evaluation of qualifications, and certification of applied psychologists. Implicit in all of this was the need to explore and define the role and function of the professional psychologist. Concurrently, while the American Psychological Association was continuing as essentially a scientific society, other psychological organizations, devoted to specific interests, were being formed.

World War II had a profound effect on professional psychology and its attempts to find its own areas of application. The widely applied uses of psychology during the war provided much of the stimulation for the scope of today's professional activity. It was under the impetus of military needs that a tremendous shift in interest from academic to applied fields occurred among psychologists themselves. At the same time, the pressure and demand for psychological services led the way to co-operative and co-ordinated activity among the various national psychological organizations, who might otherwise have drifted apart, and established a favorable atmosphere for forming a unified national psychological association dedicated to the promotion of psychology as both a science and a profession. Between 1942 and 1944 various informal and formal steps were taken toward this end and, in 1945, the reorganized American Psychological Association came into being.

This reorganized American Psychological Association represents a true alliance of both academic and professional groups. The vitality of the professional growth of psychology today owes much to this unification and the consequent endowment of a continually widening scientific foundation for professional practice. Although we can make no real assessment of trends which are still very much in progress, there is no doubt that this structuring of a national organization is good assurance that professional psychology will continue to assess theory, clinical knowledge, and technical skill against each other to the mutual development of all.

All of which reaffirms the complexity involved in describing psychology as a profession and brings us back to the fact that there is no quick answer to the question, "What is a clinical psychologist?" As this book will show, the clinical psychologist is many things to many people in many places. With increasing knowledge and activity in the field, the clinical psychologist is finding himself increasingly able to offer valuable services in the observation, analysis, and readjustment of human behavior. It is, therefore, a changing and expanding role that he plays and any attempt at some general over-all definition may either be so broad as to be meaningless or so close-fitting as to be soon outgrown.

What we have attempted here is not so much a definition of clinical psychology as a composite description of the activities of clinical psychologists. We have tried to make a comprehensive survey of what, where, and how the clinician is practicing. This is neither a handbook on current theory nor a manual on the latest techniques, although both theory and technique are basic to clinical practice. Instead, we have sketched a corporate picture of the present professional status of clinical psychology by presenting a series of reports on the functioning of clinical psychologists in various settings and organizations. We have asked each contributor to discuss the relationship of clinical psychology to the particular setting in which he practices and to describe the functions of the clinician which characterize his operation in that setting or organization.

The chapters are arranged in three groups. The first section is devoted to a presentation of the development and present status of clinical psychology in some of the institutions and agencies which have been of significant importance in the long-range professional development in clinical psychology. The second section presents the role of the clinical psychologist as he operates in some of the large-scale programs in government agencies. The third section is composed of a series of descriptions of the role and function of clinical psychologists in a number of important additional and different settings in which clinical psychologists are active.

We offer this volume not only to the clinical psychologist, but to our fellow psychologists in other applied and academic areas and our associates in psychiatry, social work, anthropology, and sociology. The clinical psychologist, busy in his own particular setting, may not be aware of how much is being done by other busy psychologists in other settings. Our colleagues in other branches of psychology, and also members of other professions with whom we work, often have a vague idea of someone with a set of Rorschach cards under one hand and a Wechsler-Bellevue kit under the other, about to write a long psychological report which no one else will understand. It is from these persons, in sincere curiosity, that the query comes as to what constitutes a clinical psychologist.

The editors would like to express their appreciation to the contributing authors. In the most literal sense, this volume is theirs and could not have become an accomplishment without their generous and continuing co-operation. The editors served merely as catalytic and refining agents to fuse the material and bring the individual productions into a single publication.

The reader will note from the list of contributing authors that almost all hold important administrative positions in their respective organizations. It is important, in view of this fact, and especially in a survey of this nature, to make it clear that these psychologists are speaking for themselves and that their opinions or assertions should not be construed as reflecting the official view of the organization with which each author may be affiliated.

We are indebted to a number of colleagues for helpful comment toward the final structuring of the book. Dr. Thomas G. Andrews, Dr. J. Q. Holsopple, Dr. H. Max Houtchens, and Dr. John W. Stafford each read the entire manuscript and made constructive criticism. Dr. Albert C. Cornsweet, Dr. William W. Michaux, and Dr. Mary Tatom each read various chapters and thereby improved our editing.

Acknowledgment is made to the publishers who have granted permission to quote. In each case the source is individually cited in the text.

Eli A. Rubinstein
Maurice Lorr

CONTRIBUTING AUTHORS

1. Joseph M. Bobbitt, Ph.D., Chief, Professional Services Branch, National Institute of Mental Health, National Institute of Health, Public Health Service, Department of Health, Education, and Welfare, Washington, D.C.
2. Joseph E. Brewer, Ph.D., Director, Wichita Guidance Center, Wichita, Kansas.
3. R. A. Brotemarkle, Ph.D., Professor of Psychology, Director of the Psychological Laboratory and Clinic, University of Pennsylvania, Philadelphia, Pennsylvania.
4. Salvatore G. DiMichael, Ph.D., Executive Director, National Association for Retarded Children, New York, New York.
5. Albert Ellis, Ph.D., Clinical Psychologist in the Private Practice of Psychotherapy and Marriage Counseling, New York, New York.
6. Norman Fenton, Ph.D., Deputy Director—Classification and Treatment, State of California Department of Corrections, Sacramento, California.
7. James F. Garrett, Ph.D., Chief, Division of Program Services, Office of Vocational Rehabilitation, Department of Health, Education, and Welfare, Washington, D.C.
8. Jeanne G. Gilbert, Ph.D., Chief Psychologist, St. Charles Church Guidance Clinic, Brooklyn, New York.
9. William M. Gilbert, Ph.D., Director, Student Counseling Bureau, University of Illinois, Urbana, Illinois.
10. David Grossman, Ph.D., Co-director, Los Angeles Psychological Service Center, Los Angeles, California.
11. A. Arthur Hartman, Ph.D., Director of Psychology and Research, The Psychological Institute of the Municipal Court of Chicago, Chicago, Illinois.
12. Karl F. Heiser, Ph.D., Coordinator of Research, The Training School at Vineland, New Jersey.
13. Robert S. Herrmann, LCDR., Head, Clinical Psychology Section Neuropsychiatry Branch, Professional Division, Bureau of Medicine and Surgery, Navy Department, Washington, D.C.
14. Harold M. Hildreth, Ph.D., Chief, Clinical Psychology Division, Psychiatry and Neurology Service, Department of Medicine and Surgery, Veterans Administration, Washington, D.C.

15. Samuel Kavruck, M.A., Consultant, Office of the Surgeon General, Department of the Air Force, Washington, D.C.
16. Edith S. Lisansky, Ph.D., Psychologist, Connecticut Commission on Alcoholism, New Haven, Connecticut.
17. Martin Mayman, Ph.D., Director of Psychological Training, The Menninger Foundation, Topeka, Kansas.
18. Helmer R. Myklebust, Ph.D., Director, Children's Hearing and Aphasia Clinic, School of Speech, Northwestern University, Evanston, Illinois.
19. Frances C. Perce, M.S., Chief Psychologist, Institute for Juvenile Research, Chicago, Illinois.
20. Leslie Phillips, Ph.D., Director of Psychological Research, Worcester State Hospital, Worcester, Massachusetts.
21. Maurice Rapkin, Ph.D., Co-director, Los Angeles Psychological Service Center, Los Angeles, California.
22. Milton A. Saffir, Ph.D., Director, Psychological Guidance Center, Chicago, Illinois.
23. Herbert J. Schlesinger, Ph.D., Chief Psychologist, Department of Adult Psychiatry, The Menninger Foundation, Topeka, Kansas.
24. Stewart B. Shapiro, Ph.D., Co-director, Los Angeles Psychological Service Center, Los Angeles, California.
25. Katherine Keneally Stefic, Ph.D., Director, Remedial Clinic, Catholic University of America, Washington, D.C.
26. Matilda E. Steiner, M.A., Research Psychologist, General Electric Company, New York, New York.
27. Clare W. Thompson, Ph.D., Assistant Clinical Professor of Medical Psychology, University of California Medical School, San Francisco, California.
28. Kirk Torrance, M.A., Supervising Psychologist, Illinois State Training School for Boys, St. Charles, Illinois.
29. Marvin Waldman, A.B., Head Psychologist, Worcester State Hospital, Worcester, Massachusetts.
30. Joseph M. Wepman, Ph.D., Lecturer, Clinical Instructor in Otolaryngology, University of Chicago, Chicago, Illinois.
31. Frederick A. Zehrer, Lt. Col., Chief, Clinical Psychology Branch, Professional Division, Office of The Surgeon General, Department of the Army, Washington, D.C.
32. Stanley B. Zuckerman, Ph.D., Clinical Psychologist, State of Minnesota Department of Public Welfare, Minneapolis, Minnesota.

Part I.

CENTERS IN WHICH CLINICAL PSYCHOLOGY HAS BEEN OF LONG-STANDING SERVICE

The early history of clinical practice in psychology is closely related to the concurrent history and growth of four specific institutions: the university psychological clinic, the child guidance clinic, the mental hospital, and the institution for the mentally defective. It was within settings such as these that the clinical psychologist first developed his professional skills and initially demonstrated what he could contribute to the study and understanding of human behavior.

Of these four types of institutions, the university clinic is most closely identified with the inception of clinical psychology. Clinical psychology had its birth in a psychological clinic in 1896 and clinical psychologists, in turn, had an important role in the early development of psychological clinics. Thirteen years later the first child guidance clinic was founded and clinical psychology, from the very beginning, has functioned as an integral, important part of the expansion of the child guidance movement. At about the same time psychological testing was introduced in the mental hospital and the psychologist, since that time, has played an increasingly important role in the evaluation and treatment of psychiatric patients. The turn of the century also found psychological testing started with the mentally defective and, with this group too, the clinical psychologist has had a continuing and vital part in the total care and treatment.

It is therefore most appropriate that this survey begin with descriptions of the functioning of the clinical psychologist in representative centers within these four groups of institutions.

I.

THE PSYCHOLOGICAL CLINIC, UNIVERSITY OF PENNSYLVANIA

R. A. BROTEMARKLE

In the autumn of 1896, Lightner Witmer (1) presented to the meetings of the American Psychological Association a "new method of research and instruction" which he called "The Clinical Method in Psychology and the Diagnostic Method of Teaching." His program suggested "the examination of physical and mental conditions of school children," "the study of defective children," "the establishment of a psychological museum with a collection of specimens of work done by defective children and of instruments, apparatus, and results of investigations of normal and defective children," and "the establishment of an experimental training school for the remedial treatment of deviates."

Witmer had returned to Pennsylvania in 1892, after study abroad with Wundt, to become Director of The Psychological Laboratory. Within four years the emerging concept of "clinical psychology" resulted in Witmer's founding the world's first Psychological Clinic at the University of Pennsylvania in 1896.

Witmer's methods with and discussions of individual cases were directed to three basic procedures. The first was the "diagnostic" procedure seeking to obtain an "understanding of the behavior of the individual." It was based upon a thoroughgoing genetic point of view. It included a comprehensive examination with quantitative test results, qualitative evaluations of the test performance, and information from sources such as medicine, education, and sociology. The second was the "prognostic" procedure directed toward the "prediction of human behavior." Witmer, insisting that "every diagnosis is a prognosis," placed great weight upon the determination of the range of variability both in the individual pattern of behavior and in the situation or environment. The third was the "treatment" procedure directed toward enabling the "individual to make the best possible adjustment." The consideration of human adjustment revealed to Witmer several challenging aspects; the "creative" emphasis requiring the unfolding of the individual's insight; the "developmental" emphasis requiring continuing study of the stages of adjustment; the "corrective" emphasis necessitating more or less extensive retraining; and the "preventative" emphasis requiring manipulation of the individual's behavior and environmental situation.

Immediately Witmer announced the establishment of a basic program for training specialists for the "new profession" of "clinical psychologist." The program included "training from other sources than the usual course of instruction in psychology." From the beginning he emphasized the fact that this specialized training must be based upon a thoroughgoing grounding in the scientific knowledge of general systematic and experimental psychology, and extensive course and practicum training in a psychological clinical facility.

During the next ten years Witmer had the co-operation and inspiration of many leading medical authorities at the University, including Drs. S. Weir Mitchell, Charles K. Mills, William G. Spiller, Harrison Allen, Alfred Stengel, William C. Posey, George C. Stoutt and Joseph Collins; each recognized for his expertness in a wide variety of medical specializations. He likewise had the co-operation of Miss Clara H. Town, Resident Psychologist at the Friends' Asylum, public school superintendents and special class teachers in the city and nearby metropolitan area, and a number of special class teachers for the blind, the deaf and the mentally retarded.

Recognizing that the "greater number of students, equipped to carry on the work of clinical psychology" were to be found in the neighborhood of the University, Witmer entered upon a period of extension of the new work. In 1907 he established a new journal, *The Psychological Clinic,* hoping thus to extend the work, and secure the co-operation of those who were "developing clinical psychology throughout the country."

THE DEVELOPMENT OF THE PSYCHOLOGICAL CLINIC

During the formative years of the Clinic, Witmer had more than adequate co-operation and consultation of a number of outstanding medical examiners in the diagnostic work of the Clinic, as well as the insistent pressure of public and private class-room teachers—the primary source of many early cases—for developing methods of specialized training. Witmer's interest in the remedial treatment of curable or "restorative" cases, and his recognition of his own lack of experience, resulted almost immediately in his securing the services of a teacher skilled in the tedious continuing study and training of deviates. Through continued development this specific phase of remedial teaching took on the more important aspects of "diagnostic teaching," suggested by Witmer in his earlier discussions and slowly set the pattern of development for several years. The development of special remedial methods resulted in the continuing appointment of a Clinic Teacher as a member of the Clinic staff, and the effectiveness of thorough medical examination resulted in Witmer maintaining a Medical Examiner on the Clinic staff for some years, until referral to the various divisions of the Medical School and University Hospital became a satisfactorily established practice.

In 1909 the University administration recognized the importance of this new development and established it more firmly with status and financial support. At this point the general pattern of the staff of the Psychological Clinic took on the form which has continued with only slight variations, dependent upon individual experience and special training, to the present. The Staff included the following:

Director
Assistant Director
Executive Officer
Psychological Examiners (Clinical Psychologists—Ph.Ds.)
Psychological Examiner Assistants (Psychometricians)
Social Workers
Clinical Teachers (Diagnostic Remedial Teachers)
Medical Consultants
Psychological Consultants
Recorders (Stenographic and Clerical)

From the beginning the dual purpose of the Clinic included the maintenance of the highest level of effective individual clinical service commensurate with the training of students in a large variety of clinical activities. The individual case load, at first limited, grew as trained staff became available and the variety of clinical activities slowly developed as specialized divisions or separate clinics within The Psychological Clinic.

Witmer's primary and continuing interest was with children—defective, normal, and superior. His clinic program included a large variety of childhood problems more recently characterized as Special Class problems. It included the diagnosis, clinical teaching, training, and treatment of educational and behavior problems of normal, inferior, and superior levels of mental ability, and a wide range of speech, hearing, sight and other physical, mental, emotional, and social maladjustments. This division of the Clinic was later designated the General Mental Clinic, and was scheduled in one to three sections during the week to afford practicum training and service at the childhood level.

The second division or special clinic was the result of the challenged interest of Edwin B. Twitmyer (1) in the problems of speech. The demands for service and training in speech correction warranted the establishment of a separate Speech Correction Clinic in 1914. This special service extended beyond the child level, and has maintained two sections for service and practicum training for many years.

Morris S. Viteles (1), having developed a comprehensive interest in the special problems of vocational and industrial selection, guidance, and adjustment, established a special division of the Clinic in 1920 to become known as the Vocational Guidance Clinic. This division has maintained service and practicum training at the teen-age and adult level in one or two sections; and was the primary source of emphasis of the clinical point of view in vocational guidance and industrial psychology.

Following an increasing interest in college personnel problems, one of Witmer's students and colleagues was appointed Personnel Officer of the College at the University of Pennsylvania in 1926. He immediately adapted the clinical point of view and methodology to the problems of the college-adult level in the work of the College Personnel Office. In 1932, Robert A. Brotemarkle (1) established a separate division of the Clinic known as the Personnel Clinic to extend this clinical service to the other undergraduate schools of the University and to nearby college and secondary school students. This division at the same time established specialized practicum training facilities within the program of The Psychological Clinic. Later broadened to include personality adjustment problems of the college-adult and adult level, this division has been carried on in one or two sections throughout the ensuing years.

During the years the Department of Psychology regularly announced in its program of professional courses the Field Work or practicum courses in each of the above separate specialized division of The Psychological Clinic. During the early years in each new application or division the Department was dependent upon this pattern of training until a number of agencies or institutions had developed facilities with trained staffs in which such training might be supplemented. While in recent years the Department has frequently sent students to a variety of agencies for specialized training and internship experience, The Psychological Clinic has consistently made available extensive training under the direct supervision of members of the clinical staff who were members of the instructional staff of the Department.

Included among the earlier facilities available were the Neurological Clinic and the Psychiatric Clinic of the University Hospital manned by many of Witmer's closest medical supporters. Because of Witmer's close association with the staffs of the Medical School, the Department of Biological Sciences, and the University Hospital, it was to be anticipated that Witmer would insist that his students majoring in clinical psychology have immediate contact with and limited training in the areas of abnormal behavior regularly dealt with by the medical profession. This was long secured through a close relationship with the University Hospital Clinics and medical school courses. Advanced students attended medical school lectures, demonstrations, and from time to time received limited training commensurate with medical responsibility. Within the years, increased enrollments in both the Medical School and Department of Psychology necessarily limited this co-operative training. In time, supervised psychological training was limited to the work of the several divisions or special Clinics of The Psychological Clinic itself, and full-time internship training was limited almost entirely to postdoctoral "on-the-job" experience. The "team" concept and function had fallen short of complete development.

With the development of the medical or mental hygiene emphasis in clinical psychology during and following World War II it was a readily acceptable step to meet the need for special training in the team situation in established University Hospital Clinics.

In 1947 the Department of Psychology announced practicum courses for majors in clinical psychology in co-operation with the University Hospital Clinics in Neurology and Psychiatry. The Department of Psychology secured the appointment of Dr. George Gammon, Professor of Neurology in the Medical School, and Director of the Neurological Clinic in the University Hospital, and Dr. Kenneth Appel, Professor of Psychiatry, and Director of the Functional (Psychiatric) Clinic in the University Hospital to the instructional staff of the Department of Psychology. A practicum for the training of clinical psychologists in the Neurological Clinic was established under the supervision of a clinical psychologist, a member of the instructional staff of the Department of Psychology and a psychological examiner in the Psychological Clinic. This dual arrangement established clinical psychological service in the Neurological Clinic and made available practicum training for clinical psychology majors in a team setting in a neurological clinic. At the same time a practicum for training clinical psychologists in a functional (psychiatric) clinic was established under a clinical psychologist, a member of the instructional staff of the Department of Psychology and a psychological examiner in the Psychological Clinic. This dual arrangement established clinical psychological service in the Functional Clinic and made available practicum training for clinical psychology majors in a team setting in a functional clinic. At this time the Department of Psychology announced in the graduate Bulletin, field work on practicum courses for clinical psychology majors in a neurological clinic and a functional (psychiatric) clinic for the first time.

In light of the above developments it is readily apparent that no completely satisfactory psychological internship training in the team situation was available in the proximity of the University and that the Department was under the necessity of taking responsibility for the establishment of such a training center. Accordingly, in 1947, the Department of Psychology established a Psychological Internship Center in the Philadelphia General Hospital, under the supervision of a clinical psychologist, a member of the instructional staff of the Department of Psychology, and a pyschological examiner in the Psychological Clinic. The Philadelphia General Hospital is a large city hospital making available experience in neurological and psychiatric clinics and in the entire range of related medical services. This arrangement made available for the first time a postdoctoral level of psychological clinical service to the Philadelphia General Hospital, and an internship practicum for majors in clinical psychology in a team situation, thus affording opportunity for advanced training in diagnostics, research, and orientation in psychotherapy with a large population of wide age range and in a variety of general medical and medical specialization settings.

At this time the Department of Psychology discontinued the former custom for its graduates to secure internship experience in a medically oriented status subsequent to the doctoral degree, and required that majors in clinical psychology preparing for service in the team setting complete a year of internship training as part of their training for the doctoral degree. The announcement informed candidates that they might complete such internship requirement in the Department Internship Center at the Philadelphia General Hospital or any other internship center approved by the Group Committee. No satisfactory certification program having been established to date, final approval rested upon the recognition of standards fully acceptable to the Group Committee upon recommendation of the staff of The Psychological Clinic.

THE PRESENT STATUS OF THE PSYCHOLOGICAL CLINIC

The policy of The Psychological Clinic is toward the maintenance of the most effective psychological clinical service commensurate with the training of advanced graduate students to the level of professional clinical proficiency in a variety of clinical applications, with high skill in the basic clinical approach in a single area of specialization, and with background knowledge available for and adaptable to related areas of professional activity. This statement of dual purpose on occasion has been ordered in a primary and secondary emphasis. Present policy is determined upon the conviction that the two purposes are concomitant and of equal importance and significance in a university setting.

Such policy can, in all probability, be understood only in light of the fact that the Department of Psychology is an autonomous department responsible for all instruction in psychology within the several undergraduate and graduate schools or divisions of a large university. It is not readily found in diversified or separated departments or psychological groups frequently observed in some university settings.

The basic methodology revolves about the individual case study. Witmer's original choice of the term *clinical* was for the single purpose of giving emphasis to the individual approach. In the broadest sense this is the "client-centered" method. In a specific psychological technical sense it involves the use of the most effective tests and techniques in individual examination. Quantitative measurements are obtained and estimates made in terms of known reliability and established indicators of variability. The clinical examiner, experienced in the observation of test performance, arrives at a qualitative interpretation of the individual's behavior, and thus gains a judgment of individual competency, efficiency and proficiency. This information is studied in light of the entire case record, including family and individual history, medical record, school and/or work history, social investigation record, and all pertinent facts obtainable through original application for service, original interview, and previously established individual case problem.

The resultant prognosis leads directly to recommendations necessary to conclude the most effective solution of the case problem. In line with the direct responsibility of the clinical psychologist, this may include his co-operative participation in, direction of, or actual execution of treatment procedures. The level of responsibility will in most instances be determined by the clinical psychologist's skill in the effective use of directive and/or nondirective counseling techniques and a wide range of insight producing and retraining procedures.

In many instances the insistent demand will be for the use of established and proven techniques; however, one must not lose sight of the fact that all professions dealing with human reactions and behavior must frequently resort to well-considered and objectively controlled experimentation. The latter necessity is not a professional deterrent or limitation. It is the challenge which calls upon the thoroughgoing and continuing scientific knowledge and experience of the professional worker. It is the grass-roots research source of progress in all applications of science.

In reviewing my former writing and discussions of clinical psychology, I find that my efforts were largely directed to the consideration of an operational definition in terms of the functions involved. I now find that I cannot deviate greatly from my former statement of the over-all functions of the Clinic. In 1931 I wrote:

The specific details of functions which characterize the activities of the Clinic as the writer has frequently said, may be summarized as follows:

(1) to make an analysis of individual reaction patterns and capacities; (2) to discover the etiology of these reaction patterns and capacities; (3) to interpret the integration of their inter-organization in individual behavior; (4) to study the adjustment of the individual on the basis of the above; (5) to outline methods and detail procedures of adjustment; and (6) to recommend, assist with, or, on occasion, to direct the application of these methods [1, p. xix].

THE PSYCHOLOGICAL CLINIC

THE GENERAL MENTAL CLINIC

The General Mental Clinic is the oldest division of The Psychological Clinic and continues the clinical activity with children of approximately three to fifteen years. It has been traditionally the initial source of individual clinical experience with resultant emphasis upon basic orientation.

It is well planned to give the student his first opportunity to apply his knowledge in a real life situation. It presumes upon basic training or laboratory drill in the use of more commonly employed test techniques, sound applicable knowledge of developmental psychology, and knowledge of, and orientation to the nature and causes of maladjustment. It is structured under the strict supervision and responsibility of a clinical examiner or clinical psychologist.

Dealing with children presenting a wide variety of intellectual, educational and behavior problems, it presents considerable flexibility of service and training. In almost every case the necessity of dealing with the parents, in regard to their contribution to the understanding of and dealing with the problem, tends to set the course along a more over-all directive type of counseling. The development of insight and co-operation frequently requires a considerable degree of informality.

Rapport is most frequently established on the basis of parental need, and by transfer to the child. The initial interview permits the completion of the case history, an estimate of social maturity by the social worker, and observation of the child's test-entrance feelings and attitudes.

The student trainee must be highly motivated to maintain the formalized procedures of standardized tests, and at the same time develop skills in the observation of test performance. He must become adept in the use of less formalized testing and investigation of reactions. Overcoming the preoccupation with test procedures he must rapidly bring to bear upon the case problem his full background of pertinent knowledge and keenness of analysis.

The diagnostic interview, varying with the feelings and attitudes of parents, proceeds to relate the findings to the entire range of activity involved in the case problem, including the home, school and community. This may require an extension of testing, or study under clinical teaching, referral to other divisions of the Clinic, or referral to appropriate community agencies for further examination, counseling or treatment.

The counseling interview, following staff conference, seeks to arrive at a practical, feasible and productive program of treatment. The great breadth of problems necessitates a wide range of flexibility for the Clinic, including more or less extensive clinical or remedial teaching and training, individual or parental counseling, school or other community agency referral, or minimal informal parent report.

The student trainee, having been under continuing supervision, and in frequent conference, finds his knowledge and experience established best by the necessity of integrating it in a comprehensive report. Tedious training in reporting cases is the most specific device for motivation to thoroughness in clinical examination, observation, discussion and overall clinical effectiveness.

Probably the most challenging and threatening experience of the student trainee is the sudden recognition of the protection assured him by the presence and final responsibility of an accredited clinical psychologist, and the awakening of the awareness of responsibilities which he must slowly accept, in anticipation of the time when he must assume final and full responsibility.

The variations within this division of the Clinic are slight in terms of the previous historical discussion, since it is the earliest and continuing basic area of application of clinical philosophy and methodology.

Remedial teaching and treatment. Concurrent with trainee progress through a variety of clinic practicums and course work in theory and research in psychotherapy, the majors in clinical psychology are trained in the specialized remedial teaching of young children, and the treatment of behavior and personality problems of children. The age range is usually below fourteen years, and a wide variety of case problems encourages a considerable breadth of experience.

The trainee is disciplined in establishing a good relationship with the child in a permissive but controlled and supervised atmosphere, and the use of nondirective permissive play therapy in a warm but "controlled freedom within limits" environment. Direct supervision and intense conference study and discussion lead to training in interviews and conferences with parents.

Frequent referral of more disturbed cases requiring long-term therapy develops an understanding of responsibility levels, and the patterning of reports for referral conference and follow-up. Such referral experience leads to an understanding of the type of complex problems which the trainee will meet in advanced internship training.

The clinical psychologist in charge of this program of service and training is experienced in the specialized techniques and procedures of remedial teaching and therapy.

THE SPEECH CORRECTION CLINIC

The Speech Correction Clinic continues one of the earliest applications of clinical psychology to a specific problem area. Speech correction is herein considered to be a special area of clinical psychology. It is established upon the acceptance of the speech therapist as a professional specialist, rather than a school teacher with an area of specialized preparation and limited training. This specialization presumes upon the previous knowledge and training basic to advanced specialization in clinical psychology, the added knowledge of certain specific course content in speech problems, and orientation to the special area.

The student trainees under strict supervision receive training in speech examinations of children and adults, including the formal and informal procedures now effective in the area. The evaluation of speech in a clinical setting necessitates the interviewing of the client, and frequently his parents, relatives, colleagues, teachers, or employer, in order that a final evaluation of the present status and effectiveness of speech may be ascertained.

Since such procedures are readily productive of diagnosis, they lead quite directly into the necessity of the Clinic proceeding to therapy in a large variety of speech disorders. This most frequently requires extensive training within the clinic situation. Basic student trainee experience in speech correction and therapy requires intensive work in a variety of given emphases, usually obtained during progressive stages over two or three years. Dependable skill must be attained in dealing with stuttering, cleft palate, aphasia, and other specific speech disorders.

In a number of instances the therapeutic procedures must be clearly delineated to school teachers, parents or others, who will assist in the training of the individual, and frequently requires the training of parents in certain specialized procedures.

The problems of rapport in this area are belabored by the added disturbances of normal speech communication, and the student trainees must rapidly meet the difficulties arising from the patient's feelings and attitudes based on such embarrassing limitations. Among his rewards will be the rapid progress attainable in simpler problems, and among his challenging threats the failure of progress in more complex and difficult cases. The assurance based upon the presence and supervision of an accredited speech correctionist, who is also a clinical psychologist, is most fundamental to his development of self-responsibility.

The Vocational Guidance Clinic

The Vocational Guidance Clinic continues the application of the "dynamic concepts" of clinical psychology in the field of vocational psychology. The "individual is made the point of departure for a thorough examination" (2) of every factor bearing upon his vocational interests and the development of insight for individual vocational choice. The present age range is from senior year secondary school through adults, and includes the entire range of vocational adjustment problems. The Clinic is conducted primarily as a practicum for graduate students; however, a limited number of outstanding senior undergraduate majors, who have expressed an interest in industrial, vocational or personnel psychology, are given limited orientation in the work in anticipation of graduate training. Vocational and industrial adjustment is studied with "due regard for the unity of the organism," and the "whole personality adjustment against a background of objective conditions to which the client is called upon to adjust himself." Herein an "adequate diagnosis involves interpretation of a trained psychologist, based on observation of performance, and a consideration of related data." The clinical psychologist must be "grounded in the principles and techniques of general and applied psychology," and have a "thorough knowledge of the theoretical and practical aspects and procedures of abnormal psychology." Orientation is directed toward "the normal" based on the "inherent objectivity of the psychological approach."

Student trainees receive supervised practice in the administration, scoring, and interpretation of tests of general and special aptitudes, interests and personality adjustment; attend regular staff conferences for the presentation and discussion of case reports; conduct initial interviews; participate in counseling interviews; and are trained in the writing of comprehensive case reports. Conference hours also include reports and discussions on procedures, techniques and basic information, including occupational information, interviewing, aptitude testing, guidance counseling, research and follow-up programs.

The over-all limitations of the usual trainee's educational process and employment experience, and the lack of breadth of necessary occupational information, as well as the lack of work experience basic to the interpretation of the latter, inherently limits the speed of progress toward the "counseling interview" training level. Such progress usually requires two or three academic terms of practicum experience, frequently in conjunction with special summer employment experience of an internship type.

The expressed and tested interests of the individual in terms of occupational activity, hobbies, extracurricular activities in school, and other

pertinent activities are weighed in relation to the many factors of educational history and status, physical history and status, competency, aptitudes, personality factors, economic and social factors, in the integrated
study of the individual problem. On occasion certain information may
be more readily obtained from his home, parental, school or occupational
contacts.

Recommendations are particularly pertinent to appropriate occupation, preparation for and entrance into the chosen occupation, and the
frequent need of extended counseling of a formal or informal nature.

The age level warrants a considered use of nondirective interviewing
and counseling, leading first toward a complete understanding on the
part of the individual as to his participation in the procedures of the
clinic, and, secondly, toward the development of individual insight directed toward the individual's final determination of his own vocational
choice.

The College Personnel and Personality Adjustment Clinic

The College Personnel and Personality Clinic continues clinical psychological service to college undergraduates, graduate students, and
college adults in a variety of educational and personal problems. The
educational problems frequently include varied aspects of vocational and
professional training and adjustment; the personal problems include the
entire range of socioindividual problems related to academic and professional training and adjustment.

The interviewing and examining techniques include extensive use of
measures of intellectual competency, interests, attitudes, study habits,
personality analysis and specialized techniques. The Clinic lends itself
to the development of such specialized techniques as "An analytical technique for use in the guidance of the multi-job-experienced college adult."
This is fundamentally a projective device leading to an insightful understanding of the relative significance of intellectual and emotional factors
in the work adjustment of the individual who has moved through a
variety of job experiences; and most frequently directing the solution of
deep-seated personal reaction patterns which were disturbing factors in
the previous work experience and adjustment of the individual. The age
range and educational status of the clients warrant a considerable emphasis upon nondirective interviewing and counseling techniques.

The diagnostic interview is frequently extended over two or three
sessions, and supportive and analytical therapy may extend over several
sessions. Long-term therapy is seldom attempted.

The practicum training of this clinic is based on prerequisite academic
knowledge and drill in a large variety of testing procedures and interpretation of measurements. Rapid progress in entrant or problem inter-

viewing is attained by supervision, conferences and discussions based on observation and recorded data. Counseling interview training is dependent upon development of rapport and basic knowledge of the problem area. The close proximity of the educational problem—a recent and continuing experience of the student trainee—is more productive of progress in counseling interviews in this clinic situation than in most other immediate clinical experience. This proximity of experience warrants the opportunity to develop the most basic attitudes of objectivity of observation of test performance and the development of "nondirective" insights. Direct supervision is maintained, and indirect supervision is secured by use of the one-way observation facilities of the Clinic and is participated in by the staff and other student trainees.

Levels of responsibility are essential elements of trainee experience in light of the referral of many cases by personnel officers and other administrative contacts of the University or nearby colleges. Certain cases, so referred, are in the pattern of screening procedures to determine the necessity of referral to medical responsibility. Referrals are frequently made to the Student Health Service, or directly to the Functional Disease Clinic of the University Hospital. Since cases carried by this Clinic are solely within the range of normal considerations, the student trainee receives basic training in the comprehension of necessities of referral. Proceeding from this Clinic to training in a clinic in a medical setting, the trainee has some preliminary understanding of the simpler level problems which he will contact in the medical orientation.

The development of personality structure reports, recommendations, and thorough case reports is oriented to the transmission of reports to appropriate referrants and continuing referrals, and is basic to entrance into the team pattern clinical experience.

THE PSYCHOLOGICAL CENTER IN THE NEUROLOGICAL CLINIC

This division of the Psychological Clinic was established in the Neurological Clinic in the University Hospital for the dual purpose of rendering psychological service to the Neurological Clinic, and giving practicum training to advanced graduate majors in clinical psychology in a neurological setting. It is of the basic interdisciplinary pattern of university educational and research training. The clinical psychologist in charge is an individual experienced in service and research in extensive neurological investigations. The case range in the Neurological Clinic and related hospital divisions such as Neurosurgery and Pediatrics, presents service and practicum training in a wide variety of medical problems.

The primary function of the practicum training is of the team pattern, with emphasis upon the job of the clinical psychologist, and for the purpose of broadening clinical experience and development of confidence in responsibility levels of the psychologist. Most basic is the recognition of the levels of responsibility in a specialized medical setting.

The student trainee has previously developed skills in a large variety of clinical examining techniques, interviewing and counseling techniques, and preparation of reports. He has acquired basic knowledge in abnormal psychology, internal medicine, and physiology; general experimental systematic psychology and research; and has had orientation in simple levels of psychotherapy. He is here faced with the challenge to develop sophistication in the application of clinical psychology in a specific medical orientation.

The basic philosophy of this practicum relates to the fundamental concept that a patient's problems are best understood when medical, psychological and social work-ups are co-ordinated in a complete team activity. To this end basic training is given in establishing rapport with patients and staff, formal and informal interviewing techniques, consultation and conference techniques, and the preparation of specialized reports.

The Psychological Center in the Functional Disease Clinic

This division of the Psychological Clinic was established in the Functional Disease Clinic of the University Hospital for the dual purpose of rendering psychological service to the Functional Disease Clinic and giving practicum training to advanced graduate majors in clinical psychology in a psychiatric setting. The clinical psychologist in charge is an individual experienced in service and research in extensive psychopathological investigations.

The case range is from approximately two years and upward, and includes a wide variety of functional, organic, and psychosomatic disorders. Most frequently, cases referred to the clinical psychologist are of the more difficult type classed as borderline between neurosis and psychosis. Referral is entirely on the basis of the case problem and necessitates the selection of a variety of specialized techniques and procedures.

The clinical psychologist, appointed with his department rank in the Department of Psychiatry in the Medical School, is responsible for the teaching of medical residents and fellows in psychiatry. This is carried on by individual conferences, staff discussions, lectures and group discussions. The content includes projective techniques, experiments in group therapy, interpersonal and group relations, psychological health, experimental design and research problems.

The practicum training of majors in clinical psychology is based on former prerequisite academic course work, drill or laboratory work in a variety of examining techniques, practicum experience in normal personality problems, and related medical and physiological knowledge. The case method of teaching is employed. The breadth of case experience varies with the regular case load of the Clinic.

Case studies are oriented toward a dynamic, but not necessarily historical, description of personality. Results of specific tests are seldom presented in staff conferences in lieu of an attempt to integrate all results of the psychological examination in an internally consistent pattern, and without rigid theoretical orientation. Interviewing and examining are under direct psychological supervision. The writing of reports is carried on under repeated consultation with the clinical psychologist. Great care is taken to differentiate between interpretation of findings, inferences and speculations. Case reports are presented under supervision, in the team staff conferences. Comprehensive training is given in the levels of responsibility, and the trainee is thoroughly oriented to the status of the clinical psychologist and psychiatric medical staff.

Limited facilities are available for psychological research, and an extensive research program on objective measures of psychopathology and learning in psychopathology are now in the initial stages of organization of space and equipment. Trainees will in this way be introduced to the basic psychological research problems within the medical setting of a functional clinic.

Opportunity for psychotherapy under medical supervision is abundant. Work in psychotherapy is limited on the part of the clinical psychologist solely by other duties and responsibilities. Trainee participation is limited to observation orientation in preparation for internship experience.

The Clinical Psychology Internship Center at the Philadelphia General Hospital

The Clinical Psychology Internship Center of the Department of Psychology is established in the Philadelphia General Hospital. It is directly connected with the Neuropsychiatric Department therein, and participates in the function of the large number of medical departments found only in such large city hospital units.

The clinical psychologist is a member of the Department of Psychology instructional staff and staff of The Psychological Clinic. He is experienced in the medically oriented psychological service and research of the team pattern. While rendering service to the Hospital in the present internship activity the presently expanding psychological staff of the Hospital is relieving the burden of service, and permits concentration on the primary purpose of internship supervision.

The internship program has as its purpose the development of "sensitive" and "disciplined" observers of psychological adjustment. "Sensitivity" has to do with the ability to discriminate those more or less subtle patterns of behavior—whether responses to a test or spontaneous verbal expression in an interview—which reflect a client's pattern of adjustment. "Discipline" has to do with the rigorous application of empirical and logical criteria in evaluating the meaning and significance of various behaviors.

The attempt of this fourfold program is: First, to familiarize the trainee with the numerous patterns of psychopathology; second, to increase his skill in the application of various diagnostic instruments, particularly the projective techniques; third, to increase the trainee's awareness of the significant psychological problems demanding further research, to develop his research skills, and afford him an opportunity for basic research; and fourth, to introduce the trainee to the practical aspects of psychological therapy and develop skills in handling therapeutic relationships with individuals and with groups of children and adults.

The training program is based upon the policy of the Department of Psychology, which requires that a major in clinical psychology shall have completed his course requirements, practicum requirements, and preliminary doctorate examinations before entering upon internship experience. This is a practical reflection of our long historical relationship with the medical faculties of the University, and reaches toward an internship in which the trainee can anticipate the most effective and comprehensive training experience. Upon completion of this program it is anticipated that the clinical psychologist will be able to assume a responsible position in a clinical, research or teaching setting.

This then is the picture of the functioning of clinical psychology at The Psychological Clinic. It has been a program of steady development and consistent expansion. Present trends include the extension of teaching responsibility to include instruction of undergraduate Medical School students, particularly on the part of clinical psychologists connected with the practicums in the Neurological Clinic and the Functional Disease Clinic, the development of basic research and experimentation with clinical techniques, the extension of interdisciplinary service and training in the newly established Rehabilitation Clinic in the University Hospital; and the heightened recognition of professional responsibility for the job which the clinical psychologist can do best.

REFERENCES

1. Brotemarkle, R. A. (Ed.) *Clinical psychology—Studies in honor of Lightner Witmer.* Philadelphia: Univer. of Pennsylvania Press, 1931.
2. Viteles, M. S. *Industrial psychology.* New York: W. W. Norton, 1932.

II.

INSTITUTE FOR JUVENILE RESEARCH, STATE OF ILLINOIS

FRANCES C. PERCE

By 1900 Chicago was showing serious concern over the problems of its delinquent and dependent children. The need to control and assist these children resulted in the establishment of the Cook County Juvenile Court, but this, it was soon discovered, only partly met their needs. In 1909, therefore, a group of public-spirited citizens furnished the funds necessary for a team of professional persons to make a five-year study of the children who came into the court. Dr. William Healy was chosen as the director of the clinic, which was first called the Juvenile Psychopathic Institute.

At the end of the five-year demonstration period, during which time the team diligently pursued its studies into the reasons for children's misbehavior, the Juvenile Court assumed responsibility for the clinic and maintained it until 1917, when it was taken over by the State of Illinois.

Meanwhile Dr. Healy and his assistant, Dr. Augusta Bronner, had returned to Boston to organize the Judge Baker Guidance Center. The state chose Dr. Herman M. Adler of the Psychiatric Department of the Harvard University Medical School as the new director of the clinic to which it gave the name of The Institute for Juvenile Research. As a state institution, the services of the Institute were made available to any child in the state up to the age of eighteen, and its focus broadened to include the prevention of personality disorders as well as their correction. The following quotation from the statute which established it indicates the magnitude of the charge and responsibility placed on the Institute by the state:

The Division herein created shall conduct scientific studies, diagnose and promote the treatment of children who are delinquent, mentally ill, mentally defective, or socially maladjusted, or who are in danger of becoming so, to the end that delinquency, crime, mental disorders, and other forms of human maladjustment may be prevented. In the administration of this Act, the Division shall make personal examination and social studies of such children and shall make its services and treatment available to children in the custody or under the control of the Department of Public Welfare, or of any court, school, public or private social agency, or parent or guardian [3, p. 379].

Historically, the Institute for Juvenile Research was the first child guidance clinic in America to study and treat personality and behavior disorders of children. Its beginnings and growth reflect the child guidance movement. From the first, recognition of the need to study an individual child from many different viewpoints and to use as many techniques as warranted has been basic.

The original staff, in addition to Dr. Healy, included a psychologist and a social worker, the latter being loaned from a private agency. Thus, the psychiatric team, as it is known today, began functioning in the examination of the child. Obviously, since pioneer work in the testing field had just begun, the early efforts of the staff were directed not only to investigating the applicability of the few available instruments, but to devising and standardizing its own. In addition to tests of general intelligence and achievement, tests for special abilities and functions, such as memory power, attention, language, foresight, and planfulness, were included in the battery used. In interpreting the test results, the need for caution and a constant awareness of the life experiences of the child were stressed.

As a state agency, the Institute, while it maintained its headquarters in Chicago, soon had the responsibility for meeting requests for the examination of children from 102 counties. In the Institute's early years awareness of its existence was limited pretty much to workers in children's agencies, both public and private, institutions, and local schools. In addition to the diagnostic examinations given as part of the team approach, the psychology department was asked to make surveys of ungraded rooms and institutions. A few down-state clinics were held. (Any clinic outside of Chicago is considered a down-state clinic.) These clinics were at that time called "traveling" clinics and were arranged at the request of the local communities. It was the belief of the Institute that the clinic's chance of success was much greater if there were enough interest and unity in a community to organize and plan for the visit of the team. Further, as soon as a community had raised sufficient funds to hire its own psychiatrist, psychologist, or social worker, the Institute staff worker from that profession could be relieved from work in the local clinic to serve elsewhere. This arrangement worked out successfully in several of the large communities. Most often it was the social worker who was hired locally, but in several instances the community was able to supply the services of a psychologist and a social worker. However, experience over the years has demonstrated the difficulties the local community finds in setting up a complete unit in the child guidance field without outside help.

By 1921, the annual report of the Institute included a description of the work of the psychologist in the clinic and the surveys undertaken in certain state institutions. The work at that time was chiefly diagnostic, but there was also participation in staff decisions. The test most frequently used was the 1916 Revision of the Stanford-Binet, but there were also supplementary tests for the "higher mental processes" which included association, attention, apperception, memory, special ability, language, and mechanical aptitude.

During the 1920's there continued to be surveys of state institutions and the individual examinations proceeded along much the same lines as formerly. At the same time, the psychology department was developing specialists in educational and vocational counseling to meet the demand for these services which were lacking in the community. So many children with special reading disabilities were being referred that several members of the department were asked to assume the responsibility for their examination. Dr. Marion Monroe was a member of the staff and was working on the standardization of her diagnostic reading tests. Her presence in the Chicago area so stimulated the interest in children with reading difficulties that for several years one-fourth of the referrals made to the clinic had as their chief reason for referral a reading handicap, or it was included as one of the problems. Although the interest in arithmetic disabilities never reached such proportions, a good many children were also being referred for whom arithmetic was a special problem.

After completion of the diagnostic work-up, it was almost impossible to find tutors and teachers who had the time and training to undertake remedial work in these two fields. To meet this need, the staff, who had intensive training under Dr. Monroe, undertook the training of tutors. At first this was accomplished on an individual basis with the tutors carrying remedial work under the supervision of a staff psychologist. However, as the work became well known the Institute became a training center and for several years offered a six-weeks summer course in remedial work. Because the Institute had no direct relationship to the education department of any university, no education credit could be granted for this course, and as soon as the local universities became interested and gave courses in remedial reading for which teachers could secure academic credit, the Psychology Department of the Institute discontinued its training in this field.

Two scholarship associations made arrangements to refer children in whom they were interested to the clinic for group evaluations. These groups were seen monthly. Tests of general intelligence, interest inventories, group vocational tests, and personality questionnaires were administered. Evaluation was made on the basis of the findings, the social history supplied by the agency, and the school report. If, on the basis of these data, an individual child seemed to need a more thorough examination, he was then referred to the clinic for a full work-up. The final decision as to whether or not a scholarship should be granted remained with the scholarship associations. Later, when the agencies were combined, a change of policy followed and the new agency made arrangements for its own psychological consultant. Requests to the Institute were made only on the basis of the needs of an individual adolescent.

For many years after the Institute became a state agency it continued a full unit staff at the Juvenile Court. The court, however, has gradually built up its own psychiatric department with the Institute giving only supplementary service. The county board first created a position for a psychologist, later adding a social worker, and finally a psychiatrist. While the Institute was supplying the services of a psychologist to the Juvenile Court, the psychologist together with the psychiatrist served on the "Feeble-Minded Commission." All children and parents who were to appear before the judge on the Feeble-Minded Call were seen first by the Commission. It was the Commission's responsibility, after reviewing clinical findings and hearing the report of the probation officer, to decide whether or not the child should be considered for institutional placement.

From its inception the Institute became increasingly aware that if it were to do preventive mental hygiene, there was need for the early recognition and study of behavior problems. Pioneer work with children of preschool age was begun with the establishment of a preschool branch in the Mary Crane Nursery of Hull House and later expanded to several other centers. The work was under the direction of a psychologist who had on her staff a psychologist, social workers, and a consulting psychiatrist. In 1930, the preschool branch was moved to Institute headquarters and more closely integrated into the functioning of the clinic. However, for some time it had its own staff, since the examination of preschool children was considered a specialty.

The Institute, in following its policy of giving service to communities which were already aware of the help it could give, and had requested it, assigned staff to hold regular clinics in the two school districts of La Salle Township High School and the Winnetka Public Schools. In both these districts the local school boards employed social workers and the Institute supplied the psychological and psychiatric services. Later, changes in the local administration of these two districts, together with additions to their clinic staffs made it possible for the Institute to withdraw from these specific commitments.

Over the years the changes which have taken place in the function and philosophy of the Institute have been due chiefly to the progress and growth of staff thinking. Administrative changes have been made by the Department of Public Welfare. At the time the Institute was established as a state agency, its director also served as state criminologist and its examination and treatment of children with behavior difficulties represented the preventive work of the Division of Criminology. This combined role of the director continued until 1941. Thus, the psychology department was asked to include in its work the early services to state hospitals, children's institutions, and, as psychologists were added to its staff, to the state prisons. In that year the state's institutions were reorganized and the Division of the Criminologist was placed in the Department of Public Safety. In the meantime the state hospitals gradually had built up their own psychology departments with a psychological consultant as supervisor. As psychologists in the children's institutions were assigned to the individual superintendents, the head of the psychology department at the Institute has served as consultant to the superintendents and their psychologists.

In 1944 the Institute decided to undertake a more careful screening of applications. There were a number of reasons for this. The team approach to the examination of a child had been accepted from the beginning. However, the waiting list was increasing each year—as early as 1921 the period of waiting was reported as four weeks—and the pressure for emergency examinations was constantly greater. One of the results of this more careful screening was the decision that staff psychologists should take complete responsibility for certain types of referrals. For example, it was often not advisable for a county judge to detain a child in the local jail until a regular scheduled clinic could arrange for an examination. If the judge needed immediate advice on a juvenile offender, a senior psychologist was assigned to make the examination and to consult with the authorities. This examination involved an evaluation of available social history material, the obtaining of further data, if necessary, administering appropriate diagnostic tests, interviewing the child and parents, if they were available, and holding a conference with the judge. If an application to the clinic indicated that the presenting problem was chiefly retardation in which the need was for education, counseling and planning, a psychologist was scheduled to complete the examination. If later the problem seemed more complicated than at first thought, the psychologist could request a full study of the case.

In 1935, in response to a request from one of the state's teacher training colleges, a senior staff psychologist was assigned to work closely with the colleges to plan a co-operative program between clinic staff and the school's faculty which would introduce to the college students the concepts of mental hygiene in the child guidance field. Although there were slight variations from one college to another in the functioning of the program, in general the sequence was about the same. The freshmen were presented with a discussion of children's needs and emotional and intellectual growth; the sophomores were given a review of the development of mental hygiene with special reference to the functioning of the Institute as a state agency. Then, as practice teachers, the students were asked by the faculty to prepare individual case studies. In one college these were discussed at conferences with the clinic staff. For advanced students a case demonstration was planned, using appropriate case material chosen from the files at headquarters. This general program continued until 1942 under the direction of a psychologist, and in each of the colleges a psychologist took an active part in lecturing and in the demonstration staffs. As the local situations changed, so the co-operative program underwent changes, and at the present time the Institute is participating only with the Southern Illinois University at Carbondale.

The year 1942 marked the celebration of the 25th Anniversary of the Institute for Juvenile Research under state sponsorship. The psychology department had grown both in number of staff and in the responsibilities it had assumed. Many new individual tests and techniques had been adopted as they became available. At no time, so far as can be ascertained, has there ever been a required battery of tests administered to each child. The individual psychologist has, under supervision when necessary, always been allowed to choose the tests he considered most appropriate.

About this time a new clinic practice was worked out in relation to school contacts. Because of the psychologist's training and closer liaison with education, it was decided that school conferences and visits would be made by members of the psychology department.

In 1942 the Institute undertook an experimental and research study of very disturbed children who were housed on a ward of the Illinois Neuropsychiatric Institute. To the psychology department was given the responsibility for the psychological examinations of these children before their acceptance on the ward, and also for whatever examinations were needed during their stay, as well as for the supervision of their education. The schooling of these children was conducted by two staff members, one a psychologist, and the other a teacher. The psychology department carried these responsibilities for the ten years of the ward's research experiment.

In the decade since 1942 the major changes in the functioning of the department have been in the continued acceptance and use of new diagnostic techniques, especially in the field of projectives, and also in the undertaking of more responsibility for therapy. It was always possible for any interested staff member to carry treatment, but a limited amount was done by psychologists during the 20's. In the next decade the cases accepted by the psychologist were those in which, in addition to remedial work indicated, the child needed more of a therapeutic climate in treatment than could usually be found in the more classic tutoring situation. With the opening of the children's ward, however, a number of the senior psychologists were asked to accept the individual treatment of a few children. There was no rigorously planned supervision of this treatment, but it was always possible for the therapist to have conferences with the psychiatrist who directed the ward. There were also frequent staff conferences in which the therapist took an active part. As the public schools built up their own facilities for detecting special educational problems in children and in planning programs for them, the number of referrals to the department for diagnosis decreased considerably and the need for treatment in the clinic correspondingly diminished. Therefore, with the increase in the treatment of children with behavior problems by psychologists, therapy for children with educational difficulties was gradually discontinued.

THE INSTITUTE TODAY

At the present time, the staff of the Institute numbers approximately one hundred persons and of these, fourteen are psychologists. There are five professional departments: psychiatry, psychology, social service, sociology, and psychophysiology. The sociology department was created in 1926 and is known as the Chicago Area Project. It concentrates its efforts in areas of high delinquency in the metropolitan community, and although its work is not closely identified with the clinic, the area workers are instrumental in referring individual children for examination. The work of the psychophysiological laboratory (established 1941) involves both service and research, which are considered inseparable. Much of the general work of the laboratory is being directed toward the development of principles of interpretation of the records to understand what is actually happening both cortically and subcortically within the brain. Also, to find out what are the relationships of recordable brain activity to mental life and behavior, and to establish principles for a "functional" interpretation of the electroencephalogram is a primary research objective of the laboratory.

Throughout the four decades of the Institute's existence, there never has been a period when growth and development have not taken place. Since it is a public agency, certain limits have been superimposed on its functioning, but the staff has kept pace with accepted child guidance procedures and has experimented with new concepts. Over the years, the criteria and postulates which can be used for determining treatability, have been discussed and in the recent past, in a series of meetings, senior staff personnel from the three disciplines have focused on this subject. Again and again reviews of intake and diagnostic procedures take place to sharpen staff thinking and render the best service. Psychology is always represented in these appointed policy and planning committees, which then submit their thinking and recommendation to the administrative staff. The department heads meet regularly with the superintendent to discuss administrative problems, to effect changes in staff functioning, and to integrate the services to best meet state-wide needs.

The service functions of the psychology department are in two areas, diagnosis and therapy.

DIAGNOSIS

From the time that an application is received, a psychologist is always one of a team to plan for the child. All applications are reviewed by a scheduling committee after the intake department has sent for the adjunctive reports which are considered important for the study. In considering referral, the psychologist decides from the reports and information available, the particular staff member to be assigned to it. Very often new psychologists come to the clinic with a rather specialized type of experience and it is the department's plan eventually to develop each staff member to the point where he can handle adequately any type of problem in a child of any age. Because of the waiting list certain cases are considered for assignment to a psychologist alone. In addition to children presenting problems of poor school adjustment and mental retardation, the psychologists may be asked to examine and plan for children with physical handicaps. To evaluate the mental maturity of children with single or multiple handicaps is most difficult and yet agencies and medical clinics need this information to plan therapeutic programs. The last group to be seen by the psychologist is that referred to establish adoptability. Following the diagnostic examination, the psychologist interprets his findings and discusses the presenting problems with the parents or agency workers. The majority of cases, however, are seen in collaboration with social service and psychiatry. The first appointment is made for the child and mother, and the second appointment is scheduled two weeks later, at which time both parents and child are interviewed by the psychiatrist.

On a typical day, the psychologist may be examining children with severe school phobias, insomnia, truancy, temper tantrums, destructiveness, learning problems, and possible psychosis. The problems are manifold and appear to be more involved and severe as time goes on. Furthermore, the age of referral is dropping, with many more preschoolers being seen. The impact of the severity of the problems is recognized when it is difficult to schedule cases for externs. No longer is the psychologist faced with the "simple problems" of the past.

The psychologist may choose the tests or techniques which he believes will be most useful. No definite battery is stipulated. With the increase in the number of psychologists employed by schools and agencies, particularly in metropolitan areas, reports of intelligence, achievement and sometimes other tests are available. Projectives or special tests, as for aphasia, may be indicated to aid in a differential diagnosis at the clinic. Each day a senior staff psychologist is in charge to act as a supervisor for externs and new staff members and also to meet emergencies.

There is much flexibility permitted in writing the psychological report. Over the years there have been many changes in the type of report to be included in the record, with the trend toward permitting the psychologist more individual freedom to include what he wishes. Factual data are, of course, recorded, and in the summary the examiner is expected to state his findings and recommendations in such a way that they can be included in a letter or report if one is written to an outside agency.

Upon completion of the psychiatric examination, the case is staffed with a psychiatric moderator and with each of the examiners reporting and integrating his findings. The psychologist is expected to take an active role in planning for the disposition of the case. Letters and contacts with schools are routinely the obligation of the examining psychologist, reports to physicians and medical agencies the responsibility of the psychiatrist, and reports to social agencies the duty of the social worker. This liaison between psychologist and the school continues as long as the case is active in the clinic. If the situation requires a school contact it is the psychologist who makes the investigation or interpretation for the therapist even though the child may be in therapy with a member of another discipline.

The decision reached by the diagnostic staff may be a recommendation for treatment, placement, referral to another agency, or for closing the case after a series of service interviews or a single conference with the parents. The psychologist may be asked to undertake the service interviews or the completion conference.

TREATMENT

If a case is referred to treatment, it has been found expedient, in a clinic as large as the Institute, to have a second review by a treatment committee made up again of a person from each of the disciplines. The treatment committee has an opportunity to re-evaluate the treatability of the case and may ask the examining team to reconsider the case or replan for the child. The committee must bear in mind the maturity and availability of staff for treatment. If a psychologist prefers to do no treatment, his wish is respected. However, those who undertake therapy may carry a case load from two to six. Usually, weekly appointments are scheduled, although they may vary as to the needs of the child and parental interest and ability to make several weekly trips to the clinic. Therapy with parents as well as children is undertaken in the department. There is no "typical" case for psychology. A few of the presenting problems that have been treated by the psychologist are: enuresis, soiling, masturbation, school phobias, and separation anxieties.

Psychiatric supervision or consultation on a regular basis is made available to members of the psychological department, the frequency of the conferences depending upon the needs of the case and upon the psychologist. Because of the nature of the problems many of the cases are carried collaboratively by two different staff members, with one seeing the parent and the other seeing the child. Staff lines may be cut across in the assignment of a case with the psychologist frequently working with a member of one of the other departments. Routinely, treatment cases are scheduled for staff review. At these meetings the therapists summarize the treatment, indicating trends and changes, and raise questions which they would like answered by the committee. The review committee in conjunction with the therapists may make such dispositional decisions as that another member of the family be treated or that the case be closed. Again, as is usual in Institute functioning, the review committee is composed of a member from each of the disciplines.

PLACEMENT

A second review of diagnostic decisions is held when the recommendation is placement of the child outside his home. The placement committee (psychiatrist, psychologist and social worker), in addition to reviewing the material in detail, keeps current with the available facilities for placement decided upon. Since the staff considers placement as its most serious recommendation, the committee also serves as a further check of staff thinking before such a plan is proposed to the parents.

TRAINING

Although the clinic is service oriented, it has two other functions which it has always considered an important part of its work. These are training and research. In the department of psychology the training of students was begun as early as 1923. The annual report of that year states that students were accepted from three local universities and the work offered them was correlated with courses they had just taken. They spent from three weeks to four months in the clinic. By 1928, the University of Illinois was giving credit for three months' experience at the Institute. In addition to the students accepted directly from the universities, there were, during the year, nine volunteers who stayed three months or longer. The next year a closer liaison was worked out with the University of Chicago through the head of the psychology department and Chicago students were accepted for three half-days a week in the clinic, with credit being given for the work. Also, that year a stipend was offered to one student for a fellowship of six months. Volunteers were still in training and were accepted after receiving a Bachelor's Degree only if their undergraduate work offered sufficient basic training for beginning work in the clinic.

During the period 1930 to 1935, the University of Illinois worked out an arrangement whereby clinical students took their academic work on the campus at Champaign, and in lieu of a thesis, spent six months at the Institute in obtaining their M.A. Degree in psychology. At the end of that time an evaluation was written for the university by the head of the department.

From 1937 to 1941, in addition to the students in training, the psychology department offered a summer course in "Problems of Children's School Adjustment." This course was open to interested counselors and school principals.

In 1942, a questionnaire was sent to 122 psychologists who had received training at the Institute during the preceding ten years. This was done as part of a review of the work of the Institute during its first twenty-five years as a state institution. From the responses it was learned that 97 were engaged in the professional work for which they trained, of whom 24 were teaching courses in universities, 16 were engaged in work in Departments of Public Welfare, 5 were in child guidance clinics, and 27 were holding executive positions.

During the period since 1942 the acceptance of volunteers has terminated and the externships have been extended from the early prescribed six months to one year. Students are now accepted if they are in the third year of their Ph.D. program or have received their M.A. Degree. Their activities include as wide an experience in diagnostic work as can be offered, two therapy cases, one carried under a supervising psychologist, and the other under a psychiatrist, participation in all the regular staff conferences, and a test work-shop. Because of the demands on the time of the supervisory staff, the number which can be accepted is small. Five externs are thought to be the maximum that can be trained at one time.

RESEARCH

The department has always been engaged in some research. Early annual reports mention such studies: The Intelligence of Delinquents, Stability of the IQ on Re-examination, Suggestibility of Mental Defectives, Possibility of Effects of Nursery Schools on the Intelligence Ratings

of Children, and The Effect of Treatment on Ability to Function on
Intelligence Tests. These are but a few of the studies. In addition, the
Chicago Non-Verbal Test as well as tests for the deaf and blind were developed and standardized by Dr. Andrew Brown and co-workers. There
have been some studies undertaken co-operatively with members of the
other departments, such as Personality Patterns and Family Relationships
Found in Allergic Children. In process is a clinical study of nondisturbed
eight- and nine-year olds. Although the Institute does not take final
responsibility for master's theses and doctoral dissertations, it has made
case material available to psychologists working for these degrees, and
shared co-operatively with the universities in their supervision. A wealth
of material is contained in the 50,000 case records on file at the Institute
and with the aid of a coding system it is possible to pull those records
which are suitable to each particular study.

Perhaps the most intensive period of research at the Institute dates
back to the establishment of the Behavior Research Fund in 1926. At
that time Dr. Herman Adler secured private resources to establish the
Fund for five years. The research undertaken varied greatly and was not
necessarily allied to clinic functioning. The work of Dr. Marion Monroe
perhaps had the closest relationship to the clinical study of children.
Among the psychologists who were on the staff of the Behavior Research
Fund were Karl S. Lashley, Chester W. Darrow, Heinrich Klüver, C. P.
Stone, L. L. Thurstone, Luton Ackerson, Carney Landis, and Simon
Tulchin.

OTHER ACTIVITIES

Although in 1940, the first permanent down-state clinic was established in East St. Louis, it was not until 1943 that a regional staffing
plan on a state-wide basis was contemplated. As the program developed,
the regional staff has been located in five of the larger communities outside of Chicago and holds regularly scheduled clinics in other centers.
It has not been possible always to provide regional psychological coverage and, therefore, by necessity, psychologists from headquarters have
been assigned on a traveling basis. The work includes not only the
diagnostic testing but conferences and consultations with responsible
local agencies. The individual psychologist's responsibility is greater than
at headquarters since supervision is not available.

In addition to the activities described, the psychologists have many
other extraclinical assignments. These include committee participation
in planning for outside speakers, inservice training, library, equipment,
and newsletters.

FUTURE PLANS FOR THE INSTITUTE

In October, 1952, ground was broken for the Healy School, a residential treatment center for 48 children. The Department of Public Welfare has already provided for the care of extremely disturbed youngsters in one of its state hospitals. The Healy School will treat less disturbed children, but those who still need more intensive therapy than can be given them on an outpatient basis. The Institute has been asked to assume administrative and professional responsibility for the center. The present staffing plan includes two psychologists who will do both diagnosis and treatment. Parents of the children in residence will need treatment, too, if the return of the child to the home is contemplated. However, since the total therapy load cannot be carried by the school personnel, the regular Institute staff will share in the treatment program. The opening of this school is the most ambitious and important undertaking planned for the immediate future.

REFERENCES

1. *Annual Reports of the Department of Public Welfare, State of Illinois.* Springfield, Ill.: Dept. of Public Welfare, 1918-1953.
2. Healy, W. *The individual delinquent.* Boston: Little, Brown, 1929.
3. *Illinois Revised Statutes, 1949.* Chicago: Burdette Smith Company, 1949.
4. The Staff of The Institute for Juvenile Research. *Child guidance procedures.* New York: D. Appleton-Century, 1937.
5. Witmer, H. *Psychiatric clinics for children.* New York: Commonwealth Fund, 1940.

III.

THE TRAINING SCHOOL AT VINELAND, NEW JERSEY

KARL F. HEISER

The contributions of psychology to the field of mental deficiency are many and varied, and it can be said, equally, that the field has made many contributions to the development of psychology as a science and profession. The great concern shown by psychology in measuring intellectual functions and individual differences has resulted in the relative pre-eminence of psychology as a professional discipline in dealing with the problem of mental deficiency. Also, the work of psychologists in handling the problems of retarded and handicapped children has had an effect on psychological theory and method. Although psychology's concern with "feeble-mindedness" antedates the work of Binet, it seems fair to say that Binet's work, followed by Goddard and then Terman, marked the beginning and basis of most of the work now done by psychologists in this field and largely determined the kind of approaches made by psychologists in their work and thinking.

The field is currently of interest to a relatively small number of American psychologists. A check on the interests of members of the American Psychological Association, as indicated in the Directory for 1951, revealed that about 3 per cent were concerned with mental deficiency, brain-damaged children or cerebral palsy. It has not been possible to assess the comparable proportion of the members of thirty years ago but it is probable that a much larger proportion of the psychologists of that time were interested in what was called feeble-mindedness. It would seem from the 1922 Directory of the American Psychological Association that over 9 per cent had such an interest. This could have been due, if true, to the relative newness and appeal of the mental testing approach made possible by the work of such men as Goddard and Terman.

A number of definitions have been constructed by leading psychologists in the field as to the essential characteristic of mental deficiency. While there is still no general agreement, the following definition by Doll is probably as satisfactory as any: "Mental deficiency is a state of social incompetence obtaining at maturity, . . . resulting from develop-

32

mental mental arrest of constitutional (hereditary or acquired) origin; the condition is essentially incurable . . ." (6, p. 217). This definition is quite adequate for all work which is concerned with the description of a condition from the point of view of intellectual efficiency. From certain other standpoints, however, it seems desirable to focus attention on etiology, on process, and on the dynamics of the condition and its treatment.

In actual practice in the institutional care of mental defectives the term "mental deficiency" often covers a large variety of psychopathologies, such as organic or structural damage to the nervous system, the destruction and disturbance in function caused by disease and infectious states, specific pathologies of the sensorimotor system, a variety of personality disturbances varying from situational aberrations of behavior to deep-seated neuroses and psychoses, a low level of intellectual functioning due to cultural or environmental poverty, and a generalized lack of intellectual potential which seems to be due to heredity.

BRIEF HISTORY OF INSTITUTIONAL WORK

It is not easy to say when psychological work, as psychology and by psychologists, began in American institutions for the feeble-minded. G. E. Johnson, fellow in pedagogy, Clark University, published his "Contributions to the Psychology and Pedagogy of Feebleminded Children," in 1895 (12). The article contains data on free association reaction time as well as a discussion of educational principles and practices. It appears that the first actual laboratory was established at the Minnesota School for Feebleminded at Faribault, where A. R. T. Wylie, Ph.D., was the first institutional psychologist. Beginning in 1899, Wylie published a long series of articles on physical measurement and acuity in all the senses (16, 17, 18). Wylie devised the first record form for psychological examinations (1). It contains space for data organized under the following major headings: Anthropological, Sensations, Perception, Memory, Emotion, Instincts, Volition, Association of Ideas, Attention, Judgment, Reasoning, Imagination, Special Talents, and School Record.

In a "Plea for Expert Psychological Investigation" Miss Bancroft (2) argued in 1901 for psychological examination of all children in all schools and institutions according to a standard form. This "Plea," no doubt, was the first of many attempts which, unfortunately, fifty years later have not yet resulted in uniformity of psychological procedures or the ready communicability of psychological data from one agency to another. In 1904, E. R. Johnstone, Superintendent of The Training School at Vineland, in his presidential address to the National Association of Medical Officers of American Institutions for Idiotic and Feeble-minded Persons said "I plead for a staff of psychologists, also, and thus we may hope to give to education as we give to medicine . . ." (13, p. 67).

Johnstone's words were not empty, as two years later, in 1906, he was able to establish the Research Department at The Training School under H. H. Goddard. The writer has not been able to check early catalogues and directories and cannot vouch for the accuracy of the following chronology but it is believed to be approximately correct.

The third institution to engage psychologists for clinical work and research was the Lincoln State School in Illinois where E. B. Huey was the first psychologist in 1910. Dr. Huey left for Johns Hopkins University and was succeeded by Clara H. Town in 1912. The publications by Drs. Huey and Town were probably more influential even than those of Goddard in the development of widespread usage of the Binet tests.

In 1910 Fred Kuhlmann succeeded Dr. Wylie at the Minnesota State School. In the meantime Wylie had obtained the doctorate also in medicine and in 1911 he became Superintendent of North Dakota's institution. Kuhlmann is best known for his revisions of the Binet scale which extended the age range downward to infancy.

The decade of the 1920's saw psychological work begun at Letchworth Village in New York by Grace Taylor, at Laurelton Village in Pennsylvania by Mary Vanuxem, at the Fernald School at Waverly, Mass. by Elizabeth Conners, at Lapeer, Michigan by Z. Pauline Hoakley, at the Sonoma State Home in California by George Ordahl, at the Vineland State School by Dorothy Bassett, at the New York City school on Randall's Island by Louise Poule (under whom the writer had his first practicum training), at the Indiana State School in Fort Wayne by Edna Jatho, at the Carswell Training School in North Carolina by Elsa Ernst, at the State Home For Boys at Jamesburg, N. J. by Margurite D. Hulbert, at the Wayne County Training School, Michigan by Miss Hoakley who transferred from the State School at Lapeer, at Pennsylvania State Schools at Pennhurst and Polk by Anne Kohn and H. Ramona Parmenter, respectively.

These people set the pattern which has been generally followed by psychologists in institutions for mentally defective children. It would not be fair to say that the early promise of those pioneers has not been fulfilled, yet one cannot say that knowledge of the field or the discoveries of the psychologists have advanced as rapidly as was expected during the early years of enthusiasm. Possibly the field would have developed more rapidly had the early sensorimotor experiments, such as were done first by Wylie at Faribault, been followed up or if more experimental and physiological psychologists had seen the great opportunities of work in the field. With the exception of a few isolated studies such as those of Kreezer on electrical brain potentials at The Training School (14), the preponderant efforts of psychologists in institutions for the mentally defective have been confined to the use of tests for purposes of: (1) classification, into intellectual levels; (2) assignment to educational and vocational training classes; (3) research on the tests themselves; and (4) better understanding of the children by the psychologists.

The major differences between psychological work in 1920 and in 1950, in these institutions, consists in the use of different tests, although it must be understood that there are a few noticeable exceptions to this statement and some individual psychologists have administrative or other functions somewhat outside the field of strictly psychological work. Wechsler's scales are probably more widely used now than the Stanford-Binet, although the only reason one finds for the shift is a matter of personal preference. The wide use of projective techniques in recent years and the concern with personality has not meant any essential change in the work of psychologists in this field, although it seems to have led many to wish they could do more with the children in the way of psychotherapy.

THE TRAINING SCHOOL AT VINELAND, NEW JERSEY

This institution was founded in 1888 on the principle that training for useful occupation was possible and desirable for the social adjustment and happiness of the child. It was the first institution to develop the cottage system with "house parents" to simulate a family pattern of living. Although these principles may seem self-evident today, they represented quite a radical position in contrast with the principle of custodial care in large dormitories as was the practice sixty-five years ago. The School is a private, nonprofit institution run by a Board of Trustees who are elected by the Vineland Association to which anyone may belong. The institution is located on 1600 acres of land, 600 of which are under cultivation.

Beginning with 7 boys in March 1888, the population grew rapidly to 550 and has been kept constant at about that figure. Approximately two thirds of the "children" are male and somewhat over half of them are wards of the State of New Jersey which pays a per diem tuition fee for each "State" child in residence for a period of training and education. This fee always has been on what might be called a "scholarship" basis as it has never covered the full cost of maintenance and training. The balance of the cost for State children has been made up out of endowment and the margin above cost paid by the parents of "private" children.

There are several ways of classifying an institutional population which would be of interest to the psychologist. Table 1, below, gives a breakdown of the current population by age, sex, training status and possibility of outside adjustment. It may be seen that the majority receive some form of training, either in the school or the job. The problem of return to the community is complex. Its answer depends much more upon the home and the community to which the child must adjust and in which he may work. Children who are wards of the State seldom have homes in which they can receive acceptance, guidance and care. "State" children may be returned to the State authorities for either permanent custodial care or for placement out in the community. In the latter case, the State provides a follow-up by social workers who provide a certain amount of guidance. In the case of children from private homes, the wishes of the parents must be considered as well as the needs of the child either for trial at home or in a job or for continued care and training in the institution.

TABLE 1

Some Characteristics of The Training School Population—1953

	5-10	11-20	21-50	Over 50
1. Age	5%	35%	44%	16%
2. Sex			Male	Female
			72%	28%
3. Age on admission			Under 11	Over 10
			35%	65%
4. Attend academic and manual arts classes			Yes	No
			48%	52%
5. Have occupational training at The Training School			Yes	No
			37%	63%
6. Probably can be returned to home or community			Yes	No
			25%	75%

Table 2 gives the kind of information about the population which may be of more concern to the clinical psychologist. It must be remembered that this Table represents the population only approximately, as diagnoses frequently change. Of particular interest may be the figures on neurosis and psychosis, as most people, even psychologists, seem to think of "the feeble-minded" as a homogeneous group whose chief characteristic is represented by a low I.Q. Another team of examiners would undoubtedly differ in the exact number to be called psychotic and neurotic. In the case of the figures in Table 2, the psychiatrist's diagnosis was taken as authoritative.

TABLE 2

Clinical Data on Training School Population—1953

Personality Pattern	Current I.Q.	Endog.	Exogenous Mongoloid	Other	Mixed	Unknown	Totals
Normal	Below 50	27	38	56	8	35	164
	50-75	41	5	46	11	56	159
	Above 75	15		13	2	22	52
Totals		83	43	115	21	113	375
Neurotic	Below 50	4	4	22	7	13	50
	50-75	6		19	1	24	50
	Above 75	3		2	1	14	20
Totals		13	4	43	9	51	120
Psychotic	Below 50	2		14	1	12	29
	50-75		1	5		9	15
	Above 75					1	1
Totals		2	1	19	1	22	45
Total	Below 50	33	42	92	16	60	243
	50-75	47	6	70	12	89	224
	Above 75	18		15	3	37	73
Totals		98	48	177	31	186	540

Some readers may be surprised at the presence of psychotic patients in a school for the mentally deficient. While very few such schools or institutions are prepared to deal with or to treat psychotic children—and, in fact, few are able to make a careful differential diagnosis—there is no doubt that every such institution cares for many psychotic children who have been mistakenly diagnosed as mentally defective.

As is indicated by Table 1, there is a large proportion of adults, some of whom are elderly and senile. This is a condition to be expected in any school unless it has a rigid policy for dropping children at a certain age. At the Training School, moreover, there has been the principle of providing a permanent home, if needed, and of adjusting the child to a self-respecting niche in this home community. While many children are able to leave and to use their training in productive work outside, there are many more who are not able to do so.

The Education Department has always been prominent. It handles the training program which has involved kindergarten, elementary grade school subjects, manual arts, on-the-job or vocational training and recreation. Between 1902 and 1933 this Department offered summer courses in the special education of the handicapped. Nine hundred and fifty teachers from various parts of the United States and some foreign countries have attended these courses.

The staff of the Education Department consists of two groups: teachers who give full time to classes, and employees in various maintenance departments who instruct in on-the-job training. For example, the painters have boys assigned to them somewhat as apprentices to work under supervision on different painting jobs. Children have part-time jobs in most all departments: shoe shop, mattress shop, cannery, store, etc.

The Research Department has been outstanding in the history of this field of work. It was founded in the fall of 1906 with the employment of H. H. Goddard, who had done his doctoral work at Clark University. In 1908, Goddard began what became a long and impressive bibliography of his work in mental deficiency with a report advocating careful longitudinal studies of: (a) growth, (b) the anatomy of the brain through autopsy, (c) metabolic changes during life, and (d) "the mental condition of the child" by methods of psychological appraisal (7). It is probable that the major characteristic of psychological work in institutions was largely determined by the work of Goddard in translating and revising the Binet Scale for American use. Goddard's first reports on this work were published between 1908 and 1910 (8, 9, 10). When they were followed eight years later by Terman's Stanford Revision of the Binet Tests, the die was cast in the sense that, from that time forward, the preponderant work of psychologists in institutions for the mentally deficient has been concerned with intelligence testing. The intelligence testing approach captivated the interests of psychologists, teachers, and administrators so that at present it would be a very unusual experience to visit an institution and be unable to get the I.Q. scores or classifications of all the children.

Following the leadership of Dr. Goddard, Dr. S. D. Porteus, 1918-1925, and Dr. E. A. Doll, 1925-1949, each served as head of the Research Department. Except for two short periods the professional staff of the Research Department has been consistently psychological in training and orientation. Between 1914 and 1916 the staff included a neuropathologist and a physiological chemist. Since October 1952 the staff has included a child psychiatrist on a part-time basis and, if present plans materialize, the staff will be augmented by representatives of other fields who may make their joint contributions to the solution of problems in this clinical field.

It would be difficult to assess adequately the actual contributions to knowledge that have been made by the Research Department. The studies which are best known are not necessarily those which have had the greatest or the most permanent influence upon the field of mental deficiency. If one were to choose the major studies that have been landmarks or have led to advancement in the field, the following might be of most significance.

(a) Goddard's translation into English of the Binet intelligence scale in 1908, and its revision for use at The Training School (8, 9).

(b) Publication of the Kallikak Family (11), which unfortunately gave further support to the erroneous but wide belief in the genic origin of intellectual defectiveness.

(c) Studies in anthropometry and anthropology (15).

(d) Studies in brain injury or cerebral palsy (4).

(e) Studies in the development of self-sufficiency and social adequacy through the development of the Vineland Social Maturity Scale (5).

The Army Alpha and Beta tests developed during the first World War were partially standardized in the Research Department. The Training School provided space and other facilities for the work of the committee of psychologists who developed the tests and, of course, the Department staff assisted materially in the project.

Other work of considerable significance, since it was the first of its kind in the field of mental deficiency, though relatively unknown, was the encephalographic study by Kreezer (14).

Some indication of the role in American psychology played by the Research Department of The Training School may be seen in the list of forty-seven living members of the American Psychological Association who have been members of the staff.

THE WORK OF THE PSYCHOLOGIST IN THE TRAINING SCHOOL

Over the years since its beginning there has been a steady trend in the direction of increasing psychological services for the children. During its first twenty-five years there were very few clinics or clinical psychologists in the United States who used their knowledge and skills in the interests of their subjects. Psychologists were more concerned with what they could learn to advance their science, naturally, than with the use of their knowledge in making decisions concerning their subjects. The very terminology used indicates the difference in the psychologist's orientation. In the early days, clinical psychologists spoke of "subjects," a term borrowed from experimental psychology; now they speak of "patients," or "clients," indicating an interest in the person rather than in the experiment. In the early years of The Training School almost all the children were tested by a variety of procedures, some children several times a year, but the results of these tests were not used in making decisions on admission, dismissal, cottage placement, education, training or treatment. Gradually, as clinical psychology learned how to use its findings practically, and learned how to communicate the significance of its findings to others, the psychologists took more and more part in the day-to-day work of the institution. Now, staff time in the Research Department is divided roughly 60 per cent to clinical work and 40 per cent to research. Each psychologist devotes time to both interests, but some spend as much as 80 per cent of their time in one or the other kind of work. Administratively all psychologists are members of the Research Department and both their clinical and research functions come under the supervision of the head of the Department. This represents a slight change from an earlier situation in which there were "clinical" psychologists and "research" psychologists with more or less independent functions. At present, all members of the psychology staff are expected to develop both their research and clinical interests under the hypothesis that each area of interest supplements or enriches the other. The clinical and research work of the psychiatrist, and of such other specialists as may be employed in the future, come also administratively under this same Department.

The staff positions currently are as follows: a department head, a chief psychologist, a part-time child psychiatrist, two psychologists, three junior psychologists, two doctoral interns, a part-time social worker, a part-time research assistant, and three stenographic and clerical positions. Some of these positions are supported by a research grant from the United States Public Health Service. This group now occupies about 3000 square feet of floor space in offices, research rooms, and examining and therapy rooms in its own building.

Clinical work consists largely of diagnosis and psychotherapy. Diagnostic studies are done periodically with the use of interviews, psychological tests, and information supplied by cottage, school and hospital personnel. These studies are reported to the Superintendent, to the head of the Cottage Life Department, and to the head of the Education Department. They are then discussed at weekly meetings of the Children's Committee, a group of department heads which advises the Director on care and disposition of the children. The reports are discussed before the Committee by the psychologist who wrote them rather than by the Chief Psychologist or the head of the Research Department, who is a member of the Committee. It is thought that this system stimulates caution and responsibility in the psychologist since he may and must stand on his own feet. This matter of responsibility is the more serious because each report ends in specific recommendations for the disposition of the child under review. Since these recommendations may conflict with those of other departments or with the ideas of the administration, the psychologist soon learns that he must be able to communicate verbally as well as in written form; not only communicate, but he must be able to persuade by the force of his arguments.

Every report is discussed in draft form with at least one colleague before final typing. This procedure has three purposes: (a) acquaintance of more than one psychologist with the problems and traits of each child, (b) an educational device for the growth of the clinician, and (c) a means of catching minor technical errors that might be overlooked by the report writer.

In addition to these diagnostic studies there are three kinds of reports prepared by the psychologists: "special referrals," "end-of-observation period" reports and outpatient clinic or preadmission reports. Each child admitted to The Training School has a three-months observation period during which extra efforts are made to establish a thorough diagnosis and to plan the most beneficial course of training either at The Training School or elsewhere. Before the end of this period, the Director, on the advice of the Children's Committee, reports to the parent or guardian as to the acceptability of the child and, if acceptable, the plans for care and training and the prognosis.

The "special referral" reports may be called for at any time by the Director or the Children's Committee in case a child shows disturbances or changes of behavior with which the cottage parent cannot cope or is unfamiliar.

There are also diagnostic studies made of children brought to the outpatient clinic. Some of these studies are very brief clinical impressions while others involve several interviews and techniques. Many of the outpatient cases are candidates for admission, but the psychologist's objective is to establish as true a diagnosis as possible and so aid in the guidance of the parents in the best interests of the child and his family.

Consonant with a marked trend in American clinical psychology away from what is called psychometrics toward what is called dynamic or analytic or interpretative clinical study, the reports prepared by Vineland psychologists are generally concerned with interpretation of behavior or personality dynamics rather than with metricized descriptions of traits, capacities and performances. We believe that it results in better psychological work with respect both to determining appropriate disposition of the children, and to providing more useful information and knowledge.

In addition to the usual types of psychological examination which are included in the clinical reports, the Research Department does electroencephalographic work. It has an eight channel instrument and one of the senior psychologists has been trained as a technician. A professor of neurology at a nearby university acts as consultant and interprets all records for both diagnostic and research objectives. The psychologist devotes half time to EEG work.

PSYCHOTHERAPY

Pschotherapy is practiced by the staff psychiatrist and by most of the psychologists. The role of the psychiatrist in relation to the psychologists may be called supervision or consultation depending upon the experience of the psychologist in therapy, the complexities of problems dealt with, and the level or depth or type of therapy attempted. For the most part the psychiatrist supervises because he is the best prepared by training, skill and knowledge for that role. The psychologist has, on the average, one hour of individual supervision for each three hours spent with the patient. In addition there are case conferences. Among our psychotherapists only the psychiatrist has been analyzed.

Psychotherapy is carried on through group work, play therapy and individual interview. We have substantial evidence of the efficacy of all types with a number of cases. This statement must be interpreted in terms of the hypotheses and predictions and objectives which are written before therapy begins. Some therapy is aimed at treating certain behavioral disturbances and thus promoting better social and emotional adjustment, some is aimed at releasing what are thought to be potentials for higher levels of intellectual efficiency, and some is aimed at removing or ameliorating certain neurotic and psychotic trends.

RESEARCH

The research done at The Training School at the present time may be characterized as having one of three different types of goals: (1) practical applied research aimed at learning how to do the institution's job of care and training better, e.g., a study of the effects of a certain drug upon enuresis; (2) studies aimed at better diagnosis and determination of etiology, e.g., a study of the effects of difficult labor; (3) advances in psychological theory, e.g., a study of stages and patterns of intellectual development.

The history of the Research Department, as discussed previously, indicates that much impetus to important work in genetics, intelligence testing, brain damage and cerebral palsy, and "social maturity," derived from small beginnings in the laboratory at Vineland. Certain areas, however, have been lacking. Among them are the problems of etiology, prevention, education or training, and psychotherapy. A beginning has been made recently in psychotherapy and it is hoped that financial support from outside may make it possible to develop research programs in the relatively neglected areas.

It is a principle of the Research Department to develop a staff of psychologists whose interests lead them into both clinical work and research. It is obvious, in this field at least, that more knowledge is needed rather than more service based on untested belief and practice.

STAFF DEVELOPMENT

While all psychologists at The Training School, except the interns, are employees who are paid for their work just as are any other professional staff members, there is some consideration given to staff development while on the job. This means that a year on the staff should result in more than incidental learning. There are frequent staff conferences which average about two hours per week. Sometimes a program is planned; sometimes discussions are extemporaneous. At recent conferences there have been a demonstration of endocrinological symptoms, instruction in EEG principles and interpretation, and discussion of problem diagnostic cases. Other staff conferences are, frankly, mere "bull sessions."

In addition to full staff conferences there are weekly therapy conferences involving the psychologists who do psychotherapy, the psychiatrist, and the Department head.

Internship training is a part of the staff development program. While it would be less expensive to employ experienced psychologists to do the actual work done by interns, there are felt to be intangible benefits of intern training which outweigh the economic problems. A staff member who has responsibility for supervising, criticizing, and stimulating a predoctoral intern has a constant stimulus to self-improvement, obligation to keep up with the literature (at least, to keep ahead of the intern!), and a ready audience on whom to vent his needs to teach.

At The Training School, internships are filled only by students who are recommended by a graduate school as being in good standing as a candidate for the doctorate. Recommendations have been solicited only from graduate schools whose clinical doctorate programs have been "approved" by the American Psychological Association. While there is no such thing as a conviction that good interns can come only from such schools and according to such procedures, there is the determination to follow in spirit as well as letter the recommendations of the American Psychological Association in regard to practicum training in clinical psychology. According to these recommendations, the internship is designed for integration with the graduate education on the campus; it is not intended to produce a test-technician nor an accomplished psychotherapist, although the intern may concentrate on these two sorts of clinical work. It is not necessary that the intern come to The Training School with certification in this or that test; it is much more important that he come with enthusiasm to broaden his knowledge, and that he continue to think of himself as a student rather than a forty-hour-per-week worker.

A program of staff development usually results in a high rate of staff turnover. In some respects this is not good, for there are real values in continuity of personnel; but in other respects it is not bad, for it spreads the reputation of the school and the Research Department as being a good place to gain experience and to do research and from which one may advance rapidly to good positions elsewhere.

TRENDS FOR THE FUTURE

It would seem likely that the psychologists of the future in institutions for mentally defective children will be less isolated than in the past from the trends and thinking represented by the American Psychological Association. A larger proportion of them will belong to the Association than at present and the standards of education and training will probably be considerably higher than they have been. With the passage of legislation which sets standards for psychologists in more and more states there will be less and less opportunity for the B.A. degree to qualify a person for a position as psychologist in public and private institutions.

It seems to be a truism to say that job opportunities create a desire on the part of students for that kind of training in the graduate school which will help qualify the student for the jobs. The graduate schools will, inevitably, go on serving the interests of the students and the needs of society as the school administrators see them. If both the students and the administrators find that there is a demand for psychodiagnosticians or for psychotherapists in our institutions, more and more schools will concentrate upon the technical and professional aspects of psychology as contrasted with the theoretical and research interests. It is likely that graduate education in psychology will become more and more a matter of training and will be placed under the control of the schools of medicine. The writer believes that medical control of clinical psychology is inevitable unless clinical psychology can demonstrate its independence as a science and the social value of its contributions as differing from those of the psychiatrist.

The above views of the writer may be biased and wide off the mark. However, if they are approximately correct, one may foresee the nature of future psychological work in institutions for the handicapped. There will be the descendants of clinical psychology working as psychiatric aides and technicians in diagnostic and therapeutic work. Every institution will have them and they will be ten times as numerous as institution psychologists are at present. Their status in the salary hierarchy will be comparable to that represented now by the social worker.

What may be the duties of these psychiatric aides or technicians in

The Training School or similar institutions? It is likely that they will routinely give a variety of tests to determine the presence and nature of organic pathology, the level of intellectual functioning, the readiness for academic education, the skills which may be utilized in vocational training, and the personality characteristics. Under psychiatric control, though not necessarily with supervision, they may carry on group and individual psychotherapy.

The Training School at Vineland and a few other institutions may have their laboratories and research psychologists who will work as colleagues of scientists from other disciplines. They may have relatively little to do with the institutional life and program; they will not know the names of their subjects or the problems of this child as compared with that one, but they will succeed gradually in contributing to such knowledge of etiology as will lead to prevention of some of the dozens of different pathologies which are now so unfortunately grouped together in the conglomerant field called "mental deficiency."

REFERENCES

1. Association of American Institutions for Feebleminded, Committee on Psychological Research. Report. *J. Psycho-Asthenics,* 1901, 6, 21-26.
2. Bancroft, M. Plea for expert psychological investigation. *J. Psycho-Asthenics,* 1901, 7, 50-53.
3. Binet, A. & Henri, V. La psychologie individuelle. *Année psychol.,* 1895, 2, 411-465.
4. Doll, E. A., Phelps, W. M., & Melcher, Ruth T. *Mental deficiency due to birth injuries.* New York: MacMillan, 1932.
5. Doll, E. A. *The Vineland social maturity scale. Manual of directions.* Vineland, N. J.: The Training School, 1935.
6. Doll, E. A. The essentials of an inclusive concept of mental deficiency. *Amer. J. Ment. Def.,* 1941, 46, 214-218.
7. Goddard, H. H. Psychological work among the feebleminded. *J. Psycho-Asthenics,* 1908, 12, 18-30.
8. Goddard, H. H. The Binet and Simon tests of intellectual capacity. *Train. Sch.,* 1908, 5, 3-9.
9. Goddard, H. H. A measuring scale for intelligence. *Train. Sch.,* 1910, 6, 146-155.
10. Goddard, H. H. Four hundred feebleminded children classified by the Binet method. *J. Psycho-Asthenics,* 1910, 15, 17-30.
11. Goddard, H. H. *The Kallikak family.* New York: MacMillan, 1912.
12. Johnson, G. E. Contributions to the psychology and pedagogy of feebleminded children. *Ped. Sem.,* 1895, 3, 246-301.
13. Johnstone, E. R. President's address. *J. Psycho-Asthenics,* 1904, 8, 63-68.
14. Kreezer, G. Electric potentials of the brain in certain types of mental deficiency. *Arch. Neurol. Psychiat.,* 1936, 36, 1206-1213.
15. Porteus, S. D., & Babcock, Marjorie E. *Temperament and race.* Boston: Badger, 1926.
16. Wylie, A. R. T. Investigation concerning the weight and height of feebleminded children. *J. Psycho-Asthenics,* 1899, 4, 47-57.
17. Wylie, A. R. T. Taste and reaction time of the feebleminded. *J. Psycho-Asthenics,* 1900, 5, 109-112.
18. Wylie, A. R. T. A study of the senses of the feebleminded. *J. Psycho-Asthenics,* 1900, 5, 137-150.

IV.

WORCESTER STATE HOSPITAL

MARVIN WALDMAN and LESLIE PHILLIPS

The growth of clinical psychology in the state hospital parallels the development of clinical psychology in general. Initially, areas of function for the clinical psychologist developed out of an academic and experimental background of an early tradition of interest in psychophysical and psychophysiological relationships. Within the mental hospital, however, the psychologist was influenced by the medical tradition of meeting the immediate needs of the individual patient. Consequently, there was an increasing emphasis on the use of psychological tests and of clinical service. To date, the latter role has remained the dominant activity of the clinical psychologist in the state hospital. The increasing influence of the university with its traditional research orientation in the training of clinical psychologists has again brought up for review what constitutes the legitimate function of the clinical psychologist. His work either in research or as a practicing clinician is still not universally recognized as the reason for his placement within the hospital setting. Whether the clinical psychologist is to serve exclusively in one of these areas or whether some balance will be struck between them is one of the problems which faces the field of clinical psychology today.

HISTORICAL DEVELOPMENT

The first psychological laboratory in a mental hospital was established in 1904 at McLean Hospital with Shephard Ivory Franz (3) as its director. It is interesting to note that the then superintendent of McLean Hospital, Edward Coles, conceived of psychologists as functioning in a research team (4) whose other members were to be physiologists, biochemists, and pathologists (13). The proposed structure of this group demonstrates the physiological bias in the psychiatric research of that period. Franz' own training and early work at McLean Hospital were primarily in physiological psychology (1). In a modern sense, his early research was somewhat divorced from an understanding of psychopathology since it centered in the areas of fatigue and nerve physiology. Due to his contacts with mental illness, however, Franz' interests soon became focused on more strictly psychological problems and their relations to psychopathology. These studies were of reaction time, cerebral function, aphasia, attention and memory. The establishment and work of the psychological laboratory at McLean was, in Franz' words, "generally accepted" (3), and a tradition of the psychologist as a research worker in the mental hospital was established.

Franz became interested in what might be the optimal form of relationship between psychology and psychiatry in the mental hospital. He wrote many articles dealing with the relationship between these two professions and became known as the "protagonist of the rapproachment of psychology and psychiatry" (3). However, his attempts to bridge the gap between psychology and psychiatry met with a good deal of resistance from both sides. On the one hand, psychologists did not consider Franz as one of them, and the psychiatrists felt that Franz did not have the medical knowledge and experience to deal with mental disease.

Franz' contacts with a patient population seem to have stimulated his interest in the potential service functions of a psychologist in state hospital practice. In 1907, while at St. Elizabeth Hospital (then known as the Government Hospital for the Insane), he developed and introduced the first systematic routine psychological examination of psychiatric patients. This was put into book form and published in 1912 (2). It included tests of sensation, motor movement, speech difficulties and aphasia, attention, perception, memory, association, reaction time, intelligence, emotional stability, life history, and symptomatology. Some of these tests were devised by Franz; others he had borrowed and used either in their original or modified form. For example, he made use of the Kent-Rosanoff association test and adapted parts of the Binet Intelligence test. The Woodworth personality questionnaire was employed to evaluate what he called emotional stability.

Another early pioneer in the history of clinical psychology in the state hospital was F. L. Wells (12), who succeeded Franz at McLean. Subsequently both Wells and Robert M. Yerkes were associated with Boston Psychopathic Hospital (11). Grace Kent and David Shakow at Worcester State Hospital were also early workers in the field. It was primarily at these three hospitals in Massachusetts and at St. Elizabeth in Washington, D.C. in which the function of the clinical psychologist in a mental hospital was developed.

The state hospital has provided the psychologist with invaluable opportunities for his professional development. This has proceeded along two main lines, research and clinical. Both have been made possible by the rich source material of a state hospital population. The role of the clinical psychologist traditionally has been considered to be one of service to the individual patient. For a long time, perhaps into the 1930's, he was conceived as a mental tester, whose activities centered about the measurement of isolated psychological functions, intelligence level, memory function, temperament, and the like. Under these conditions the psychologist experimented, developed and applied various psychometric tests. From the 1920's on there has been increasing concern with systematic programs of research in state hospitals.

WORCESTER STATE HOSPITAL

Worcester State Hospital, founded in 1832, is the oldest center of training and research in psychiatry in Massachusetts. Worcester State Hospital is approved for psychiatric residency training by the American Board of Psychiatry and Neurology. The psychiatric training program is affiliated with Tufts College Medical School and the Psychiatric Training Faculty of Massachusetts. There are similar programs offered by the School of Nursing for affiliate nurses and the Occupational Therapy department, affiliated with the Boston School of Occupational Therapy. Students in sociology, theology, and medicine are also systematically trained as part of the hospital's function.

To a large extent, this role of teaching and training provides the framework for the clinical activities of the hospital. Somewhat over 800 adult patients are admitted each year, and the hospital has a bed capacity of approximately 2850. The hospital also conducts a psychosomatic clinic which provides experience in outpatient psychiatry. An affiliation is maintained with the Worcester Youth Guidance Center (a state clinic liberally aided by Community Chest funds) which provides treatment for the psychological disturbances of children.

The Psychology Department at Worcester State Hospital is administered by the Director of Psychological Research. The department consists of six staff psychologists, three psychology interns, and one postdoctoral fellow. Three staff psychologists concern themselves with full-time research activities. The interests of another staff member are in group therapy, half time being devoted to research in this area, the other half to actual group therapy. One staff member concentrates almost exclusively on supervision of the intern training program. The Director takes administrative responsibility for the department as well as for its research and clinical activities.

The Psychology Department is situated in two locations within the hospital. The departmental members involved in administrative and clinical functions, and in those research activities utilizing the more usual clinical techniques, work in the hospital administration building. This section of the Psychology Department occupies eleven offices. Of these, one is an observation room equipped with a one-way vision window and recording equipment. A filing system is maintained in which the records of all patients having psychological tests are indexed on approximately 100 variables by means of a key-sort technique. Research using more experimental procedures is undertaken in a nine-room section located close to the psychiatric wards. This contains five experimental rooms including a constant temperature and humidity room.

A medical library of over 10,000 volumes, with a full-time librarian, is maintained by the hospital. The library subscribes to 122 general scientific, medical, psychiatric, and psychological journals. In addition, the Psychology Department maintains its own library.

RESEARCH

The Psychology Department at Worcester State Hospital has been committed for many years to studies in the field of psychopathology. Its philosophy is that the role of the clinical psychologist is fundamentally one of research in the clinical area.

The Research activities of the Psychology Department at Worcester State Hospital function as a part of the Hospital Research Service. This was established in 1927 as an administratively separate interdisciplinary unit organized for the study of schizophrenia. The Research Service functions under a Medical Director of Research and is organized into medical-psychiatric, biochemical, and psychological components. Over-all policies are established through a Research Council for which the Director of Research serves as chairman. Thus, psychologists participate as part of a scientific team that includes kindred specialists in biochemistry, physiology, neurophysiology, endocrinology, neurology, psychiatry, and sociology.

Research was initiated at relatively simple and even reflex levels of function of the human organism to delimit those factors in which presumed differences existed between normals and schizophrenics. Gradually, investigations were brought to include some of the more complex functions such as thinking and intelligence. Recently, studies of reaction and adaptation to stress, factors in social survival, determinants of symptom choice, and psychophysiological relations have become central points of interest for research. The more strictly biological studies have been undertaken in collaboration with the Worcester Foundation for Experimental Biology. Considerable collaborative research has been undertaken in conjunction with Clark University, particularly in an investigation of developmental processes and their relations to mental disorder and social adequacy. Regularly scheduled seminars and conferences are integral functions of the Research Service and Psychology Department at Worcester State Hospital.

A postdoctoral training program has recently been initiated in conjunction with the Psychology Department of Clark University. The program is primarily designed to provide intensive training in areas not ordinarily covered in graduate study. The postdoctoral fellowship permits the psychology student to participte in integrated research programs with workers in related disciplines. In this way he is able to integrate his academic background in research and clinical training with the investigation of specific and pertinent problems in the clinical field. The particular emphasis in the postdoctoral program depends on the needs and interests of the individual. While the main emphasis in the postdoctoral program is on research, opportunities are always available for the student to participate in the clinical activities of our Department. As now conceived, the postdoctoral program is a two-year program of training.

On the predoctoral level also, emphasis is placed on student participation in the departmental research program. In the majority of cases, the intern usually selects some part of the departmental research program as his special interest. A number of these projects have been turned into doctoral dissertations. Difficulties in communication have sometimes arisen in terms of acceptance of such problems as thesis material. In part this is based on the difficulties of working out complex material by letter. It arises also from a lack of familiarity on the part of university faculties with the aims and objectives of our Department. Many of the difficulties that arise with research in psychopathology are special problems in design and methodology which are almost unique to research in a clinical setting. Despite this, correspondence has always resulted in an attitude of acceptance on the part of the university faculty, and we have felt that the exchange has been mutually profitable. Nevertheless, in terms of research, the optimum resolution of difficulties appears to be the selection of students for training whose doctoral dissertations are either partially or fully completed. In this way, the student may make the fullest use of the hospital research program as a learning process without regard to the complexities inherent in obtaining university approval for a specific problem.

CLINICAL TRAINING

The clinical activities of our Department are structured to meet the needs of the training program. An emphasis on training has been one of the continuing and central interests of clinical psychologists, and this has perhaps made one of the most effective contributions toward the growth of clinical psychology as a profession. To a large extent, the nature of that training has been in the form of internships, and state hospital programs have led the field in providing that training. The first internship (7) in a mental hospital was established in 1913 at the Boston Psychopathic Hospital under the supervision of Robert M. Yerkes and was continued by F. L. Wells. In 1922 intern programs were initiated at McLean Hospital by Helge Lundholm, and at Worcester State Hospital under Grace Kent. In 1928 the Worcester program came under the direction of David Shakow, whose thinking and philosophy have been fundamental in the development of graduate training in clinical psychology (9, 10). To a large extent, the current training program in clinical psychology in our Department is an outgrowth of his eighteen years as chief psychologist. At the present time our Department offers training at both the predoctoral and postdoctoral level. These programs are supported in part by the U.S. Public Health Service.

At both the predoctoral and postdoctoral levels, we prefer to train those students whose primary interest is in the field of experimental psychopathology. Nevertheless, even though it is our opinion that the clinical psychologist's main contribution lies in research, we believe that the student should learn to know and understand the difficulties of patients from whom, after all, arise the problems in psychopathology. In general, the internship program is designed to provide competency in the usual psychological methods of personality evaluation, but even more important to provide the opportunity to learn the various approaches and assumptions which are made by workers in allied fields, and to sensitize the intern to the complex of function which makes possible the operation of a modern mental hospital. The internship program exposes the student to a broader range of experiences than can be provided in his prior practicum or clerkship placements. He is placed in a situation where he can apply the knowledge and techniques learned in an academic setting both in a practical fashion and at a professional level. During the internship year he directly observes psychopathological behavior and develops the seriousness and sense of responsibility required in dealing with the intense and living problems of patients. He learns to appreciate at first hand the complexities of clinical evaluation and treatment. Throughout the year, the student concurrently becomes sensitized to relevant problems in psychopathology which may become the focus for research. During this year of training attitudes are established, in dealing with members of allied professions, which will remain relatively permanent. Consequently, the appropriate habit patterns for smooth working relationships should be established at this time. We believe this cannot be established by lecture, although casual discussion at appropriate moments is beneficial. Most influential is the example of harmonious and productive relationships among members of the whole professional staff. The pattern should be set of the clinical psychologist, in a setting of a mental hospital, as a member of a professional team. The very real problems associated with an interdisciplinary approach need to be worked through during the internship year. Recently we have decided to begin our psychology training year at the same time as the psychiatric residency training program. Hospital procedures are thus introduced to the psychology and psychiatric students simultaneously. This serves as a mutual introduction and affords a good opportunity for the establishment of working relationships. Of equal importance, however, is the opportunity for personal and emotional growth which the experiences of the internship year provide.

An orientation period of approximately three to four weeks starts the psychology training program, during which time the intern becomes acquainted with the daily routine of the hospital. This includes participation in ward rounds, diagnostic interviews, staff conferences, interviewing of relatives, observation of admission procedures, physical therapies, occupational ward rounds, and lectures on administrative routines. A weekly discussion group composed of the new psychiatric residents and the psychology students is held throughout the year. The function of this discussion group is twofold: (1) didactic discussion and practical demonstration of cases of mental disorder, and (2) to explore their own attitudes in relation to each other as individuals and of the roles of psychology and psychiatry. Experience has shown that the latter activity is by far the more valuable, and in fact has proven to be one of the most beneficial features of the training program.

Immediately subsequent to the orientation period the intern is assigned a case for psychological testing by the supervising psychologist. Referrals for psychological testing are usually made by the Director of Clinical Psychiatry at the staff conferences where newly admitted patients are seen. The bases for such requests are varied. A referral may be made when a problem of differential diagnosis arises, to clarify prognostic material, or to provide an understanding of the patient and his problems which may be useful in a psychotherapeutic relationship. Very often the psychologist will be asked relatively specific questions such as, "Is the patient a suicidal risk?" or "How severely depressed is the patient?" In other cases a general personality evaluation may be requested or it may simply be a referral for intellectual evaluation. Sometimes cases may be referred for psychological testing because a patient may have symptomatology which is classically characteristic of a certain disorder and as such may be used for demonstration or teaching purposes.

Our psychology students receive intensive training in descriptive psychiatry. This has been seen as a necessary precaution since these students are expected to undertake psychotherapeutic sessions. It is felt that the student must become sensitized to the types of patients with whom he deals and the risks and care needed in dealing with patients. The Director of Clinical Psychiatry periodically assigns newly admitted patients to the psychology interns and postdoctoral fellows who then undertake psychiatric examinations, write up complete diagnostic evaluations, interview relatives for anamnestic purposes, and present these cases at hospital staff conferences. The Director of Clinical Psychiatry intensively reviews and supervises these cases with the psychology students prior to presentation at staff meetings.

Training in psychotherapy is a central aspect of the internship program. Patients for psychotherapy are chosen from the hospital population and the outpatient clinic on the basis of student readiness for such training. One afternoon a week is spent in supervision by a practicing psychoanalyst. A second psychoanalyst conducts a weekly workshop in which psychotherapeutic and interviewing techniques are discussed. These latter sessions are attended by the psychiatric residents as well as by the psychology interns. The aim of this training and interviewing in psychotherapy is more than a teaching of therapeutic procedures. The attempt is to develop a clinical evaluative approach toward psychotherapy and to lay a basis for future research if the students should subsequently wish to investigate the nature of the therapeutic process.

Approximately one third of the intern's time is spent in diagnostic testing. This includes the whole procedure of test administration, interpretation, report writing, and presentation of the case at staff conference. All of these activities are supervised by a staff psychologist. The supervising psychologist observes the student's first test session which is then followed by a discussion period. This reveals strong and weak points in test administration, but equally stressed is the meaning of the student's and patient's behavior in the test period toward each other. The student then writes a case evaluation, which is followed by an intense supervisory session with an emphasis on detailed analysis. The student's report is also discussed and evaluated from the viewpoint of the amount of information it contributes toward an understanding of the case and to its final disposition. Each case is then staffed by the responsible psychiatrist, the psychology student and his supervisor. This is considered to be a teaching session for both psychiatric and psychology students, one in which the complementary contributions of both disciplines are integrated. Subsequently, the student presents his case report at a full staff conference.

Emphasis is placed in the psychological test program on an intensive analysis of a relatively small number of patients. The intern is assigned cases to represent a wide variety of psychopathological conditions. These are drawn from the State Hospital population, an outpatient clinic, or are referred from the County Jail. For approximately the first six months the student evaluates each case with no knowledge of the patient's case history. This permits the student to learn the strength and limitations of psychological test instruments, to develop confidence and skill in his handling of test procedures, and to avoid the subtle influence which knowledge of case-history data may have on interpretation of test material.

The clinical activities of the Psychology Department are rounded out by a wide variety of seminars and staff conferences. These are conducted not only within the Psychology Department, but also in other departments of the hospital, the Psychology Department of Clark University, and the Worcester Foundation for Experimental Biology. Weekly classes in neurology are open to psychology students as well as a weekly staff on neurological cases. There are also seminars on case history analysis, the theory and practice of psychoanalysis, theory and practice of projective techniques, various case demonstrations, discussions in various medical fields related to clinical psychology, the psychiatric staff conferences of the hospital, weekly outpatient clinic staffs, and special teaching conferences of the Worcester Youth Guidance Center.

The Psychology Department participates in the general hospital teaching program. Staff members of the Department contribute to the training of students in nursing, occupational therapy, sociology, theology, and medicine through both formal and informal lectures and discussions.

Thus, the activities of the Psychology Department at Worcester State Hospital fall into four main categories: (1) research in psychopathology, (2) clinical services, including psychiatric case work-up and psychotherapy, and case evaluation through psychological tests, (3) training of student psychologists, and (4) participation in the general hospital teaching program.

FUTURE OUTLOOK

In retrospect, the psychologists in state hospitals served initially as research workers; only gradually was their function broadened to include more clinical activities. Today the psychologist in the state hospital is primarily thought of as a clinician, one whose role is of service to the individual patient. The relative emphasis and time spent by psychologists in state hospitals in the functions of research and clinical service has to a large extent, been governed by: (1) the pressure, needs, and environment in which he works; and (2) the personal interests and motives of the psychologist. Today, most clinical psychologists spend the major part of their time in responding to the demands of the hospital clinical services.

The present functions of the clinical psychologist in the state hospital are not unique but correspond very well with the activities of clinical psychologists in general. The psychologist in the state hospital is today a more adequately trained and a professionally more responsible individual than his predecessors. This stems, first, from the increasing professional acceptance of the clinical psychologist since the end of World War II, and secondly, from the more intensive and higher level of training which the clinical psychologist now brings to his work.

There has been a series of influences which has recently affected the interests and activities of the clinical psychologist operating within the state hospital. The hospital psychologist of today receives more intensive academic training than he did previously. The orientation of the university with its research interests has stimulated the clinical psychologist toward research, all the more since the academic psychologist has recently come to undertake experiments in problems which have clinical relevance. Within the state hospital setting, however, increasing professional demands have been made of the psychologist for psychiatric evaluation and psychotherapy. Thus, the state hospital psychologist is finding himself beset with simultaneous demands for more research and more clinical service. Few psychologists function comfortably in both roles. This may be due to limitations in available time, but also, it may be because different personality constellations seem needed to function in these diverse roles.

In the state hospital, these increased demands have been met primarily in two ways: (1) by an increase in the number of psychology staff positions, and (2) by an increasing specialization of function.

Whether these solutions are temporary or permanent is not yet clear. The ultimate functions, identifications, and loyalties of the clinical psychologist remain largely unsettled. These are problems which face the whole field of clinical psychology. The state hospital programs in clinical psychology can play an important role in determining these future directions.

REFERENCES

1. Franz, Shephard Ivory. In C. Murchison (Ed.), *The Psychological Register*. Vol. III. Worcester: Clark Univer. Press, 1932. Pp. 171-173.
2. Franz, S. I. *Handbook of mental examination methods*. New York: Macmillan, 1919.
3. Franz, S. I. Shephard Ivory Franz. In C. Murchison (Ed.), *A history of psychology in autobiography*. Vol. II. Worcester: Clark Univer. Press, 1932. Pp. 89-113.
4. Hall, G. S. Laboratory of the McLean Hospital. *Amer. J. Insanity*, 1894, 51, 358-364.
5. Holzberg, Jules D. The practice and problems of clinical psychology in a state psychiatric hospital. *J. consult. Psychol.*, 1952, 16, 98-103.
6. Moore, T. V. A century of psychology in its relationship to American psychiatry. In J. K. Hall (Ed.) *One Hundred Years of American Psychiatry*. New York: Columbia Univer. Press, 1944. Pp. 443-477.
7. Morrow, W. R. The development of psychological internship training. *J. consult. Psychol.*, 1946, 10, 165-183.
8. Raimy, V. C. (Ed.) *Training in clinical psychology*. New York: Prentice Hall, 1950.
9. Shakow, D. An internship year for psychologists (with special reference to psychiatric hospitals). *J. consult. Psychol.*, 1938, 2, 73-76.
10. Shakow, D. The functions of the psychologist in the state hospital. *J. consult. Psychol.*, 1939. 3, 20-23.

11. Watson, R. I. A brief history of clinical psychology. *Psychol. Bull.*, 1953, 50, 321-346.
12. Wells, F. L. In C. Murchison (Ed.), *The Psychological Register.* Vol. III. Worcester: Clark Univer. Press, 1932. Pp. 535-537.
13. Whitehorn, J. C. A century of psychiatric research in America. In J. K. Hall (Ed.), *One hundred years of American psychiatry.* New York: Columbia Univer. Press, 1944. Pp. 167-193.

V.

THE MENNINGER FOUNDATION

MARTIN MAYMAN and HERBERT J. SCHLESINGER

The Menninger Foundation is a nonprofit organization devoted to psychiatric treatment, research, and training. The Foundation today is a complicated and rather extensive organization which bears little resemblance, except in spirit, to its modest start in 1919 as a partnership for the group practice of psychiatry. The Foundation now includes a small, psychoanalytically oriented hospital and outpatient clinic, a department of child psychiatry, a department of neurology and neurosurgery, a research department, a department of education, and a department of social applications of psychiatry.

Up to 1941 almost the sole concern of the Menninger Clinic was diagnosis and treatment, although some education and research were carried on from the first. By 1941 it had become clear that a major expansion in education and research was needed to help meet the growing demand for psychiatric services in both the armed services and civilian life. It was proposed that the Menninger Clinic partnership be dissolved and a nonprofit foundation be incorporated in its place which could devote itself to the expansion of education and research. The reorganization was accomplished by 1946. Several major research programs were formalized and others inaugurated under the auspices of the new Research Department (5, 6, 8, 9, and 11), and training commitments were greatly extended through the establishment of the Menninger Foundation School of Psychiatry and the Menninger Foundation School of Clinical Psychology. From January 1, 1946, to December 31, 1953, 390 psychiatrists, 52 psychologists, 20 social workers, 77 psychiatric aides, 93 adjunctive therapists, and 9 marriage counselors have received clinical training in programs sponsored by the Menninger Foundation.[1]

Current research, education,[2] and clinical functions are carried by a staff of 36 psychiatrists, 11 psychologists (in addition, there are two post-

---

[1] All statistics cited in this chapter are as of December, 1953.

[2] The Menninger School of Psychiatry is maintained with the collaboration of the staffs of the Topeka State Hospital and Winter V.A. Hospital where psychiatric residents obtain the bulk of their clinical experience.

doctoral fellows, two part-time staff members, and five research assistants), 14 social workers, 21 nurses, 21 adjunctive therapists, and 42 psychiatric aides. Most of the professional staff members at the Foundation carry research or teaching functions along with their clinical responsibilities, but all remain closely involved in clinical practice and devote the major segment of their time to clinical services.

Clinical services are provided on both an inpatient and outpatient basis by the Departments of Adult Psychiatry, Child Psychiatry, and Neurology. Some statistics may help the reader visualize the clinical setting. The Menninger Foundation Hospital is a relatively small unit compared with the average psychiatric hospital. The completion of its new wing in 1954 will boost its capacity from 70 beds to 113 beds for adults. Ground has also been purchased for the construction of a new Southard School, which would enable it to accept 28 children for residential care as compared with its present capacity of 16. The largest department of the Foundation is the Department of Adult Psychiatry which is responsible for the psychiatric evaluation and treatment of all adult patients. In 1953, 562 adult patients were in treatment at the Foundation either as outpatients, inpatients, or "day patients" who use the hospital treatment facilities during the day but live in town. In addition, 400 patients were seen for diagnostic evaluation or for consultations involving anywhere from one to fifteen interviews. In the Department of Child Psychiatry there were 55 outpatient evaluations and 29 consultations completed last year. There were twenty children in treatment, four as outpatients and sixteen in residence.

Not all of the staff psychologists at the Foundation are attached to the Department of Adult Psychiatry. Some are assigned to the Department of Child Psychiatry, others to the Departments of Research and Education. Regardless of the primary departmental assignment, however, there remains considerable overlap of function. Staff psychologists in the Research Department do some psychotherapy, diagnostic work, or teaching outside of their Research Department commitments. Similarly, most psychologists in the Department of Adult Psychiatry spend some time in research as well as in psychotherapy or diagnostic testing. Only the relative proportions of these time commitments vary with the department and assignment. It should be noted, however, that regardless of the amount of time spent in other functions by psychologists in the Department of Adult Psychiatry, diagnostic testing is considered to be their most important and unique contribution to clinical operations. Although a psychologist may become a skilled psychotherapist or researcher, he does not give up his identification as a clinical psychologist with primary skills in diagnostic testing.

DIAGNOSTIC TESTING

Diagnostic testing is the oldest and best established function of the Menninger psychologist. The first diagnostic tester, Mr. John Stone, was employed in 1923. Mr. Stone for many years did all of the Clinic's psychometric testing, which at that time was directed largely at the measurement of intelligence. From 1934 to 1940, there was a handful of psychologists here, some of them full-time staff members at Southard School, and some, under the direction of J. F. Brown of the University of Kansas, were part-time diagnosticians in adult psychiatry. In 1940, David Rapaport came to join the psychology department and became its first full-time psychologist in adult diagnostic testing. It was largely under his leadership that the role of the psychologist as a diagnostician was first crystallized.

Initially, diagnostic psychological testing was on a rather tentative footing. Psychiatrists were not convinced of the contribution that diagnostic testing could make to their work with patients. Test reports were cautious, test-oriented and self-consciously prone to citing test "evidence" in support of diagnostic inferences. Moreover, reports were written according to a strict policy of blind diagnosis.

With the publication of *Diagnostic Psychological Testing* (9), in 1945, and with the progressive accumulation of more and more diagnostic "successes," the original need for primarily research-oriented, test-validating reports diminished, and an essentially pragmatic, service-oriented, problem-focused, advice-giving approach took its place. In part, this change was associated also with the introduction of therapy training for psychologists, which necessarily led to a fuller appreciation of the kinds of issues most pertinent to therapy planning.

The diagnostic testing role of the clinical psychologist today can be best discussed within the context of the major clinical operation. For this purpose we shall describe briefly the operation of the Department of Adult Psychiatry to which most of the clinical psychologists are assigned.

The diagnosis and treatment of adults is handled largely by four semi-autonomous teams called Clinical Sections. Three of these deal with inpatients and day patients, and are made up of one senior psychiatrist, two or three junior psychiatrists, a resident psychiatrist, one or two psychologists, a social worker, nurse, and adjunctive therapist. Sections meet regularly two or three times a week to discuss the evaluation, treatment planning, and progress of the patients assigned to their care. A fourth Section deals solely with outpatient evaluations, consultations, and short-term treatment. It does not include a nurse or activities therapist but is augmented by several psychiatric consultants.

Most of the psychologist's diagnostic work in the Department of Adult Psychiatry is done in connection with the clinical Section of which he is a member. Here the psychologist functions as a clinician. Although he may test about half of the patients seen for evaluation and most of the patients in treatment with his Section, he participates in *all* group discussions and decisions. He uses his testing skills when they seem likely to contribute to the understanding of a patient's problem or to plan more effectively for his treatment.

Testing is occasionally done to corroborate the psychiatrist's findings or to provide an independent clinical judgment, but far more often as an integral part of the Section's work with the patient. Psychiatrists and psychologists and other Section members exchange data, impressions and opinions at every stage of evaluation or treatment. The psychologist may raise questions to be answered through further psychiatric or neurological examination, as well as attempt to answer questions that may grow out of these examinations. The collaboration of the Section members is in fact so close, and the final case summary so often a full synthesis of the several sets of findings, that the question of who contributed what to the total picture becomes both difficult and academic.

This degree of integration presumes several prior conditions which have developed over the years. Most important of these is that the psychologist and psychiatrist speak the same language. Both use the same clinical-descriptive terms and work within the same conceptual-theoretical framework, psychoanalytic ego and instinct psychology.

Despite this common theoretical orientation and frequent overlap of functions, there is still considerable distinction in professional roles. The psychologist is specially equipped to do a microscopic study of the patient in action and certain aspects of the patient's functioning fall particularly within the purview of his diagnostic methods: (1) the impact of emotional disturbance on intellectual functioning, which often reveals trends in an illness not yet apparent in grosser clinical behavior; (2) the characteristic defensive or coping behavior of the patient when confronted with a challenging problem or a frustrating situation; (3) general personality dispositions and "character" traits; (4) fantasy material which may reflect important inner pressures and conflict areas. Since no single test is sufficiently comprehensive in its sampling of behavior to permit a reliable evaluation of all of these areas of the personality into which the illness may make intrusive inroads, a battery of tests is always used for diagnostic evaluations. In adult work, this includes the Wechsler-Bellevue, Rorschach, TAT, Word Association, Story Recall, and Object Sorting tests. The Bender-Gestalt and Draw-a-Person tests are used frequently, especially when there is a possibility that a patient has some organic brain damage. With children, the tests used vary with the age and intelligence level of the child being tested. The Cattell Intelligence Scale for Infants and the Gesell Developmental Schedule are used routinely with infants, and the Revised Stanford-Binet and Merrill Palmer Scale of Mental Tests with all other children. The Rorschach, Children's Apperception Test, and TAT are frequently used with children three years of age or older, and the Bender-Gestalt, Children's Wechsler-Bellevue, House-Tree-Person, Word Association, Sorting Test, and Sentence Completion tests are used with children about six years of age or older.

A second important condition for successful collaboration between the diagnostic tester and clinical interviewer is a common purpose or direction for the total evaluation. In this connection, both psychiatrists and psychologists have been preoccupied for several years with some very troublesome questions: What is the purpose of evaluation? What function does diagnosis serve? What do we mean by "diagnostic testing"? What *should* we mean by diagnostic testing? The answers to these questions, if not expressed, are certainly implicit in the reports which we have been writing. Psychologists still use nosological terms, but do not stop at labeling. They do not believe in trying merely to identify the patient's "disease." Patients do occasionally manifest identifiable symptom syndromes, but this does not indicate the presence of a *disease;* rather, it indicates the presence of a particular constellation of defense mechanisms directed against a particular constellation of impulses in a particular personality. Psychologists try to use their tests to understand the person and his misdirected efforts to achieve some measure of psychological equilibrium. This point of view has been expressed recently by Karl A. Menninger, with important consequences for the entire procedure of psychiatric diagnosis (7).

In practice, all of this means that we believe it is not as important to find the proper label as it is to help answer such questions as these: What constellation of defenses is the patient using at present? How rigidly fixated are they? Is there sufficient control over impulses to permit treatment on an outpatient basis? What strengths are there which can be capitalized upon in a hospital treatment program? How much use will this patient be able to make of intensive psychotherapy? What kinds of resistances is he likely to use, and how rigidly will he cling to them? Are there any significant indications or contraindications to any particular type of treatment for this patient? What seem to be the areas of greatest conflict at present?

At the same time, testing is used to determine the kind and degree of pathology present in any patient. Here too, the attention is directed to functional capacities and functional disturbances, rather than to "differential diagnosis." For example, the psychologist may be called upon to help answer such questions as: Is there latent schizophrenic thought disorder beneath this ostensible neurotic syndrome? Is there any evidence that organic brain damage contributes to this patient's disorganization? Is this patient's narcissism and immaturity part of a deep-seated ego deficit, or are there latent ego strengths in the character structure which are masked by the manifest infantile behavior?

In order that he may better explore questions of this nature, the psychologist has learned to become a participant-observer in the diagnostic process, one who seeks not only to understand, but also to use his relationship with the patient during the diagnostic process. Without destroying the basic psychological equivalence of the testing situation for patients, the psychologist tries to relate to his patient not in a rigidly mechanical "standardized" fashion, but rather as a clinician who enters into a special kind of relationship with the patient in order to find answers to some of the questions cited above. He approaches the patient as a clinician, not a psychometrist.

Development and change are still taking place in both the philosophy and the practice of diagnostic testing. Some psychologists are experimenting with the value of new testing procedures which may be more fruitful methods for learning more about a person's self-concept, perceptual style, manifestations of organic brain damage, and prognostic criteria for patients in psychotherapy. The active pursuit of such clinical explorations leaves little doubt that diagnostic testing continues to be the primary function of the clinical psychologist at the Menninger Foundation.

TRAINING

Teaching occupies a relatively smaller proportion of the psychologists' time than other functions, although psychologists do participate actively in a number of training programs, including the Menninger School of Psychiatry and the Topeka Institute for Psychoanalysis. Training in clinical psychology has been provided uninterruptedly by the Menninger Foundation since 1935. The history of these efforts has been described in some detail in previous publications (10, 12).

Whether training beginners or more advanced clinical psychologists, we try to help the psychologist-in-training to develop diagnostic skills, learn a set of concepts which will enable him to use these skills to best advantage, acquire a clinical (helping) attitude which will give purpose to these skills, and work closely and co-operatively with members of other disciplines in psychiatry. These we consider to be the cornerstone of professional competence and the core of the professional identity of the clinical psychologist. Since diagnostic testing forms the nucleus of this professional role, it is stressed at every level of training. The skillful exercise of this function in a way which contributes materially to patient care gives the young psychologist a conviction which he can get in no other way—that he, as a psychologist, can make a unique clinical contribution.

Several years of experience with one-year predoctoral internships demonstrated how little can be accomplished in such a short time compared with what must be taught to assure professional competence. This experience seems to be widely shared since the trend in clinical training is more and more in the direction of supplemental training at the postdoctoral level. At present, the Menninger Foundation devotes itself exclusively to such intensive, advanced training by offering two-year postdoctoral Fellowships for psychologists who have had at least one year of previous (often predoctoral) clinical experience. The Fellowship program is supported by Public Health Service funds and is available not only to recently trained psychologists but also to more experienced psychologists who desire additional specialized training. At present only two postdoctoral Fellows are accepted for training at any one time.

The most important medium of training, we believe, is individual supervision. The integration of skills and attitudes, the change and growth which mark the maturation of the professional self can be accomplished only through this special kind of teaching relationship. Through this relationship, the psychologist-in-training can come to recognize blind spots in the way he sees himself and his function, can look closely at his attitudes about patients and illness, and can deal with the resistances to professional growth which these may represent. Much thought has been given to the process of supervision as it helps the psychologist-in-training to accomplish such objectives of professional growth at the same time that he is acquiring a firmer grasp of skills and concepts (2, 3).

Considerable training is also accomplished through lectures, seminars, discussions and reading. These include a number of basic seminars on psychopathology, psychodynamic theory, and test rationale, as well as other courses offered regularly in the Menninger School of Psychiatry on the theory and practice of psychotherapy. The small number of psychologists taken for training permits the program to be individualized to a considerable degree. Special seminars are arranged to meet the special interests and needs of the psychologists being trained. It has been the practice to limit the time spent in didactic training to approximately eight hours per week.

The psychologist-in-training is given the opportunity to work with almost all members of the psychology staff and to be supervised by several of the senior members. He usually works with any one supervisor for at least a six-month period. During periodic evaluation meetings, usually at the start and end of each six-month period, the psychologist with the help of his supervisor tries to make explicit his current level of competence, the specific learning problems he has encountered, and the objectives for the next six-month period of training.

After a period of single-minded concentration upon diagnostic testing on the Admissions Section and one hospital Section of the Department of Adult Psychiatry, usually toward the end of his first year, the psychologist is encouraged to diversify his activities and explore at least one other area of specialization. He may wish to develop some skill as a child psychologist; there may be a research project he would like to pursue; or he may wish to concentrate on acquiring skill in psychotherapy. Before he chooses his area of secondary concentration, the psychologist is encouraged to sample all of these areas of specialization.

PSYCHOTHERAPY

Psychotherapy is one of a number of treatment methods available to patients at the Menninger Foundation. Patients accepted for psychotherapy at the Foundation span a broad range of diagnostic categories and include symptom neuroses, character problems, addictive, homosexual, and other behavioral disorders, and borderline and manifest psychoses. Relatively few severely regressed patients are seen in psychotherapy. The availability of hospital facilities within the same administrative structure makes it possible to accept certain classes of patients for whom psychotherapy is possible only in a hospital setting. When a recommendation for psychotherapy is made, the case may be assigned to any of the staff trained in this specialty. The assignment is made on the basis of the skills, level of training, special interests of the therapist, and the needs of the case, rather than on the basis of the therapist's professional discipline.

At the Menninger Foundation all psychotherapy, whether done by psychiatrists or psychologists, is supervised. It is felt that all psychotherapists should have the opportunity to discuss their cases and their psychotherapy problems with more experienced staff or, at the highest level of skill, with equally experienced staff. This attitude reflects the belief in the group practice of psychiatry which characterizes all of the Foundation's clinical work. The nature, extent, and frequency of supervision varies, of course, with the skill, level of training, and needs of the psychotherapist as well as the complexity of the problems with which he deals.

Psychotherapy supervision is offered by the most senior staff members of the Foundation, functioning as a supervision committee with a senior psychiatrist at their head. The work of each psychotherapist, as well as general problems in psychotherapy and its supervision, are discussed and handled by this group. Psychotherapy supervision assignments are made, where possible, with an eye toward matching particular training needs of the psychotherapist with particular strengths among the supervisors. Psychotherapy supervision assignments are rotated periodically to provide varied training experience. At present, the integration of clinical psychologists into this psychotherapy structure is complete. Certain psychologists of long experience and particular teaching skill now function as supervisors in this structure.

Psychologists may seek training in psychotherapy with any of several motives. Some psychologists with a deep interest in helping patients directly have a primary interest in doing psychotherapy. Others are primarily interested in doing research in this or other clinical areas. It is widely recognized, too, that well-supervised psychotherapy is an excellent medium to enrich the clinical acumen of the psychologist. It provides him with first-hand knowledge of the psychotherapy process, in the planning for which, through his diagnostic function, the psychologist must participate. The extent of the training that a psychologist receives in psychotherapy will depend upon his interests, talents, and aspirations as well as upon the need of the Foundation for other of his services.

Full psychotherapy training for any staff member typically extends over a period of years. Long before a patient is assigned to him, the psychologist or psychiatrist will have taken part in a training sequence with both didactic and clinical aspects. Formal lecture courses on the theory and practice of psychotherapy are offered in the Menninger School of Psychiatry. Following these introductory experiences (which may be waived, if adequate didactic preparation has already been acquired) the psychologist is assigned to a psychotherapy supervision group in which five to ten psychiatrists- and psychologists-in-training, under the leadership of an experienced psychotherapist, review the on-going work of one or more advanced members of the group. It is one of the functions of the group leader to recommend further training for any member of the group on the basis of the kind and quality of the contributions he makes as a participant in the group. Thus, after some period of attendance at psychotherapy group supervision meetings the psychotherapist-in-training may be assigned a supervisor by the Psychotherapy Supervision Committee. His first interviews with the supervisor are spent in selecting a suitable case as well as in discussing the various technical and personal problems related to the beginning of a psychotherapeutic relationship. Psychotherapists customarily meet with their supervisors at least one hour a week.

Some psychologists now spend about half of their time as psychotherapists. For others, psychotherapy practice is more limited, often because the psychologist himself prefers to commit his time to other functions. On the principle that the richest possible training should be made available to those who would specialize in the area of clinical research, psychoanalytic training is available to psychologists in the Topeka Institute of Psychoanalysis.

RESEARCH

From its birth as a group practice, the Menninger Foundation has leavened its clinical practice with a strong research bias. Through the years clinical papers have marked the range of interests that have captured the curiosity of the staff (1, 13). With the reorganization of the institution as a Foundation came also the first commitments to organized, programmatic research. Psychologists have usually been most active in the conduct of these projects. But it is recognized that clinical research, like clinical practice, may often best be served by the collaborative efforts of workers from several disciplines and recently several such clinical investigations have been undertaken by multidiscipline groups.

Formal research projects now occupy the full time of several psychologists and a part of the time of a larger number of psychiatrists, psychologists, and social workers. Others of the staff pursue exploratory research as part of their daily clinical work, and such explorations occasionally lead to more intensive and directed investigations. A multidiscipline Research Advisory Committee has been set up to encourage the staff to pursue their research interests. The Research Department also provides opportunities for several graduate students in psychology to obtain training in research by carrying out research projects under supervision or assisting in one of the large research projects.

Among current research activities is the "psychotherapy project." This study began as an investigation of the factors which make for success and failure among various psychotherapies. Gradually, this line of investigation prepared the way for research into three areas: (1) accuracy of prediction of the probable direction and success of psychotherapy from information available in the initial psychiatric evaluation, (2) interviews with patient and therapist upon termination of therapy to learn both about the process in psychotherapy and the benefits derived, (3) long-term follow-up studies of the patients treated in psychotherapy. As of this writing these studies are in their beginning phases.

The perception project (5) has for some years been an investigation of the highly individual ways in which a person perceives his world. Principles have been sought, using a variety of clinical and laboratory techniques, that could explain these highly idosyncratic perceptual styles. Paralleling this approach to perception is a series of studies investigating the unlearning or modification of perceptual biases (14). Several projects deal with children, one on understanding the psychology of the shifting ego states seen in some borderline-psychotic children (14), and another on the way in which essentially normal children learn to cope with their own problems (14). The "coping" project follows and builds upon the work done in the infancy project, a nonnormative investigation of infant behavior, and studies many of the same children who were studied previously as infants (8). A study now nearing termination is the investigation of criteria for selection of applicants for psychiatric training (6). These are but a few of the wide variety of clinical problems now being investigated by groups of the staff.

Conspicuous among the recent trends in research at the Menninger Foundation has been a sharp increase in interest and investment of time of psychiatrists in research projects. In the last year, training in research has been offered to psychiatric residents in the Menninger School of Psychiatry in order to stimulate this movement.

The Menninger Foundation offers excellent opportunities for research in clinical problems. Extensive clinical records are kept, a large staff permits extremely close observation of patients, and the multidiscipline spirit permits close collaboration on all facets of clinical problems. The Foundation maintains a psychological laboratory equipped with a wide variety of standard and specially designed experimental-psychological apparatus as well as well-equipped electronics and machine shops. Sound recording, photographic facilities and one-way vision rooms are available.

Plans for future development in research include the co-ordinating of psychological with physiological and neurological investigations. The present laboratory facilities are being expanded to take care of the growing commitment to research.

REFERENCES

1. *Bull. Menninger Clinic*, Vols. 1-17, 1936-1953.
2. Ekstein, R., & Sargent, H. Preliminary report on an experimental project in supervision in clinical psychology. *Trans. Kans. Acad. Sci.*, 1949, 52, 232-243.
3. Ekstein, R., Brown, Wm., Greenbaum, B. N., Hollingsworth, I., Kobler, A., & Sargent, H. A method of supervision for psychotherapy. *Trans. Kans. Acad. Sci.*, 1950, 53, 254-267.
4. Gill, M., & Brenman, M. *Hypnotherapy*. New York: International Universities Press, 1947.
5. Klein, G. S. The Menninger Foundation research on perception and personality, 1947-50, a review. *Bull. Menninger Clinic*, 1953, 17, 93-99.
6. Luborsky, L., Holt, R., & Morrow, W. R. Interim report of the research project on the selection of medical men for psychiatric training. *Bull. Menninger Clinic*, 1950, 14, 92-101.
7. Menninger, K. Psychological aspects of the organism under stress, Parts I and II. *J. Amer. psychoanal. Assoc.*, 1954, 2, 67-106, 280-310.
8. Rapaport, D. The future of research in clinical psychology and psychiatry: annual report to board of trustees, 1945-1946. *Amer. Psychologist*, 1947, 2, 167-172.
9. Rapaport, D., Gill, M., & Schafer, R. *Diagnostic psychological testing*. Chicago: Yearbook Publ., 1945.

10. Rapaport, D., & Schafer, R. The psychological internship training program of the Menninger Clinic. *J. consult. Psychol.*, 1946, 10, 216-220.

11. Schafer, R. *The clinical application of psychological tests.* New York: International Universities Press, 1948.

12. The Menninger Foundation School of Clinical Psychology: an experiment. *Bull. Menninger Clinic*, 1947, 11, 109-140.

13. Psychological research at the Menninger Clinic. *Bull. Menninger Clinic*, 1937, 1, 201-231.

14. Research number. *Bull Menninger Clinic*, July 1954, 20.

VI.

WICHITA GUIDANCE CENTER

JOSEPH E. BREWER

The Wichita Guidance Center is chartered under the laws of Kansas as a nonprofit corporation. As stated in its constitution: "The purpose of the corporation shall be the rendering of psychological and psychiatric services to the community, including the promotion of public understanding of the emotional problems of all ages and groups, the promotion of sound mental hygiene practices, consultation with and treatment of individual cases and the carrying on of research work in the problems associated with the various activities of the organization" (6, p. 1). Despite this very broad definition of services the Guidance Center has been essentially a child guidance center from its inception. In 1952, for example, only 9 per cent of the cases served were eighteen years of age or older.

The Wichita Guidance Center was founded in 1930 under the name of the Child Research Laboratory. This name reflected an attitude of close affiliation with the academic stream of thought, perhaps attempting to capitalize on the prestige of research as an important value in society and to ease the separation from the university laboratory. This same identification is seen in such organizations as the Institute of Juvenile Research in Illinois and the Bureau of Juvenile Research in Ohio. There must have been some awareness of the tentative nature of judgments in the field of applied psychology which made psychologists cautious in assuming a strictly service role. However, there was apparently no serious question that the main job of the Center was service to the community.

The Center began through the combined efforts of Dr. Edwina Cowan, who was in private practice of clinical psychology, and a group of women who had organized and helped staff an institution for the hospitalization of physically ill children. When this institution was no longer needed they transferred their interest and energy to the mental health of children with Dr. Cowan as director and virtually the entire staff. The financial status of the Center was directly in the hands of this group of women who constituted the Board of Directors. In 1932 the net receipts of the Center amounted to $3,606.11. All but $620.20 of this represented savings or money earned by the Board through sponsorship of lectures, dances, sales, etc. By 1934 the Center had been accepted as a member of the Community Chest and began its integration into the more formal support of community social services. In 1952, 57 per cent of the budget of $69,870.00 came from the Community Chest with the remainder coming from local, state and federal tax funds and fees.

There has been a stability in the management and direction of the Center as witnessed by the fact that there have been only three directors of the Center during its twenty-two years of existence, and by the presence on the Board of Directors in 1952 of two of the original group who formed the Center. Dr. Cowan served as director from 1930 to 1941. On her resignation Dr. Jerry W. Carter, Jr. was appointed director and served until 1948. Dr. Joseph E. Brewer, the present director, who had served as assistant director since 1946, was appointed director at that time.

The original conception of the staff of the Center in 1930 envisaged a team of psychologist, social worker and consulting psychiatrist. During most of the early years this was not realized. Dr. Edwina Cowan and one or two assistants with a minimum of training made up the basic staff.

During succeeding years this staff has undergone considerable growth to the extent that, in 1952, it consisted of four clinical psychologists, two junior psychologists, four consulting psychiatrists, two social workers, and four psychological interns.

The history of the standards of training required of personnel at the Center reflects the changes in the conceptions of the profession as a whole. The direction of the Center has always been in the hands of an experienced clinical psychologist trained at the doctoral level. During the early years psychometrists with no more than the A.B. degree were employed as assistants. At present no staff member has less than two years of graduate work and a year's supervised experience.

This concern with standards of training is reflected in the development of an internship program in 1946. In the beginning the M.A. was set as the educational requirement and in 1949 the completion of two years in a doctoral program was set as the requirement. The year 1949 also marked the beginning of a training grant from the U.S. Public Health Service.

A review of the case records indicates that, in 1932, the psychologist was dealing primarily with problems of placement, speech defects, school retardation and juvenile delinquency. The job of the psychologist was one of psychological study and direct recommendations. While testing played a dominant part in the study, an evaluation based on social history, parent interview and clinical impression was also essential. Definite and detailed recommendations, usually in the form of written reports, were made directly either to parents or to referring agency. For the most part there was little continuing contact with the child or family. Treatment was thought of primarily as habit re-education, speech training or remedial teaching. The approach was more an intellectual, direct attack on the problem than an attempt to help the child and parent with their feelings. There was an emphasis on effects of physical limitations such as visual and hearing defects and poor motor co-ordination. This emphasis is shown in the development of a test of motor co-ordination by the staff of the Center (5).

By 1942 the Guidance Center was functioning as, and considered itself, an "agencies' agency." Only 13 per cent of the cases seen that year were referred directly by parents or relatives. There was still much emphasis on diagnostic testing and interviewing for the purpose of helping to make plans for the child—plans mostly in the nature of environmental changes. There was emphasis on the possible importance of physical conditions influencing behavior as shown by the practice of requiring a medical examination and physician's report prior to acceptance at the Center (3).

The present-day program shows a definite emphasis on treatment of children and parents and somewhat more direct referral. Forty per cent of the cases served in 1952 were referred directly by parents or relatives. Many of those referred by physicians and schools are accepted with the understanding that the parent is to assume responsibility for the relationship with the Center and in turn the Center is responsible primarily to the family. There is a continuing service to all agencies in the community who are dealing with children. This service becomes more specialized as the training and skills of the personnel in these institutions and agencies improve.

Treatment methods have changed from direct recommendation and environmental manipulation to play therapy with children and counseling or therapy with parents and adults. The changed emphasis of referrals and treatment and also the greater emphasis on the parental role in children's behavior problems is reflected in decreased time spent in diagnostic testing and increased time in therapy with both children and parents.

At the Center diagnostic testing has developed in keeping with general trends. It is apparent that a wider choice of diagnostic tools is available to the clinician and the techniques of personality evaluation have been increased at the expense of co-ordination and achievement tests. Instead of a fairly standardized battery of tests the clinician now selects a series of tests for the particular problems presented by the client.

The job of the psychologist today is seen to fall in six areas as outlined in 1950 by Brewer (1): (1) clinical services to individual clients and families; (2) consultation to agencies and individuals; (3) preventive work through group programs; (4) community planning; (5) professional training; (6) research.

1. CLINICAL SERVICES TO INDIVIDUAL CLIENTS AND FAMILIES

At the Wichita Guidance Center the clinical psychologist is presented with a wide range of diagnostic and therapeutic tasks. The diagnostic problems range from evaluation of developmental status of infants prior to adoptive placement to the diagnosis of childhood psychosis. The treatment problems range from counseling with parents regarding normal development of young children to intensive, long-term therapy with prepsychotic children and psychotherapy of neurotic parents. The clinical psychologist functions co-operatively with social workers, psychiatrists and other psychologists in handling specific cases. Staff presentation of findings and treatment plans and therapeutic problems occur regularly. When a child and his family are accepted for service at least two persons work directly with the family. This means that continuous interaction of clinicians is necessary in carrying out diagnosis and treatment. The psychologist does not function as an independent person in serving the usual parent-child problem.

The actual population of clients being served by the Wichita Guidance Center can be described in several dimensions. The statistics utilized here are based on the referred case. If a parent or parents refer a child he is counted as one case and the tabulations are about the child. During 1952, 622 cases were served by the Center. In over 95 per cent of these the psychologists played a major or significant part.

The percentage of clients in different age groups was as follows: 20 per cent one year and under, 14 per cent between two and five years, 38 per cent between six and eleven years, 11 per cent between twelve and fourteen years, 7 per cent between fifteen and seventeen, 4 per cent between eighteen and twenty-four, 5 per cent twenty-five years and over. Virtually all the children were accompanied by their natural parents or boarding parents.

All economic levels of the community were represented by the families served, with the breadwinner of 50 per cent of them classified as a skilled workman. Only 5 per cent were nonwhite.

There are no adequate classificatory schemes for the problems encountered in a guidance center. The usual psychiatric classifications are not ordinarily meaningful and a final diagnostic label on a case is not useful. A classification in terms of presenting problems has been used at the Wichita Guidance Center, and the clinical tasks can be illuminated by referring to the proportions of cases falling in these categories. Data unless otherwise noted refer to 1952.

Evaluation of developmental progress is used to designate the service in response to those requests for some estimate of intellectual development and emotional maturity, or as a means of understanding a child who is felt to be deviant by the referring agent. This referring agent may be parent, teacher, physician, social worker, probation officer, or agency to whom is entrusted the child's placement. Thirty-seven per cent of the cases in 1952 were of this sort. Of these, two thirds were clearly referred for such evaluation as part of the planning for a suitable placement for the child in a home or institution. Most of these were infants being considered for adoptive placement. Of the others, a number were being considered for placement in an institution for the feeble-minded and a few were thought to be exceptionally bright and in need of special attention. A number were referred because of concern on the part of the parents about retarded development. Parents of retarded children often seek some cure for the retardation and frequently resist accepting the facts of retardation. The psychologist uses a therapeutic approach in interpreting psychological findings to such parents.

Problems of school adjustment constituted 12 per cent of the case load during 1952. The symptom seen in these cases is primarily a failure to achieve in a manner commensurate with ability. Bill, age nine, who was referred by his mother at the suggestion of the family physician is illustrative of this type of problem. A congenital malformation of the spine had required wearing braces from the age of six months until a year before his referral. He reacted explosively to frustrations at home and maintained a very hostile relationship with a sister two years younger than he. He would do no work at school unless someone was constantly with him. His poor achievement was of concern to Bill as well as his family. Diagnostic testing revealed him to be of average intelligence. Bill's problems appeared to result from parental rejection and guilt because of his malformation and their overprotection led to a dependent reaction which was being exploited by the boy. Treatment consisted of play therapy for sixteen months with one psychologist, and concurrently, remedial reading for eight months with another psychologist. Treatment of the mother by a third psychologist was centered around Bill and her relationship to him. The father was seen briefly by a fourth psychologist.

Withdrawing behavior (daydreaming, fears, feeling of inferiority, psychosomatic reactions) characterized the presenting problems of 23 per cent of the 1952 case load. Five-year-old Janet illustrates this type of problem. She was referred by her aunt with whom she lived. Janet was extremely withdrawn and whiney. Her behavior at kindergarten was isolated but the teacher did not feel this was occasion for concern. Janet felt rejected by a passive father and a cold hostile mother who placed her with the aunt when mother went to work. A favored younger sister aggravated the feelings of rejection. Play therapy was planned beginning with the initial contact. The aunt was seen by another therapist in weekly sessions focused on her relationship with the girl. Toward the end of therapy the aunt joined one of our therapy groups but attended only three sessions. Janet's play behavior duplicated that reported at home and school during the initial sessions. As her relationship with the therapist developed she was helped to express her feelings and take initiative in the play session. Janet took an active role in continuing therapy at a time when the aunt wished to terminate and also took an active part at termination. The child made full use of a permissive therapist who offered to help her become happier. The aunt was able to support the changes in Janet through her own growth and understanding. Therapy extended over an eight-month period.

Acting out behavior is the major symptom of 19 per cent of the case load in 1952. Rick, age seven, was referred by the school counselor because he was hostile and aggressive toward other children. Rick's mother had been to the Center two years previously but for only three visits. The referral problem was the same then as now. After two diagnostic interviews, which revealed superior verbal ability and average performance ability with aggression immediately available at any frustration, Rick was seen in therapeutic play once a week. He accepted his interviews as a means of helping him with his "mads." The expression of feelings was intense and disorganized. He progressed to where he could concentrate for most of the hour on a constructive task. The mother dealt with her overimpulsive and immature behavior and spent much time at first in talking of how Rick had always annoyed her and her husband. Gradually she came to the point of feeling they had unjustly blamed Rick for interfering with the settled way of life they had fallen into during eight years of childless marriage. Soon after reaching this point she reported a much more sympathetic attitude toward her son and before long was finding that "he just isn't a bother any more." Therapy was continued over a five-month period.

The remaining 9 per cent of the cases included family problems, vocational guidance problems and a few not classified in the above schema.

At the Wichita Guidance Center the experience and philosophy of psychological examining described in Carter & Bowles' monograph (4) has continued to the present. The purpose of a psychological examination affects its content and procedure. The individual referred for evaluation per se is given a more formal series of tests and the resulting report is designed to meet the needs of the referring agency or individual. The so-called blind psychological diagnosis is rarely attempted except as a training device. Normally the psychologist is responsible for assembling and/or evaluating the necessary case history data as well as administering and interpreting the tests.

The individual referred for treatment or treatment planning is approached in a more flexible manner than the out-and-out diagnostic case. When the problem is not clear or the child's psychological status uncertain, diagnostic study often begins with intelligence and projective tests. When, on the basis of the intake interview, the problem seems relatively clear, and parent and child seem ready for treatment, diagnostic testing is usually omitted or introduced at some later time during treatment to answer specific questions.

Some diagnostic testing, primarily using the Rorschach, has been done with parents during the course of their treatment. This has usually occurred when there were apparent blocks to treatment or when depression or anxiety pointed to the possible need for hospitalization or psychiatric treatment.

Psychotherapy with children emphasizes the relationship between child and therapist, with the philosophies of Allen, Taft and Axline being used rather than those of Klein or Anna Freud. The use of play as release and a medium for the relationship rather than as a source of unconscious material for interpretation is characteristic. When remedial work is undertaken it is conceived and carried out as therapy rather than education. Reading or any other school subject can be a medium for therapy as well as doll play, guns, clay, or construction.

Parent interviewing has several aspects that may occur separately or in various combinations in particular cases. Parent interviews at times are primarily a method of gathering information about a child and his history. In some diagnostic studies this may be the sole function. Another function is that of interpreting the findings of psychological study. A third function is that of therapy, which may occur at several levels. The focus may be maintained on the parent-child relationship itself, it may be focused on the relationship of husband and wife, or it may be focused on the parent's own early development, relationship to his own parents, or basic personality problems.

2. CONSULTATION WITH AGENCIES AND INDIVIDUALS

A community clinic is in interaction with a variety of persons in the community who are concerned about particular cases. The clinical psychologist obtains information from, conveys information to, and effects changes in attitudes and behavior of these various persons. The psychologist may obtain a medical report from a physician that will clarify certain traumatic events in a child's life or that will illuminate the attitude of a parent toward her child's physical condition; a public health nurse wishes help in understanding a child in whose home she is visiting; a probation officer desires recommendations regarding institutional placement or the return of a delinquent girl to her home; a social worker desires further understanding of a mother-child relationship in a family receiving financial assistance; the psychologist requires more information from a school teacher about peer relationships of an aggressive child being seen in play therapy. These types of situations require considerable flexibility in the clinical psychologist's approach. His role may shift from case to case as the needs of the different cases vary.

While many of these interactions with other professional persons in the community are by telephone, letter, or formal report, the most effective means of communication is through a conference with these interested persons. During 1952 there were more than one hundred such case conferences at the Wichita Guidance Center in which psychologists were leaders or participants. The number of other agencies involved in a single conference has ranged from one to seven.

The beneficial results of these conferences are not restricted to the particular case. The interchange of information broadens the understanding of the teachers, social workers, physicians and nurses regarding the diagnostic and therapeutic help available from the Center. Such understanding enables them to make more adequate referrals. It also changes their own handling of other children. Such conferences help the psychologist by providing valuable information and also keeps him aware of the realities outside the clinic walls.

Consultations are not limited to individual cases.

Through his knowledge of personality dynamics and developmental processes, the psychologist can be helpful to many individuals without performing direct diagnosis or treatment. A teacher may wish to talk with someone about a classroom situation that is not focused on one child. On occasion this becomes in effect a therapeutic experience for the teacher. The essential parts of such a consultation would be the defining of the problem, the uncovering of the feelings aroused by the situation and the development of a plan of action within the teacher's ability to carry out. In one instance a principal asked if the teachers of her school might have a series of staff meetings with a psychologist to talk about some of their problems. They presented individual cases and used these as the basis for discussion of general problems of meeting the needs of individual children. The county welfare department requested consultation for its social workers and supervisors to be used for presentation of specific family situations for discussion regarding personality dynamics and possible procedures to deal with the problems [1, p. 359].

A nurse who was teaching in a local school for nurses requested help in teaching methods and ways of interpreting psychological aspects of illness to student nurses. Ministers have requested help in meeting emotional problems in their congregation and ways of handling groups within the church.

3. PREVENTIVE WORK THROUGH GROUP PROGRAMS

The Wichita Guidance Center has developed a program of community education to interpret the clinical services of the Center and promote mentally healthful parent-child relationships. Any community-supported program needs continually to keep in touch with those groups that support it. The psychologist must be able to describe the clinical program in ways that will elicit support and will enable individuals to refer appropriate problems for help. One method that has been found very effective is that of showing the film "Angry Boy," which illustrates the operation of a guidance center, and following this with discussion and interpretation of the Wichita program.

When something more than interpretation of the Center's program is desired a series of meetings is often planned. In our experience these have been organized primarily by the Parent Teachers Association of various schools, and the local health department. Parent Teachers Association programs usually include the showing of mental health films from the Center's film library and the stimulation of discussion among the members of the group with the psychologist serving as moderator and interpreter. A series of six sessions at weekly or bi-weekly intervals can be directly helpful to parents with their own attitudes and feelings. The experience of sharing problems and solutions with other parents breaks down the isolation many parents feel in facing difficulties within the family.

The health department programs are of two sorts. One is a series of meetings with the parents of children who will be entering school for the first time. The psychologist leading these discussions, co-operatively with public health physicians and nurses, has a task focused on a rather specific adjustive problem. The participation in well-child conferences organized by the health department is another approach to preventive work. Group discussions and individual interviews are combined to reach those who want help with normal problems of child rearing as well as those who have more pressing and unique problems. Some of the formal supports of ordinary clinical practice are absent in the well-child conference. The clinician must be able to meet parent and child without these supports.

There is a continuing demand for talks to clubs, church groups and other groups about mental health and child guidance problems. While such individual talks are limited in their effectiveness, they are an additional method of modifying individual and community attitudes.

4. COMMUNITY PLANNING

The psychologist functioning in an agency like the Wichita Guidance Center must take part in community planning for the total health and welfare program of the community. The staff of the Center has taken an active role in the local community planning council throughout its history. In this manner the mental health needs of the community are brought to the attention of a wider group through surveys and reports on mental health problems. The psychologist assists in the solution of even broader community problems by contributing his knowledge of personality development and research methods to the planning groups. Participation in such community activity prevents the psychologist from becoming isolated in his interview room. The Center's own program of psychological services is subject to the scrutiny of the planning council and thereby benefits from the evaluation of a representative community group.

5. PROFESSIONAL TRAINING

The professional training of clinical psychologists has been a responsibility assumed by the Wichita Guidance Center since 1946. By 1953, twenty-one trainees from sixteen different universities had completed internships at the Center. The goal of the training program has been to prepare the trainees to function in the roles described above. The program has been outlined by Brewer (2). The psychologist as supervisor of trainees has a responsibility to several groups. In the service setting of the Center the primary responsibility is to the clients, to see that they receive the most adequate help possible for their problems. The psychologist has an obligation to the trainees to provide full opportunities for professional development. To the universities he has a responsibility to assist the trainees to integrate their theoretical and technical knowledge with their practical experience.

The first responsibility is discharged in several ways. The selection of cases for assignment to trainees is the first step in protection of the client. The psychologist and the intake social worker evaluate both trainee and client before making an assignment. By assigning a senior staff member to work with the trainee and provide continuing supervision the client is further assured protection. The presentation of the case to staff conferences is another method of giving the client the benefit of the best skill that is possible within the Center's organization.

The trainee is gradually integrated into the total service program of the Center. For any one trainee certain phases of the program may be no more than sampled while others will be experienced throughout their internship. The varied case load and community program provide a wide selection to meet the individual needs of trainees. The psychologist's responsibility to the trainee includes a sensitivity to his personal needs and goals and making available to him opportunities for their realization whenever possible. The development of a community-minded attitude in the trainee is felt to be especially important.

The individual case may provide an avenue to integration of theory and practice during the supervisory sessions or staff presentation. Seminars in therapy and diagnosis as well as reviews of current literature are used to maintain contact with the current research in psychology. Research opportunities within the Center's program are available to the trainee. However, the supervision of research on a doctoral problem is not felt to be a responsibility of the Center.

6. RESEARCH

Research cannot be claimed as a major function of the Wichita Guidance Center. There are from time to time surveys and analyses of current case loads and specific types of cases for administrative purposes. The current infant testing program is based in part on research carried out at the Center, resulting in a scale for two- and three-month-old infants with norms on a local population. Two projective tests for children have been devised and are still in a developmental stage. All of these have remained at the level of practical, intrainstitutional research. Several trainees have carried out pilot studies of possible thesis research and have expanded their own research conceptions.

FUTURE TRENDS

The Wichita Guidance Center represents a program conceived and carried out by clinical psychologists, using the resources of social work and psychiatry as co-operating disciplines. The psychologists have carried administrative responsibility as well as the greater part of the clinical services. The Center's future development should parallel that of the profession of clinical psychology with which it has been identified from the beginning. This means a continued advancement of clinical theory and technique together with an increased capacity for self-determination by the psychologists.

While there seem to be no radical changes in prospect in the near future, there are some specific trends that are apparent in the Center's program. Group therapeutic techniques are being explored and their greater use seems indicated. Groups of parents who have referred their children for treatment are being organized. This does not offer a short-cut to treatment because the most effective use of group therapy seems to be in conjunction with individual therapy. Often the two approaches complement each other.

The expansion of essentially preventive techniques is a necessity. It is not clear yet whether the clinical psychologist will make a major contribution to meeting this problem. In any event, he is looked upon as a reasonable source of help by the interested citizen. A continued exploration with public health and school personnel of preventive techniques is part of the Center's future plans.

REFERENCES

1. Brewer, J. E. A community program of psychological services. *J. clin. Psychol.*, 1951, 7, 357-360.
2. Brewer, J. E. Supervision of interns in a community guidance center. *J. consult. Psychol.*, 1951, 15, 268-270.
3. Carter, J. W., Jr. The Wichita Guidance Center. *J. consult. Psychol.* 1944, 8, 27-30.
4. Carter, J. W., Jr. & Bowles, J. W., Jr. A manual on qualitative aspects of psychological examining. *Clin. Psychol. Monogr.*, 1948, No. 2.
5. Cowan, E. A., & Pratt, Bertha M. The hurdle jump as a developmental and diagnostic test of motor coordination for children from three to twelve years of age. *Child Developm.*, 1934, 5, 107-121.
6. Constitution and By-laws of the Wichita Guidance Center. Wichita, Kansas: Wichita Guidance Center, 1949.

Part II.

GOVERNMENT AGENCIES WITH LARGE-SCALE PROGRAMS OF CLINICAL PSYCHOLOGY

With World War II, all of professional psychology entered its present period of very rapid expansion. Psychologists were utilized in increasing numbers during the war by all the armed services. Many of these psychologists had, at the time they entered service, a purely academic rather than professional background. They were called upon to apply their psychological knowledge to specific practical problems and situations, many of which fell into the area of clinical practice. Not only did wartime experience introduce many young psychologists to clinical practice, it resulted in influencing them to continue functioning in a professional and clinical capacity after the war. At the same time, the entire area of clinical psychology was given considerable impetus as a result of the services rendered during World War II. One of the most important postwar developments is the use being made of clinical psychologists in government agencies. Prior to World War II there was no extensive use of clinical psychologists in these settings. The establishment of the large-scale clinical psychology program in the Veterans Administration, the expanded use of clinical psychologists in other government agencies concerned with mental health, such as the Public Health Service, and the continuation and augmenting of clinical psychology programs in the various armed services are all reflections of this recent development.

It is therefore most pertinent to this survey to present descriptions of the functioning of the clinical psychologist in these government agencies.

VII.

CLINICAL PSYCHOLOGY IN THE VETERANS ADMINISTRATION

HAROLD M. HILDRETH

Clinical psychology was introduced into the Veterans Administration in 1946. Like the new medical program of which it is part this development was a direct outgrowth of World War II, and coincided with the great expansion of the Veterans Administration which took place at that time. In 1945, the Congress, faced with the immediate prospect of millions of servicemen soon to become veterans, took legislative steps which profoundly changed the size and nature of the Veterans Adminstration, the agency responsible for the administration of all veterans' benefits authorized by law.

One of the most extensive changes took place in the Medical Department. Separate legislation established a Department of Medicine and Surgery, independent of many customary Civil Service restrictions. Physicians, dentists and nurses under the new law could be appointed and paid on the basis of individual qualifications without reference to grade levels of classified positions as had previously been required. The Administrator of Veterans Affairs was also authorized to establish such standards as were necessary or desirable for any professional group within the new Department of Medicine and Surgery. Concurrent with this legislative and administrative change a vast hospital building program was launched, which only now is nearing completion. A new philosophy, new concepts, and new patterns of training energized the new Department of Medicine and Surgery. In short, there was brought into being in 1945 and 1946 the largest single medical program in the world, with the announced mission of providing veterans with "medical care second to none."

The postwar expansion of the Veterans Administration as a whole, and the Department of Medicine and Surgery in particular, took place in an extremely short period of time and under great pressure. History had little precedent for a development of this magnitude, at this speed, in a permanent governmental organization. About the only comparable event was wartime mobilization of professional personnel; and mobiliza-

83

tion by its temporary nature provided no adequate pattern for permanent organization. Given these circumstances, it is not surprising that this large federal agency with its far-reaching medical program should have gone through three major reorganizations to date and experienced a somewhat less than tranquil existence since 1945.

The current reorganization, now nearing completion, promises to provide a pattern for efficient functioning, with the establishment of three fairly independent bureau-type departments: Medical, Insurance, and Veterans Benefits. Although most of the funds appropriated annually for the Veterans Administration are disbursed through the latter two departments, the Medical Department has the largest number of employees, currently some 120,000 of the total of 170,000.

Against this backdrop, we may consider the establishment of clinical psychology in the medical program of the Veterans Administration. Its inauguration, development, difficulties and achievements necessarily have been influenced greatly by the setting in which they took place. The magnitude of the major agency changes was constantly reflected in a multitude of smaller problems with which psychology early found it necessary to deal.

For one thing, the pace of events in the new medical program forced upon the new clinical psychology program the necessity for early decisions on matters of far-reaching consequence. The fateful nature of these decisions for the future was clearly recognized; the need to make them at an early stage could not be avoided. One major effect was to force upon those responsible for the program a constant awareness of the organizational aspects of a psychology program in a large agency. Attention could not be confined solely to scientific and professional matters with which psychology had heretofore been almost exclusively concerned. The history of psychology, both as a science and, in more recent years, as a profession, had little to offer in the way of guide lines for the organizational aspects of a large-scale program. Conscious of this fact, the psychologists in the Veterans Administration have deliberately taken upon themselves the continuing obligation of reviewing and reflecting upon their experience and evaluating it as objectively as participant observers can.

HISTORY

There was no formal clinical psychology program in the Veterans Administration before World War II.[1] In the fall of 1945, a number of

---

[1] A few psychologists had been previously employed by individual hospitals, the earliest known instance being that of George Van Ness Dearborn, M.D., Ph.D., who established a psychological laboratory at the Veterans Administration Hospital, Bronx, in the 1920's.

psychologists on duty in Washington were consulted in regard to the new program, and in December 1945, Dr. George A. Kelly, just released from the Navy, came to the Veterans Administration in a consultant capacity to get the program under way. It was during this period that the initial standards for clinical psychologists were developed. Later, in the spring of 1946, Dr. James G. Miller was released from the Office of Strategic Services to become the first full-time head of the new Clinical Psychology Program, serving in this capacity until December, 1947. He was succeeded by the writer in January, 1948.

During 1946 and 1947, standards were developed further, procedures were established and the program given shape and form. One of the most important steps of this early period was the establishment of the Clinical Psychology Training Program. The number of qualified clinical psychologists in the nation was extremely small, and, with the widespread demand for their postwar services in many agencies, it was clear that there would be a shortage for years to come. In the spring of 1946, the Chief Medical Director met with representatives of leading universities to ask them to undertake the training of clinical psychologists for the Veterans Administration. This they agreed to do, and with the co-operation of an initial group of twenty-two universities the first 200 trainees went on duty in the fall of 1946. Subsequently the Veterans Administration, with the support of the United States Public Health Service, asked the American Psychological Association to undertake the accrediting of universities for doctoral training in clinical psychology, as a guide to federal agencies involved in training activities. This development, which subsequently led the American Psychological Association to establish an Education and Training Board, was of inestimable value to the psychology program of the Veterans Administration. It placed the responsibility for basic educational decisions in the hands of an impartial and appropriate scientific organization, and provided a solid foundation for the free and co-operative relations which have since existed between the Veterans Administration and the training universities.

The growth of the Veterans Administration program as a whole has been due to this training program. From the beginning, the stature and strength of the training program offered its own recruiting incentive, and gave sure indication to already qualified clinical psychologists that employment in the Veterans Administration held much professional challenge. At the same time, of course, it afforded a large number of graduate students in psychology an unprecedented opportunity for combining academic work and extensive clinical experience. The response at both levels, students and professional psychologists, was immediate and has continued strong. The training program has been, and remains, the primary source of qualified clinical psychologists for the Veterans Administration, and has been integrated closely with the staff program.

CURRENT ORGANIZATION

At the present time, the Department of Medicine and Surgery of the Veterans Administration operates 168 hospitals, with a few more still under construction. Of the present number, 38 are predominantly neuropsychiatric hospitals, 21 are tuberculosis hospitals, and 109 are predominantly general medical and surgical hospitals. Almost all of these latter have been built with neuropsychiatric units, with units varying in size from a few beds to as much as one fifth of the total hospital. At the present time, there are approximately 50,000 neurologic and psychiatric patients, 14,000 tuberculosis patients, and 36,000 general medical and surgical patients in Veterans Administration hospitals.

In addition to its hospitals, the Department of Medicine and Surgery operates 17 domiciliaries. Almost without exception these domiciliaries, successors to the Old Soldiers Homes of earlier days, adjoin a general hospital which provides medical care for the domiciled members. About 17,000 veterans are now in these domiciliaries.

The outpatient facilities of the Department of Medicine and Surgery are housed partly in the Regional Offices of the Veterans Administration, 13 of which are administratively combined with hospitals into centers, and partly in hospitals. The 70 Regional Offices are primarily business offices taking care of such matters as veterans' insurance, claims, educational and other benefits. Housed in the separate Regional Offices, Centers or hospitals are the general medical clinics of the Veterans Administration. Included in these installations are 63 Mental Hygiene Clinics.

In addition to these stations, providing direct care for patients, the Central Office of the Veterans Administration, located in Washington, D.C., and the six Area Medical Offices, located in Boston, Washington, Atlanta, St. Louis, St. Paul, and San Francisco are charged with certain administrative and co-ordinating responsibilities.

Organizationally, Clinical Psychology is one of three Divisions of the Psychiatry and Neurology Service, which in turn constitutes one of the Professional Services of the Department of Medicine and Surgery. As of December 31, 1953, there were 476 staff clinical psychologists on duty in the Veterans Administration. Approximately 30 per cent of these were in clinics and the remainder in hospitals. Stations vary considerably in number of psychologists, ranging from one clinic with 17, to stations with only one person. In about one fifth of the stations, there is not yet a single clinical psychologist. There are 3 clinical psychologists in the Central Office and one in each of the six Area Medical Offices.

All staff clinical psychologists in the Veterans Administration have the doctorate in psychology. This requirement was established in the earliest days of the program, and the wisdom of the decision has been amply confirmed by the passing years. However, concurrent with the initial doctorate requirement, provision was made in the first two or three years of the program for temporary employment of individuals who had clinical experience but lacked the academic requirement. Such individuals were notified upon employment that the degree eventually would be required, and provisions were made for assisting them in the attainment of this requirement. By the end of 1951 the goal set almost six years earlier was achieved and the clinical psychologists of the Veterans Administration have since been an entirely doctorate group.

Staff psychologists contribute in a variety of ways to the Veterans Administration medical program in general and to patient welfare in particular. Through a varied and changing psychological testing program, they contribute to patient diagnosis and prediction of improvement. Under psychiatric supervision they provide group and individual psychotherapy in hospitals and clinics. They are responsible for the continuing graduate practicum training and work experience of the trainees. They also assist in the psychiatric residency training program, in the training programs of other disciplines, and in almost all in-service training. Nearly all carry out research activities themselves or stimulate and assist others to do so. They assist managers in the screening, selection, and placement of such necessary personnel as psychiatric aides, volunteer workers, and others. The psychologist contributes consultative advice to specialists in nonpsychiatric areas such as speech pathology, dietetics, tuberculosis, and paraplegia.

The daily individual program of any clinical psychologist in the Veterans Administration is compounded primarily of such activities and a few others related to them. There is no fixed standard pattern. The patients a clinical psychologist sees and the type of relation he has with them, the staff members with whom he confers, the questions he tries to answer, and the immediate purposes he tries to achieve—these are determined by many factors operant in the setting in which he is working. The most pressing needs recognized by the hospital or clinic, the availability or lack of other personnel, the presence or absence of additional clinical psychologists: such factors as these are the determinants of his immediate work program. The pattern of his activities and efforts varies from time to time, depending upon changes in the work situation and his own best judgment. As a professional person he is responsible for evaluating his own efforts and, within the latitude which the situation permits, for choosing constantly the most effective focus of his efforts. This is particularly important in situations where there is much more work to handle than there are personnel available—and such situations seem to be nearly universal. Because he does utilize his broad professional skills in response to the needs of his own particular work setting, it is impossible to give any specific description of the actual functioning of the clinical psychologist in the Veterans Administration.

Although the variety of activity of clinical psychologists in the Veterans Administration precludes any description of "typical" duties, some closer appreciation of actual functioning may be obtained from a description of their diverse work settings. Given below are background data and a brief survey of the major types of stations in the Veterans Administration. In each instance is included a sample report for a single station of the type being described. No one report is fully characteristic of the entire class of stations for which it is used as an illustration. Yet it is hoped that these sample reports, taken together, will give some over-all picture of the nature of the clinical psychology program in the Veterans Administration.

MENTAL HYGIENE CLINICS

The first Veterans Administration mental hygiene clinic was established in Los Angeles in 1945. This was the beginning of a unique nation-wide treatment program that is today an important aspect of the medical program for veterans. The 63 mental hygiene clinics now in operation are staffed by approximately 175 full- and part-time psychiatrists, 135 staff clinical psychologists, and 160 psychiatric social workers. In addition, about 200 psychology trainees and 40 residents in psychiatry are assigned to these clinics.

There is considerable variation among clinics, both as to number of full-time professional staff and number of patients treated. The smallest clinic has two full-time persons while the largest has forty. Not including part-time personnel and trainees, the median clinic has two psychiatrists, two psychologists, and two social workers. The fact that, at any one time, as many as 21,000 veterans are receiving treatment in these 63 clinics gives an indication of the magnitude of this phase of the total program.

A majority of the veterans who come for treatment to these clinics are either self-referred or are referred from other units of the Regional Office or hospital Medical Division. Veterans Administration hospital service organizations, contact representatives, and community agencies refer most of the remainder of the clinic patients. It is interesting to note that 20 per cent of these outpatients have a diagnosis of a psychotic condition.

Following is a report, prepared in August 1952, by the Chief Clinical Psychologist of a mental hygiene clinic established in 1946.

The clinical psychologists in this Regional Office function as an integral part of the Mental Hygiene Clinic. In that capacity they work in close co-operation with the psychiatrists, social workers, and the other members of the Psychiatric Division. In addition, although administratively a part of the Mental Hygiene Clinic, the five staff psychologists and eight trainees also perform services for other sections of the Medical Division, the Vocational Rehabilitation and Education Division, and the Personnel Division.

Psychotherapy continues to form an important function for the psychologists. In addition to individual treatment, a considerable portion of the training activity is centered around this function. Two consulting psychiatrists spend four hours each week in seminars on psychotherapy with the psychologists. At these seminars the ongoing process of treatment of cases by trainees and staff is presented and discussed. This affords expert supervision for psychotherapy done by the staff psychologists and those trainees who are skilled and thoroughly acquainted with psychodynamics. Other patients in treatment not discussed at these seminars are carried under individual supervision of the psychiatrists of the Mental Hygiene Clinic. Still another method of continuing study of individual cases and treatment is accomplished by means of the team approach. These teams are made up of one staff psychiatrist, one clinical psychologist, and a social worker, as well as one clinical psychology trainee, one social work trainee, and resident psychiatrist. Each team meets at least once a week for an hour in a discussion of patients treated by the respective disciplines. The several approaches discussed insure the patient more expert treatment, and also further the development of the psychologist in all areas.

A very important part of the diagnostic work done by the psychologist is concerned with testing of veterans as a part of the examination for disability rating. All veterans with neuropsychiatric disabilities, and other veterans who show some mental disturbance, are referred by the various rating psychiatrists of the Outpatient Medical Division for complete psychological evaluations. In each case testing is not routine but varied as to the extent and selection of the instruments according to the specific problems of the patient. The test report is then sent to the psychiatrist and the findings are incorporated in the rating examination. In connection with this work, a research project is now being conducted to give a descriptive picture of this group of patients and also to find significant similarities and differences in the psychological reports as compared to earlier diagnostic evaluations. A sample of 150 rating cases seen over a period of six months is being used for this study.

Similarly, diagnostic testing for the Mental Hygiene Clinic patient does not conform to any routine battery but is developed for each case in accord with the referral and the presenting disturbance of the patient. Much testing is concerned with the problem of evaluating veterans as to their potentiality for psychotherapy in the clinic, and other aspects of treatment planning. Another area of diagnostic work is the testing of patients during the course of treatment as an aid in therapy. Final evaluations of special problems are made in weekly diagnostic conferences. Services to other divisions broaden the professional experience and the usefulness of the clinical psychologist. The Psychology Section has co-operated with the Personnel Division of the Regional Office in the development and administration of a battery of tests to assist in the selection of personnel for promotion. In addition, from time to time, various staff clinical psychologists have been consulted by the Personnel Division on individual problems of personnel relationships which are psychological in nature. The relationship with the Vocational Rehabilitation and Education Division involves mainly diagnostic testing and evaluating veteran applicants who are applying for training and education and who have some emotional disturbance or who present some unusual psychological problems. Here, too, planned consultations about these veterans with their vocational advisors have allowed the Psychology Section to assist in handling those specific problems. A psychologist from the Mental Hygiene Clinic serves on the Rehabilitation Board.

The training accomplished at the clinic is multidimensional. Trainees attend from ten to twelve hours a week of conferences and individual supervision. In addition to the therapy seminars mentioned before, time is spent by each trainee with an assigned supervisor from among the staff psychologists for individual discussion of diagnostic patients and test reports. Each testing case handled by a trainee is thus directly reviewed and supervised by a staff member. On alternate weeks there is a two-hour clinic conference with all of the disciplines in attendance, at which time current clinic matters, administrative, professional, and scientific, are discussed. Finally, there are the neurological conferences where the resident psychiatrists make case presentations and where staff members and trainees in the Clinical Psychology Section attend.

Research and training in research is a continuous activity. The trainees at the clinic are all actively engaged in research projects in connection with their postgraduate degrees. Three doctoral dissertations are now being conducted, all of which include factorial studies. One is an analysis of the alcoholic personality, one is a determination of the validity of the Rorschach Test by factor analysis, and another is a factorial study of verbal content associated with several types of group behavior. Staff psychologists are formally and informally assisting in these projects. In addition, staff research projects are an integral part of the over-all activity. At the present time, three large projects are being conducted as well as several smaller ones. The survey on a sample of rating examinations over a six-month period is one of the projects which is under way. The use of content analysis on early and later interviews to evaluate treatment is also being developed. Over the last year, the staff psychologists, and actually the entire Mental Hygiene Clinic, have co-operated with the Central Office Psychiatry and Neurology Research Section in the development of a series of rating scales. Considerable work has since been done on those rating scales and is being continued. A report has been made of the study at the last Eastern Psychological Association meeting. At the present time a paper relative to this study is being submitted for publication.

A special project is under way at the present time for evaluating patients from other medical services as to their potentialities for treatment in group psychotherapy. Seven or eight groups are to be formed from these referrals. The psychosomatic problems presented by these veterans require a new approach in treatment for the Outpatient Medical Division. The results and observations in group therapy will permit new and varied group dynamic studies and research. Finally, it is anticipated for the late fall that a symposium will be set up of well-known professional leaders including those in psychology, psychiatry, neurology, social work, and other allied medical sciences.

Neuropsychiatric Hospitals

Of the 38 hospitals which are predominantly psychiatric, the largest has about 2,500 beds, the smallest 670; the median hospital has 1,500. Of patients hospitalized at any one time, schizophrenics represent about 67 per cent, severe psychoneurotics 3 per cent, and neurologic cases approximately 10 per cent, with the remaining 20 per cent distributed among the various other severe mental disturbances.

There are approximately 700 physicians assigned to psychiatric or neurologic wards or services. In addition there are consultants in psychiatry and neurology, and about 140 residents in psychiatric training. All of these hospitals have at least one full-time clinical psychologist. The median psychiatric hospital has four psychologists; the range is from one to eleven. All told, there are 170 full-time staff clinical psychologists and 250 social workers. About 200 psychology trainees currently are assigned to these hospitals.

The following report comes from a neuropsychiatric hospital with a staff of eleven psychologists where, in addition to its existing program, there was initiated in 1952 a special project designed to explore the increased utilization of clinical psychologists in the treatment of long-term patients.

At this hospital we regard the service to the veteran and the training of the clinical psychology trainees as interlocked parts of the same service. The trainee comes for his practical training in hospital clinical psychology. As in most neuropsychiatric hospitals, he carries a fair share of the service demands, under the strict supervision and guidance of the staff psychologists. It is difficult, therefore, to delineate which is service and which is training. For this reason, the functions of service and the functions of training are herein regarded as an entity.

SERVICE FUNCTIONS

I. *The Admissions Screening Service.* Here psychological group tests are given to patients referred for initial diagnostic screening. It is possible through this service to give a rapid, preliminary diagnosis and psychodynamic picture of each patient within a period of forty-eight hours. This facilitates the work of the Admissions Service Psychiatrist in the disposition of the patients. The psychologists also attend and participate fully in the psychiatric admissions conference where each patient is seen as soon as possible after his arrival at the hospital. Both staff psychologists and trainees also undertake psychiatric case reports of patients. This helps greatly in the work load of the Ward Psychiatrist and, additionally, provides the psychologist with an experience which places him in a better position to understand the problems facing the Admissions Psychiatrist. Occasionally, these patients are maintained in psychotherapy by the psychologists.

II. *The Consultation Service*. This provides a psychological service for psychiatrists upon request. Most of this testing is undertaken by the trainees assigned to the various wards, in order that the psychologist may function as a member of the ward staff rather than as a "visiting tester." Each trainee is expected to discuss each referral with the psychiatrist before and after testing and not to restrict his report to written file data. This is a service which extends throughout the hospital.

III. *The Psychosomatic Service*. This provides an initial diagnostic testing of referred patients on the Medical Service. Following the testing, a brief psychotherapy service may be provided by the clinical psychologists.

IV. *Psychotherapy*. Many staff psychologists and clinical psychology trainees carry patients in individual and group psychotherapy. The Assistant Chief for Therapy screens all the cases referred to him by psychiatrists for individual psychotherapy. He then allocates one or more of these patients to a psychology trainee or a clinical psychology staff member. The patients are seen regularly at least three times per week. Strict supervision is maintained in the case of both staff and trainee psychologists. The former work with visiting consultants and the trainees are under the supervision of staff psychiatrists of the hospital. They also have the opportunity of attending three seminars in psychotherapy given by the psychiatric consultants.

V. *Personnel Screening*. It has been the practice for the clinical psychologists to play a major role in the screening of personnel applying for positions as hospital aides and for positions in the Dietetic Service. These are referred to the Psychology Service by the Personnel Officer. They first receive a small battery of tests. Following the scoring of these tests, each applicant is interviewed by the clinical psychologist. Combining the results of the screening and the interview, the psychologist makes a decision as to whether this individual should be hired for the position in question, and makes a recommendation, accordingly, to the Personnel Officer and Manager.

Other facilities are also provided by the Psychology Service in the area of personnel screening. At the moment, for example, there is a study under way of persons on the hospital staff who may be regarded as accident-prone. There is study being given to the problem of excessive sick leave. The Personnel Officer has requested the Psychology Department to study the entire "problem of the supervisor" in the hospital. Many chiefs of departments in the hospital further feel that the Clinical Psychology Service is a department to which they may bring their personnel problems when they feel that personality problems are involved. These contacts, we are confident, provide a very valuable service to the hospital.

VI. *Research*. The general field of research is under the control of the Assistant Chief for Research, who is mainly engaged in providing the facilities for trainees working on their university dissertations. These studies, although primarily research, often provide a direct service to the hospital, as many more patients are tested and seen than would be otherwise given such attention. The psychologist is also available to other hospital personnel for research discussion. He is called upon frequently to set up the methodology for research investigations being made by members of the psychiatric and medical staff.

The second category of research undertaken at the hospital is in connection with the psychophysiology laboratory, which is under the direction of a noted neurophysiologist. Here the psychologist undertakes research, including some experiments with animals, bearing on problems of psychophysiological functioning.

VII. *Lecture Programs.* Lecture programs in the hospital provide a much-needed service, as they are sources of information for all hospital personnel. There is a continuous program of seminars structured specifically for members of the Clinical Psychology Department. These include test seminars, case seminars, psychotherapy seminars, neurology seminars, psychosomatic seminars, psychology theory seminars, research seminars, and general case conferences. These seminars are always open to other interested hospital personnel. In addition, the Department is frequently called upon to give general and specific lectures to groups of personnel in other departments of the hospital. These have included talks to the nurses, to members of the Registrar Division, and to the Personnel Division. The Clinical Psychology Service also participates in the orientation program for all new employees.

GENERAL MEDICAL AND SURGICAL HOSPITALS

Of the 109 general medical and surgical hospitals, 65 now have psychiatric and/or neurologic sections in operation. Of all the operating beds in these hospitals some 8,000 are in psychiatric and neurologic sections. At present there are about 150 full-time clinical psychologists and 200 trainees assigned in Veterans Administration general hospitals.

The clinical psychologist's functions vary a great deal depending upon the size and organization of the hospital, the number of staff members and trainees, and the length of time the section has been in existence. In some of the general hospitals diagnostic referrals come principally from the Psychiatry and Neurology Service. In others, referrals for diagnostic and consultative services come primarily from the medical and surgical wards and from physical medicine and rehabilitation services. Patients with psychosomatic illnesses, orthopedic, tuberculous, and geriatric cases, and domicilary members are referred for psychological evaluation.

In addition to diagnostic services, individual and group therapy are provided, with both psychiatrists and clinical psychologists participating. Acute psychotics are likely to receive individual treatment; psychosomatic patients frequently are handled in groups. Psychologists are also likely to participate in physical medicine and rehabilitation activities by assisting in the planning of treatment programs.

Training opportunities in the medical and surgical hospitals are stimulating and unusual. The wide variety of cases provides the trainee with an opportunity for clinical experience with all types of patients. Research activities tend to be collaborative with participation of medical as well as psychiatric personnel. Investigations of personality factors associated with favorable and unfavorable response to radical surgical procedures, such as duodenal gastrectomy, and studies concerned with the personality patterns of specific psychosomatic patient groups, or with the comparison of slow- versus rapid-growing cancer patients, are representative.

The following report is from a general medical and surgical hospital with a staff of nine clinical psychologists.

Since the last report, the psychologists are now assigned to wards and are geographically stationed on the ward. This plan was effected with the move into the new building. As a result, progressively greater responsibility in the administration of the ward has been assigned to the psychologist.

All medical residents and interns rotate on the Neuropsychiatric Service. During their month assignment to the Neuropsychiatric Service, from three to four hours are given to each resident or intern by the psychologist demonstrating the use of tests, method of analysis, and function of psychology under a general medical and surgical hospital. There are two psychiatric residents on the Neuropsychiatric Service at this time and these spend approximately two hours per week with the Chief of the Psychology Section reviewing selected readings and discussing problems of mutual interest. The residents in psychiatry take advantage of the opportunity extended to the residents and medical interns that are on rotation to the service. All their patients that are seen in therapy, or become their responsibility, are given extended psychological evaluation and the findings are discussed personally in addition to the regular full reports. Since the last report, a dental residency program has been started in this hospital. The psychologists participate in the residency training program by recommended readings and discussion of problems in psychology for a period of not less than two months with two hours per week per dental resident. The dental residents bring in problems with which they are concerned in dealing with patients and personnel and these problems are discussed. The dietetic intern training program is now in its second year at this hospital. The psychologists during the second year of training have been called upon for a series of six lectures dealing with problems of personal relationships. In addition to this, near the close of training, the dietetic interns will be participants in discussion groups (group therapy) in which they will discuss the problems they have run into in dealing with people and what happened to them in these situations.

Ceiling is available for additional psychologists, and positions for which there is pressure for placement are: (1) a position for a psychologist on the Neurology Service with some training in language difficulties and in language retraining; (2) psychologist for the open-admission-ward type of patients. Under the present program of expansion of this hospital, there is a demand upon psychology to consider the placing of more than one psychologist per ward, the second position being a psychologist who is primarily interested in service function and whose time will be primarily devoted to that of carrying patients in therapy and in testing. In addition to added staff for full ward coverage on Neurology and Admissions (NP), it has been decided that an open neuropsychiatric ward will be established with a psychologist in charge of program under the administrative supervision of a psychiatrist. Medical and psychiatric consultations will be continuously provided. Staff psychologists will be assigned to this ward, one of them with the primary responsibility of administration and one primarily responsible for evaluating the effects and problems that develop in such a situation.

Research projects under way are as follows: personality defenses of patients with neurodermatitis; concept formation in schizophrenic and brain-damage groups; behavior and unconscious fantasies of patients with rheumatoid arthritis; vocabulary knowledge and usage among normals and schizophrenics; fantasies of patients receiving shock treatment.

Members of the Psychology Section of this hospital have been requested to present a symposium at the regional psychological association meeting.

TUBERCULOSIS HOSPITALS

In tuberculosis hospitals, and on tuberculosis wards of other hospitals, psychologists now are generally seeing all patients soon after admission, getting acquainted with them, and helping them as needed in making their adjustment to hospitalization and in handling the accompanying emotional reactions. In one tuberculosis hospital the psychologist's work is almost entirely staff-centered rather than patient-centered; that is, he spends his time talking with the medical staff about the problems of special patients, and dealing with aspects of the physician-patient relationship, particularly the emotional components of it, which hinder further successful treatment.

The greatest single problem in the successful treatment of tuberculosis is that of irregular discharge. Patients progressing well often decide to leave the hospital before a lasting recovery has been achieved. Following the almost inevitable relapse, subsequent treatment is more difficult and prolonged. The problem is basically psychological, consisting on the one hand of identifying on admission those patients who subsequently will become irregular discharge problems, and on the other hand the devising of means to interrupt or prevent this tendency. Clinical psychologists in the Veterans Administration are moving rapidly in gaining the knowledge essential to the solution of both aspects of this problem. The same approach used in selecting recruits for pilot training, high-school graduates for college, or employees for specialized industrial jobs is being adopted for identifying potential irregular-discharge patients on admission. For patients so identified, programs are being developed for effective attitude change and behavior modification.

The number of clinical psychologists in tuberculosis hospitals and on tuberculosis wards is still relatively small but is expected to increase fairly rapidly. It is significant to note and important to record that clinical psychologists who have moved into this new area of psychology-in-medicine are extremely enthusiastic regarding the potential contributions which psychologists can make, and prefer their assignments to the many other opportunities constantly open to them. It appears that the tuberculosis hospital challenges, and offers opportunity for the expression of, almost the entire range of a psychologist's knowledge and skill.

Following is a report from one of the first tuberculosis hospitals in which psychologists have functioned.

I. *Patient Services*

    A. *Direct.* Interview, test, and treat patients whose emotional problems are considered to be beyond the skill of trainees. Accept all referrals by physicians made specifically to the staff psychologist.

    B. *Indirect*

        1. *Unscheduled Conferences with Staff*

        Impromptu consultation with staff members has become an activity of major importance. In any given day, they may include discussions with the Chief of Professional Services, Chief of TB, Chief and staff of Physical Medicine Rehabilitation Service, two or three ward physicians, social workers, and various members of the Patient Education Committee. Because all staff members are busy, it is important to be in the office much of the time and available without previous appointment. These discussions are usually in regard to matters of immediate importance and often require immediate decision.

        2. *Scheduled Conferences with Staff*

            a. *Psychosomatic Conference.* Weekly meetings requiring preparation in notifying participants, arranging psychological workup of case, and preliminary consultation with ward physician, social worker, and psychiatric consultant. Preparation of record of conference which includes medical history, social history, psychological report, PMR and nurse's report, verbatim account of discussion, psychiatric evaluation, summary and recommendations.

            b. *Admissions Conference.* Weekly meetings of all professional personnel who routinely interview new patients (ward nurse, social worker, psychology trainee, occupational therapist, educational therapist, and vocational advisor). The purpose of these meetings is to avoid the duplication of effort and to bring together in one report all information pertaining to the adjustment of the patient to hospitalization. The report includes verbatim transcript of the discussion, with specific recommendations to each participant as to the part he can play in assisting the patient. Need for patient education is particularly noted and included in the recommendations. These meetings are moderated and the transcript prepared by the psychology department.

c. *Patient Education*. Assistant to the Chairman of the Patient Education Committee in over-all co-ordination of the program. Membership on Family Forum and Radio subcommittees. Responsibility for publicity. Attendance at Sunday meetings of the Family Forum. Supervision of work of trainees who are members of Publications subcommittee. Participation in family and radio programs as occasional guest speaker.

d. *Conference with Staff Nurses*. Bi-weekly discussion of problems submitted by group members and considered to be of primary concern in their understanding and handling of patients (e.g., methods of tactful and effective enforcement of TV curfew; problems arising in assignment of beds to patients of minority groups). These meetings are conducted jointly by a field representative from the county Tuberculosis and Health Association and by a psychology trainee. Supervision of the latter includes planning before meeting, using role-playing techniques, and discussion following it.

e. *Conference with Occupational and Educational Therapists*. Weekly discussions with staff and students about problems arising in work with patients. Assistance in setting up research design to study the relationships between participation in occupational and educational therapy and response to medical treatment.

II. *Training and Supervision*

Two trainees are regularly assigned to this hospital for training. This has made possible an extension of services which would otherwise be prohibitive. In addition to the extensive psychological testing and interviewing they do, these trainees carry patients in psychotherapy under psychological and psychiatric supervision, obtain data for research, assist in conducting meetings with other staff members, and serve on subcommittees of the Patient Education program. Each activity of the trainees must be discussed and approved, not only to assure their professional growth, but also to avoid any action which might have an adverse effect on patients or on the attitude of other staff members toward the psychology service.

III. *Administration*

In addition to the usual administrative reports, there are regular written evaluations of the trainees' progress and regional meetings regarding the training program. An increasing number of days or half days have been spent with official visitors from other Veterans Administration installations, and with consultants from the universities, the State TB Associations, and State Department of Health. Correspondence with psychologists at other Veterans Administration tuberculosis hospitals has become frequent and informative.

IV. *Research*

At present, three studies are under way—factors involved in irregular discharges, relation of psychological test scores to response to medical treatment, and autonomic nervous system factors in response to treatment. Both trainees and staff psychologists participate in gathering data, obtaining medical ratings from ward physicians, and making statistical analysis of the results.

V. *Community Relations*

Membership on two committees of the county Tuberculosis and Health Association. Meetings with staff of two non-Veterans Administration tuberculosis hospitals, and with staff of the city Health Department.

DOMICILIARIES

In domiciliaries the situation is somewhat similar to tuberculosis hospitals, in that clinical psychologists are not yet represented in large numbers. This despite the fact that the problems presented by the members of the domiciliaries have been recognized as basically psychological in character; and since 1946 clinical psychologists have conducted three surveys—the only ones to date—of various aspects of the problems of the domiciled veteran.

Although under the jurisdiction of the Department of Medicine and Surgery domiciled veterans are not patients; any veteran who is without a home may apply for admission as a member. As a point of fact, many members suffer from some form of medical disability and the intermittent but rather frequent medical attention which they require is usually supplied by the general hospital located on the grounds of, and administratively connected with, the domiciliary. Only the urgent priority of acute illness has delayed the assignment of clinical psychologists in greater numbers to the domiciliaries, for the need for psychological treatment and rehabilitation is recognized and the prevalence of geriatric problems is pronounced.

The domiciliary, joined with a general hospital, constitutes a Center. In such a Center, clinical psychologists customarily function both in the hospital and in the domiciliary. The following report reflects the character of such activity, and to a degree supplements the description of activities in general hospitals given above.

The Chief Clinical Psychologist is directly responsible for all clinical psychology activity. The second staff psychologist carries responsibility for all psychological functions on the Tuberculosis Service, two of the medical wards, and two of the neuropsychiatric wards. Also, the senior trainee, functioning as a staff psychologist, is carrying the responsibility for all psychological functions in the domiciliary, three medical wards, and two neuropsychiatric wards. The domiciliary responsibility consists of admission screening, rehabilitation and research. The Chief Clinical Psychologist is personally responsible for the work with outpatients and with hospital staff. It is planned that the staff psychologist and the senior trainee will shift assignments in six months. The other trainees' schedules are planned so that they will work with each of these staff members for three months at a time and so rotate that by the end of a year they will have spent six months with each supervisor on two different assignments. It is believed that such a rotation plan allows for greatest diversity in training as well as maximal service to the hospital.

The basic premise of the program here is that clinical psychology trainees assist the full-time staff members and receive training commensurate with their level of professional development and the existing hospital services. Training is an integral part of the actual functioning of the psychologist. The actual volume of work done by the trainees during this period has been very considerable. The Clinical Psychology Section at this station is extremely active in the professional activities of the entire hospital and domiciliary. The Chief of Psychiatry has insisted from the beginning that he wanted full utilization of the clinical psychologist in the over-all total patient care program. Also, he has given unsparingly of his time in teaching activity, with special instruction in physiology and neurology. He is of the opinion that psychologists cannot be completely effective unless they have a good realization and knowledge of these phases of medicine.

While the major part of training revolves about the actual hospital activities of the staff psychologists, specific training plans are also included in terms of needs of individual trainees. Each trainee receives two hours of individual supervision per week and participates in four weekly seminars in Therapy, Research, Tests, and Psychological Theory. In addition, there are also two monthly didactic psychodrama sessions oriented to the professional problems of a psychologist in interpersonal relationships. The seminars are conducted by the Psychology Staff and are also attended by Social Service, Physical Medicine Rehabilitation, Special Services, and Nursing. Physicians from the various medical services also attend these meetings and are very active in their participation. The entire orientation of the trainees is directed toward a team approach.

At the suggestion of the medical staff, the Psychology Section has applied its research techniques to three of the important problems of medical management: (1) rehabilitation of the domiciliary member, (2) the prediction and prevention of irregular discharges among the tuberculous, and (3) evaluation of a treatment program for geriatric cases.

Reports on the first phase of the domiciliary project have already been forwarded to Area and Central Office. Data are now almost complete for the tuberculosis project and the study of a control group for the domiciliary research, and reports of these will be available in the near future. Analysis of the second phase of the domiciliary program is well under way. The third project has just been initiated and data will not be complete for several months.

SPECIAL PATIENT GROUPS

The description of the five major types of stations has, it is hoped, given some picture of the nature of functioning of the clinical psychologists in the Veterans Administration. Not mentioned so far, however, are duties involving special patient groups, or special interstaff relationships.

One of the patient groups receiving special attention are the paraplegics, where psychological factors are understandably important. The major problems of the amputees are also frequently psychological. The same is true of the blind, and the hard-of-hearing. Such patients, and those with severe neurological, cardiac, or other permanent conditions which greatly restrict and alter the patterns of life activity—these are individuals who need sustained psychological help. For such individuals there comes a time when surgical and medical care has been completed, or largely so. The patient is in many instances no longer primarily a patient but rather a human being who must face life with a given set of serious limitations. Under other circumstances he would no longer be considered a medical responsibility. But if he is a veteran the Department of Medicine and Surgery of the Veterans Administration necessarily has a degree of lifelong responsibility for him. The agency must do what it can to provide him the type of help that he needs. This help is, of course, in the simple business of living—his emotional problems, his outlook on life, his motivations, etc. The need to help such patients with their life problems, and to assist them in achieving and maintaining psychological equilibrium, is thus one of the special responsibilities of the clinical psychologists as part of the medical program of the Veterans Administration.

The clinical psychologist also functions helpfully in a number of special interstaff relationships. Illustrative of these is his work with the dietitian. The dietetic service of the Veterans Administration is a splendid one, and nothing is left undone in providing meals which are both nutritious and pleasing. However, the patient's emotional reactions to food often frustrate an important aspect of his treatment. The delusions of the psychiatric patient that may center around food are neither the only nor major aspect of the problem. Medical and surgical patients come into Veterans Administration hospitals from a wide variety of subcultures in the nation, carrying with them a wide variety of food habits and customs. Add to these the idiosyncrasies of individual patients, and the various types of psychosocial significance attached to food and the process of eating, and it is evident that this problem is by no means a small one. Both on the wards and in the area of training, clinical psychologists and dietitians are working together to understand and solve some of the problems in this area.

THE TRAINING PROGRAM

The Veterans Administration Clinical Psychology Training Program, as mentioned earlier, is of primary importance to the total functioning of clinical psychology in the Veterans Administration. Established in 1946 to meet and anticipate the desperate demand for qualified personnel, it is now a continuing and integral part of the Veterans Administration's medical program. It seems worth while to describe it in some detail not only for this reason but for whatever value it may have for the development of state training programs now already under way.

Selection of the trainees is made by the university, and upon concurrence by the Veterans Administration these students are enrolled as part-time employees. During their four-year program trainees work at the university toward the completion of their doctoral degrees in the same manner as other students. They also work part-time in Veterans Administration hospitals and clinics, where they are paid for the actual number of hours worked. Inasmuch as this combination of academic and clinical work creates a heavy load for the student, it usually takes him five years to complete the doctorate and at the same time to accumulate the equivalent of two years' clinical work needed to qualify him for a staff position.

For this reason universities generally recommend for the Veterans Administration program only those who have already completed at least one year of graduate work. Such students are enrolled as *first year* trainees so that they may spend the last four of the needed five graduate years in the Veterans Administration program. This arrangement has many advantages for the student. It means that once he is in the Veterans Administration program he will usually have time to finish both academic and experience requirements for a full-time staff position, and can move into such a position without a break. This continuity is advantageous in cases where for one reason or another there is a temporary delay in filling a staff vacancy. In such instances the individual can continue in training status, detailed to the station where he eventually will go on duty, until all of the rather complex arrangements for staff appointments are completed.

The selection of more advanced students for the Veterans Administration training program also has advantages for the university, and for the agency. For the university, it means that selection can be surer because the capabilities of individual students are better known. This means lower attrition in the training program. It also means that first-year trainees are capable of making a greater immediate contribution in the hospital to which they are assigned.

In the Veterans Administration, it is the Area Chief Clinical Psychologists who carry primary responsibility for the conduct of the training program. It is they who, along with the Chiefs of Training Units, provide the major liaison between the universities and the Veterans Administration stations, and make the assignments of trainees to hospitals and clinics. Trainee assignments must have the concurrence of the university, for the basic responsibility for the education of trainees has been delegated to the universities. They must also have the concurrence of the station concerned. The Area Chief Clinical Psychologist, with his training unit chiefs, not only makes certain that all training assignments are mutually agreeable but performs a further highly valuable function. Working both with the universities and with the stations, he devises patterns and sequences of training assignments which will be as nearly optimal as possible from the standpoint of training, and at the same time maximally contributive to the hospitals and clinics. This careful and often intricate planning by persons familiar with and sympathetic to the goals of both the universities and the stations has been a major factor in the development of a highly efficient program.

In connection with training assignments, it should be pointed out that these may be brief, or may run for six months or a year. They may be for ten hours a week or for thirty-nine hours (i.e., just short of full-time). They cover different types of stations in rotation. This flexibility allows for the adaptation of the Veterans Administration program to many different university patterns. Depending on geographical location and other factors, one university may prefer to have its trainees on straight twenty-hour-a-week assignments throughout their four years, while another will prefer ten-hour-a-week assignments during the first trainee year and a six- to twelve-month internship at thirty-nine hours a week in the third or fourth year of training. Some universities find that the most suitable arrangement is a block system in which trainees spend one term on campus, and then one term at a Veterans Administration station working thirty-nine hours a week. All of these arrangements have their points of advantage, and the choice among them depends upon many factors within the university. But the important fact is that from the standpoint of the Veterans Administration all are feasible. Co-operation in training continues as long as it is mutually satisfactory. The implied contractual agreement may be terminated by either party at any time. This system of checks and balances, and the establishment of machinery for formulating plans and reaching decisions, has proved highly effective.

Trainees are not limited to assignments to nearby stations; on the contrary, they are urged to accept at least one assignment to a distant station. Such arrangements not only permit a wider variety of experience during the training period, but also enable the trainee to become acquainted with a different section of his country and with the psychologists and universities in that area. If he is in the final stage of training, it may help him to select the station to which he will go upon graduation.

Trainees may be assigned to any station in the Veterans Administration, provided it is agreeable to all concerned. The Area Chief Clinical Psychologists work together in effecting interarea assignments. In like manner, they function togther in arranging staff placement for trainees who are graduating. Each Area Chief knows the needs, characteristics and present staffs of stations within his own area; he also knows each individual trainee and his preferences and potentialities. Being in possession of both types of information he can work with other Area Chiefs in arranging highly satisfactory interarea placements of individuals. Through such interarea co-ordination, graduating trainees can be assured that all stations within the Veterans Administration are brought within their range of consideration; and conversely, hospitals and clinics desperately needing additional staff know that there can be full selective recruitment for their stations from the entire group of graduating trainees in the Veterans Administration as a whole.

One other aspect of the training program should have comment. What do trainees do when they are assigned to hospitals and clinics? The simplest answer is that they serve as junior staff members. They are assigned to and function directly under the Chief Clinical Psychologist of the station, working side by side with him and his staff on all of the problems handled by the Clinical Psychology Unit of the station. They are at the station as part-time employees, and as such are expected to share in the work load of the staff unit. Customarily starting with simpler forms of diagnostic testing, they are given additional responsibilities as rapidly as they are able to handle them. Older staff members are always available for consultation and guidance, but the trainee begins early to carry the burdens of professional responsibility. It is a protected situation for him, but also one in which he is expected not only to learn rapidly but also to carry his share of the work of the group.

There are no psychometrists or others at a technician level in the Clinical Psychology Program of the Veterans Administration. Trainees do the work for which technicians would otherwise have to be employed, and are paid at a corresponding rate.

For psychology this training pattern is of particular importance, for the field is growing rapidly and methods are being outgrown at a rapid pace. If anything, this pace will increase because clinical psychologists are research-trained, and it is an integral part of their job to work constantly at the development of more efficient methods. The organizational fact which aids this development in a scientific group is the absence of a permanent technician group, and the handling of the entire work of the staff program solely by professional and preprofessional personnel. It would be difficult to overestimate the importance of this pattern of organization.

Another value of the training pattern lies in the *concomitance* of academic and clinical experience. It is the opinion of most psychologists in the universities and in Veterans Administration stations that this combination of experience for four years accelerates progress in both areas. Academic subject matter becomes more meaningful when one is exposed early to the realities of practical situations. And an early direct grappling with clinical problems tends to mature scientific and research thinking.

Furthering the relation of academic and clinical experience are the faculty members of the universities who serve as Veterans Administration consultants. This essential part of the total training program was initiated at the very beginning, and has played a major role not only in achieving efficient training but in providing further liaison between the universities and the hospitals and clinics of the Veterans Administration.

Inasmuch as trainees have never been under legal obligation to remain with the Veterans Administration upon graduation, the question of "return" from the training program was a matter of some apprehension in the early days of the program. Such fears were needless, for the return has been exceedingly and gratifyingly high and there is every reason to expect that it will continue to be so. The last tally in this regard showed that 80 per cent of all graduates had remained with the Veterans Administration. Another 12 per cent has accepted faculty positions where, by augmenting university training resources, they were of equal value to the Veterans Administration. This 92 per cent still does not give the full picture of social return from this governmental training program. Of the remaining 8 per cent most have gone with state, and some with county or city, hospitals or mental health units, some have taken commissions in the U.S. Public Health Service, a few have gone into clinic practice, and the rest are in the uniform of one of the branches of the armed forces. As a result of this record, some 60 per cent of the clinical psychologists now on duty in the Veterans Administration have come from the training program. Furthermore, graduates have proved willing to go in gratifying numbers to remote and isolated stations where the need is most acute. Needless to say, continuing thought is given to ways of assisting such individuals and protecting their professional development and future.

RESEARCH

Training and research are very closely related in the Veterans Administration program in psychology. Inasmuch as all trainees are doctoral candidates at a university, each is required to complete a dissertation which adds to the basic knowledge of the field. Many of the dissertations of Veterans Administration trainees evolve from the problems confronting the professional staff of the hospital or clinic. However, there is no obligation to select such a problem for study. The trainee is entirely free, in so far as the Veterans Administration is concerned, to work on projects requiring brass instruments or mathematics, rats or monkeys, and his thesis does not need to be "clinical" in nature. But the basic underlying responsibility of the psychologist to contribute throughout his lifetime to the growing knowledge of his field, through his own work or by facilitating the efforts of others, is indelibly impressed upon the trainee. This extremely close co-ordination between research and training is easily translated upon graduation to the concept of research-and-service which characterizes the activity of the full-time staff clinical psychologist.

One of the most important early decisions made in regard to the functioning of clinical psychologists in the Veterans Administration was the inclusion of research as a normal activity of the staff psychologist. This step represented a major departure from the conventional use of scientific and professional personnel in government, where small numbers of scientists customarily have been employed as full-time research workers and larger numbers of professional personnel for full-time service. The new pattern laid down for clinical psychologists combined research and service for the entire group. This early step on the part of the Veterans Administration was subsequently incorporated in the U.S. Civil Service Commission Classification Specifications of 1949, which apply to clinical psychologists in all federal agencies.

The actual number and variety of research projects is considerable. At any one time there are perhaps 500 studies in progress at Veterans Administration stations undertaken by staff members and trainees. More than a third are concerned with the development or refinement of measuring devices or techniques for differential diagnosis and prognosis. Some seek a better understanding of the nature of particular mental disorders, while others are directed toward an evaluation of factors underlying specific therapeutic or rehabilitative procedures. Many are directed at a better understanding of personality and psychodynamics.

In addition, there are basic studies of learning, of the effects of special conditions of learning, of sensory and perceptual phenomena, and of concept formation. There is much interest in the understanding of the clinician himself as diagnostician and therapist, and in the development of new therapeutic methods. One substantial advantage in the Veterans Administration is the widespread opportunity for interdisciplinary and collaborative research.

More effective co-ordination of research and the prevention of unnecessary duplication of effort is promoted by the interchange of information among psychologists working on related problems. To this end each investigator is asked to prepare a Research Project Report which contains data descriptive of the investigators, the title of the project, the problem or hypothesis, and the plan of study. One copy of this report is filed with the Central Office, and one in the appropriate Area Office.

One special development should be noted bearing on the recognized need for more objective and reliable methods of evaluating the results of psychotherapy. Recently there has been established, in the Washington, D.C. Regional Office, a Neuropsychiatric Research Unit, under the direction of a clinical psychologist, for the purpose of developing such methods. This unit, the first of its kind in a Veterans Administration outpatient setting, is developing a program aimed at the study of the effectiveness of present methods of mental hygiene clinic treatment, and the selection of appropriate methods for treating particular types of patients.

THE FUTURE

A number of trends in the developing activities of clinical psychologists can already be identified. In the diagnostic area, there is increasing concern with an understanding of the basic perceptual processes. In lieu of diagnostic categories, which are more useful for legal than for research purposes, multidimensional rating scales have been developed within the Veterans Administration. These provide a means for charting and profiling the behavior of patients, and already are proving most useful in the measurement of behavioral change.

In neuropsychiatric hospitals the trend has been in the direction of bringing clinical psychologists out of a central group of offices and assigning them directly to wards where they now have much closer and more continuing contact with patients and where they assume greater responsibility for work programs. Much attention is being given to the long-term continued-treatment patient, with particular emphasis on ways of developing more group activity among these patients. Customarily such patients are those who have been through the acute-intensive treatment program of the hospital upon admission and have failed to respond. Clearly what they need is not more of same, but some different type of treatment. The need for new methods for these patients is clear; this in turn calls for new thinking and fresh approaches, including reconsideration of basic assumptions. This problem, which is a most important one, is already the subject of intense interest and study in a number of hospitals, and it is likely that it can be brought under sustained attack in the not too remote future. In one hospital the establishment of a special ward is under way which will provide special preparation for patients approaching discharge from the hospital—a counterpart of the intensive treatment program developed for them on admission. Group testing of psychotics, an almost unexplored area until the postwar years, is now rather generally used. This development has been a major contribution to the therapeutic program because it provides means for eliminating the unavoidable two- to four-week delay between admission and full initial study which formerly was necessary before a treatment program was instituted.

In the first few years after the establishment of the program in 1946, clinical psychologists were drawn rather rapidly and extensively into individual psychotherapy. Subsequently, increasing emphasis has been given to group psychotherapy. Now, a trend is discernible in the direction of more intensive study of group processes among patients, and ways and means of organizing a therapeutic social world for the patient within the hospital setting.

As part of this trend, it appears that clinical psychologists may find themselves spending an increasing amount of time with other staff members rather than directly with patients. Already there is a fairly widespread feeling among medical personnel in the Veterans Administration that developments *within* each of the specific therapeutic modalities have tended to advance at a much faster rate than the co-ordination *between* them. The full cumulative effect of the contributions of diverse specialists will be achieved in the degree to which their efforts are fully integrated. In this effort the psychologist has special skills to contribute to group functioning and must assume a corresponding degree of responsibility.

In the widening and deepening attack upon basic problems, it is clear that all the resources of the science of psychology must be brought to bear. It is not only the techniques of the clinical psychologist which are needed, but also the methods and approaches of those in physiological, social, and personnel psychology. Plans for bringing into the Veterans Administration psychologists with these varying backgrounds are under way. Counseling psychologists are already being employed in large numbers as a result of a new Vocational Counseling Service established a year and a half ago. To provide more qualified personnel for these positions, a Veterans Administration training program in counseling psychology is now well under way. In such matters as level of training, university relations, selection of trainees, and so forth, it parallels very closely the pattern of the longer established Clinical Psychology Training Program. Administratively, the new Service is separate and distinct from the Clinical Psychology Program, both in training and staff aspects.

The basic determinant of the future, both in regard to direct service to patients and in respect to the development of more effective methods, is the caliber and number of persons involved. This brings us to the outlook for the future in regard to personnel. The Veterans Administration is still far short of its needs, having at the present time only about one third of the clinical psychologists it requires. Even with a training program of the present size, it will be many years before these needs can be met. For a number of years, the Clinical Psychology Training Program has run at the level of 700 trainees; at the present time it is 625, but restoration to the earlier figure in the near future is anticipated. Even at the 700-level, however, it means at most no more than 175 trainees graduating each year, and this number is considerably greater than the number which can be counted upon as a yearly staff increment. Considering attrition from all causes, and the number of graduates who must go into universities to maintain capacity to train, the Veterans Administration cannot safely count on more than 100 a year; and 125 would be the most optimistic possible limit. At this rate of accession, it is clear that it will take quite a number of years to meet minimal needs, even without staff attrition. But staff attrition cannot be disregarded, and the larger the program and the longer it is in existence the more important this factor becomes. It seems likely that at whatever point staff needs level off, the continuing replacement problem will be of such magnitude as still to require, if not to tax, a training program of the present size.

VIII.

CLINICAL PSYCHOLOGY IN THE
UNITED STATES ARMY

FREDERICK A. ZEHRER

On the day World War I was declared a group of experimental psychologists met at Harvard University to consider ways and means of providing opportunities for psychologists to serve effectively in the interest of defense. The letter which they wrote on 6 April 1917, addressed to the Council of the American Psychological Association, resulted in a proposal through the National Research Council, that The Surgeon General of the Army utilize psychologists to assist medical officers in discovering and eliminating men from the Army who were mentally unfit for military training and duty.

In August 1917, The Surgeon General provided for the commissioning of officers to serve as psychologists in the newly created Sanitary Corps. Major Robert H. Yerkes, the first commissioned psychologist in the Army, was assigned to the Office of The Surgeon General as chief of the newly established Division of Psychology (January 20, 1918).

Within a short time the function of the psychologist was expanded to aid in segregating the mentally incompetent, classifying men according to their mental capacities, and assisting in the selection of competent men in responsible positions. Army-wide psychological testing was established for all personnel through the rank of Major. By the middle of 1918 there were at least 118 officers and approximately 350 enlisted men serving on active duty as psychologists in the Medical Service.

The military psychologists in World War I tested over 1.5 million men using group examinations Alpha (for literate men) and Beta (for illiterate men) in addition to having examined 83,000 men individually, using such instruments as the Point Scale, Stanford-Binet Scale, and Performance Scale.

Clinical psychology in the Army came into being in early 1918 when several psychologists were assigned to military hospitals to work in close co-operation with neuropsychiatrists. The Surgeon General sent out orders which included instructions that reports of individual psychological examinations "shall be accepted by the psychiatrist as part of the medical examination and included in the case record if an individual is to be recommended for discharge or special assignment."

Despite the excellent contributions of psychologists in the Army during World War I and the recommendation that provision be made for officer psychologists in the permanent military organization, when wartime demobilization was completed in 1920 there was no provision for the retention of psychologists in the Medical Department. Development of *clinical* psychology in the Army during the period of 1921 to 1941 is not a matter of record.

In the early stages of preparation for World War II (1939-1941) psychologists were used by the Army in the area of personnel selection, classification, and assignment procedures. There were several clinical psychologists in military units, but only a few were assigned and used as clinical psychologists.

During the first year of World War II (1942), several clinical psychologists were appointed as civilians (in uniform) in the Army Specialists Corps to serve in Induction Stations and Reception Centers. Within a few months, these officers were granted commissions and assigned to The Adjutant General's Department, but remained in the same duty stations. The functions of this group of psychologists were essentially those of a psychometrist and interviewer, with limited opportunity for clinical appraisal during the rapid screening examination of Selective Service registrants except in the performance of individual examinations of suspected malingerers and illiterates.

Other individuals, with wide variations in training and experience, were commissioned as psychologists in The Adjutant General's Department and six clinical psychologists were commissioned in the Sanitary Corps of the Medical Department. The former were assigned, generally, as personnel consultants and personnel psychologists, whereas the latter were assigned to psychiatric services in Army general hospitals.

Many officers who had training and experience as clinical psychologists performed duties in special training units (slow learning and illiterate), Army Specialized Training Program STAR units (college special programs), induction stations, reception centers, separation centers, and mental hygiene units, as well as in other military units throughout the Army in a variety of military assignments. Some of the assigned duties called for extensive use of professional skills; others limited markedly any opportunities for clinical service.

In the performance of their duties at induction stations, the psychologists briefly interviewed the men while they were in the line awaiting phases of the medical examination. The purpose was to screen out those who were possibly illiterate, non-English speaking, or mentally retarded. A rapid review of their Selective Service forms revealed formal educational level and occupation. Those about whom there was doubt as to their meeting current induction standards in the aforenoted areas were tabbed to be examined by the psychologist at the end of the physical examination if they met the medical criteria for acceptance for military service. Generally, those who had completed at least ten grades of school were not selected for examination.

Those examined by the psychologist were administered a group qualification test which was essentially a nonliteracy scale of ascending difficulty wherein some intellectual functions were sampled. A brief literacy test was usually given to determine reading ability. Those who did not attain a qualifying score were then tested, in small groups, through the administration of a nonverbal scale. Directions were given in pantomime. Those who failed this test were examined individually. The individual battery consisted of short tests to sample ability to follow verbal directions; to reproduce block designs; and to count the number of blocks in piles in pictured form. Those who failed this battery were rejected.

In borderline cases, and where the clinical impressions were not in agreement with the test data, the registrant was interviewed, the key elements in his history were reviewed, and a decision was made to accept or reject the man. If it was determined that an individual was mentally deficient, even though he had attained a score above the critical range, a conference was held with the psychiatrist who had seen the man earlier. Since mental deficiency is a medical diagnostic item, the psychiatrist could enter this as the reason for rejection when applicable.

By 1943, when the aforenoted tests were used in all examination stations, it became apparent that clinical psychologists were not needed. Many with training in this field were transferred to units where their training and experience could be better utilized. They were largely replaced by "personnel consultants" who could perform the tasks set for the administrative selection and rejection of personnel on the basis of literacy and estimated ability to learn in the military service.

In reception centers, where men who had been accepted for military service were sent, the psychologist generally interviewed and examined individuals referred by medical officers and those whom they screened out as of doubtful ability to adapt successfully to the military service. These officers typically employed various examination instruments and techniques. Their principal function was to assist in the selection of men who were functionally illiterate (below standard 4th grade level of reading and writing) in order that they would be sent to a special training unit prior to basic training.

The special training units, established in 1943, included a personnel consultant on the staff. These officers generally had had some training in psychology. They often performed duties similar to those generally conducted by school psychologists. Test administration and interpretation was a frequent duty. Analysis of reading disability was not unusual. A trainee was assigned to the unit until he learned to read and write at least to grade four level, if this could be accomplished in not more than twelve weeks. Instruction was conducted six days a week generally by trained schoolteachers, many of whom had remedial reading training. Individualized programs of instruction were guided by the psychologist. Personal counseling was a frequent function in these units.

When mental hygiene clinics were established in 1942 psychologists were included as members of the staff. The psychologists assigned to the few clinics in operation during World War II generally had more training in clinical psychology than those assigned to induction stations, reception centers, and special training units. They examined patients, conducted individual and group therapy, and advised personnel officers concerning reclassification or reassignment of trainees.

With the establishment of rehabilitation centers and a large neuropsychiatric patient load, there were increasing demands for the services of clinical psychologists in medical service units. Brigadier General William C. Menninger, MC, who served as Chief of the Neuropsychiatric Consultants Division in the office of The Surgeon General during most of World War II, advocated the establishment of neuropsychiatric teams (psychiatrists, clinical psychologists, and psychiatric social workers) in the Army. Upon his recommendation to enhance the effectiveness of psychiatric services, The Surgeon General formally established the use of clinical psychologists in Army medical installations in September 1944. Those officers qualified to serve as clinical psychologists were detailed to the Medical Administrative Corps under the jurisdiction of The Surgeon General and assigned as members of psychiatric teams in Army general hospitals, convalescent hospitals, station hospitals, regional hospitals, correctional organizations, rehabilitation centers, and mental hygiene clinics in troop training centers. On 1 September 1945 responsibility for all Army *clinical* psychological activities was transferred to the Office of The Surgeon General and personnel qualified for duty in this field were assigned to the Medical Service. In effecting this change the Clinical Psychology Branch was established in the Office of the Chief Psychiatry and Neurology Consultant in the Professional Division of the Office of The Surgeon General.

In an Army policy statement to the field in 1945, it was stated that clinical psychologists assigned to Army hospitals, mental hygiene clinics, and disciplinary barracks were to be assigned to duty with the neuropsychiatrist. Their duties were to: aid in the development and administration of a program of counseling designed to prepare patients to remain on duty or for return to military units; assist in the preparation of clinical records, particularly including those requiring the use and interpretation of psychological examination techniques; assist in studies of special psychological problems related to classification and retraining of neuropsychiatric casualties; assist in the determination of the appropriate military occupational specialty of patients with special difficulties; assist in the treatment of patients under the supervision of the psychiatrist; and perform such other professional duties as would most effectively assist the neuropsychiatrist in the accomplishment of the best management and disposition of patients. This gave official recognition to what many psychologists already had been doing in the areas of psychodiagnosis, therapy, and counseling as well as to stimulate the more extensive utilization of professional skills of clinical psychologists.

In the latter months of World War II (1945), a total of approximately 250 officers were assigned to duty as clinical psychologists in Army medical units, to fill that many of 346 authorized spaces based on requisitions for clinical psychologists. A survey of their duties and functions indicated that the transition from a multiplicity of duties in psychology to *clinical* psychology had been made rather effectively when the clinical psychology program was finally set up as a Medical Service responsibility.

When postwar plans were made for the permanent structure of the technical services in the Army, it was apparent that clinical psychologists had proven their value on the psychiatric team in the Army Medical Service. In the legislative action (1947) which created the Medical Service Corps, there were included clinical psychologists in the Allied Sciences Section of the Corps as a part of the permanent Medical Service organization. This was the first time that clinical psychologists became an integral element in the Regular Army.

An effective career pattern, allowing for professional growth and development, was soon adopted to insure a satisfying field of professional service. This provides military schooling at appropriate intervals; sequential assignments to mental hygiene consultation service units, disciplinary barracks and hospitals with increasing responsibility and opportunity for professional experience; for tours of duty as instructors in the Medical Field Service School and as research personnel in the Army Medical Service Graduate School; for postdoctoral refresher training at appropriate intervals or to meet specific needs; and for duty as consultant in The Surgeon General's office or Army Area headquarters. The assignments are made in terms of individual officer's status and need as well as the requirements of the military service. Clinical psychologists are assigned and utilized as recommended by the Office of The Surgeon General.

In 1949 authority was granted to procure career Regular Army clinical and medical research psychologists during the ensuing six years. To implement this action an effective clinical psychology internship program was established and developed in three Army hospitals. This program is conducted in the same hospitals where American Psychiatric Association approved residency programs in psychiatry and neurology are conducted.

The Army clinical psychology intern program is based upon the recommendations and criteria as determined by the Education and Training Board Committee on Practicum Training of the American Psychological Association. It provides for one full calendar year of training for selected graduate students matriculated at institutions which have doctoral training programs in clinical psychology approved by the American Psychological Association Education and Training Board. Those appointed as interns (as 2nd Lieutenants in the Medical Service Corps) must have completed all doctorate degree requirements except the dissertation and examinations usually conducted subsequent to the submission of the dissertation. They then return to the university (in active military student status) to complete the remaining degree prerequisites.

Those considered best qualified and apparently well motivated for a professional career in the Army are appointed. Each year there are several times as many applicants as intern spaces available. Of the total of 75 appointments made in the last five-year period, there were but two who were unsuccessful in completing all Ph.D. requirements. The full year in residency offers an excellent opportunity to provide intensive and extensive training experience in a high standard medical setting. A ratio of better than one qualified staff supervisor to two interns is maintained at all times. At Walter Reed, Fitzsimons, and Letterman Army Hospitals, where the internship program functions, there are, in each case, three staff clinical psychologists and not more than five interns.

The program provides for orientation to the functions of the Army clinical psychologist; psychodiagnostic examination practicum; research opportunities; seminars and conferences; therapy (introduction); and instructional experience. Ward rounds, management of patients, journal clubs, observation of various forms of therapy, consultation with medical and social work personnel, and opportunity to examine patients of all ages and both sexes are some of the items in the experience of the intern. Interns are rotated for duty on the neurosurgical ward, open ward, closed ward, outpatient clinic, and child guidance clinic to provide opportunity to observe and examine patients manifesting the widest possible range of disorder and illness. Interns who have university-approved dissertation projects which allow for the gathering of data in the military setting have an opportunity to work on the project in so far as practicable. Each hospital where the intership program is conducted has highly qualified civilian consultants who make regular visits to the unit for guidance and didactic purposes.

In 1950, the academic prerequisite for a commission as a clinical psychologist (with minimum grade of 1st Lieutenant in the Medical Service Corps) was raised to the doctorate degree with major field of study in psychology. No exception is made to the doctorate degree requirement in the consideration of applicants. Although the appointing authority regulation specifies major field of study in "psychology," the interpretation for appointment in the Medical Service Corps is "clinical psychology" and the institution from which the degree was granted must be on the list approved by The Surgeon General.

In 1951, an Army Technical Manual (TM 8-242) was published for the guidance of clinical psychologists on duty and to orient their medical and allied sciences colleagues concerning their duties and functions. This 197-page manual "outlines the functions and procedures of the clinical psychologist in the Army and Air Force hospitals, Mental Hygiene Consultation Services and in the Disciplinary Barracks. There is a discussion of the diagnostic, research and psychotherapeutic functions of the clinical psychologist in the installations to which he is assigned. The Administration, scoring and evaluation of some of the more commonly used clinical psychological instruments and techniques are discussed, namely: Wechsler-Bellevue Intelligence Scale, Thematic Apperception Test, The Rorschach, Goldstein-Scheerer Tests, and Minnesota-Multiphasic Personality Inventory" (3, p. 1).

The residency training in psychiatry for medical officers conducted concurrently with the clinical psychology internship program manifestly has contributed to a present situation wherein the psychiatrists, clinical psychologists, and psychiatric social workers work together exceptionally well as effective professional teams in Army organizations.

CURRENT STATUS

The Army clinical psychologist serves in the department of neuro-psychiatry of hospitals; in mental hygiene consultation services located in troop training centers; in the psychiatry and neurology sections of U.S. disciplinary barracks (i.e., Army prisons) and rehabilitation training centers; and in the combat area with psychiatric units. In addition, clinical psychologists are assigned to the faculty at the Medical Field Service School and in research positions in the Department of Psychology at the Army Medical Service Graduate School. Other assignments include the Research Division in the Office of the Secretary of Defense; as Chief, Human Resources Research Branch in the Medical Research and Development Board, Office of The Surgeon General; and Chief of Clinical Psychology Branch in the Professional Division, Office of The Surgeon General. This variety of assignment allows opportunity for career progression with responsibilities commensurate with rank. The military rank (as an indication of status and acceptance) of clinical psychologists ranges from 1st Lieutenant through Colonel in the Medical Service Corps (Allied Sciences Section).

As a member of the neuropsychiatric team in the different types of units, the clinical psychologist works collaboratively with other staff members toward the common goal of maintaining effective mental health among military personnel utilizing professional skills in the prevention, diagnosis and treatment of mental illness.

The clinical psychologist's function is fundamentally similar in the various military units in so far as clinical examination, therapy, research, and expert consultation are involved. However, the emphasis and amount of time devoted to these activities varies in the different units. This is due to the primary mission and location of the organization as well as to the differences in personality, adaptability to conduct therapy, and the theoretical orientation of the clinical psychologist.

In mental hygiene consultation services (i.e., mental hygiene clinics) the clinical evaluations are less extensive than in neuropsychiatric services of Army hospitals, and more time is devoted to group therapy with patients. In addition, the clinical psychologist, with other clinic staff members, provides guidance for officers and enlisted personnel in the field of mental hygiene through group sessions and individual interviews. The clinical psychologist is responsible to the chief psychiatrist as is the psychiatric social work officer. He is assisted, typically, by enlisted men who are qualified clinical psychology technicians. He conducts in-service training, supervises the technicians, and prepares reports for the psychiatrist with special reference to the reason for referral.

In correctional organizations (i.e., disciplinary barracks and rehabilitation training centers) psychodiagnosis is a major function. Each newly arrived prisoner is examined by the psychiatric staff for the purpose of making recommendations concerning trainability, education needs, and potential concerning clemency, parole and restoration. The psychologist focuses as strongly upon the man's assets as upon his limitations and deficiencies. Also, much time is devoted to consultation with other personnel concerning rehabilitation methods, plans for individual training and education, preparole orientation, and preventive psychiatric functions among prisoners and custodial personnel.

In Army hospitals a large proportion of time is generally devoted to psychodiagnostic functions. Therapy on an individual basis, in co-ordination with the psychiatrist, is conducted more frequently in hospitals than in the aforenoted military organizations where group therapy is more generally utilized.

Generally, the psychologist in an Army hospital administers and interprets standardized psychological examination techniques and instruments essential in the evaluation of the individual patient's intellectual potentials, efficiency of intellectual function, personality structure and key dynamics, special abilities and disabilities, primary interests, and motivation. In addition to examination of the patient, the medical and psychiatric social history is reviewed prior to the preparation of a clinical report. The report, which becomes part of a patient's medical record, is written to assist the medical officer in making a differential diagnosis, prognosis, and specific treatment and disposition plans. The psychologist supervises technicians and less experienced officers; conducts training on psychological subjects; participates in staff professional conferences; and conducts research on psychological aspects of problems related to the Medical Service.

In combat zones, the clinical psychologist is used as an assistant to the psychiatrist in his multiple duties involving diagnosis, therapy, and disposition of patients as well as preventive aspects of mental health among troops. There is little time for Rorschach evaluation and intensive psychometric explorations under field conditions, although these are used frequently as needed. Clinical observations, and suggestive forms of treatment in co-ordination with the psychiatrist are typical duties performed. The methods of utilization of the clinical psychologist in the combat zone are under study. Empirical determinations to date have indicated that the skills brought to the field by the clinical psychologist determine the extent to which he can be used in this very new role. In time, it is anticipated that experience will reveal the specific attributes and skills deemed to be most essential in clinical psychologists assigned to such duties.

In mental hygiene clinics located in troop training divisions and in correctional units the clinical psychologist works primarily with patients who are adult males. However, in Army hospitals he sees patients— male and female—who range in age from preschool to senility. There are four child guidance clinics in hospitals located in the United States, one in Japan, and three in Europe. Outpatients and inpatients are referred to the clinical psychologist not only on neuropsychiatric service, but from all of the various services and clinics in the hospitals. The widest possible range of mental health conditions is manifested among the patient population. As a result, the clinical psychologist in an Army hospital may examine in any one week a patient who is psychotic, neurotic, emotionally immature, disabled as a result of cerebral damage, or presents problems of school adjustment to mention only a short typical sample. He may see for treatment purposes a soldier with neurotic symptoms; a boy who has a reading disability; a young woman who presents problems in behavior adjustment; a soldier who suffered cerebral damage in combat and is now aphasic; or a soldier who has a speech defect. Also, he may conduct a study group for parents concerned with child guidance. The range of function in the military setting provides ample opportunity for challenging forms of efficient service.

Expert civilian consultants in the various disciplines, including clinical psychology, are available at all large Army hospitals and specialized treatment centers. In addition, the professional libraries are maintained at high quality levels. To supplement local facilities, the Armed Services have a medical library which provides reference books and photostatic copies of professional articles not readily available locally. The military clinical psychologist is provided the means to enhance and refresh his knowledge through enrollment in universities as well as attendance at professional conferences, workshops and seminars.

In all types of medical organizations research projects are conducted, and clinical psychologists serve as consultants to other professional staff members concerning research design and methodology. As an indication of the very considerable interest and morale of Army clinical psychologists in the field of professional activity and contribution, these individuals have had accepted for publication a total of sixty-eight articles during the three-year period, 1949-1952.[1] The productivity is rather remarkable in view of the shortage of personnel (in terms of demands for professional service) during this period which necessitated much "after hours" work to collect data, keep professional reading current, evaluate findings and prepare the manuscripts. The Surgeon General encourages research and professional contributions among Medical Service personnel.

At the Walter Reed Army Medical Center in Washington D.C., there has been established a Department of Psychology in the Division of Neuropsychiatry at the Army Medical Service Graduate School. This Department is staffed with civilian and officer psychologists. Among the psychologists on duty in the unit there are those who have specialized in experimental, comparative, physiological, social, and clinical psychology as well as statistics. Not only is developmental research conducted of special interest to medicine in a military setting, but also extensive basic research is carried on. In addition to the studies of the psychological aspects of morale, motivation, and stress conducted in combat (as they were in Korea), there are studies under way to develop more effective psychodiagnostic devices to determine the existence and extent of cerebral damage. The unit is conducting research to determine the environmental influences concomitant to various forms of somatic therapy among psychotic patients. A project is under way to attempt to isolate etiological factors of mental illness in selected geographical areas. These are but a few samples of the activities of the large staff.

---

[1] This total does not include the thirty-nine Ph.D. dissertations written by officers in the Army Senior Psychology Student Program.

This Department is in a strategic position, almost unique among existing civilian or military research organizations. In the same organization, neurologists, neuroanatomists, psychiatrists, biochemists, and sociologists work together closely to pool interdisciplinary knowledge. Further, on the same post (next door) there is located one of the largest Army hospitals (Walter Reed) which has a large Department of Neuropsychiatry with locked wards, open wards, neurology wards, outpatient psychiatry and neurology clinic, and child guidance clinic. In addition, there is a large audiology and speech center in the hospital. The psychologist, and clinical psychology interns, hold regularly scheduled interstaff conferences and work together on many projects. The resources for research are as extensive as is the Army.

To insure proper utilization of officer clinical psychologists (and other specialists), military personnel are normally limited to career pattern assignments to the extent consistent with the best interests of the Army and the individual. Without exception, officer clinical psychologists in the Army Medical Service Corps are assigned to primary duty in the field of their specialization. There are a minimum number of demands on their time for duties not related to clinical psychology: in the hospital, clinic, correctional institution, Army school, and headquarters staff. A survey made among clinical psychologists on duty in 1952 revealed no instance where more than 8 per cent of a typical duty week's time was devoted to functions not related directly to the practice of clinical psychology.[2] In view of the dual role (i.e., clinical psychologist and military officer), this is considered to be an optimum situation.

Since early 1951, the quality of enlisted personnel (inducted via Selective Service) assigned to duty as clinical psychology technicians has contributed markedly to the effectiveness of the clinical psychology aspects of the psychiatric services. The minimum prerequisites for assignment to the intensive (graduate level) course conducted at the Medical Field Service School have been a Bachelor's degree with major field of study in psychology, manifestations of emotional maturity, and strong motivation for duty as a clinical psychology technician.[3] During the period 1952-1953, six articles prepared by enlisted technicians were accepted by professional journals for publication. These men serve in the same manner as subdoctoral personnel in civilian psychiatric agencies under the supervision of clinical psychologists. Despite their military grade, they are given opportunities for clinical experience and develop-

2 Among clinical psychologists in the large Army hospitals the range was from 2 per cent to 4 per cent of time devoted to duties not directly related to clinical psychology.

3 In 1953 at least 89 enlisted technicians on duty had completed two years of civilian graduate study or held a Master's degree with major field of study in clinical psychology prior to entering the Army.

ment commensurate with their training backgrounds and demonstrated abilities.

FUTURE DEVELOPMENTS

In this relatively new Army utilization of clinical psychologists in medical units, attention is devoted constantly to the maintenance of highest professional standards, enhancement of contributions as members of a psychiatric team, provision of opportunities for research, and continued growth in clinical proficiency.

Plans are being formulated for a sound postdoctoral refresher and training program utilizing civilian and in-service resources; the establishment of career patterns for the clinical psychology technician; publication of a technical bulletin concerned with the duties and functions of a clinical psychology technician; and development of an adequate program for Reserve officers who are clinical psychologists.

In addition, plans have been made for the rotation assignment of career clinical psychologists to a research unit where they can devote full time to research as members of a multidisciplinary team in the broad field of neuropsychiatry.

REFERENCES

1. Cohen, R. R. Mental hygiene for the trainee. *Amer. J. Psychiat.*, 1943, 100, 62-71.
2. Berlien, I. C. Neuropsychiatry in Armed Forces induction stations, reception centers, and combat divisions. *Bull. Menninger Clinic*, 1944, 8, 146-149.
3. Departments of the Army and the Air Force. *Military clinical psychology*. TM 8-242—AFM 160-45. Washington, D. C.: U. S. Government Printing Office, 1951.
4. Freedman, H. L. The services of the military mental hygiene unit. *Amer. J. Psychiat.*, 1943, 100, 34-40.
5. Freedman, H. L. Unique structure and function of the mental hygiene unit in the Army. *Ment. Hygiene*, 1943, 27, 608-653.
6. Gilbert, G. M. The personnel consultant in an Army training center. *Psychol. Bull.*, 1944, 41, 180-186.
7. Henderson, R. W. Psychological consultation service in an Army specialized training program STAR unit. *Psychol. Bull.*, 1944, 41, 395-399.
8. Layman, J. W. Utilization of clinical psychologists in the general hospitals of the Army. *Psychol. Bull.*, 1943, 40, 212-216.
9. Menninger, W. C. *Psychiatry in a troubled world*. New York: Macmillan, 1948.
10. Patterson, C. H. Clinical psychology in the Army. *Psychol. Bull.*, 1945, 42, 393-395.
11. Rosenberg, S. J. The psychiatric service of an Army station hospital. *Amer. J. Psychiat.*, 1943, 99, 864-868.
12. Seidenfeld, M. A. Clinical psychology in Army hospitals. *Psychol. Bull.*, 1944, 41, 515-518.
13. Smith, L. H. Treatment activities in war psychiatry. *Amer. J. Psychiat.*, 1944, 101, 303-309.
14. Yerkes, R. M. (Ed.) *Psychological examining in the United States Army*. National Academy of Sciences, XV, Washington, D.C.: U.S. Government Printing Office, 1921.
15. Yoakum, C. S. & Yerkes, R. M. *Army mental tests*. New York: Henry Holt, 1920.

IX.

CLINICAL PSYCHOLOGY IN THE
UNITED STATES NAVY

R O B E R T   S.   H E R R M A N N

The inherent and varied problems of personal adjustment encountered in the Naval Service undoubtedly date back to the illustrious era of "Wooden Ships and Iron Men," but it was not until the turn of this century that any psychological evaluation of incoming personnel was made. Most of those early efforts were conducted by medical officers and were concerned with the detection of mentally subnormal men. The majority of tests utilized were self-constructed devices drawing heavily upon the Binet-Simon scale and adaptable only to individual testing (4).

The rapid expansion of the Naval Service during World War I created an imperative need for acceleration of the psychological examination and efforts were directed toward the formulation of personality inventories and questionnaires which were more amenable to group administration, rapid scoring and simple interpretation. This emphasis continued during the ensuing years and was conducted under the auspices of the Training Branch of the Bureau of Navigation (Personnel). The importance of classification and educational and vocational placement problems within the Navy was thus recognized and led to the development in 1924 of the General Classification Test. For the next fifteen years this test and its subsequent modifications served as the basic psychological tool for acceptance or rejection of Naval recruits, classification procedures, and disposition from the Naval Service for inaptitude and related nosological conditions.

During the period of increased recruiting in the two years prior to the outbreak of World War II it became more and more apparent that the rapid change of environment and resulting trauma to the personality incident to entering the Naval Service could not be predicted with any degree of significance by the simple criterion of a paper and pencil test score (1). Rather, a more accurate appraisal could be afforded only by the observation of the recruit's ability to adjust himself to the rigid and demanding environment of a Navy or Marine Corps recruit training activity.

With the disproportionately high incidence of neuropsychiatric casualties from World War I still in mind, the Navy Department moved to meet the crisis by placing several Naval Reserve H(S) commissioned clinical psychologists upon active duty. These clinicians were strategically placed in the various recruit training facilities to assist the medical officers in the neuropsychiatric screening of all incoming personnel. From this rather unprecedented origin an extensive clinical psychology program was developed and established as an integral part of the neuropsychiatric services in naval hospitals, training stations, retraining commands and disciplinary barracks during World War II.

Those Navy clinical psychologists stationed at the hospitals, retraining commands and disciplinary barracks functioned with administrative and professional responsibilities much the same as their civilian counterparts. However, the majority of Navy clinicians were placed in the Neuropsychiatric Units of the Navy Training Stations and the Marine Corps Recruit Depots. The primary mission of these units was the early detection for separation from the Naval Service of recruits who, by reason of psychiatric defects, would be a continual handicap to the Navy through their chronic inaptitude and inefficiency; or who, by breaking down at some critical moment, might seriously disrupt the functioning of their entire unit (9).

For the first time Bureau of Medicine and Surgery directives governing the establishment and operation of the Psychiatric Units gave full recognition to the professional competence and rightful place of the clinical psychologist in the hierarchy of the "psychiatric team." These authorizing directives made it clear that the clinical psychologist was not to be utilized purely as a psychometrician but that objective and projective test results would be supplemented by clinical interviews and interpretations of social histories and exercising clinical judgment in the usual sense of the term (2).

It was also at this time that Naval clinical psychologists, because of the selection and screening procedures unique to the Naval Service, were directed, by the following section from the original directive, to divert some energies toward research: "From the very beginning, the Psychologist should undertake to collect data on such scales which can later be studied in relation to the psychiatric findings and service records for purposes of establishing validity" (8, p. 3). It should be noted that these studies, commenced early in the war, have provided the Neuropsychiatric Branch of the Professional Division, Bureau of Medicine and Surgery with a wealth of criterion data for present-day policies and procedures (11).

By 1946 all Naval Reserve clinical psychologists had returned to civil life. However, the desirability of continuing the clinical psychology program as an integral part of the neuropsychiatric service required augmentation of this depleted military structure with a number of civil service clinical psychologists.

In 1947 Congress established the present Medical Service Corps of the U.S. Navy, abolishing the old Hospital Corps H(S) specialists (10). The Allied Medical Sciences Section of this newly formed Corps embraces a host of ancillary fields including that of Clinical Psychology. Administratively this section is under the direction of the Neuropsychiatric Branch of the Professional Division of the Bureau of Medicine and Surgery. At this time the first opportunity was presented to organize a long-range career plan for clinical psychologists. Procurement of officers for this program has been, and will continue to be, upon a very limited basis to insure an even rank structure and equality of status with other segments of the Navy officer personnel. With the program just six years old, the number of career psychologists is small and is complemented by a large component of well-qualified and experienced reserve clinicians upon an active duty status plus an increased number of permanent civil service personnel.

The following two years were formative years for the clinical program with the major emphasis placed upon training facilities of the Navy and Marine Corps. The postwar austerity program had reached its peak in 1949 and very little expansion was possible within the drastically reduced size of the Naval establishment.

The commitment of Naval and Marine Corps personnel and equipment to the United Nations effort in Korea in 1950 found Naval neuropsychiatry and clinical psychology again faced with the critical problems associated with intensive military combat. However, a drastic change in emphasis from World War II practice was instituted from the very beginning. Combat psychiatry for the Naval Medical Department became literally combat psychiatry and found the clinical psychologist operating as a member of the neuropsychiatric team with the U.S. Marine Corps in the forward areas of combat. This new philosophy emphasized early treatment of neuropsychiatric casualties; treatment on the spot, minimizing opportunities for any secondary gains, with no mention of evacuation to the safer confines of a rest camp or Naval hospital located outside of the combat periphery. This methodology placed an extremely heavy responsibility upon the clinical psychologist, requiring rapid yet accurate clinical evaluation under the most trying of circumstances. The major emphasis in the psychological appraisal was placed upon ascertaining the man's potential for further service and the likelihood of the facilities in the forward area (dry clothes, warm food and reassurance) being able to assist the patient to materialize this potential. Axiomatically, it was found that the farther from combat a man goes before receiving any type of treatment, the less probable it is that he can be salvaged for any additional effective service (7).

To this end a system was devised whereby the clinician utilized an extremely mobile psychological office. His "office" consisted of a foot locker containing nonmedical supplies such as stationery, playing cards, athletic equipment (5), and a field kit especially designed to carry an adequate battery of both objective and projective psychological tests.

With the procurement and assignment of more professionally qualified clinical psychologists and psychiatrists, the Navy combat psychiatric program increased its effectiveness by setting up an interim treatment facility located approximately two miles to the rear of the actual combat area. This location enabled the psychiatric service to provide clean tents, bedding and clothing and more time for supportive therapy. It also enabled the psychologist to make every effort to get the individual functioning again as a member of a group; be it in group athletics, games or interviews.

Those cases not amenable to front-line, or near front-line, treatment were evacuated to the Naval hospital ships in the area and returned to the Naval hospital in Japan. This facility's neuropsychiatric service is organized and staffed in the conventional manner, allowing more time for psychological evaluations and providing the patients with more secure environment. Once more the major emphasis is placed upon getting the man to a duty status and an eventual return to his original organization.

The clinical psychologist contributed immeasurably to the success of the Naval combat psychiatric program during the past three years of hostilities in Korea. Taking with him the traditional concepts of diagnosis, research, and therapy, he soon added instruction as a fourth concept to facilitate the evaluation of his patients. This was accomplished by instructing battalion and regimental medical officers, Marine Corps line officers and other staff personnel in methods for recognizing and handling potential neuropsychiatric casualties. The clinical psychologists and psychiatrists who served with the Marine Corps in the Far East can look back upon a job well done. Initial and unofficial statistics for the Korean war indicate that less than 10 per cent of all psychiatric referrals were evacuated to the United States and, of more importance, less than 10 per cent of those returned to duty were readmitted to the sick list for psychiatric reasons and 96 per cent of all psychiatric admissions remained upon the sick list for less than fifteen days.

PRESENT FUNCTIONING OF THE NAVY CLINICAL PSYCHOLOGIST

The present-day assignments of the clinician in the Navy are quite diverse and call for widely varying backgrounds as the duties range from teaching psychology at the Naval Academy to working with Marine combat medical teams in the battlefield. There are few, if any, specific functions which the clinical psychologist performs in civilian life that are not also found among the duties of his Navy counterpart. In addition, by providing the opportunity to study group dynamics and the effective functioning of the "normal" and "marginally normal" personality, military clinical work offers a challenge not often found in civilian practice.

Past experience has shown that the most effective Naval clinicians are those who have an understanding of the over-all functioning of the Navy as well as a sound professional background. In fact, it is considered highly desirable for the psychologist to have served at sea either as an enlisted man or a line officer. Psychologists who are procured directly from civilian life are sent to the Officer Candidate School at Newport, Rhode Island for an eight-week period of general indoctrination as Naval Officers. After this orientation to the Navy these officers, as well as those new psychologists with previous commissioned experience, are ordered to the National Naval Medical Center, Bethesda, Maryland for a ninety-day period of indoctrination to Navy psychology and the functioning of the Naval Medical Department; thence to their first permanent duty station.

Teaching programs exist at all field activities with supervised training for men who have had little previous clinical experience. Moreover, Navy psychologists are strongly urged to participate in civilian professional activities and may, on occasion, be ordered to professional workshops and professional meetings at government expense. Provisions also exist for the career military psychologist to complete his Ph.D. degree at the university of his choice.

The basic orientation of Navy psychiatry is toward improving selective, predictive and prophylactic techniques so as to obtain maximum effectiveness from the individual members of the service. The philosophy in this connection is a preventive policy of psychiatric care rather than the development of an elaborate therapeutic program for the treatment of mental illness. As a result of this policy, the psychiatric patient population tends to be somewhat different than that found in most civilian settings and there are relatively few situations where the Navy psychologist deals with the long standing, chronic and severe psychoses or deteriorated organics. These individuals are transferred to Veterans Administration hospitals once the severity and prognosis of their cases has been established.

As the duties and problems are so vastly divergent in the billets which are occupied by Navy clinicians, each type of duty will be described in detail and an attempt will be made to place it in context with the service situation in which the particular billet is found.

NAVAL TRAINING CENTERS AND MARINE CORPS RECRUIT DEPOTS

The Neuropsychiatric Unit functions as an integral part of the Medical Department, charged with the responsibility for the health and welfare of recruits at that particular training center. This medical department is an entirely separate organization from the Naval hospitals which are usually found nearby or at the training center itself. As opposed to the hospital setting, the Recruit Training Command psychiatric unit occupies a dispensary building which is centrally located within the training area. There are no locked wards in this dispensary, nor are there provisions for hospitalization of the overtly psychotic or severely neurotic patient who could not safely be handled on an open-ward basis. When such serious cases are detected, they are transferred immediately to the Naval hospital for treatment and further disposition. Although primarily concerned with recruits, the Neuropsychiatric Unit also serves the training center staff personnel on an outpatient and consultative basis.

The mission of the training center Neuropsychiatric Unit is twofold. The first major task is weeding out the psychiatrically unfit before their condition may become aggravated by being exposed to the rigors of training. The second task is the "screening-in" of marginal manpower so that individuals who might otherwise be lost to the service can be effectively utilized. The extent to which this mission is successfully carried out with any particular group of recruits will be reflected in the rate of medical discharge for psychiatric reasons and the number of disciplinary cases which find their way to the psychiatric services after the specific group has completed two or three years in the fleet.

The staff at a Neuropsychiatric Unit varies from time to time, according to the needs of the service, but a typical organization in full operation during the Korean conflict period might consist of five to nine psychiatrists, two to five psychologists and a psychiatric social worker. In addition, several hospital corpsmen with psychological training may be assigned to work as psychometricians. In order that such a small staff may operate effectively under the rather pronounced stress of the everyday work load, there is no formally structured psychology department. All staff members of the Unit, regardless of professional discipline, are responsible directly to the senior psychiatrist. The senior ranking military psychologist is responsible for the co-ordination of psychological work and works closely with the senior psychiatrist in planning the over-all operation of the psychiatric unit. There is a maximum of informality and opportunity for interchange of ideas and opinions on patients and other professional matters. In essence, the organization promotes a team approach and interdisciplinary co-operation of maximum effectiveness and it is considered that the Neuropsychiatric Unit, when in full operation, nears the ultimate in the classical "team approach" to psychiatric problems.

The specific duties of the psychologist in the above setting are quite varied and include considerable administrative details, not only in the Neuropsychiatric Unit, but with the training command proper. As newly enlisted recruits enter the training center they are administered a rather detailed questionnaire and personal history form which gives background information for use during the psychiatric screening interview which follows. The psychologist sometimes gives this screening interview on the basis of the preliminary data, and those individuals who are suspected of possible psychiatric defects are marked for recall and further examination at a later date. During the course of training, these recruits will report to the Neuropsychiatric Unit for an extended examination to evaluate and predict their adjustment to the military service. It is at this interview that the psychologist can probably perform his greatest service. The time available for examination is limited and it is often necessary that an objective evaluation be obtained of the individual's basic ego strength, defense mechanisms, and personality dynamics by means of psychological examination. This examination is especially helpful when cultural factors, language handicaps, defensive façades, or other complications make the short psychiatric interview nonproductive.

No attempt has been made to standardize a battery of tests to be utilized in the recruit training station; rather the tests used and the extensiveness of the testing are dictated by the particular problem at hand. A recruit can be referred for psychological examination with a minimum of formality and reports are returned in the same manner. One technique which has been found to be particularly useful in the evaluation of large groups of individuals is the group Rorschach with the individual inquiry. Intellectual evaluation is greatly facilitated by use of an abbreviated scale such as the one developed for the Navy under a research grant at a civilian university (3). As with the Rorschach, when the rapid intellectual evaluation indicates a need for further study, standard test procedures are followed. It is often the result of the psychological examination that gives the information necessary either to admit an individual to the psychiatric unit or to return him to duty.

The population with which the psychologist works is of primary interest. As has been the case for many years, men are entering the Naval Service from every area of the United States and its possessions. These men may come from isolated sections of the country where their cultural and social backgrounds are almost foreign to individuals raised in a urban environment. Further, many groups in large cities preserve their old-world cultures and customs to a surprising degree, so there may be many adjustmental problems in their assimilation into the military service.

The range of pathology seen in this setting is considerable and many problems are brought to the surface that would never receive medical or psychiatric attention in civilian life. Furthermore, in spite of wide cultural variations, the population with which the Recruit Training Command psychologist works might be considered to be within the hypothetical concept of "normal" as the subjects were all making an adjustment in civilian life, albeit the adjustment may have been quite marginal.

Another major duty of the psychologist in the training center consists of the extensive evaluation of those individuals who have been admitted to the unit for consideration of separation from the Naval Service. This evaluation may be as complete as any which are done in intensive treatment hospitals, especially if it is decided that the individual is unsuitable for service. He will then be brought before an Aptitude Board for a hearing prior to disposition and a clinical psychologist is required to be one of the five members of this board. Here again, the psychologist may contribute a great deal of professional information and understanding to the individual case presentation.

The Recruit Preparatory Training Program. During the manpower shortage that always occurs at a time of mobilization it is necessary to lower enlistment standards and accept individuals who would not be allowed to enlist during times when the Armed Forces are small, compact units. At present, the services accept a sizeable number of illiterates and through organized training programs attempt to give them sufficient educational background to function as effective military personnel. This area is one which is particularly rich for the psychologist to explore and with the examination techniques available he can make a unique contribution to the evaluation of this group. Therefore, even though procedures vary somewhat with local conditions, in most training centers the psychologist plays a major part in the evaluation of illiterates. The psychiatric casualty rate is disproportionately high among recruits in this group. For example, unofficial statistics show that about 3 per cent of the recruit population for one center was assigned to the illiteracy program during a particular period that was studied. However, this preparatory training group of 3 per cent contributed 20 per cent of the total men admitted to the Neuropsychiatric Unit during this same period.

The primary problem in dealing with the vast majority of illiterates coming into the Navy today is not one of simply providing them with further education; rather, it is to determine why the individual has been unable to assimilate the education to which he was exposed in civilian life and then to evaluate his capacity for learning in the Naval environment. Recent studies at a Naval Training Center have shown that the number of illiterates who are unable to read because of a lack of opportunity to learn has markedly decreased since World War II, and there appears to be a far greater proportion of recruits at the present time whose illiteracy is on an emotional basis. The evaluation of the Navy illiterate's capacity to profit from further training must of necessity be drawn out over a period of time as the training program usually has a psychotherapeutic effect on the recruit.

A good number of illiterate recruits fail to reach the required fourth grade level of reading proficiency by the end of the thirteen weeks allocated for literacy training, and a further evaluation of these individuals and their suitability for service must be made. Persons who fail to profit from the extensive academic training in this length of time almost without exception reveal pronounced emotional learning blocks. The intellectual, emotional, social and vocational assets of the recruit are weighed against the severity of his symptomatology and the likelihood of his becoming a psychiatric casualty in determining whether he should be allowed to continue into regular training. It is considered that if a man has compensating assets for his illiteracy which are sufficient to allow him to complete regular recruit training, he should be able to serve satisfactorily in a seaman's billet.

In order to maintain an effective working relationship with the instructors who are responsible for the training of this extremely marginal group, periodic meetings are held with the staff of the Recruit Preparatory Training Unit. Not only are specific cases discussed, but a continuing program is carried on in the area of the psychodynamics of emotional reading blocks, motivation of the marginal group, and overcoming of the secondary gain which is so frequently found in this body of recruits. Efforts are also made by the psychologist in conducting this program to prevent the school staff from becoming so emotionally involved with their pupils that they lose perspective of the fact this group will be expected to function without special consideration once they leave the school.

In an advisory capacity, the psychologist also serves to help maintain the basically psychological approach to the illiterate recruits along with the very necessary military climate of the school. It can be seen that if a careful balance between the military and psychological approaches is not maintained, the whole program would be in danger of losing its value. Overemphasis of the military aspects results in an instructor-pupil void which greatly impairs learning in this psychotherapeutic situation, and failure to keep a general military setting in the daily routine causes extreme difficulty when the recruits are placed in regular recruit training with its rigid authoritarian environment.

The Recruit Retraining Unit. All training centers maintain a Recruit Retraining Unit wherein an effort is made to bring men whose performance has been unsatisfactory up to a par with their shipmates. A recruit may be sent to the retraining unit for any number of reasons, such as failing tests, having dirty clothing, and inability to march, but their one common factor is the inability to perform at an acceptable level in training. These men are frequently referred to the Neuropsychiatric Unit for psychological evaluation to determine whether they should be allowed to continue in training. The technical problems encountered during such evaluations are numerous, but one of the most frequent is that of distinguishing between personality inadequacy, poor motivation, and mental deficiency as a cause of poor performance in culturally deprived individuals. In addition to the above conditions it is not unusual to detect severe but well-concealed emotional disorders among the men in the retraining units.

While the retraining unit does not deal primarily with disciplinary problems, infractions of regulations are markedly high among this group of recruits. Again, the psychologist is called upon to aid in ascertaining the underlying causes of the behavior which has resulted in disciplinary action. Distinction between deep-seated character disorders which will not benefit from disciplinary action and the immature or adolescent personality who will be benefited by corrective action is usually the key problem presented. On occasion there is also a question of legal competence and responsibility for disciplinary infractions. Regardless of the question which is presented, the commanding officer's disciplinary action in the individual case will probably be based on the recommendations of the Neuropsychiatric Unit. Frequently the detailed psychological and psychiatric reports will be forwarded to line officers, making it most important to express psychological test results in clearly understandable lay terminology, relating all interpretations to the problem at hand.

Educational duties. In order effectively to implement the Navy's program of preventive psychiatry, it is necessary to conduct an organized and intensive course of indoctrination for the noncommissioned officers who work directly with the recruits. The psychologist is often given all or at least part of the responsibility for carrying out the educational program of the Neuropsychiatric Unit. The first Navy Company Commander and Marine Corps Drill Instructor lectures are conducted while the new leaders are undergoing their formal period of indoctrination. Further instruction sessions are conducted after the petty officers have actually taken over the training of a recruit company or platoon.

The time consumed in preparing and actually conducting the company commander's indoctrination program is relatively short. However, there is no other area of the total recruit psychiatric program where the clinical psychologist can make a greater contribution. The proper guidance and psychological handling of new recruits has a profound effect on their future development and personal adjustment.

In addition to explaining the basic functions of the screening program considerable time is spent in setting forth the need for utilization of the marginal man and the part a sound mental hygiene approach can play in obtaining the maximum service out of these persons. Once the lecturer has overcome the initial resistance to the very existence of a psychiatric program the remainder of the indoctrination is usually carried out without too much difficulty. The basic mechanisms of adjustment to recruit training are discussed with small groups of company commanders where specific examples are brought up by the group. Technical terminology is avoided as is any attempt to place the various syndromes into diagnostic categories. Rather, emphasis is placed on a recognition of the various adjustive mechanisms and the proper approach to the individual in which they are displayed. All of this must be placed into the framework of a military setting which has fairly specific boundaries on the extent to which recruits may receive individual attention. Of further importance is the setting up of a rough framework which will aid the company commander or drill instructor in his recognition of the more serious emotional disturbances which should be brought to the attention of the Neuropsychiatric Unit.

Research. A rather extensive program of in-service psychological research is carried on by training center psychiatric units. The majority of this research is concerned with the development of new screening techniques and the improvement of the existing implements. While Navy clinical psychology is oriented toward the use of projective techniques rather than paper-and-pencil tests, the screening questionnaire is considered to be of value for use in the rapid processing of large numbers of men. Therefore, a great deal of work has been directed toward the development of a screening instrument which will be reasonably accurate in detecting men who are in need of further, intensive evaluation by the psychiatrist. The limitations of this type of instrument are fully realized and it is not intended that the questionnaire ever be used as more than an aid in the clinical appraisal of all incoming personnel.

The recruit training center is a natural setting to conduct research on intelligence tests, projective techniques and, more important, studies on various factors in the psychological adjustment of the "normal" individual. While the majority of research must be conducted in conjunction with other psychological duties, there are exceptions where the primary duty of the psychologist will be research in nature. A group of experienced civilian consultants work closely with the service personnel in carrying out the program of recruit training research.

NAVAL HOSPITALS

Clinical psychology in the Naval hospital embraces the same duties and responsibilities that are found in the leading psychiatric installations of other government agencies as well as in comparable civilian institutions. Thus, the psychologist is an integral part of the neuropsychiatric service and concerns himself with the areas of diagnosis, consultation, research, therapy and training as demanded by the local situation.

As there are a few military clinicians in Naval hospitals, the majority of the psychological positions are filled by civilians. All Navy clinicians operate under the administrative supervision of a medical officer (psychiatrist) and in a few of the larger hospitals a higher grade supervisory clinical psychologist also exercises the technical supervision over the lower grade psychologists within a formal department of psychology. In psychological evaluation and psychiatric treatment the clinician works closely with, but professionally independent of, the psychiatrist in establishing and presenting basic data on mental levels, personality dynamics, behavior deviations, and over-all personality configurations. The contributions of the psychologists are usually accepted as authoritative and are utilized by the psychiatrist and other medical officers in devising an over-all treatment plan. An analysis of representative Navy positions indicates that performance in the areas of diagnosis, research, therapy and consultation is typical at all hospitals. Many psychologists are also responsible for training and consultation duties. This training is of both a formal and an informal type, in addition to "on-the-job training" of trainee psychologists. In some hospitals clinical psychologists train other specialists, e.g., nurses or psychiatrists, in the application and significance of psychological findings in their specialties.

The duties of the clinician in the Naval hospital duplicate the functioning of his civilian counterpart more closely than in any other Navy situation. The major differences lie in the patient population rather than in the professional functioning of the psychologists as the bulk of the patient load in Naval hospitals is composed of the severe personality disorders, psychoneurotics, and individuals with acute psychoses.

NAVAL RETRAINING COMMANDS

The problem of military delinquency is as old as the service itself, but it is only since the early days of World War II that Naval psychiatry and clinical psychology have actively participated in the retraining program. At the present time, psychiatric teams are staff members of all the major disciplinary facilities and are principally concerned with the psychological characteristics of individuals who have failed to meet the disciplinary requirements of the military service.

The objectives of the retraining command are twofold. The primary task is to salvage the maximum number of these offenders for future Naval service. In those instances where this is clearly impossible, the command endeavors to improve the individual's chances for a conforming and productive civilian existence.

From the moment a man arrives at the retraining center the psychiatric service makes every effort to foster his personal growth and maturity. The task is to free the man as quickly as possible from his personality and emotional disturbances so that he can initiate his own restoration plans (6). Psychologists and psychiatrists assist the individual with an extensive therapeutic program consisting of individual testing and psychotherapy, orientation films and lectures, on-the-job training, adult education courses, and occupational and vocational counseling; all aimed at helping the retrainee decide what he wants to do in his present situation better to prepare himself for life in or out of the service.

OTHER DUTIES

Of no less importance, but involving few psychologists in any given installation, are the following diversified clinical billets in the Naval Establishment:

U.S. Naval Academy. The clinical psychologist at Annapolis is a member of the faculty and, with the psychiatrist, conducts courses for the midshipmen in mental hygiene and the psychological principles of good leadership. Providing the future line officer of the Navy with an understanding and appreciation of the basic psychological concepts of leader-follower situations is another firm cornerstone in the long-range preventive psychiatry program of the Navy.

Administrative assignments. Psychologists are assigned within the Bureau of Medicine and Surgery to administer the Clinical Psychology program and assist with staff policy formulations at this level. These duties call for a thorough working knowledge of the entire Navy and involve a close liaison with other branches of the Navy Department. It is through this chain of command that the everyday, routine and practical aspects of the Navy psychiatry program are effected.

THE RESEARCH STORY

In retrospect, the original authority establishing the position of clinical psychology in the training activity's psychiatric unit proved most fortuitous. Specific attention was given to the need for a constant gathering and processing of research data for the continued improvement of selection techniques in use at any given time. This was the rather inauspicious beginning from which the Navy's expanded psychiatric and psychological research program of today was started. The tremendous press of work in the days that followed the promulgation of the authorizing directive precluded any systematic processing of data but did not prevent the methodical collection of a large body of psychological and psychiatric material for future reference.

Approximately two years after the end of World War II the Office of Naval Research consummated the first research contract for the purposes of processing and analyzing these medical and service records. As this project progressed, Bureau of Medicine and Surgery plans began to crystallize for a long-range psychiatric research program. This program, initiated and stimulated by the Neuropsychiatry Branch, was developed in accordance with four guiding policies:

(1) The program must supplement rather than duplicate psychiatric and psychological research conducted by other Federal agencies, and by civilian agencies.

(2) It must meet specific service needs, either directly or indirectly.

(3) It must be interdisciplinary and in all instances involve the discipline of psychiatry.

(4) It must utilize in-service facilities, directly or in collaboration, in so far as it is possible to do so.

Developing from these policy guides, research projects are organized around a 10-point program in the preventive aspects of psychiatry and clinical psychology as promulgated by the Neuropsychiatry Branch in 1949.

(1) Evaluate each man psychiatrically, initially and as necessary, to determine the continuing level of his Naval performance.

(2) Evaluate Naval billets in terms of psychiatric factors involved, as well as of skills and aptitudes required.

(3) Assist in the assignment and reassignment of personnel on the basis of personality resources, as well as of aptitudes and skills.

(4) Provide opportunity for the psychiatrically handicapped to participate in the fleet effort without enhanced protection or undue advantage.

(5) Assess each phase of training and operation to determine the group dynamics unique to each setting.

(6) Assist in the modification of training and operational personnel techniques to minimize psychiatric stress and to capitalize on positive group resources.

(7) Collaborate with line personnel to incorporate concepts of preventive psychiatry in policy and planning.

(8) Establish psychiatric facilities at all strategic levels of Naval operations to provide joint preventive and rehabilitative services.

(9) Establish laboratories for psychological and psychiatric research, with special attention to the cultural and social factors influencing motivation and adaptation in the Navy.

(10) Provide professional training to produce Naval psychiatrists and clinical psychologists oriented to preventive psychiatry in group setting, as well as psychiatry of the individual.

Under this general program, research is conducted by contract and inservice facilities in the areas of policy and planning, operational and basic psychiatry. Special attention is given to the old problem concerning lines of communication between research and operational activities which enables inservice facilities to incorporate reliable and valid research results into operational policy with a minimum of delay.

The Neuropsychiatry Branch utilizes the services of its contract research investigators in the role of consultants on actual planning and operations in Navy and Marine Corps psychiatry. By this method, topflight professional people with full staffs have been made available to the psychiatric program and have been fully utilized. Each of the principal investigators under research projects has had special experience in Navy and/or Marine Corps procedures that materially enhances his value to the program.

It is the philosophy of the Navy that research in this sphere is never in a static condition, nor is it readily amenable to the traditional "hardware" concepts so necessary to procurement of financial support. It has, however, been firmly established as an integral aspect of the Medical Department of the Navy and is considered to be a continuous process that must accompany the proper administration of the neuropsychiatric program. This is a continually changing world with an ever-increasing premium being placed upon the complexities of mechanical and atomic warfare. The selection procedures utilized during World War I were manifestly unsuited for use during World War II; these same selection procedures of 1942-1945 were found to be no longer applicable for the recent Korean conflict; and the procedures for any future emergency must be geared to the needs of that particular moment. Research in the manpower selection field must be continued if the Navy is to remain abreast of the times and fully discharge its responsibilities to the American people.

FUTURE PLANS

The Clinical Psychology Section of the Neuropsychiatry Branch is still a young organization and must continue to undergo some of the "pains" of maturation. Fortunately, a solid foundation is its inheritance from the wealth of World War II experience, and its growth is being carefully planned.

Personnel plans call for the gradual and controlled formation of a nucleus of qualified and experienced career psychologists. As the needs of the service dictate, this necessarily small number of military psychologists will continue to be supplemented by academically qualified and experienced civilian psychologists in Civil Service positions. Of vital importance will be the continued maintenance of many experienced and informed Naval Reserve commissioned psychologists in an inactive status who can be quickly mobilized should a national emergency so warrant. Efforts are presently under way to provide more of the inactive reservists with active duty training periods for reorientation purposes, thereby insuring a standby reservoir of informed professional persons who would be of immediate value should their services be required upon a moment's notice.

Future plans within the professional sphere are for increased emphasis upon the use of clinical psychology for preventive treatment within the Naval establishment. This means a partial break with the traditional hospital concepts involving only diagnosis and treatment and moving more psychologists into the field situations. Here, rigorous preventive hygienic programs are being established and opportunities afforded for first-hand observation and detection of the potential psychiatric casualty. Here too is where immediate treatment will result in a far greater restoration percentage than has been experienced heretofore. Manpower is the one commodity of this country that is not inexhaustible and every effort must be made to preserve an adequate and well-trained Naval Service for the protection of our National security.

REFERENCES

1. Bell, R. A. Recruit selection. *U.S. Nav. Med. Bull.*, Wash., 1940, 38, 301-306.
2. Hunt, W. A. The psychologist in the psychiatric program at the Naval Training Stations. *Psychol. Bull.*, 1944, 41, 557-560.
3. Hunt, W. A. and French, E. G. The CVS abbreviated individual intelligence scale. *J. consult. Psychol.*, 1952, 16, 181-186.
4. Louttit, C. M. Psychological examining in the United States Navy: An historical summary. *Psychol. Bull.*, 1942, 39, 227-239.
5. McMichael, A. E. and Fowler, D. K. An equipment chest for a field psychiatric service. *Med. Tech. Bull.*, 1952, 3, 117-118.

6. Murphy, J. M. and Grant, J. D. The role of psychiatry in Naval retraining. *Armed Forces Med. Jour.*, 1952, 3, 631-634.

7. Stouffer, G. A. W. and McMichael, A. E. The Naval psychologist in the Far East Command. *Armed Forces Med. Jour.*, 1954, 5, 196-200.

8. U.S. Navy, Bureau of Medicine and Surgery. The inauguration of a procedure to eliminate the neuropsychiatric unfit. BuMed letter of Feb. 1, 1941.

9. Wittson, C. L., Harris, H. I., and Hunt, W. A. Detection of the neuropsychiatrically unfit. *U.S. Nav. Med. Bull.*, Wash., 1942, 40, 340-346.

10. *Army-Navy Medical Services Corps Act of 1947. Public Law 337.—80th Congress.* Washington: U.S. Government Printing Office, 1947.

11. *Psychiatric Unit operational procedures.* (Rev. Ed. 1954) Washington: U.S. Navy, Bureau of Medicine and Surgery, 1954.

X.

CLINICAL PSYCHOLOGY IN THE
UNITED STATES AIR FORCE[1]

SAMUEL KAVRUCK

The need for a program of clinical psychology in the U.S. Air Force began at the time American planes were being considered as potential military weapons prior to World War I. The use of planes as bombing devices was probably considered to be secondary to their value as aids to observation, and military aviation served as an arm of the Signal Corps. However, the problems which currently face psychologists in the Air Force undoubtedly arose when the first Army aviators prepared for flight. The first reference to the development of a program of psychology for aviation, appears in the Memoirs of the National Academy of Sciences, Volume XV, *Psychological Examining in the United States Army,* as follows: "The Division of Military Aeronautics has recently requested the General Staff to authorize the application of psychological methods to its enlisted personnel. This request was indorsed by the Surgeon General with the recommendation that the existing organization and personnel for psychological service, Medical Department, should so far as possible be used for conducting this work in the Division of Military Aeronautics" (5, p. 51).

The present structure and organization of the U. S. Air Force program of clinical psychology is a direct outgrowth of the Army Air Force Aviation Psychology program developed during World War II. Two training manuals were published prior to the entry of the United States into World War II, which are of historical interest. The first was *TM 8-325, Outline of Neuropsychiatry in Aviation Medicine* (3), which was concerned chiefly with psychiatry and psychiatric examination. The second, *TM 8-320, Notes on Psychology and Personality Studies in Aviation Medicine* (4), was more applicable to clinical psychology. These publications are evidence of the need for general guides for use in training individuals who would be concerned with the problems of psychological adjustment.

---

[1] The clinical program in the Air Force is, at the time of this writing, still in the process of implementation. This is an interim report and necessarily in less detail than will be possible in the near future.

A recent publication, joint *AFM 160-45* and *TM 8-242, Military Clinical Psychology* (2), published in 1951, is an excellent guide to current organization and procedures in clinical psychological services offered by the Army and Air Force.

The first convalescent training program began in 1942 in the station hospitals of each AAF base, as well as in larger regional hospitals. By September 1943 special convalescent centers were organized. These differed in scope from the original convalescent training program in that many of the patients were combat veterans. In March 1944 the Air Technical Service Command was given jurisdiction of the program. By June 1944 the newly constructed AAF Personnel Distribution Command was given direction of the program.

The origin of this program, its psychological services, research accomplished, techniques, and functions of key personnel are excellently summarized in an Army Air Force publication edited by Bijou (1). In describing the program, Bijou and Heathers state that the purpose of the psychological services program in AAF convalescent hospitals was to contribute to the psychological skill and knowledge of the psychologist, to the accomplishment of the mission of these hospitals, which mission was to treat the whole man, bringing about improvement both in his physical condition and in his mental condition, attitudes, morale, and readiness for duty. The program entailed the following areas of activity: convalescent orientation, initial evaluation, special evaluation, individual counseling, and group counseling. Research was accomplished using adjustment inventories, attitude studies, biographical surveys, interest inventories, measures of mental functioning, projective techniques, and evaluation of personal adjustment group conferences.

A great amount of research was accomplished using such paper-and-pencil instruments as the Cornell Selectee Index, the Personal Inventory, the Shipley-Hartford Retreat Scale, the Rorschach, the Bender Visual-Motor Gestalt Test and an Incomplete Sentences Test. A major objective of the research program was the evaluation of convalescent services. Techniques for objectifying and quantifying interpersonal behavior in personal adjustment group conferences were evolved.

In evaluating the AAF psychological program in convalescent hospitals, Bijou and Heathers point out that though the program was in operation for only a little more than one year, and handicapped by a lack of trained personnel, psychological services were rendered to about 30,000 convalescent patients.

The present clinical psychology program of the U.S. Air Force began with the establishment of a separate Medical Service of the U.S. Air Force, on 1 July 1949. This was a direct outgrowth of the National Security Act of 1947, which established the Department of the Air Force and which authorized the Secretary of Defense to transfer responsibility for its own medical support to the Air Force. The immediate problem of this newly created service was to build a structure to serve best the unique needs of the flyer, to initiate a career program, and to develop a program that would insure the optimum level of health in the Air Force.

Qualified clinical psychologists in the Medical Service Corps of the Army were given an opportunity to transfer to the newly organized Medical Service Corps of the Air Force. Air Force clinical psychologists function within the Neuropsychiatry Branch which is part of the Consultant's Group. Psychologists with a background in clinical psychology also function with the Psychological Medicine Branch under the Aviation Medicine Division, chiefly in research. It is possible to serve in clinical psychological work in either an officer or enlisted status. Officers are designated as Clinical Psychologist, with Air Force specialty number 9186. They may range in rank from second lieutenant to colonel. Enlisted men who start as medical helpers may attend the neuropsychiatric training course and become neuropsychiatric apprentices (AFSC 90231). They may then qualify for advancement to neuropsychiatric specialist and senior neuropsychiatric specialist (AFSC 90251). The function of enlisted personnel in the neuropsychiatric framework is currently being clarified. Officers may be commissioned from enlisted ranks or directly from civilian status.

The primary mission of the Air Force clinical psychologist is to serve within the neuropsychiatric framework of the Air Force, and as a member of the psychiatric team under the supervision of the neuropsychiatrist, to engage in: (a) psychodiagnostic testing; (b) individual or group therapy aimed at the readjustment of habits, or treatment of psychoneurotic complaints; (c) counseling of a remedial or rehabilitative nature such as remedial educational retraining or vocational advisement with patients facing reassignment or discharge; (d) research, designed to evaluate and improve the predictive instruments used in psychodiagnostic testing and the effectiveness of therapeutic techniques; (e) training of technicians and assistants in psychological principles and techniques.

The clinical psychologist in the Air Force serves in one of three major organizational units: the Neuropsychiatric Center, the Psychiatric Unit, or the Mental Hygiene Clinic. At the time of preparation of this report, these three organizational units were only recently put into operation. A typical Neuropsychiatric Center is now in operation at Parks Air Force Base in California. The staff includes three clinical psychologists and nine psychiatrists. A Psychiatric Unit exists at Westover Field in Massachusetts with one clinical psychologist and three psychiatrists. A Mental Hygiene Clinic has been established at Sampson Air Force Base, New York, with one clinical psychologist and two psychiatrists.

THE NEUROPSYCHIATRIC CENTER

The Air Force Neuropsychiatric Center is designed to handle the major psychiatric and neurological problems requiring hospitalization for prolonged periods of observation, diagnosis, and treatment, and clinical psychologists in these centers are equipped to function within the entire range of psychological services. This includes all types of psychodiagnostic testing with a variety of patients including schizophrenics, depressives, psychopaths, aphasics, conversion hysterics, etc., with cases ranging from mildly disturbed to seriously disturbed.

The clinical psychologist generally makes three types of evaluations: diagnostic, follow-up, and terminal. Referral for diagnostic evaluation is made to determine intellectual level, nature of mental disturbances, severity of disturbance and prognosis, and determination of special disabilities. Follow-up evaluation is concerned with determination of the patient's program in relation to his therapeutic program. A terminal evaluation is conducted when the patient is considered ready for disposition either for return to duty or for separation from the service. The terminal evaluation provides a measure of the degree of improvement during the patient's stay in the hospital.

In addition to the psychological testing, psychologists in these centers assist in a program of indoctrination of professional personnel entering from civilian life into the program of military psychiatry. Psychiatric attendants, medical corpsmen, nurses, occupational therapists, and related medical specialists are given broad training in the principles and practices of the program of clinical psychology. Such personnel are encouraged to become aware of the value of careful observation and reporting of patients' symptoms and behavior which are often so valuable in determining diagnosis, prognosis and therapeutic measures.

Individual and group therapy sessions are carried on at the direction of the neuropsychiatrist. Group sessions have been found to be effective with either homogeneous or mixed patients with a maximum of twenty-five to thirty men. The therapy is in the form of flexible lectures or open discussion from the group co-ordinated by the therapist with goals planned in advance and based on the nature of the group represented. Careful reports of the proceedings, with observations of change, are recorded for inclusion in the individual case folder. Individual therapy is reserved for those cases requiring intensive treatment as indicated by the psychiatrist.

The Neuropsychiatric Center represents the best establishment for the design and facilitation of research projects in psychiatry and psychology. Because of its large population, varied clinical groups, provision for prolonged and intensive therapy, and availability of specialized equipment, the Neuropsychiatric Center should be the focus of research. Clinical psychologists in Mental Hygiene Units and Psychiatric Units, because of the urgency of maintaining effective operating rates and the transient nature of personnel in these units, will have less opportunity for research, though they can often contribute much to the improvement of techniques and procedures.

THE PSYCHIATRIC UNIT

The Psychiatric Unit, which functions within the zone of combat or the zone of communications, provides mental hygiene facilities at Medical Group level and limited hospitalization of psychiatric patients. The clinical psychologist in psychiatric units assists the neuropsychiatrist in psychodiagnostic screening of serious and chronic cases of emotional and mental illness, brief psychotherapy aimed at restoration of the patients to duty, maintaining a program of mental hygiene and preventive psychiatry, preparing the psychological summary for presentation to courts-martial and discharge boards, and providing personal counseling in the maintenance of combat effectiveness.

The psychologist must be prepared to perform diagnostic testing with cases of simple exhaustion, severe or overwhelming exhaustion, confusional states, diffuse dissociated states, localized dissociations, acute anxiety states, acute emotional outbursts, visceral disturbances, and acute psychotic and psychopathic reactions. In this unit he is concerned with a military program of mental hygiene aimed at detection and removal from service of actual or potential neuropsychiatric Air Force misfits and prevention of development of serious neuropsychiatric disorders, and which may include morale, enemy propaganda, leadership, rumor, military vocational efficiency, and food and sex as military problems.

The Psychiatric Unit presents an opportunity for the collection and analysis of data involving emergency psychiatric conditions and therapy. The clinical psychologist makes every effort at setting up a system for the collection and analysis of data wherever possible.

THE MENTAL HYGIENE UNIT

The Mental Hygiene Unit in the Air Force functions to provide a consultation service to medical processing and other departments in induction, reception, training, and rehabilitation centers of the Air Force. It serves as an outpatient service apart from the base hospital and will not provide hospitalization of any kind.

The clinical psychologist in the Mental Hygiene Clinic provides a psychodiagnostic service with recruits, trainees, prisoners, etc., who present emotional difficulties or maladjustments. Where the results of testing indicate, the psychologist recommends referral to the base hospital with cases requiring hospitalization or prolonged therapy. In the Mental Hygiene Clinic, the psychologist provides assistance with personnel who continue on a duty status.

Counseling and guidance services not requiring prolonged psychotherapy are also part of the psychologist's function. Referrals to the Mental Hygiene Clinic usually involve intrapersonal problems associated with the transition from civilian to military life. Trainees presenting symptoms of anxiety, insomnia, fears, homesickness, nervousness or somatic complaints such as headaches, back pain, and malaise are referred to the Mental Hygiene Clinic. Referrals are also made for interpersonal problems involving violation of military law, or inability to get along in group living or training.

The psychologist in the Mental Hygiene Unit is concerned, as in the Psychiatric Unit, with detection and removal from service of actual or potential neuropsychiatric Air Force misfits (such as alcoholics, homosexuals, psychopaths, addicts) and prevention of development of serious neuropsychiatric disorders.

Psychodiagnostic testing is employed to determine the level of intellectual functioning, the determination of the presence and extent of deterioration, an analysis of the structure of personality, its efficiency, and areas of conflict, assistance in determining personnel requiring hospitalization and evaluation of failure in the Air Force assignment. Planned lectures as part of a program of preventive psychiatry and mental hygiene are given to all incoming personnel.

The clinical psychologist also functions in close co-operation with classification personnel, chaplain's units, and Red Cross services in planning talks to airmen on fear, discipline, sex behavior, aims of war, drinking, recreation, and fatigue.

Relationship within the psychiatric team. The psychiatrist accepts medical responsibility for the patient and is the chief of the psychiatric team, which includes the psychiatrist, the clinical psychologist, the psychiatric social worker, and any other members of the hospital or facility concerned with the adjustment of the patient. The latter may include medical attendants, psychiatric nurses, occupational therapists, and physiotherapists. Each member of the team is expected to know and make suggestions about any individual patient. The team meets at regular intervals in staff conferences to discuss new patients, progress in therapy, and research. There is a free exchange of opinions and observations, and the resulting decision is a co-ordinated one.

RESEARCH

In addition to research which is carried on by psychologists in the organizations described above, research in clinical psychology is also conducted at the Air Force's School of Aviation Medicine at San Antonio. A typical investigation included a study of the value of projective techniques in the selection of pilots and other crew personnel. It is not difficult to imagine some of the areas in which clinical psychologists of the Air Force will make contributions as the problems of flight become increasingly complex. Such problems will entail studies of human adjustment under conditions of ultrasonic flight, the ability to function under extremes of temperature and pressure, and analyses of factors, yet unknown, related to mental breakdown and psychotherapy under such flight situations.

REFERENCES

1. Bijou, S. W. (Ed.) *The psychological program in AAF convalescent hospitals. Report No. 15. AAF Aviation Psychology Program Research Reports.* Washington: U.S. Government Printing Office, 1947.
2. Departments of the Army and the Air Force. *Military clinical psychology. TM 8-242—AFM 160-45.* Washington: U.S. Government Printing Office, 1951.
3. War Department. *Outline of neuropsychiatry in aviation medicine. TM 8-325.* Washington: U.S. Government Printing Office, 1940.
4. War Department. *Notes on psychology and personality studies in aviation medicine. TM 8-320.* Washington: U.S. Government Printing Office, 1941.
5. Yerkes, R. M. (Ed.) *Psychological examining in the United States Army.* National Academy of Sciences, XV. Washington: U.S. Government Printing Office, 1921.

XI.

PSYCHOLOGY IN THE PUBLIC HEALTH SERVICE

JOSEPH M. BOBBITT

The Public Health Service is an organization with many functions composed of highly diversified programs. Psychologists, some of whom represent the clinical area and some of whom do not, are utilized in many of the activities of the Service and in a variety of ways. It should be made clear at the outset that there are no centralized administrative structures responsible for psychological activities throughout the Service. Psychology, on the other hand, is utilized by the Service in activities where it is perceived as a useful professional area. This utilization is very extensive in terms of the number of activities involved, although the actual number of psychologists is not large.

BACKGROUND

The history of psychology as an important professional area in the Service can be said to be a development following World War II. On the other hand, psychologists have been active in or for the Service for many years. In order to describe one of the early uses of psychologists by the Service it is necessary to indicate that the Public Health Service supplies the medical care of Federal prisoners in the institutions operated by the Bureau of Prisons, Department of Justice. Public Health Service medical officers are assigned to the Federal penitentiaries and correctional institutions, and an officer is also detailed to the Bureau of Prisons as its Medical Director. For over twenty years psychologists have also been assigned to the medical installations in the Federal penal institutions. The early work of psychologists, beginning in the early 1930's, involved testing of intellectual functions and a considerable amount of clinical work. It was in this period that an intelligence test for prison use was developed, known as the Public Health Service Classification Test. As time went on, psychologists assigned to the prisons increased their scope of activity. The clinical work was continued and considerable research activity was developed by some of the psychologists. For instance, one psychologist did a

145

great deal of work in the prisons on the problem of the psychopathic personality.

The arrangements described above still exist today. The concept of what the psychologist can do in the prison medical installation has been greatly broadened over the years. At present, the desire is to secure fully qualified clinical psychologists to perform the full range of duties of this class of personnel. Particular interest exists in securing research-trained clinical psychologists to work upon the problem, for instance, of the rehabilitation of young offenders. It must be admitted that recruitment for prison assignments is not easy, and the number of psychologists utilized in the prisons is smaller than the number that could be utilized. It should be mentioned that the budget for these activities in the prisons, both medical and psychological, comes from the Bureau of Prisons, but the Public Health Service is responsible for the professional personnel and the professional services.

One of the earliest instances of the utilization of psychologists as Public Health Service employees in Service installations occurred in one of the two Public Health Service Hospitals for narcotic addicts established by the Service in the mid-1930's. The Public Health Service Hospital at Lexington, Kentucky, 'has utilized psychologists almost since its opening. The Fort Worth hospital did not do so until about a year after it opened. The hospital at Fort Worth has at the moment only one psychologist, a fully trained person in the clinical area. His function is that of a clinical psychologist as presently envisaged. Also, this hospital is only to a small extent devoted to narcotic addicts at present. Most of the patients at this institution are psychiatric cases, treated under contract with the Veterans Administration.

The Lexington hospital has utilized psychologists for nearly twenty years. Some emphasis upon psychometrics may have been involved in the early days at the Lexington hospital; but, as a matter of fact, the utilization of the skills of the clinical psychologists at this institution in the early days was probably well ahead of that at most other hospitals in the country at that time. Both research and therapeutic responsibilities were assigned to the Lexington psychologists from the outset. One fully trained clinical psychologist is currently on duty at the Lexington hospital, and it can be fairly stated that the Service is aware of the fact that more personnel of this kind could be used to advantage.

In this connection it is necessary to mention the Addiction Research Center maintained by the National Institute of Mental Health at the Lexington hospital. Originally, the Lexington and Fort Worth hospitals were administered by the Division of Mental Hygiene which was located in the Bureau of Medical Services and which at a later date (1949) became the National Institute of Mental Health and a part of the National Institutes of Health. When this organizational change occurred, the Division of Hospitals became responsible for the operation of the two hospitals, but the Institute maintained the addiction research activities which it had initiated as the Division of Mental Hygiene. The Addiction Research Center is perhaps the outstanding laboratory in the world dealing with addiction from the standpoint of the pharmacological, physiological, clinical care, psychiatric, and psychological problems involved. At the present time a physiological psychologist is on duty at this institution. In the recent past, a clinical psychologist has worked there with a psychiatrist on an intensive study of the personality characteristics of young addicts hospitalized at the Lexington hospital. He later was assigned to New York City to secure comparable data concerning other young addicts to check the possible bias in the Lexington sample.

During World War II, the Service assigned a group of psychologists to perform psychological screening and assessment functions for the War Shipping Administration in co-operation with its training of officers for the Maritime Service. These psychologists worked at several training centers and were involved in the assessment of both intelligence and personality. This activity was, of course, terminated at the end of the war. It is perhaps worth noting that these psychologists were given reserve commissions in the Public Health Service Commissioned Corps, marking the first time that psychologists have been utilized by the Service on other than a Civil Service basis. This fact is of interest since at least half of the psychologists now in the Service are commissioned officers, and over one half of these officers are in the Regular Corps.

The post-World War II period has seen a rapid growth in the utilization of psychologists in the Public Health Service. Much of this development may be attributed to the passage of the National Mental Health Act in 1946 and to the subsequent program developed by the Division of Mental Hygiene which later became the National Institute of Mental Health simultaneously with its transfer from the Bureau of Medical Services to the National Institutes of Health. It should be made clear, however, that trends toward greater utilization of psychologists during the postwar period have also existed throughout the Service. It is gratifying and important that clinical and other types of psychology have received support in recent years throughout the Public Health Service, although greatest development has been in the National Institute of Mental Health.

Since 1946, the number of psychologists, both in the clinical and other areas, has increased markedly. At that time there were only two or three psychologists in the predecessor organization of the Institute, the Mental Hygiene Division. It appears that one or possibly two clinical psychologists were on duty at that time at the Public Health Service Hospital for narcotic addicts at Lexington, Kentucky. One clinical psychologist had recently been assigned to the Public Health Service Hospital, Fort Worth, Texas.

In July 1946 a chief psychologist was acquired by the Mental Hygiene Division in connection with the development of the new program under the recently enacted National Mental Health Act. It was his responsibility to plan for the utilization of clinical and other psychologists in the new program, to recommend standards, to indicate the proper and possible areas of activity in which clinical and other psychologists could be of use, to assist in formulating actual areas of activity for the program whether they were primarily psychological or not, to recruit additional psychologists, and to act as a general consultant with respect to psychological problems within the Division and, upon request, elsewhere in the Service. Pending the recruitment of additional personnel, he had to meet operating needs of all parts of the program during this interim period. Another important part of his function at this time was that of informing the psychological profession of the new program, its actual activities at that time, and the planned and hoped-for expansion. It was felt that an accurate perception of objectives, goals, and potentialities by the members of the profession was a *sine qua non* of the effective development of a successful mental health program. The fact that the Institute has enjoyed remarkably fine co-operation and understanding from the psychologists of this country is a reflection, not so much of skillful work upon the part of this newly appointed chief psychologist, as it is of the readiness of American psychologists to learn and understand, of university departments to co-operate, of the American Psychological Association to help and to open channels of communication, and of individual psychologists to serve as consultants and advisors.

The development of the National Mental Health program did result in increased numbers of psychologists in the Public Health Service. This fact is, however, one of the least important aspects of this development as far as psychology is concerned. In the first place, the role of psychologists in this program was quite different from what they had experienced before. The creation of a chief psychologist position placed psychology in the position of one of the recognized major mental health professions responsible for planning and implementing the new program. This organizational status has been fully reflected in all operations and in all developments. The thinking of psychologists has been utilized intimately and completely throughout the last eight years. Psychology is now represented in every relevant program activity and at all levels of operation. There has never been any failure to utilize or to accept in planning or in activities what psychology has to offer. The limits of the involvement of psychologists have been set by the limits of their knowledge and skills.

It should be added that the other major mental health professions have been utilized in a similar manner. There has been a real joining of forces.

PRESENT FUNCTIONING

Today, clinical psychologists are doing a large variety of jobs at the National Institute of Mental Health. To understand these activities, it is necessary to indicate the general organization of program operation at the Institute.

First, the Institute supports training at the doctorate level in the field of clinical psychology and provides graduate traineeships through graduate schools and internship centers as well as support for some of the teaching activities of these educational institutions. Applications for these grants are first reviewed by a consultant group known as the Training Committee. This Committee is subdivided into subcommittees in the fields of psychology, psychiatric social work, psychiatric nursing, and psychiatry. The recommendations of the Training Committee are reviewed by the National Advisory Mental Health Council whose favorable action is necessary before the Surgeon General can make the grants. The Council is established by law and consists of outstanding persons, both lay and professional, in the mental health field. Psychology has been represented on the Council since 1950.

Within the Training and Standards Branch of the Institute there is a psychologist who is responsible for administering the part of this program devoted to psychology. The other fields are psychiatry, psychiatric social work, psychiatric nursing, and public health. The training specialist in psychology is responsible for informing psychological training centers of the nature of the Service's program in this field, for securing detailed information about the needs, potentialities, and activities of the various training centers expressing an interest in participating, and for handling all of the communications and liaison work with the participating institutions. The position is primarily an administrative one, but one for which a person is qualified only if he is sophisticated as a psychologist, knowledgeable with respect to the nature of universities and graduate departments of psychology, and possessed of an ability to perceive the needs for psychological training and the way in which the Service can be of assistance in this matter.

The psychologist in the Training and Standards Branch is also responsible for recommending and arranging conferences and other activities designed to help the profession improve and clarify training procedures and standards. The Service carefully avoids intruding itself into these functions, but it does assist them. The Boulder Conference on the Training of Clinical Psychologists, sponsored and conducted by the American

Psychological Association, was supported by a Public Health Service grant from the Institute training grant funds. It was developed in part because the psychological consultants to the Institute and the psychologist in the Training and Standards Branch perceived the need for such a conference. Similarly, the two conferences upon the role, function, and training of counselors held by the University of Michigan in 1949 and 1950, were supported by an Institute grant. The idea for such a conference originated outside the Public Health Service, but it was recognized by the Institute that these conferences could do much to improve the effectiveness of the Institute's contribution to the field of clinical psychology. Most psychologists are familiar with the fact that the Institute has for several years also supported with grants the accreditation activities of the American Psychological Association in the field of clinical psychology. Other instances could be cited, but it should be clear that the psychologist in the Training and Standards Branch has an important role to play in working with the profession to improve the standards and effectiveness of training in clinical psychology.

The National Institute of Mental Health also supports, on a grant basis, research at universities and other research organizations on mental health problems in the medical, biological, and behavioral sciences. These grants are made in a manner similar to that described above for training grants, with the difference that the first review is conducted by a consultant group known as the Mental Health Study Section. In addition, research fellowships at the postdoctoral level are awarded in various disciplines relevant to the problem of mental health. The Research Grants and Fellowships Branch is the organizational unit of the Institute which administers these activities and the chief of this branch has for the last five years been a psychologist. It is obvious that the chief of such a branch needs to be a person conversant with one or more of the mental health disciplines, but the position has not been filled by a psychologist upon the basis of any assumption that this discipline represents the only proper recruiting ground. In other words, the psychological training of the person involved has been of great significance, but a person with a very different background of training and experience could also perform this function.

Third, the Community Services Branch of the Institute administers a program designed to increase and improve the mental health programs of the States and of community and voluntary groups. As a part of this program, grants are made to the States to assist their work in the mental health field. Also of great importance, however, is the maintenance of an Institute and field staff in all of the mental health disciplines to serve a consultant and facilitating role, to explore the nature of mental health problems in the community services field, and to develop and evaluate approaches that may be utilized by the States and other groups.

The Community Services Branch has a Chief Clinical Psychologist who is responsible at the Institute for the utilization and integration of psychological personnel, techniques, and methods into the pattern of community mental health activities. These functions involve, for example, clinical services, work with the schools and other community organizations, estimates of the nature and size of the mental health problems at given places, and mental health education. The Chief Clinical Psychologist of the Community Services Branch is also responsible for the development by the Institute of recommendations concerning standards and selection criteria for psychologists utilized by the States and other groups in community mental health activities. Such recommendations are not coercive requirements but statements developed by the Institute in collaboration with its consultants who comprise the Community Services Committee on which psychology is regularly represented. Such statements are also presented to the Institute's top consultant group, the National Advisory Mental Health Council, for review.

It should be clear that the job of developing community mental health programs cannot be done completely at the site of the Institute. Consequently, the Institute maintains consultants in eight of the ten Regional Offices of the Department of Health, Education, and Welfare; however, all States of the country are served. These consultants are drawn from the fields of clinical psychology, psychiatry, psychiatric nursing, and psychiatric social work. It is not possible to have each of the four disciplines represented in each Regional Office. Clinical psychologists are on duty in three of them. The clinical psychologists and other Regional Office consultants deal directly with the States comprising their Regions. They consult, upon request, with individual States concerning their community mental health activities and, when asked to do so by the appropriate State authorities, with community groups within the States. The Regional Office consultants make contributions in their own right to the planning and thinking of the States of their Regions and make available materials developed by the Institute. Through the activities of the consultants in the Regional Offices, the Institute gains a clear picture of the mental health problems of the States and areas of the country and is able, therefore, to deal intelligently with the community services aspect of the Institute's program.

Specifically, the clinical psychologists in the Regional Offices make available consultation in the area of clinical psychology as it is involved or may be involved in the programs of the States. They are in communication at all times with the Chief Clinical Psychologist of the Community Services Branch to whom they are responsible in a professional sense.

When States not served by Regional Offices to which clinical psychologists are assigned request consultation on psychological matters, the Institute arranges for the necessary services to be performed by Institute personnel or by personnel from other Regional Offices. Thus, the incorporation of clinical psychology into the community services field is accomplished by the integrated activity of the Chief Clinical Psychologist of the Community Services Branch and of the clinical psychologists stationed in the Regional Offices.

The Community Services Branch has an additional psychologist who is responsible for dealing with areas in the community mental health field where special problems exist. For instance, he has worked on the mental health implications of civil defense. In this project he worked as a staff person with a subcommittee of the Community Services Committee of consultants, reference to which has already been made. Liaison was established by the psychologist with the Federal Civil Defense Administration. The psychologist worked both with the Subcommittee and with the Federal Civil Defense Administration. The result was a document, prepared by the Subcommittee, which was reviewed, accepted, and published by the Federal Civil Defense Administration. The document is entitled *Mental Health Implications in Civilian Emergencies*. This psychologist is currently working with another subcommittee of the Community Services Committee on the problem of the evaluation of mental health programs.

The Community Services Branch also has administered since January 1948, the Prince Georges County Mental Health Center, a mental health clinic devoted to investigating the ways in which such an organization can co-operate with and be integrated with the health services of the community and the other community agencies. Not all of the personnel time is spent in clinical work, but a significant amount of such work is done. Close working relationships have been developed with all community agencies, and one objective of the Center has been that of assisting such agencies to deal effectively with mental health problems encountered in their work. The clinical psychologist at the Center has performed both diagnostic and therapeutic functions with some emphasis upon problems growing out of the school experiences of children. He also has done work in the field of remedial reading with the schools and has helped them to develop arrangements and skills for handling these problems. His work with the schools has made it possible for him to do research with their co-operation on the problem of teacher judgments of the adjustment of children and on the relationship between these judgments and other forms of assessment, including self-report techniques upon the part of the children.

The Professional Services Branch of the Institute also utilizes a clinical psychologist. The staff of the Branch, which is interdisciplinary in nature, calls for one psychologist, one psychiatrist, one social scientist, and one psychiatric social worker. It is hardly possible to describe the function of the psychologist in this case except by indicating the major functions and role of the entire Professional Services Branch. This group has a wide variety of responsibilities, the most important of which from the present point of view is its activity in the field of program development. All members of the Institute staff, but particularly the members of the Professional Services Branch, are constantly aware of the need to define areas in which program activities of the Institute and of other mental health organizations are at the moment inadequately developed. These areas fall into two rough classes. First, there are activities which are primarily of a mental health nature but which are inadequately handled in the country at the moment. An example is the problem of the rehabilitation of the mentally ill. The second type of problem is one which lies partly outside of the mental health field but for which the mental health field has some responsibility and some possible contributions that are not yet fully recognized and utilized. The problem of aging, mental deficiency, and juvenile delinquency are examples of the latter type of area. Once a problem area has been accepted as one requiring attention, the literature is carefully surveyed, and a study is made of the actual practice and operations in this field throughout the country. Such surveys frequently result in publishable articles, monographs, and bibliographies. In most cases, the first analysis clarifies the problems to the point that a pilot study, experimental study, or a demonstration project may appear desirable and feasible in order to develop or lay the basis for developing program techniques for dealing with the area. The Institute has a small amount of research grant funds that are utilized to support such projects, the purpose of which is to supply information and knowledge of program techniques valuable in developing program operations in the area involved and for making it possible to integrate such developments into present administrative structure of the Institute and operating programs. The desire is always to develop material which can be used by the operating programs of the Institute or by public, private, or voluntary groups in the mental health field. Frequently, however, nonapplied research must be performed as a part of the process of gaining such information. Consequently, the projects developed by the Branch are not always of an applied or pragmatic nature, but the final goal is always that of being able to make reasonable suggestions about the way in which some problem area can be handled. The Branch, furthermore, works with the operating branches of the Institute and with outside groups, when feasible, in order to secure application and utilization of the results obtained in these studies. Sometimes the results become substantive material for the mental health consultants of the Institute, located in Regional Offices, and working with State mental health programs. Sometimes the results influence policy decisions with respect to some aspect of operating programs, such as, for example, training. Occasionally, they stimulate specific interests and activities in the intramural research programs.

In summary, the effort is to vitalize the Institute's program and to keep it current with respect to the demands and possible demands made upon a mental health organization. The fact that a psychologist happens to be chief of this Branch is incidental, since a member of any one of the three other disciplines represented (psychiatric social work, social science, and psychiatry) could fill this position. A psychiatrist has done so in the past. It is important, however, to note that a psychologist is a part of the table of organization of the Branch. By way of final summary, it might be said that the Branch represents a kind of operations research organization with which many psychologists are conversant.

The intramural research programs of the National Institute of Mental Health—that is, research conducted in its own facilities by its own personnel as contrasted with research supported outside the Government through the use of grants—have begun to develop in the recent past. At earlier dates there were no physical facilities, and the total of planned facilities has not yet become available. About two years ago the program of basic or laboratory research in the various scientific areas relevant to mental health was initiated, and an Associate Director for Research was established in the Institute to plan and develop this activity. About one year ago a Director of Clinical Investigations was appointed to develop a broad program of clinical research in the mental health field. As already indicated, each of these large intramural research programs is still in a developmental stage, but enough has now eventuated to indicate something about the future course of events.

Each of these programs of research, the basic and clinical, will involve psychology and psychologists. Perhaps, however, the best way to indicate what they will mean for clinical as well as other fields of psychology is to describe something about these over-all research programs at present and as envisaged for the future. It should be indicated at the outset that the administrative distinction at the National Institute of Mental Health and in other parts of the National Institutes of Health between basic and clinical research does not indicate any invidious distinction concerning either type of research or a failure to see the essential unity of both approaches. However, facilities, personnel, and the kinds of problems do differ enough that there is an administrative convenience in organizing them separately. Every possible effort is being made to assure communication, co-operation, and joint efforts between the investigators in these two programs; and psychology is actually being organized in a way which essentially eliminates the distinction.

The basic research program is charged with laboratory or field studies of any and all kinds relevant to the etiology, nature, and prevention of mental illness. The areas covered are extensive, ranging at present from a Laboratory of Socio-environmental Studies under the direction of a sociologist to laboratories in the basic medical sciences, such as neurophysiology and neuroanatomy. The research space is not yet all available, but laboratories are in operation both in some of the older buildings at the National Institutes of Health as well as in the new Clinical Center about which more will be said below. There is and will be practically no limitation placed upon any investigator with respect to the type of research project he wishes to pursue. Since it is not certain what investigations may give leads to the solution of problems in the field of mental illness, the relevance criterion involved is a very broad one. The quality, rigor, and research feasibility of proposed projects will be more important considerations than their apparent potential for immediate practical results. Senior investigators will indeed have a degree of autonomy no smaller than that enjoyed by their colleagues in universities.

It should also be noted that the basic research group may utilize field study techniques if they represent the best approach to problems. The Laboratory of Socio-environmental Studies is currently conducting two such studies, one at St. Elizabeths Hospital in the District of Columbia and one at Hagerstown, Maryland. The Addiction Research Center, mentioned above, is part of this laboratory research program but is located at the Public Health Service Hospital, Lexington, Kentucky. In other words, there is and will continue to be as much flexibility as possible in accomplishing research objectives by whatever methods of study appear to be the most desirable and effective ones.

The clinical research program will utilize primarily the National Institute of Mental Health facilities in the new Clinical Center which was opened in July 1953. The Clinical Center is a resource shared by all of the separate Institutes which comprise the National Institutes of Health. The Clinical Center has a bed capacity of 500 patients. It contains additional space for laboratories, space which is, as a matter of fact, twice as great as that devoted to patient care. The laboratories, especially those that utilize patients as the primary source of data, are arranged in close proximity to the patient care area, but the hazards and inconveniences that could develop by such arrangements have been eliminated by architectural arrangements which appear to be effective and some of which are unique. A complete description of the Clinical Center is not necessary or feasible in this discussion. What has been said should indicate that it is one of the best planned and equipped clinical research centers in the country. There are high hopes that it will contribute significantly to the study of the chronic diseases, to which it is primarily devoted.

The National Institute of Mental Health has an allocation of 98 beds and corresponding laboratory space in the structure, but it will take considerable time to arrange for full occupancy. At the moment, the Children's Service is initiating a study of highly aggressive children and an adult psychotic ward has been established. Actual programs of study are not well enough developed at the moment to describe them in detail.

The basic plan is to secure patients to meet research needs rather than to adapt research activities to the nature of the patient population. This arrangement greatly facilitates flexibility in planning research. Patients are accepted only upon referral from a physician. As much as possible they will be taken from local areas to prevent their being isolated from their families. If it is necessary to do so, patients may be accepted from distant points. Patients understand before admission that they will be co-operating in research work.

Psychology has an important role to play in the arrangements described above for research and clinical care. Of great significance are the organizational arrangements that have been developed for bringing the research and clinical competence of psychologists to bear on these programs. It was decided for a variety of reasons that the organization of psychology in the research and clinical care fields should be unitary and not segmented into basic and clinical groups. Consequently, there is one psychologist who is responsible for all three aspects of the psychology program in these areas: clinical care, clinical research, and laboratory research. There will be a laboratory of psychology with sections initially in the areas of clinical, experimental, and developmental. The clinical section will utilize Clinical Center facilities, as will the section on developmental psychology. The experimental section will have facilities in the Clinical Center, and possibly elsewhere. Clinical care responsibilities will be assumed on a part-time basis by the clinical psychologists in the section on clinical psychology. There are no plans at present to have any psychologist performing service functions only. The reason for reluctance to have nonresearch personnel in a research-oriented organization such as the Clinical Center should be clear. However, each clinical psychologist will have the great preponderance of his time available for research, although the exact ratio of research to clinical duties cannot yet be stated with accuracy.

The psychologist who will head the psychological organization described above has been recruited. A small number of clinical psychologists have been recruited or assigned to the program, but only one psychologist is active in the experimental area. Two psychologists are working in developmental. It is not feasible to attempt to describe now the actual nature of research that will be done in these facilities. The interests and competences of the psychologists involved will be highly determining. It should be clear, too, that much of the research will be interdisciplinary. Psychologists will initiate and develop research of their own, which frequently may require collaboration from workers in other fields. Similarly, psychologists will be asked to collaborate on projects developed by other investigators. Both types of co-operation have already occurred.

What has been said above should indicate that there is a widespread utilization of clinical and other kinds of psychologists at the National Institute of Mental Health. The pattern of duties will probably change continuously as time passes, but there is good reason to believe that psychology is making and will continue to make a contribution commensurate with what it has to offer.

While it is true that the National Institute of Mental Health is the chief locus of psychological work in the Public Health Service, it is by no means the only part of the Service in which they are active. In fact, each of the four bureaus of which the Service is composed has some psychological activities. At the National Institutes of Health, which is a bureau level organization devoted almost completely to research, only one other Institute along with the National Institute of Mental Health has any psychological personnel. The National Institute of Neurological Diseases and Blindness has one psychologist on duty at present. It seems likely that further expansion of psychological work in that Institute will occur.

Some of the other psychological activities were mentioned in the historical introduction to this discussion. The utilization of psychologists at the Public Health Service Hospitals for narcotic addicts was mentioned earlier. Also, the assignment by the Service of psychologists to the Federal penal institutions was mentioned before.

There is one other activity which involves another part of the Federal Government. The Public Health Service supplies medical services to the United States Coast Guard. During World War II the Service supplied psychiatrists to the Coast Guard Academy, who worked with the Coast Guard psychologists during the War on a program of officer selection and evaluation. During the wartime period rather extensive research was initiated on the personality factors associated with success as an officer candidate in the Reserve Training School and in the Academy program for cadets destined to become Regular Corps Coast Guard officers. The psychiatrists and psychologists also provided clinical services to personnel and dependents. Since the War, the Division of Hospitals of the Public Health Service has supplied a psychologist to the Coast Guard Academy. His duties involve, in part, a continuation of research upon the entrance procedures used for Cadets at the Academy. He has also addressed himself to the problem of both academic performance and personality factors of cadet success, and has continued to do, under the aegis of the Academy hospital, some clinical work. As a consequence of this entire program, the basic entrance procedures used at the U.S. Coast Guard Academy have been completely revised and are based almost entirely upon the results of research which has been done over the past ten or eleven years at the Academy by the psychiatrists and the psychologists stationed there during that period of time. Personality measures are included in the entrance assessment procedures. Intensive research is still continuing, particularly research concerning personality factors associated with success as Coast Guard cadets.

The Division of Personnel located in the Office of the Surgeon General also has a program which utilizes psychologists. The Division contains a Measurement and Evaluation Branch, the professional personnel of which is composed completely of psychologists. All Regular Corps commissioned officers at the entering grades are admitted upon the basis of competitive examinations prepared by the Measurement and Evaluation Branch. The examinations are composed of professional examinations, ability measures, measures of background, training and experience, and personal interviews. The Measurement and Evaluation Branch not only develops the actual testing instruments but also develops guides and training devices for the use of interviewing officers in connection with the personal interview. Also, techniques have been developed by this group for the evaluation of the file data composed of life history material.

In addition to the entrance examinations procedures outlined above the Research Branch has done extensive work on the evaluation of officers already in the Service, especially with respect to deriving techniques that will improve original selection procedures. The Branch has spent a considerable amount of effort in assessing personality factors which influence the success of officers in the Public Health Service. The work done by this group is not a routine group testing procedure and the chief of the Branch is a Diplomate of the American Board of Examiners in Professional Psychology in the clinical area.

Finally, the Division of Public Health Education located in the Bureau of State Services is also active in the psychological field. Most of the work of psychologists in this Division is carried on by the Experimental and Evaluation Services Branch which is composed primarily of social psychologists with special interest in problems of measurement and evaluation. The work is not, as might be assumed, confined to the evaluation of educational materials; rather, it is devoted to a determination of the reasons which people have for behaviors which are of health significance. Particular interest exists in resistance to accepting suggestions involving change of behavior with respect to one's health. Consequently, this group deals much more with dynamic aspects of behavioral problems than it does with formal educational efforts. The mode of operation involves the collaboration with an operating unit of the Service which has encountered some difficulty in securing adequate dissemination or acceptance of health materials. Necessary studies are conducted and solutions to the problem suggested. Work is conducted with the operating group until the need for consultation has been satisfied.

The material presented above indicates a widespread use of psychological personnel and techniques in the Public Health Service. Predicting what will happen in the future is always a difficult job, but some trends may be noted. First, the activities at the National Institute of Mental Health will continue along the line described, and there probably will be a significant increase in the next few years in the amount of research and clinical work in which psychologists are active. Second, it seems highly probable that other Institutes at the National Institutes of Health will find a need for psychological personnel since there is already evidence that they are encountering psychological problems in some of the research initiated at the Clinical Center. Third, the assessment and evaluation activities in the Office of the Surgeon General may well be increased in scope in the future. Regardless of what the specific future history of effort may be, the writer is convinced that the Service will continue to perceive with sophistication the personal contributions of psychologists and that the Service will continue to be an effective utilizer of this class of personnel.

Part III.

REPRESENTATIVE AGENCIES AND SETTINGS MORE RECENTLY INCLUDING CLINICAL PSYCHOLOGISTS AMONG THEIR PROFESSIONAL STAFF

The clinical practice of psychology is not confined to its operation in the various settings or agencies described in the previous two sections of this survey. Even before the tremendous postwar expansion in the use of clinical psychology, it had functioned in various other settings. As a matter of fact, although it was not in wide use or thoroughly identified as clinical psychology, clinical practice existed in some of these additional settings only a few years after Witmer's Psychological Clinic was opened in 1896. However, the most considerable expansion of clinical practice in these additional areas, as in the whole of clinical psychology, occurred within the last ten years.

The diversity and number of these other settings, and the challenge they hold for the advance of professional psychology, make it most important to this survey to offer descriptions of these areas of clinical practice.

XII.

THE CLINICAL PSYCHOLOGIST IN A MEDICAL SCHOOL PSYCHIATRIC CLINIC

CLARE W. THOMPSON

Psychologists have been employed in medical schools for only about the past quarter century, with the greatest impetus coming after World War II. In trying to summarize their work, one is impressed with the great variety of ways in which such appointments can be made to contribute. There is no general pattern to the kind of appointment (e.g., to the hospital staff or the teaching or research staff of the medical school), the source from which such appointments are financed, or the duties performed. This is understandable and appropriate for, as Jacobsen says: "There are some 70 plus four-year schools of medicine. I believe one could correctly say that there are some 70 plus distinctive, and even unique, programs of medical education" (1, p. 37).

The University of California is a happy choice to illustrate the role of the psychologist in medical education for, not only does the psychologist function in many various ways, but the structure of the clinic itself introduces a necessary element of diversity into the program. The department of psychiatry of the University of California Medical School is housed in a separate building and is called the Langley Porter Clinic. The Langley Porter Clinic, however, is also a state mental hospital under the State Department of Mental Hygiene. To illustrate, Dr. Karl M. Bowman, the director of the clinic, is professor of psychiatry at the University of California and superintendent and medical director of the clinic for the State Department of Mental Hygiene. Some psychologists at the Langley Porter Clinic are civil service employees paid by the Department of Mental Hygiene, and some have academic appointments in the Medical School and are paid from University funds. Some work only on research and are attached to research projects and paid from research funds. One directs an outpatient clinic for children in the University of California Hospital building, separate from the Langley Porter Clinic, and another is employed on a research project in this building. These are all ways in which psychologists participate in other medical schools, but it seems unlikely that very often is such diversity found in a single school.

One way in which the Langley Porter Clinic situation is atypical is in the number of psychologists involved. Mensh (2) reports that fifty-eight of the seventy-nine medical schools in the country have psychologists on their staffs, and that there are 255 psychologists so employed. Thus, there is an average of 3 psychologists per medical school, or between 4 and 5 to each school having any psychologist. At the University of California Medical School, on the other hand, there are 9 psychologists, one research statistician, and 7 psychological interns. Actually, the time of these 9 staff psychologists adds up to that of only 7 people, but again this is in line with Mensh's findings. Five of the 9 are full-time and 4 half-time, which corresponds to his finding that 56 per cent of all medical school psychologists are full-time.

Thus it appears that to examine the Langley Porter Clinic Psychology Department should be an effective way to learn about the clinical psychologist in a medical school in this country. This can best be done, however, after a more detailed description of the clinic as a whole.

THE LANGLEY PORTER CLINIC

The Langley Porter Clinic was authorized by the Statutes of 1941 "to provide opportunities for the State and the University of California to co-operate in prevention, diagnosis, treatment and promotion of research in the field of mental disorder, and in advancement of the learning and knowledge of students of the university and others" (4, *1932*, p. 5). The report for the first fiscal year the clinic was open contains a list of objectives, a surprising number of which have been achieved in this first decade. They include:

1. A training center where physicians, nurses, social workers, and others can be schooled in the most modern neuropsychiatric and psychotherapeutic techniques, equipping them for positions in the state hospital system.
2. A research center in which physicians of the state hospital system and members of the University of California faculty may perfect and improve present therapeutic procedures in the field of mental illnesses and develop treatments now unknown.
3. A center for the education of the general public where they can learn the truth about mental disorders.
4. An outpatient department which:
   a. Renders immediate service to adults and children for conditions ranging from simple maladjustments to actual psychoses.
   b. Renders aftercare to person on leave from state hospitals and
   c. Develops procedures which may eventually be applied to a state-wide system of mental hygiene clinics.

And this list omits the important fact that patients who are voluntarily admitted to the hospital as inpatients do benefit from treatment, even though they may be selected as suitable for teaching purposes, or for the specific research programs being carried on by the clinic at the time, as well as for intensive treatment.

Perhaps the picture of the present day clinic can best be conveyed by following progress in each of these areas.

TRAINING

Since its inception training has been offered to students of all branches of mental health. A residency program in psychiatry not only provides training for the sixteen (regular) and two senior Langley Porter Clinic residents, but for medical officers from the Navy and the Air Force, for physicians in the Veterans Administration residency program, for veterans in residency at the University of California Medical School, and for assistant residents in medicine and pediatrics rotating from University of California Medical School. This three-year residency program is approved by the American Board of Psychiatry and Neurology and the clinic is approved as a training center in child psychiatry under the National Mental Health Act.

The training program in clinical psychology is such an integral part of this department as to be treated more effectively in the next section, but since the opening of the clinic there have been four half-time fellowships for graduate students in clinical psychology and under the Mental Health Act, the United States Public Health Service has provided two full-time third-year fellowships.

Field-work training is offered by the social service department, and twelve or more student psychiatric social workers spend three days per week for one year in this program. All student nurses at the University of California School of Nursing are assigned to the Langley Porter Clinic for eight weeks, and in 1948 an advanced program in psychiatric nursing was instituted.

Inservice training is offered to the professional staffs of the various state hospitals. Every year since 1946 an annual twelve week refresher course in psychiatry has been held by the Langley Porter Clinic in co-operation with the University of California Extension Division. This was instituted especially for physicians in the state hospital system but has been widely attended by physicians throughout California, and indeed throughout the country. Less formally, the Langley Porter Clinic neuropathologist carries on an active autopsy service for state hospitals near San Francisco. He conducts frequent clinicopathological conferences and medical staffs at these hospitals, using case material from their own populations.

RESEARCH

Research has been characteristic of the Langley Porter Clinic since its doors were opened. Clinic psychologists have pursued their own research interests, which will be discussed later in this chapter, and have also co-operated with other disciplines in assessing the efficacy of various therapeutic measures. The treatments which were studied were electric shock, insulin shock, electronarcosis, lobotomy, conditioned reflex treatment for alcoholism, antabuse, glutamic acid, and brief psychotherapy. On the basis of findings from these studies, the state hospital system as a whole has been able intelligently to plan for the treatment of patients in all its hospitals and clinics.

PUBLIC EDUCATION

By virtue both of its location in a metropolitan center and of its inherent philosophy, the Langley Porter Clinic has been a center for the education of the general public. It is difficult and perhaps unimportant to draw a sharp dividing line between these activities and the education and training offered to professional people, for it is the more informed public who avail themselves of such opportunities. Educational events are sometimes formalized, as might be done in connection with a visit from an undergraduate class in psychology. Such classes from San Francisco State College and from the University of California have regularly visited the Langley Porter Clinic. The program on such an occasion usually consists of a tour of the clinic, a discussion by members of the various disciplines of their roles in the work of the clinic, and the presentation of a case, carefully edited to prevent identification, and with the individual himself not present. Other formal activities are those arranged in conjunction with the University of California Extension Division, such as the refresher course in psychiatry already mentioned. In 1950 the Langley Porter Clinic and the University of California Extension co-operated in organizing an institute on mental hygiene and nursing.

OUTPATIENT SERVICE

The outpatient department of the Langley Porter Clinic was included in the original planning but has been enlarged far beyond these plans. Opened during the Second World War, the clinic was unable to find sufficient staff, especially psychiatric nurses, to permit the opening of all wards. The space which could not be utilized according to plan, was converted into interviewing rooms in which outpatients were treated. When it was eventually possible to open all wards, temporary buildings had to be erected to insure the continuation of this program. Applications have always far exceeded the staff to treat them, and group psychotherapy has proved one effective means of offering help to as many as possible of the people needing it. This program was started early in 1947 and has continued since then. Also since 1947 Langley Porter Clinic staff members have been detailed to the University of California Hospital, to consult with specialists in other medical specialties about patients and to offer outpatient treatment to patients who most appropriately remain on the University of California Hospital rolls instead of being transferred to the Langley Porter Clinic. The outpatient department of the Langley Porter Clinic has furnished a model for a statewide system of mental hygiene clinics. At present seven other clinics are in operation throughout California.

The inpatient service at present consists of a 100-bed neuropsychiatric unit. Six wards with from 16 to 18 beds make up this complement, and there is an additional 20-bed treatment unit for shock treatment, fever therapy, or other special methods. There are four adult wards, one children's ward, and one ward for neurosurgical patients. The inpatient service is approved as a psychiatric hospital by the American Medical Association and by the American College of Surgeons. It will have been anticipated by the reader that anything which fulfills its purposes as well as this account would indicate cannot stand still, and plans have been drawn for a 140-bed addition to the clinic.

THE ROLE OF THE CLINICAL PSYCHOLOGIST

The emphasis on teaching and research is especially apparent in the history of the psychology department. The original psychology staff consisted of a full-time Lecturer in Medical Psychology and four half-time fellows in medical psychology, all on the Medical School budget, and one full-time research psychologist, on a project sponsored by the Federal Government's Office of Scientific Research and Development. This does not, of course, mean that these people performed no service functions. A large percentage of the teaching and learning in clinical psychology is simply the supervised performance of clinical work. Moreover, the research project in question was an evaluation of the attitudes of psychiatric patients toward medicine and doctors, the carrying out of which involved a good deal of service work with psychiatric patients. Actually, psychologists saw 1230 patients in the first full year of operation of the clinic. Service was formally recognized in 1945 by the setting up of two positions as senior clinical psychologist on the pay rolls of the State Department of Mental Hygiene, but training also received further impetus in 1947 with the allocation of United States Public Health Service funds for a lecturer and two third-year fellowships. In 1952 a research technician was added to the staff. Actually, seeing the staff of the department in operation, one would have difficulty deciding not only who is in a "teaching" and who is in a "service" position, but even who is a staff member and who a student. The opportunity for each individual to do that which his interests and skills fit him for is in line with the general eclectic philosophy of the clinic.

SERVICE FUNCTIONS

Both Jacobsen and Mensh report that psychologists in medical schools perform service functions such as diagnosis and therapy. According to Mensh, psychologists, in about three fourths of the schools which have psychologists, participate in diagnosis and in one third of these schools they participate in psychotherapy. The Langley Porter Clinic psychology department performs service functions in each of the divisions of the clinic: inpatient, outpatient including the outpatient work at the University of California Hospital, and children's division. A staff member is assigned to each division, and students rotate through all of them. The emphasis varies with each division, but in general service functions consist of psychodiagnostic testing around a particular question and of psychotherapy. In performing his diagnostic work, the psychologist discusses the case with the referring person before seeing the patient, talks over his results with the referrant before writing the report, and participates in any staff discussions of the patient, as do members of all disciplines who have worked on the case.

Much of the most effective teaching about the subject matter of clinical psychology, as well as about the functions of the clinical psychologist, goes on within the framework of the referral system. A psychiatric resident who has a problem about a case, with which he thinks the psychologist might be able to help, discusses the case with the psychologist. This interaction in itself is almost invariably helpful to both discussants, sometimes to the point where no further participation by the psychologist is required. More often, of course, arrangements are made for psychological study, but the discussion has made clear to both the psychologist and the resident exactly what the psychologist can offer and why. Sometimes a decision is reached that this is not a question which the psychologist has tools or techniques to help solve. This was stated very nicely by the assistant superintendent who once said: "I try to have one of my residents not refer a case to the psychologist when the problem is something that is going on between the resident and the patient, because the psychologist can't help him. Or rather, the psychologist may be able to help him, but the Rorschach can't."

It is not uncommon for teaching and diagnosis both to be served by essentially the same activities, but at Langley Porter Clinic developments have recently been made which contribute simultaneously to teaching, diagnosis, and research. This is an innovation in report writing which serves not only to make it a much less harrowing experience for the student, but to make the data from psychological summaries as available to research methods as are the raw scores of test protocols. Twenty psychologists participated in amassing a pool of 100 meaningful items, phrased in the language of clinical description, and embracing all areas covered in psychological reports. When a diagnostic case has been seen by a student, the student and his supervisor examine the test battery together and discuss its implications. Each then independently does a Q-sort of these items, accordingly to how accurately each item describes the patient. They next compare these independent sorts and reconcile any gross discrepancies. The student then writes a report consisting of the fifteen most characteristic items for the patient in question, put together in grammatical form. The research possibilities of this method are almost limitless. Not only can simple correlational studies be done by having the patient's therapist sort the same items on the basis of his independent observations, but over a ten-year period there will be several thousand such reports. It will then be possible to select those reports written about patients with some common characteristic, such as a symptom (ulcers, paranoid ideation, epilepsy, etc.) or a kind of behavior (suicide, alcoholism, illegitimate pregnancy, etc.) and determine what items are common to most people with this characteristic. Such information should enhance our understanding of the characteristic in question and our ability to diagnose it in future patients. It should be added, however, that the more traditional report is still being written and used.

The psychotherapeutic work done by psychologists is likely to be collaborative. On children's service, a parent is seen in therapy in every case carried. With inpatient cases a social worker frequently sees members of the family on a continuing basis. And more than one family member is often seen in the outpatient department. Thus, the psychologist is likely to share a case with a worker from some other discipline. A student is supervised by a staff member as well. It is through these interactions over diagnostic and therapeutic cases that much of the educative process occurs, with the psychologist both learner and teacher. Psychologists have also participated in group psychotherapy, with the groups usually organized in such a way that the group members have common problems. Examples are a group of husbands of hospitalized women, and a group of adolescent inpatient boys.

TEACHING

Formal teaching activities are also scheduled. The psychology department has always held a weekly seminar, the content of which has shifted with the changing interests of those participating. Members of other disciplines have been welcome to attend, and have done so to varying extents. Similarly, student psychologists attend seminars arranged primarily for residents in psychiatry and conducted by psychiatrists. Most popular among these have been continuing case presentations, one led by a senior Freudian analyst, the other by a senior Jungian analyst.

Mensh (2) reports that psychologists offer courses to medical students in 86 per cent of those medical schools having psychologists, to psychiatric residents in 44 per cent, to nurses in 33 per cent, to graduate students of psychology in 25 per cent, and to medical interns and other professional students in 14 per cent. Psychologists at the Langley Porter Clinic lecture to all of these with student psychiatric social workers as the "other professional students." About twenty or twenty-five hours of the refresher course in psychiatry are devoted to material presented by psychologists. Moreover, on request, residents in psychiatry and student nurses themselves take psychological tests and discuss the results with psychologists, learning about them in this way also. Dr. Robert E. Harris, the chief psychologist, has also taught seminars in the Department of Psychology of the University of California Berkeley campus.

The greatest difference between the Langley Porter Clinic program and the general picture as reported by Mensh is in the relative emphasis on training residents in psychiatry rather than medical students. The Langley Porter Clinic was dedicated and admitted its first patient just ten years ago. It was, in a sense, added on to a medical school with a well-established curriculum, where the number of hours allotted to the various specialties has remained the same for a period of years. The actual teaching of medical students consists in fourth-year medical school students spending half time for only four weeks at the Langley Porter Clinic, working up cases. In some instances, the student continues to carry a case after this four-week period is past. During this time, three hours of lectures on clinical psychology are presented to the senior student. At present the whole medical school curriculum is being reviewed, so that this picture may soon be quite different.

The primary participation of the psychologist in the training of medical students has been in what Jacobsen (1) calls administration rather than teaching. Thus a psychologist participates in the interviewing of medical school applicants, helps to interpret the results of the Educational Testing Service's Medical Aptitude Test, is a member of the board which makes the final selection of students, and has directed a research study of the effectiveness of this selection procedure.

Consultation service in psychology is offered by the Langley Porter Clinic to other hospitals in the State Department of Mental Hygiene. Also, in line with the general policy of the clinic, psychologists have spoken before groups ranging from prisoners in a state penitentiary to members of scientific organizations, and have performed such community service as membership on San Francisco Community Chest committees.

In line with their training, psychologists are characteristically active in research. Langley Porter Clinic psychologists are no exception. Although they make up but a small proportion of the clinic staff, psychologists appear as authors or co-authors of about one fourth of the publications coming out of the clinic. In about one fourth of these, the authorship is interdisciplinary, in the other three fourths the research is by psychologists alone. Psychologists consult or co-operate in various other ways, however, on many more projects than this would indicate. Similarly, the psychologist may consult with members of other disciplines about his research.

Research at the Langley Porter Clinic, including research done by psychologists, is oriented directly toward clinical problems. It grows out of day-to-day contact with patients, and its findings contribute to their day-to-day care. As will be apparent from a review of the topics studied, this relationship is sometimes a very direct one and sometimes less so. Problems which have been studied by psychologists by research methods at this clinic group themselves into five general subheadings: the evaluation of psychodiagnostic instruments, the personality characteristics of members of various disease and behavior groups, the effects of various therapies, studies of students and of teaching methods, and the exploration of more theoretical questions which have to do with personality and its correlates.

Studies of diagnostic instruments have sometimes been simple validation studies, as for example the agreement of diagnosis by the MMPI and by psychiatric evaluation. Sometimes they have determined the effect of varying the usual method of administration, as by giving various combinations of subtests of the Wechsler-Bellevue. Other times new measures are derived from existing instruments, as in the development of a scale for the prediction of response to shock treatment on the MMPI. And occasionally entirely new instruments are devised, as in a projective test of simple drawings currently being explored.

Studies of responses to treatment methods have already been mentioned in the first part of this chapter. Attempts have been made to isolate personality factors characteristic of patients with symptoms ranging from head injury to ulcers and hypertension. Other groups have been studied on the basis of their behavior, such as alcoholics and unmarried mothers. Personality characteristics of women with postpartum psychoses have been another area of investigation, as have the parents of schizophrenic children.

A method for teaching psychotherapy through content-free interviewing was developed and was found, by research methods, to be valid. "Buddy ratings," similar to those developed during the Second World War, have been used in the assessment of residents in psychiatry, and the evaluation of the selection program for medical students has already been mentioned. Broader, more theoretical, questions which have been studied include level of aspiration and adjustment to failure, physiological correlates of fear, and personality determinants of perceptual processes.

Jacobsen gives as a prevalent problem of psychologists in medical school education "that we wish we had more time for research, but the pressure for patient service is too great" (1, p. 51). He says more fully, "During the postwar years, the number of people trained to render psychological services to patients has greatly increased, and the participation by psychologists in the teaching of medical students has similarly expanded. I fear that these developments may have taken place at the expense of *basic research*, which a review of the earlier appointments to medical staffs will show was the *raison d'être* for such appointments" (1, p. 49). Happily, it is apparent that research continues to thrive at the Langley Porter Clinic.

Mensh gives three problems mentioned by respondents to his questionnaire. "Five respondents saw a need to better integrate their programs into the medical school curricula; 8 urged the necessity of understanding the importance of 'selling' psychology by quality of its services and by increased attention to public relations between psychology and medicine in all branches; and 11 colleagues wrote that more, and better-trained, psychologists would do much to satisfy the demands of medicine as well as to improve relations with psychiatry and other branches of medicine" (2, p. 85). These are problems at the Langley Porter Clinic in inverse proportion to their prevalence nationally. The problem, given by only five respondents, of better integrating the program of the psychology department, and of psychiatry as a whole, into the medical school curriculum is a very real one which, hopefully, will be ameliorated by the current review of the total medical school curriculum.

REFERENCES

1. Jacobsen, C. Psychology in medical education. In Dennis, Wayne et al. *Current trends in the relation of psychology to medicine*. Pittsburgh: Univer. of Pittsburgh Press, 1950.
2. Mensh, I. N. Psychology in medical education. *Amer. Psychologist*, 1953, 8, 83-85.
3. *Biennial Report for 1950-1952. State of California Department of Mental Hygiene*. Sacramento, Calif.: California State Printing Office, 1953.
4. *Statistical report of the Department of Institutions of the State of California*. Sacramento, Calif.: California State Printing Office, from 1942 to 1946.
5. *Statistical report of the Department of Mental Hygiene of the State of California*. Sacramento, Calif.: California State Printing Office, from 1947 to 1951.

XIII.

PSYCHOLOGICAL SERVICE CENTER

DAVID GROSSMAN, MAURICE RAPKIN and
STEWART B. SHAPIRO

The private psychological service center represents a comparatively recent development in the practice of clinical psychology. While psychological clinics, under the directorship and administration of psychologists, have been in existence since the establishment of Witmer's Psychological Clinic in 1896, the private psychological service center is essentially a post-World War II development. According to Louttit's (1) analysis of a 1935 directory of psychological clinics in the United States, only two out of eighty-seven such clinics were "self-supported." In contrast to this, the 1951 American Psychological Association Directory lists psychologists working in at least twelve different private psychological service centers, under variations of this name, in such cities as Los Angeles, San Francisco, Washington, D.C., Chicago, and New York. These centers offer psychological services in such areas as intelligence and achievement testing, psychodiagnostic testing, vocational and personal counseling, and psychotherapy. There are probably, in addition, an equal number of private psychological service centers operating under less generic names but offering these same professional services. In the absence of a recent directory specifically of psychological clinics this is not a completely accurate figure, but it does seem a conservative estimate that the two "self-supporting" clinics of 1935 have, as of 1953, increased to at least twenty such clinics or centers. Most of these centers came into existence since 1944 and trends are for a continued increase in number.

This growth was influenced by two related but independent factors; first, the internal changes within the science of psychology, and second, the changes in the social milieu in the United States during and following World War II. Within the science itself, there was an increased professional interest in the application of clinical psychology, greatly expanded training facilities, the extension of well-established tools, and the development of new techniques. The determining forces in the social milieu during the same period were an increased awareness of psychological needs of the individual and the services which psychology had to offer to meet these needs. This awareness drew especially although not exclusively, from the applied fields of psychology.

THE LOS ANGELES PSYCHOLOGICAL SERVICE CENTER

In 1948, several clinical psychologists met to explore the advantages of a group private practice and succeeded in establishing a plan to organize a psychological service center. The over-all goal was to incorporate the advantages of individual private practice without sacrificing the real advantages of clinics supported by public funds. Two interrelated kinds of goals were formulated: those relating to services to the public and those concerning benefits to the staff itself.

The following service goals were formulated:

(1) To make psychological services available to those people who could not afford the usual private practice fee, but whose income was greater than that of the usual applicant at public clinics.

(2) To provide a wide range of co-ordinated psychological services. Both the scope and integration of the services were intended to cover areas not ordinarily available from the usual private practice or public agency. The Center was designed to be a flexible unit which would develop services according to the needs of a variety of situations.

(3) To encourage "gate keepers," people who crucially influence others in human relations, such as teachers, probation officers, nurses, and community and business leaders, to make personal use of psychological services.

(4) To provide the public with the advantages inherent in the clinical team; that is, making available the specialized skills and points of view of each discipline.

(5) To establish a facility that would minimize organizational hierarchical control and promote individual freedom and responsibility.

Goals primarily to fulfill staff needs were:

(1) To provide a setting and atmosphere in which each staff member could be personally, professionally and financially secure. Personal security was interpreted to mean individual freedom and responsibility, job stability and mutual respect for each other's personality differences. Professional security was construed to mean professional status; that is, the establishment of a center in which the clinical psychologist would be on a par with other related professions. These security factors were felt to be especially important in this field where the personality of the clinical psychologist is crucial to his effective professional functioning.

(2) To provide the opportunity, so often unavailable to the individual practitioner, for continued professional growth through staff interaction and in-service training.

(3) To offer a setting within which the staff members could carry out teaching, supervisory and research functions.

The Los Angeles Psychological Service Center opened its doors formally in January of 1950. Initially, the staff consisted of one full-time and two-part time Ph.D. clinical psychologists. Following two years of growth, an additional office was opened in the San Fernando Valley (May, 1952), to provide services to an area with a large and growing population in which there were practically no psychological services. At the present time, the Los Angeles staff organization calls for four full-time Ph.D. clinical psychologists, two full-time M.S.W. psychiatric social workers, and one part-time M.A. psychometrist. The Valley staff at present consists of two part-time Ph.D. clinical psychologists and two M.S.W. psychiatric social workers, one full-time and one part-time. Future plans for the Valley division call for a staff organization similar to the Los Angeles division. The Center also obtains the services of four psychiatrists as consultants. Two of these psychiatrists consult on diagnostic problems. The other two psychiatrists, one of whom is a psychoanalyst, provide a regular weekly consultation service.

PRESENT STATUS

Physical plant. The office facilities of the two Divisions are essentially the same, although there are differences in detail. The Los Angeles Division consists of a suite of five offices in a medical professional building. Three of these are large enough for either group therapy or staff meetings. In addition to these five offices, there is a waiting room, without a receptionist, a play-therapy room, and a large meeting room which can seat fifty or more people.

Administrative organization. The Center is headed by three Ph.D. clinical psychologists who serve as co-directors, and also function as full-time staff members. The co-directors are responsible for the total management of the Center. The remainder of the staff consists of associates: clinical psychologists, child psychologists, psychiatric social workers, and a psychometrist. As mentioned above, the Center also utilizes four psychiatrists as consultants. Central to the organization of the Center are the staff meetings. These include administrative staffs, intake staffs, academic staffs, and continuous case conferences. In addition, each staff associate maintains a direct channel of communication with one of the co-directors.

Policies. In general, the primary *raison d'etre* for the Center is to provide the opportunity for personal growth to the public and for professional growth to the staff. Therefore, all of the policies of the Center stem directly or indirectly from this fundamentally therapeutic orientation. This applies to staff interaction and personal and professional growth of the staff members, as well as services to patients. To implement this general orientation, specific staff policies and service policies were developed.

Staff policies. One of the most important staff policies is that each staff member shall obtain intensive personal psychotherapy. Experience has shown the importance of this policy from the standpoint of optimal intrastaff and service functioning of the Center.

A second major policy calls for each staff member to assume full professional responsibility for his patients. That is to say, while supervision is provided and consultation is encouraged, each staff member carries out his professional functions according to his own best judgment.

Another policy is that routine procedures are left also to the individual staff member's own discretion. For example, although there is an overall schedule for setting fees, variation in this schedule remains an exercisable prerogative of the staff member. In this way, subtler aspects of the total relationship between patient and therapist can be accorded importance and may result in a different fee. Also, each staff member sets his own work schedule within the broad framework of the Center's policy of making evening and Saturday hours available to the public.

It is a policy of the Center to arrange for remuneration of each staff member on an individual basis, taking into consideration, as far as possible, his personal needs. To those individuals who prefer a fixed monthly income, a straight salary plan is offered. For those people who work best under incentive conditions, a profit-sharing plan is provided. Others may prefer a combination of these two plans.

Service policies. One of the more important policies affecting patients is the manner in which fees are set. In accordance with the goal of making services available to moderate income groups, an appropriate minimum fee was set. With this as a base, a sliding scale was empirically derived, taking into consideration the income of the average family in this area, and basic living costs. Variations due to number of dependents, frequency of sessions per week and gross family income were reflected in the scale.

Another important service policy follows from the general theoretical orientation of the Center, which is psychodynamic. As a result of this orientation, the Center offers intensive long-term psychotherapy, when indicated. This orientation also influenced other policies, such as therapy for the therapist and consultation with a psychoanalyst.

The Center also has a policy of obtaining a medical clearance for all patients at the beginning of therapy. This consists of a medical examination to determine the general health of the patient and to determine the indication or contraindication for psychotherapy in relation to the patient's health. This examination is usually conducted by the patient's own physician. If the patient requests it, he is given the name of a physician on the Center's panel. This panel includes various medical specialists who are psychologically oriented and with whom the Center has established a working relationship. It is the responsibility of the therapist to obtain a written report from the physician, and to maintain continued contact and professional exchange with him.

Another policy of the Center has been a strong interest in providing group psychotherapy. Specialized groups are formed around core problems of patients or their common characteristics. Examples of such groups would be a marital-problem group, young-adult group, and a group with obsessive-compulsive character problems. The Center stipulates that each group patient also undergo concomitant individual treatment.

Policies regarding the treatment of children include the strong encouragement of treatment for the parents, but allow for the acceptance of a child for play therapy if at least one parent will avail himself of consultation at a minimum of once a month. Another policy regarding children is that a child psychologist is better equipped to handle the majority of parent-child cases which come to the Center. While most of the other staff members carry a few child cases, a child specialist is included in the optimal personnel team to contribute specialized knowledge in this area.

A further service policy is the participation of the staff in mental health activities in the community. For example, staff members teach courses in mental health in universities and adult education programs. Staff members are encouraged to participate in professional organizations and other community groups such as religious and fraternal organizations, co-ordinating councils and mental health associations. In these activities the clinical psychologist functions in two ways: as a member participant in lay groups interested in mental health, and as a professional consultant and lecturer to other community organizations.

Functions of the staff. The over-all function of each discipline at the Center can be stated as follows: Three of the staff psychologists serve as co-directors. All staff psychologists function primarily as psychotherapists, but, in addition, do intake interviewing, psychodiagnostic testing, public relations work, and may do some teaching, some supervising, and some research. Psychiatric social workers function mainly as psychotherapists and, secondarily, do intake interviewing. In addition, they may be responsible for some supervisory and some public relations duties. Psychiatrists act as consultants, supervisors, and occasionally do diagnostic interviewing. But perhaps the clinical psychologist's role in this setting can best be understood by a survey of his actual functions in the staff meetings, in activities involving the Center as a whole, and in public relations.

The *administrative* staff meeting is held for two hours and is attended only by the co-directors. At these meetings every aspect of the Center's function is discussed, and policies are established. These discussions cover a wide range of activities—professional, business and legal, intracenter personnel relations and community relations.

Operating an organization of this nature entails a considerable amount of administrative effort—both on the levels of broad policy and the execution of the many administrative details. A division of labor among the co-directors was arranged to carry out these duties. One co-director is primarily responsible for personnel procurement and evaluation. Another is responsible for most of the building, and business and legal arrangements, such as leases, personnel contracts, and office furniture. Still a third takes the responsibility for the financial aspects—general accounting, payroll, banking, and office supplies, etc. One of the co-directors also acts as administrative liaison to the Valley Division and attends its staff meetings. Responsibility is also delegated for items of lesser magnitude, such as play-room equipment, test equipment, malpractice insurance, and liaison with consultants. All of the co-directors may be asked to share any of these duties when they become excessive. Also, the co-directors share such responsibilities as public and community relations, arranging staff meetings, and liaison with individual staff members.

The *intake* staff meeting is attended by the entire staff and is conducted for an hour and a half weekly. As will be remembered, every staff member functions as an intake worker. Each staff member who is to present a new case to the staff prepares the material according to the following general outline: the presenting problem, major psychological and physiological symptoms, the development and family background, a formulation of the patient's psychodynamics, his probable diagnosis, his prognosis, and the proposed therapeutic plan. Following this, the staff discusses the choice of therapist. Factors considered in this choice include the prospective therapist's psychodynamics, his special interest or experience with a particular kind of problem and his availability. The final choice is made with the concurrence of the therapist and the staff. In certain cases, the staff may decide to refer the case to an outside facility. The reasons for such action might be that the patient was thought to be psychotic, suicidal or homicidal. In this event, the patient would be referred to a psychiatrist either for therapy, shock treatment, or institutionalization. Patients also might be referred for treatment requiring specialized skills such as medical services, speech therapy, family casework, psychoanalysis, and therapy with the brain damaged. It becomes the responsibility of the intake worker to arrange for the referral.

The hour-long *academic* staff meeting is designed to further the education of the staff members. Activities may include the intensive and prolonged study of a pertinent book, the presentation of a certain case to provide a point of departure for the theoretical discussion of a particular therapeutic or psychodynamic problem, a discussion of a particular psychotherapeutic technique, the study of recent advances in the field, and an intensive study of the proposed American Psychological Association code of ethics.

The *continuous case* conference which meets weekly, also lasts an hour, and includes a psychiatric consultant. This conference has three main purposes—to broaden the staff's knowledge of psychotherapy and psychodynamics, to acquaint them with procedures used by the other therapists at the Center, and to serve as a type of control or supervision of the member who presents the case. In general, two approaches have been used during the staff. A therapist may take detailed notes and present to the staff as fully as possible an account of what occurred during the preceding week's therapeutic session(s) with the patient. Staff members and consultant give their ideas and suggest alternate avenues of proceeding with the therapy. This case may be presented continuously for many months. Another approach is for a therapist to discuss a case with which he is currently having a particular problem. A resume is presented covering the entire course of therapy up to the present. The group then discusses various aspects of the problem over a period of several weeks.

Over-all Center function. The Center is called upon to perform such typical services as individual and group psychotherapy, child therapy, marital counseling, parent-child counseling, vocational guidance, psychodiagnostic testing, and over-all personality evaluations. One specific way in which the Center functions as a whole is the sponsoring of workshops for various groups, such as parents. The proposed workshop on parent-child relationships will be the result of the combined efforts of almost everyone at the Center. However, it will be conducted by one or two of the staff members. Other workshops may be conducted for probation department officers, nurses, and nursery school teachers. The Center also organizes psychological film series and conducts research. Problems connected with research in a private setting will be discussed elsewhere.

Public relations functions. The Center operates without the benefit of public funds, and therefore is financially dependent on the services which it provides. The securing of referrals becomes a major responsibility of the co-directors, and a minor one for the remainder of the staff. More specifically, this means that the clinical psychologist in this setting must devote time and energy to enlarging and maintaining referral sources. He must undertake many kinds of public and community relations activities. Some work of this nature can be done indirectly through participation in lay and professional groups, teaching, consultation, etc., as already mentioned under service policies. But there are many direct methods which a clinical psychologist can use to make the services of his organization known to the public. One avenue of contact is the distribution of printed announcements to appropriate selected segments of the population. Another method is to volunteer services as a lecturer or discussion leader to various groups. A more difficult but perhaps more rewarding method seems to be through personal contact with interested people. During these meetings the clinical psychologist has the opportunity to explain the goals and functions of the Center. This type of relationship may be mutually advantageous. Psychological referral sources for people with moderate incomes are not plentiful, and waiting lists are not uncommon. Many professional people when confronted with individuals needing help, have difficulty in making appropriate referrals. This is especially true for patients needing intensive treatment. As part of his public relations function, the clinical psychologist at the Center devotes time and effort in educating referral sources in the techniques of making referrals. This is necessary because enabling people to seek and accept psychological help takes considerable skill and information. For example, it is helpful for the referrer to know the importance of mobilizing the patient's internal motivation, the dangers of imparting unrealistic expectations from therapy, etc.

PATIENTS

Patients are referred to the Center from a wide variety of sources. The leading sources in the first two years of operation were social agencies, personal friends of staff members, university psychology departments, current and former patients, and nonpsychiatric M.D.s, in that order of frequency. Beginning with the third year, the leading source of referral was "current and former patients."

A perusal of the patient population indicates that somewhat more men than women come to the Los Angeles Division and that 85 per cent of the population has an age range of nineteen to forty-five. (In the Valley Division there is a greater proportion of people under the age of sixteen.) In a sample of 326 cases, slightly more than one third were found either not suitable or declined therapy. Of those who entered therapy, approximately 37 per cent remained from one to nine sessions, approximately 30 per cent remained from ten to forty-nine sessions, 10 per cent remained from fifty to ninety-nine sessions, and 20 per cent continued for over one hundred sessions. Diagnostically, the patient population has consisted mainly of moderate to severe symptom neurotics and character disorders. As a rule, the Center does not accept for treatment psychotic patients, even though they may be ambulatory. Financially, the majority of the patients fall in the lower middle economic stratum.

A typical (hypothetical) case. Another way to illustrate the role of the clinical psychologist and other staff members in this setting might be to follow the course of a typical (hypothetical) case.

A staff member answers the phone call of a man who had been referred by a friend whose wife had received treatment at the Center. The staff member arranges an intake appointment and the prospective patient presents the following problem:

For the last five years, tension between him and his wife has been mounting, which he felt resulted in a poor sexual relationship and considerable quarreling. Being psychologically aware, both marriage partners realize that a psychologist might be of assistance to their situation.

The husband is a thirty-four-year-old musician who has been married for ten years. A few years ago he suffered a "nervous breakdown." At the end of the first hour, the staff member feels that no psychodiagnostic testing is needed. Because this first hour is spent on the marital relationship, it is felt that he should return to give further background material. It is also suggested that his wife call another staff member for an intake appointment. At the end of the second hour, the patient's financial circumstances are discussed, and the fee set according to the sliding scale. It is explained to him that his problem will be presented to the staff and he will be contacted by the therapist whom the staff thinks will be most effective in working with him.

At the intake staff meeting the two staff members who interviewed the husband and wife present their respective findings. The case is discussed from the standpoint of the individual personality problems as well as the marital relationship. For example, what are their core problems, character traits, and major defense mechanisms? How do these factors in each partner affect the other? Should they get a supportive or an uncovering type of therapy? Should they come once a week or oftener? What kinds of problems can be expected to arise during the course of treatment? Would psychodiagnostic testing be helpful to the therapists? Might the patients work best with a male or female therapist? Or a younger or older therapist? What therapeutic goals can be set for each? The staff consensus is that the husband, because of the nature and depth of his problem, plus his strong motivation, should undergo long-term psychoanalytically oriented therapy, three times a week. Dr. X expresses an interest in treating this patient, and also has the time available. He makes some additional suggestions about his proposed plan of treatment. The staff discusses this and mentions the possibility of the patient joining a marriage-problem group at a later phase in therapy. It is also decided that the wife, considering the nature of her defenses, and her lack of motivation, should undertake once-a-week, limited-goal therapy. Dr. Y accepts the responsibility for her treatment.

Each therapist arranges with his patient to obtain medical clearance, affording the therapist a clearer picture of the etiology of the patient's somatic complaints.

From this point on, full professional responsibility for the psychological treatment of each of these patients rests with the therapist. However, he can call on the staff for assistance whenever he wishes. For example, he can discuss his case informally with other staff members, particularly the therapist of the spouse, bring up the case for formal discussion at a case conference staff meeting, request another staff member to do psychodiagnostic testing, or request a consultation with one of the regularly visiting psychiatrists.

SPECIAL PROBLEMS

In the functioning of a private psychological service center, many special problems arise. Several of these have already been mentioned in other sections of this chapter. These problems point up the role of the clinical psychologist in this setting.

One of the most difficult problems derives from the conflict between the moderate income fee policy and the basic requirement of the Center for highly trained clinical psychologists. Furthermore, the problem of personnel selection and relationships is complicated by the combination of personality characteristics required of the clinical psychologist in this setting. It is difficult to find experienced, highly trained, Ph.D. clinical psychologists who are interested in private practice, prefer an organized group setting, and at the same time, are willing to work for a moderate salary. In other words, what seems to be needed are individuals with the kind of independency strivings which enable them to pioneer and take risks along with strong enough dependency needs to desire group belongingness and some authority control. The difference in pay plans for each staff member is a testimonial to the fact that even those few who do fit the combination of characteristics vary considerably among themselves.

Another personnel problem concerns the evaluation of staff members. It has been difficult to define criteria for the selection of psychologists who are best suited in terms of personality and training to become staff members at the Center. Assessment of personnel has had to proceed mainly on an experimental basis. It has also been difficult to set for a potential staff member an evaluative probationary period when private patients are involved. This is so because the probationary period may not at all correspond with the needs of patients regarding the duration of treatment. A transfer from one therapist to another at a given time may jeopardize the progress of a patient who is in a rather delicate or deep state of transference with the original therapist.

Business and professional problems which have caused concern include such matters as partnership agreements, contracts with staff members, negotiations with insurance experts, with lawyers and accountants on tax matters, social security, and malpractice insurance. Of this group of problems, the question of malpractice insurance for clinical psychologists may be of the most general interest. As is the case with many new professions, the development of suitable malpractice policies had to proceed tentatively and experimentally. Following initial exploration, the Center arranged for individual malpractice insurance through a local agency, and underwritten by Lloyds of London. Cost of this insurance was based on preliminary information about the risks involved. However, the Center has finally been able to obtain a group malpractice plan which is considerably less expensive for the staff member.

Another problem common to clinical psychologists in private practice concerns formal and informal relations with, and recognition by, the medical profession. There was a gradual development of confidence through personal contact with individual members of the medical and psychiatric profession. But, from the very outset, obtaining formal medical and psychiatric recognition was difficult. After many contacts, it was possible to arrange for the services of two psychiatrists, primarily on diagnostic matters. Somewhat later, formal relationships were developed with two other psychiatrists for consultation on therapy cases. Part of the difficulty here lay in the lack of information which many psychiatrists have about the training of the qualified clinical psychologist. Another aspect of this problem was the implicit responsibility which a psychiatrist assumed when undertaking a consultantship with a private organization staffed by nonmedical personnel. The responsibility might involve ethical as well as legal and medical aspects, and therefore most qualified psychiatrists had to be assured of the training and stability of the organization and its staff. The development of this assurance took time and effort. Increased general recognition and acceptance of clinical psychologists by the medical profession is a problem that is far from a complete solution. Perhaps the Center policies of close medical communication, medical clearance for each patient, and the establishment of a panel of physicians for referral may aid in this process of education and acceptance.

The acceptance of a private psychological service center by members of its own profession has also constituted a problem. Not only were there doubts by influential people in the academic and nonacademic fields, but a considerable number of peers for various reasons were not especially enthusiastic about this form of professional practice. Judging from informal reports, and referrals by other psychologists, psychiatrists and social workers, it would seem that the acceptance of the Center has steadily increased.

Another professional problem of considerable concern has been the difficulty of conducting psychological research in the Center. The main problems here concern the cost involved, the time required, and the fact that some patients are reluctant to allow themselves to be treated as "subjects." Although there have been some joint research projects, most of the research has been on an individual basis. A possible solution to the financial problem may lie in research grants or community funds, but these are difficult to obtain for a relatively new private service organization. Other suggestions for coping with these problems include the employment of a research director and perhaps the establishment of a Center foundation whose purpose it would be to support and conduct research.

FUTURE OUTLOOK

In the three and a half years of its existence, the Center has undergone a number of changes. The Center is geared to encourage service requests from the community; therefore, in the future it will continue to adapt itself in such a way as to fulfill these requests. This places the Center in a potentially pioneering position in the development of the clinical practice of psychology.

One approach to speculating about future changes is to explore the ways in which the Center operations could be improved. For convenience, these might be placed into three categories: enlarging services, improving staff skills, and enhancing staff rewards.

Enlarging services. One of the most important tasks ahead is that of educating the public in mental health and the services that clinical psychologists have to offer in this area. In the next few years, the fact that mental illness is the nation's number one health problem must be brought to the attention of the public. The Center plans to contribute to this educational campaign by offering classes that are not available elsewhere to young adults and to parents. These classes might combine some of the features of the university extension course, the adult education class, and group psychotherapy. Also, the Center is considering the possibility of issuing a mental health news-letter for distribution to the community. Classes or workshops are being planned for other professional groups like physicians, lawyers, probation officers, community leaders, and religious workers.

Other areas in which services could be offered are in fields involving social group tensions and interpersonal relations. For example, the Center has been interested in problems involving minority prejudices, adult and juvenile delinquency control, and civic and community problems. Services might be applied to areas such as human relations, group development, and job satisfaction in industry and local government agencies.

Another way of providing additional services to the community is to set up centers comparable to the Los Angeles and Valley Divisions.

The Center has also thought about developing specialized service divisions in order to meet specific community needs. An example of this is a day or resident school for emotionally disturbed children.

In order to help meet the increasing demand for psychological services, the Center has been exploring the possibility of providing internships and postdoctoral training facilities for clinical psychologists and field placement for psychiatric social workers. Such a plan would call for the clinical psychologist undergoing intensive psychotherapy as well as obtaining supervision in working with patients that ordinarily are not seen in either university or public facilities.

Improving staff skills. As time and funds for research become available, it will be possible to investigate many questions pertaining to the rendering of services. Among these are the improvement of individual and group therapeutic techniques, screening of patients, problems associated with matching of patient to therapist, and the most effective methods of training therapists.

Enhancing staff rewards. As mentioned in the discussion of goals, the Center is sensitive to the personal needs of staff members. In the interest of enhancing staff rewards and security, the Center plans to provide opportunities for each member to increase his income and professional status. This might be done by enlarging his administrative responsibilities or the development of special projects. Another alternative is for the staff member to devote himself more to other activities outside the Center such as consultation, teaching or research.

In summarizing the future outlook of clinical psychologists in this setting, there seems to be an impressive number of possibilities for development. Although it is difficult to predict the future role of the clinical psychologist with a high degree of certainty, it appears that the main trends are toward educating the public, enlarging the areas of service, and increasing training and research facilities.

REFERENCES

1. Louttit, C. M. The nature of clinical psychology. *Psychol. Bull.*, 1939, 36, 361-389.

XIV.

PRIVATE CLINICAL PRACTICE

ALBERT ELLIS

By the private practice of clinical psychology we mean the psychologist's working in a noninstitutional setting, taking full responsibility for the work he does, and making fee arrangements directly with his clients or patients. Although the private practitioner may work, on a consulting or co-operative basis, with other psychologists or clinicians, he is directly responsible to the recipient of his psychological services, and is primarily an independent agent. While, in essence, the functioning of the clinician in private practice may not differ from that of his colleague in the institutional setting, his role as an independent practitioner has a distinct and important influence on the approach, the emphasis, and the scope of his professional services.

HISTORY OF PRIVATE CLINICAL PRACTICE

Whereas clinical psychology is generally considered to have begun its development with the opening of Witmer's clinic in 1896, the private practice of clinical psychology has no such apparent birth date. Seemingly, some of the early clinicians did some private work, but more probably private practice did not actually begin until around the time of World War I. In an article published in 1934 on opportunities for the psychologist in private practice, Rosen (5) noted that, in 1927, only ten psychologists out of 700 members of the American Psychological Association were described as being in private practice. In 1934, according to this same article, the Association of Consulting Psychologists recorded 25 out of 233 members as engaging in private practice.

In recent years, especially since World War II, there has been a considerable growth in the number of clinicians who are devoting most or part of their time to noninstitutional and nonacademic practice. Although only about 3 per cent of the members of the American Psychological Association, and 7 per cent of the clinicians in the American Psychological Association would appear to be in full-time independent practice (2, 6), a survey in 1951 indicated that 56 per cent of the members of the Division of Clinical and Abnormal Psychology of the American

186

Psychological Association were then engaged in some type of paid private practice (3). The growth of regional groups devoted to private practice, and the great interest shown at recent American Psychological Association and local meetings devoted to the professional problems of private practice, would also indicate that there is an increasing tendency for clinical psychologists to devote at least part of their time to independent activities.

One indication of the recent growth of the private practice of clinical psychology is the large increase in the number of psychologists successfully engaging in psychoanalysis or psychoanalytic psychotherapy. Several of the most influential analytic therapists, including individuals like Theodor Reik, Erich Fromm, Harry Bone, Rollo May, Milton Wexler, Robert Lindner, Peter Blos, and the late Géza Róheim have been privately practicing psychologists. And psychologists have been instrumental in starting several Freudian and neo-Freudian groups and institutes, such as the National Psychological Association for Psychoanalysis and the William Alanson White Institute.

WHO ENGAGES IN CLINICAL PRIVATE PRACTICE

Although available factual evidence is meager, it would seem to indicate that clinical psychologists who engage in private practice tend to have a Ph.D. degree, several years of supervised experience in an institutional setting, and personal psychotherapy (especially psychoanalysis) and supervised psychotherapy (2). This is particularly true of full-time practitioners. Practicing psychologists who do not have the Ph.D. degree tend to have considerable experience and to be eligible, under "grandfather" clauses, for the diplomate of the American Board of Examiners in Professional Psychology.

Clinical practitioners, especially full-time practitioners, tend to congregate in the large cities and states, such as New York, California, Massachusetts, and Illinois. The four local private practice groups which now exist are in New York City, Los Angeles, San Francisco, and Boston. Increasingly, however, private practitioners are opening offices in smaller cities all over the United States.

According to a survey made by the writer for the Committee on Private Practice of the Division of Clinical and Abnormal Psychology of the American Psychological Association (3), about 55 per cent of clinicians engaging in independent practice devote from one to nine hours per week to this type of activity; about 15 per cent devote from ten to nineteen hours to paid private practice; and about 30 per cent devote twenty or more hours per week to independent practice.

WHAT PRIVATE PRACTITIONERS DO

According to the aforementioned survey (3), clinical psychologists in private practice mainly do psychotherapy and psychodiagnosis, with about two thirds of those reporting saying that they engage in either or both these specialties. In addition, about one sixth of private clinical practitioners do some vocational guidance, about one sixth do business and industrial consultations; and about one tenth do remedial education. Most of the clinicians replying to this survey reported that they do two or more types of activity in their private practice, and only 40 per cent reported that they do only one type of activity.

Of psychologists engaging in only one kind of work in their private practice, the majority do psychotherapy, a slightly smaller minority do psychodiagnosis, and a much smaller minority do business or industrial consultation, remedial education, vocational guidance, or other forms of psychological practice. Of those engaging in full-time private practice (that is, twenty or more hours per week), the great majority do psychotherapy, a sizeable minority do psychodiagnosis, and only a few do other types of psychological activity. Altogether, then, it may be confidently stated that, at the present time, private clinical practice largely consists of psychotherapy and psychodiagnosis.

Although no clear-cut facts are now available, it seems safe to say that the majority of clinical psychologists in private practice who engage in psychotherapy are psychoanalytically oriented, and that the majority of those engaging in psychodiagnosis specialize in the Rorschach and other projective techniques of personality evaluation. Client-centered psychotherapy and individual mental testing are poor runners-up in psychotherapeutic and psychodiagnostic practice.

According to the same survey of private clinical practitioners previously cited, 60 per cent of independent psychologists reported that they mainly see adult clients, 24 per cent reported that they mainly see children or adolescents, and 16 per cent reported that they see about an equal number of adults and children or adolescents. Whereas, therefore, the old-time clinical psychologist was wont to do little private practice, and when he did so to engage in the mental testing of children and adolescents, the modern clinician is likely to do more private practice, and to engage in the psychotherapy and psychodiagnosis of adults.

SETTING UP IN PRIVATE CLINICAL PRACTICE

The private practitioner, in setting up practice, has problems not encountered by the nonindependent psychologist. First of all, he must open an office which is adequate for his and his clients' needs. Many practitioners, particularly when they are first getting into independent service, utilize their homes, and set up a room or two for seeing clients. More and more, however, psychologists find it necessary to have a separate office for this purpose, appropriately furnished and equipped.

The private practice of psychology, like any other private practice, becomes a business as well as a profession. The psychologist in private practice is therefore concerned with, and responsible for, all the details attendant to his independent professional functioning. He not only sets up his own office, he keeps his own records, establishes his own fees, and maintains his own sources of new referrals.

As with any professional service, setting up in private practice requires an ethical, and professionally acceptable, publicizing of the psychologist's services to the community in which he works. And as with any other professional service, the psychologist begins by letting his professional colleagues, his friends, and his relatives know what he is doing. He becomes an active member of the community. He usually maintains his source of referrals through the following kinds of channels: (1) Community physicians, including psychiatrists, to whom he may refer cases that are outside his field of training and experience, and who in turn may refer suitable clients to him. (2) Other professional workers, such as social workers, clergymen, dentists, and welfare workers, may also be a good source of referral. (3) The psychologist's own clients, when helped by him and when educated to understand the importance of helping others to realize the value of psychological services, may well become his main source of continuing referrals. (4) Friends, relatives, and acquaintances may also be educated to understand what a psychologist is and does, and who may be referred to him for help. (5) The general public may be helped to understand a psychologist's function through his participating in public talks, discussions, and symposia; through his teaching at educational institutions; and through his writings. (6) The psychologist's own professional colleagues in other branches of psychology may be a source of referral. (7) Psychologists may sometimes join special groups, such as private practice organizations or psychoanalytic groups, which receive requests for psychological services and which will act as referral sources. (8) Local universities, clinics, medical societies, and other groups may be contacted to let them know what areas of practice the psychologist encompasses. The practicing clinician who does paid or unpaid work for a clinic, hospital, mental hygiene society, university, or other center concerned with psychological or psychiatric activity will often find cases being referred to him as a result of his work.

SPECIAL PROBLEMS OF THE PRIVATE CLINICAL PRACTITIONER

Because of the nature of his psychological activity, the private clinical practitioner will often find himself involved in many special problems, some of which will now be considered.

LICENSING AND LEGAL CERTIFICATION PROBLEMS

Although licensing or legal certification of psychologists is of importance to every psychologist, academic or applied, legal control of psychological practice is particularly important to the private practitioner. Restrictive legislation is likely to be aimed directly at him and his practice; and any status gained by psychologists through legal recognition is likely to benefit him more than virtually any other psychologist. Consequently, private practitioners should be, and usually are, directly concerned with legislative actions in their states or cities. The responsible practitioner will join any local psychological organizations that are considering legislation, will support them financially to the best of his ability, and will actively participate in attempts to instigate favorable legislation or to prevent unfavorable legislation. If he does not do so, he risks real disaster.

Partly as a result of the needs and efforts of privately practicing clinicians, licensing or certification statutes have now been passed in several states and are being considered in several other states. New York State has particularly seen much recent activity in this connection. As a result of psychologists' action, a licensing bill was unanimously passed by the New York legislature in 1951, but was vetoed by Governor Dewey. In 1953 and 1954 a proposed change in the medical practice act, which might have seriously interfered with the work of practicing psychologists, was solidly opposed by the New York State Joint Council of Psychologists on Legislation and was defeated in committee. The legislative situation continues to be indefinite in New York as well as in several other states, with private practicing clinicians co-operatively joining with academic, institutional, and other psychologists to work for beneficial, and against inimical, legislation.

At the same time, the New York State Joint Council has recently fought for, and won, two tax rulings which are very important to privately practicing psychologists. It has obtained a rule whereby psychologists, along with other professional people, are exempt from paying the New York State Unincorporated Business tax, and it has obtained a ruling from the United States Department of Internal Revenue allowing patients or clients of clinical psychologists in private practice to deduct their fees as legitimate medical expenses on their income tax returns.

FEE SCHEDULES

Whereas institutional and academic clinical psychologists have few or no fee problems, private practitioners have many. They must charge fees which enable them to make a decent living, and at the same time must provide services to members of the public who desperately need such services and who are frequently in no position to pay regular fees (4). Private practitioners, moreover, must compete, today, with other professional workers who are often better established and have higher public status than they have, and must consequently often accept lower fees for essentially the same work as these other professional people perform. The practitioner, therefore, is often placed in a position where he must manage not to charge low-income patients too high fees and at the same time not unduly to exploit himself.

PROFESSIONAL ISOLATION

The clinical psychologist in private practice is in special danger of becoming isolated from the rest of psychology, particularly if he is in full-time practice in a somewhat small community. He often does not work in conjunction with other psychologists, and he may see client after client without having the chance to discuss his practice with other professional workers, as he would usually do if he were working in an institutional or agency setting. He may combat these dangers by consulting with other professional people in his community; by attending case seminars and other postgraduate activities; by being an active member of his local psychological organizations; by attending national and local psychological meetings; by engaging in activities, such as teaching or institutional work, in addition to his private practice; by keeping up with recent psychological literature; by engaging in psychological research; and by otherwise getting beyond his immediate practice into the broader field of general and clinical psychology.

RESEARCH PROBLEMS

The psychologist in private practice often has considerable difficulty engaging in research activities, even though he may be highly motivated to do so. In the first place, in his own work he ordinarily sees a limited number of clients or patients, and it is often not practical to engage in various kinds of research activities with these individuals. Secondly, he is often pressed for time, because he must do his research entirely on his own time, and must sacrifice potential income when he does so. Thirdly, he has not the laboratory, library, and other facilities with which to carry on certain research projects. Fourthly, he normally does not have supplementary personnel, such as research assistants, student helpers, and secretarial or clerical aids, to help him in his research activities. Fifthly, just because he is in private practice, and is not connected with a large university or other center, he stands little chance of obtaining sizeable research grants.

Nonetheless, there is some valuable research that can be done in private practice—as shown by Freud's pioneer studies with his private patients—and it is important for the sake of the science of psychology, as well as for the continued growth and development of the practitioner himself, that the psychologist in private practice attempt to remain a research scientist as well as a clinician. The more time and thought he gives to this problem, the further is he and his area of practice likely to develop.

RESPONSIBILITIES TO THE PUBLIC

Many psychologists, institutional and noninstitutional, come into direct contact with the public; but the privately practicing clinician especially does so, because he not only deals directly with clients or patients in his professional work, but also has no intermediary to arrange appointment times, fee schedules, publicity, and so on. All such activities are his own direct responsibility. Consequently, the impression which he gives to the public is closely related to what he says and does in his relationships with members of this public.

The psychologist in private practice would do well to realize, therefore, that he assumes, in his public contacts, responsibility for not only his own but psychology's reputation, and should guide himself accordingly. In matters of fees, of accepting invitations for public talks or appearances, of co-operating in community studies, and of engaging in other activities where the public is particularly sensitive, he may well keep in mind not only his own limited interests but those of the entire profession. That the psychologist in private practice will adhere strictly to the ethics of his profession, and conduct himself as an individual who is devoted to public service as well as to his personal goals and aims, is to be taken for granted. In addition, it is important, especially while the private practice of clinical psychology is still in its childhood or early youth, that he serve the public so scrupulously and well as to help materially in the continued growth of his profession.

A PRIVATE PRACTITIONER'S WORK WEEK

A more graphic picture of what a privately practicing clinical psychologist is and does may perhaps be gained from a description of a typical psychologist's work week. Taking, for this purpose, one of the writer's own weeks, I find that it ran something as follows.

Monday: Saw six regular psychotherapy patients and one marriage counseling case. Had a lengthy telephone consultation with a referring physician about a new psychotherapy patient. In the evening, as a representative of the New York Association of Clinical Psychologists in Private Practice, attended the regular monthly meeting of the New York State Joint Council of Psychologists on Legislation.

Tuesday: Went to see about possible jury duty exemption, to discover that clinical psychologists are not exempt (as are physicians, lawyers, and members of several other professions) in New York City and cannot be exempted until a special amendment to the jury law is passed (which is not likely to be passed, if it ever is, for many years to come). Saw seven regular psychotherapy patients and one marriage counseling case.

Wednesday: Addressed the psychology club of one of the New York universities. Saw seven psychotherapy patients and one individual where special psychodiagnostic confirmation was sought by a physician. Conferred with the physician on this case; then conferred with a neuro-psychiatrist, to whom I advised that the patient be referred.

Thursday: Spoke to a writer from a national magazine whose editor had decided that American females have recently changed their sex habits drastically and who wanted a quotation to sustain his view and to bolster his suggested story. Tactfully explained to the writer that there was no scientific evidence that his editor's view was correct, and gave him some informational leads that eventually induced him to write up quite a different kind of story (which the editor thereupon tore apart and printed in a highly bowdlerized form). Saw six psychotherapy patients, one couple desiring premarital counseling, and one psychologist whom I am supervising in psychotherapeutic technique. Had a telephone consultation with a gynecologist, to whom I had referred one of my psychotherapy patients.

Friday: Saw an executive of one of the television chains, who wanted me to write material for a show where members of the home audience would rate themselves on their success in answering psychological and marital questions. Explained carefully to him that such a program would involve the construction of exceptionally brief, thoroughly unstandardized self-rating psychological tests—and that this is dangerous to the public and is considered unethical practice under the present American Psychological Association code of ethics. He quickly saw the point and said he would try to rearrange the program so that the self-rating feature would be eliminated and the questions would be of an educational nature. Saw seven psychotherapy patients and one psychologist for supervision.

Saturday: Tried to keep the day free for research, writing, and catching up on record keeping. Had to see one unscheduled patient who became panicked and a couple who insisted on coming for marriage counseling immediately after phoning. Managed to spend the rest of the day doing the originally planned research and writing.

Recapitulating the psychological services rendered for the month which included this week, I observed that I had seen twenty-five psychotherapy patients for a total of 142 hours, seven premarital or marriage counseling cases for a total of 24 hours, one individual for psychodiagnostic confirmation, and two psychological supervisees for a total of 9 hours. I had also attended three psychological meetings, given two public talks, spoken to four representatives of mass media, and carried on about a dozen long telephone conversations with physicians or psychologists in regard to patients or counselees. Sandwiched in between (mostly on week ends) I had managed to get in some writing and research.

Of the thirty-three different patients and counselees seen by me during this month, four had been referred by physicians, four by psychologists, three by friends or acquaintances, two by professional organizations, two through reading some material written by or quoting me, one through hearing me talk at a public gathering, and seventeen had been referred by other patients or clients. Of the twenty-five psychotherapy patients seen, twenty-two were moderately disturbed individuals (five of whom had originally come for marriage counseling and had seen that they actually needed psychotherapy), while three were more seriously disturbed. Most of the psychotherapy patients were being seen once a week; some (who were in the closing stages of therapy) once every two or three weeks; and several two or three times a week.

How typical my working week or month as a private practitioner is cannot readily be said without a systematic survey of the field. It is certainly not typical of practicing clinicians who largely do orthodox psychoanalysis, and who therefore see fewer patients per week. Nor is it typical of clinicians who largely do psychodiagnosis, most of whom probably also see fewer clients per week and who spend several hours giving a battery of diagnostic tests to each client. So many and varied are the practices of psychologists today that it is quite likely that no individual's practice is typical of the whole field.

THE FUTURE OF PRIVATE CLINICAL PRACTICE

In the survey made by the present author of the private practice activities of the members of the Division of Clinical and Abnormal Psychology of the American Psychological Association (3), the respondents were asked to what extent they would like to extend their present paid private practice. Of 569 members of the Division reporting, it was found that more than half of those engaging in no private practice said they would like to engage in some. Of those engaging in private practice, about 70 per cent said that they would like to extend their private work. These figures are confirmed by recent professional meetings devoted to private practice, by the growth of private practice groups in several of our large cities, and by many conversations which the writer has had with young clinical psychologists. It would appear that not only is private clinical practice rapidly increasing, but that there exists a large number of clinical psychologists who are impatiently awaiting the time when they can begin or extend their independent activities.

Because of the propensity of clinicians to enter private practice in increasing numbers, the Committee on Private Practice of the Division of Clinical and Abnormal Psychology of the American Psychological Association has recently recommended and published standards for training and experience for all psychologists (independent as well as institutional) who engage in unsupervised practice. The Committee's report (1) recommends that psychologists engaging in unsupervised practice should (after due allowance for "grandfathers" is made) have a Ph.D. in clinical psychology and at least two years of paid full-time experience in the field of clinical psychology, at least one year of which should be in a treatment center where mildly and seriously disturbed individuals are commonly seen. The Committee further recommends that clinicians doing psychodiagnosis in unsupervised practice should have at least fifty hours of supervision in any psychodiagnostic specialty employed, and that clinicians doing counseling or psychotherapy should have at least one hundred hours of direct supervision in any counseling or psychotherapeutic specialty which they employ in their unsupervised practice.

In view of the past history of and present trends in clinical psychology, it may confidently be expected that psychologists in increasing numbers will be engaging in private clinical work, and that the time may well come when the great majority of older and more experienced clinicians will be engaging in some amount of independent practice. If so, the existing problems of private practitioners will become more and more important, and additional individual and group effort to solve them satisfactorily will be in order. The sooner that clinical psychologists begin to realize this, the better it will be for the profession of psychology in general and for that of clinical private practice in particular.

REFERENCES

1. Committee on Private Practice of the Division of Clinical and Abnormal Psychology. Recommendations of standards for the unsupervised practice of clinical psychology. *Amer. Psychologist,* 1953, 8, 494-495.

2. Committee on Psychotherapy of the Division of Clinical and Abnormal Psychology. Report. *Newsletter Div. Clin. Abnorm. Psychol.*, 1950, 4, No. 2, Supplement.
3. Ellis, A. Report on survey of members of the Division of Clinical and Abnormal Psychology who are presently engaged in paid private practice. *Newsletter Div. Clin. Abnorm. Psychol.*, 1951, 5, No. 3, Supplement.
4. Ellis, A. The psychologist in private practice and the good profession. *Amer. Psychologist*, 1952, 7, 129-131.
5. Rosen, E. K., Fisher, V. E., & Payne, A. F. Opportunities for the psychologist in private practice—a symposium. *Psychol. Exch.*, 1934, 3, 151-158.
6. Sanford, F. H. Annual report of the executive secretary: 1952. *Amer. Psychologist*, 1952, 7, 686-696.

XV.

THE CLINICAL PSYCHOLOGIST IN AN OLD-AGE COUNSELING CENTER

JEANNE G. GILBERT

Recent years have seen a marked increase in longevity and a population which is rapidly growing older. During the first half of this century there was a life expectancy increase of approximately twenty years, so that by the middle of the century almost 9 per cent of the population of the United States, totaling more than thirteen million persons, was sixty-five years of age or older. The expectation is that this number will increase to 14 per cent by 1975. Medical advances have done much to eliminate or decrease the destructive and debilitating diseases, particularly of early life, so that each year more persons can reach the years of later maturity and old age. Unfortunately, however, this increase of life span has not generally brought with it the happiness and contentment which might have been anticipated. Too many persons reach these years physically weakened, unloved, unwanted, economically insecure, and weighted down with feelings of uselessness, so that their added time in this world means no more than an added burden to themselves and to their families.

In recognition of some of the needs of older persons, medicine has worked toward alleviating their physical distress and social legislation toward alleviating their economic difficulties. Retirement plans, old-age pensions and old-age benefits have been offered as solutions to the problem, but one sometimes wonders whether the real aim is the welfare of the older person or the easing of the economic burden on the younger person. Some, more truly social-minded individuals and corporations have, of course, recognized that the needs of older persons go beyond mere physical care and material comforts and stressed the importance of vocational and avocational pursuits, hobbies, social clubs and the like. Still, progress and understanding have been slow during this first half of the twentieth century.

This same period of years has seen the rise of clinical psychology as a profession. Strangely enough, old-age counseling and rehabilitative work had its origins in psychological work with children. Dr. Lillien J.

Martin, a retired professor of psychology from Stanford University, had established a child guidance clinic for preschool children in 1920. Noting that difficulty frequently resulted from the presence of an aged and difficult grandparent in the home, Dr. Martin decided that salvaging the old person might prove more beneficial and economical than trying to forget about him or get rid of him. Therefore, in 1921 she began remedial work with the aged and in 1929 in San Francisco opened the first old-age counseling center in the United States and perhaps in the world. Martin's work with the aged was based on the theories that it is possible to grow mentally and to modify one's way of life at any age and that happiness lies not in uselessness or in an abundance of material things but in active participation in life in accordance with one's own physical strength and capacity. With these premises in mind, she labored toward rehabilitation of her older clients by helping them to become useful and active in life, to understand themselves, to readjust to the new, and to look forward to a future in this life instead of only in the next. Dr. Martin's pioneer work was notably successful but unfortunately, with her death in 1943 and that of her associate, Clare deGruchy, a few years later, the clinic was disbanded. Similar fates befell clinics in Los Angeles and New York which were patterned after Martin's clinic.

OLD-AGE COUNSELING TODAY

Today old-age counseling is carried on largely on a private basis, in mental hygiene or psychiatric clinics which treat adults of all ages, in mental hospitals, in geriatric clinics of hospitals, or in old-age homes. Occasionally, welfare agencies, industrial preretirement clubs, old-age recreational centers and adult education programs offer some counseling. There are also a few setups which deal primarily with the vocational problems and job placement of older workers.

In most setups co-operation of services is practiced and in all setups it is desirable. In working with older persons all facets of the individual's life must be understood and taken into consideration, and it is doubtful if the training in any one field is sufficiently broad to warrant having the specialist in that field dispense with the services of specialists in allied fields. The psychologist, for example, cannot expect to be equally well versed in the fields of diagnosing and counseling the emotionally disturbed person, geriatric medicine, vocational guidance, job placement, old-age benefits, housing of older persons, old-age homes, hospitals and clinics, educational programs, old-age recreational centers and clubs, etc. Rather, he must stick to his own psychological specialty and co-operate with other services, particularly those of medicine and social work, in helping the older person to effect a better adjustment. The welfare of the patient must always be kept foremost in mind, and when a psychologist has once accepted a patient for counseling, he must remember that his is the responsibilty for the welfare of that patient. The psychologist himself, if he would work in an old-age counseling center, must have a genuine liking for and interest in older persons, and have resolved his conflicts in regard to his own parents. He must be optimistic regarding the potentialities of the aged and the possibilities of working with them, and yet at the same time be realistic about their problems. He must have respect and sympathy for them, show courtesy toward them, and be very patient in his dealings with them, bearing in mind that when one is young it is difficult to understand the problems of the old. The field of old-age counseling is relatively new and one which requires considerable imagination and ingenuity; the psychologist who possesses these traits can learn and grow as he works. The old-age counselor must also be aware of community resources and know where and how he can secure the co-operation of services just discussed. It is most important to know which medical men and which clinics and hospitals specialize in geriatric problems, what housing facilities are available for older persons, what homes and hospitals will admit them, how to go about getting relief funds or old-age pensions for them, what vocational possibilities are open to them in the community, and what recreational centers cater especially to older persons.

In a counseling center offering service to older persons, all types of problems may be encountered—essentially the same types of problems which will be found in other adult groups with the added complicating factor that the patient is old. This means that he has had more time to develop and grow rigid in his maladjustment, that on the whole he is less flexible and ready for change, that he has less time to modify his behavior, and that society is less ready to accept him. Physical and particularly psychosomatic problems may be encountered frequently, and individuals will be found who are psychotic, psychoneurotic, fundamentally inadequate or mentally deficient. Housing problems, in which institutional, foster home, hospital, old-age apartment or old-age colony placement is indicated, may be found, as well as those of marital difficulties, parent-offspring conflict, loneliness and general unhappiness. The most common problems, however, seem to be those in which there is a vocational readjustment or employment problem involved. Often this is the problem of the person who, because of age, has been retired or dismissed from his job and has insufficient funds to live independent of his family, relatives or charity. Unwanted by his relatives, he resents his dependency, feels useless and inadequate, and becomes difficult and cantankerous in the home. Unhappy with his leisure time and discouraged by his failure to find a job on his own initiative, he may take the advice of someone he knows and seek outside help. Usually, of course, his problem involves much more than mere job placement but as this is paramount in his mind, it must be dealt with first and the patient helped to see and to understand his related problems as he returns for further interviews. The psychologist may be able to determine the vocational potentialities of the client but may need the help of a job placement agency to put the potentialities to practical use. If, as is the case with large numbers of older persons, a physical problem is involved, he will need the help of a medical doctor who specializes in geriatrics. If, as sometimes happens, the older person is found to be or is suspected of being psychotic, the help of a psychiatrist is indicated. In other words, the psychologist who works in the field of counseling the older person must remember at all times that the welfare of his patient is his primary concern, that co-operation of services is essential to effective counseling, and that he must always be ready both to give his services and to accept the help of allied specialties.

FUNCTIONS OF THE CLINICAL PSYCHOLOGIST

As in centers dealing with other age groups, the work of a psychologist with patients in an old-age counseling center will consist essentially of diagnosis, consultative interviews, short-term counseling, and therapy of varying depth and intensity. The type of service rendered will, of course, depend upon the problem presented by the patient, his desire for help, and his ability to respond to therapy if therapeutic aid is indicated.

Diagnosis, considered in its broadest sense, varies considerably with the older patient and the problem he presents. For example, the physically and emotionally healthy individual who seeks a job but is not sure what he wants to do or can do requires an entirely different type of diagnostic procedure than the one who feel unwanted in his offspring's already overcrowded home, and a still different procedure than the one who suspects the neighbors of gossiping about him and his relatives of trying to poison him. Effective counseling has to be based on sound diagnosis, and this can be made only after the psychologist has applied the techniques at his command for learning as much as possible about the patient.

A diagnosis may be made in one or several interviews from a careful appraisal of the patient's history and present symptoms, behavior and attitudes. On the other hand, an accurate diagnosis may require or be expedited by the use of various tests of intellectual and/or personality functioning. These tests, however, must be chosen and used with great care and with a definite plan and purpose in view. Testing with older persons should not be done for the sake of the testing itself or for the purpose of obtaining a score which may mean anything or nothing.

It is well recognized that as one grows older his efficiency in certain areas of mental functioning declines, but it may or may not be necessary to determine to what extent this functioning is impaired. If an individual seeks employment, has been out of the labor field for many years, and little verified information is available concerning his past work history or education, certainly it would seem essential to know as much as possible about his present level of mental functioning and the potentialties he may have, and in this case appropriate test procedures must be used. While the tests used will aim to appraise all aspects of the personality make-up, the emphasis will be on the intellectual and functioning areas.

On the other hand, where there is an emotional disturbance, or a psychoneurotic or psychotic process is suspected, impairment of mental functioning may be important to know, but even more important may be a thorough study of the personality structure. In cases of this sort personality tests, particularly the projective techniques, will assume greater importance than the various measures of intellectual functioning.

Again, when a healthy, self-supporting, aged individual is unhappy because of an intolerable in-law conflict within his home, it may be entirely unnecessary to use any test procedures whatsoever. In view of his obvious normality, it is not essential to determine the extent of his decline in various areas of mental functioning since this information contributes nothing to the solution of his problem. In these matters the well-trained clinical psychologist must, of course, use his own judgment.

The psychologist must, in all cases though, be careful not to over-test. Older persons, as a rule, do not tolerate tests well, so that they must be used with caution. At the mere suggestion of taking a test some react with violent antipathy and reject the whole counseling situation. Others become apprehensive and anxious and perform so poorly that their feelings of inferiority and inadequacy are intensified. Therefore, it is advisable to broach the subject of taking tests, if the need of this be indicated, in a matter-of-fact yet reassuring manner as a routine part of the counseling situation. The tests themselves should be brief and pertinent, and any prolongation of the testing situation by the inclusion of tests which contribute little or nothing to what we need to know about the client should be avoided.

An early and accurate diagnosis is basic to effective counseling. It is essential to know what the real problem is and what the personality make-up of the person presenting the problem is in order to know what to do about the problem and how to treat the personality. There is such a relatively short time left for the aged that we cannot afford to waste what there is; in so far as it is possible, each hour of counseling must be made productive. As with all age groups, but perhaps even more so with older persons, some clients may be unsuitable for counseling beyond the diagnostic level, but this can be determined only by a diagnostic study. Some may present primarily a physical or organic problem, in which case referral to a geriatric specialist, clinic or hospital would be made following the psychologist's diagnostic study. Some may be too deteriorated or mentally ill for counseling beyond the diagnostic level. Others may show inadequacy of such long standing that counseling over a prolonged period would be obviously futile. Still others may have employment or housing problems which require only a diagnostic interview by the psychologist and then referral to a co-operating service. Where therapy or further counseling is indicated the diagnostic study should point the direction along which the treatment should proceed and indicate the depth or level of therapy which should prove most effective with this particular patient. From this discussion it can readily be seen that diagnosis is a very important and unique part of the work of the clinical psychologist in an old-age counseling center. Because of the techniques peculiar to his profession, the psychologist is particularly well equipped to handle the problem of diagnosis and should consider this area one that is well within his own special province.

The psychologist can best counsel patients whose problems involve organic conditions by working in conjunction with a medical doctor. He will be most effective with employment problems if he can have the co-operating services of a job placement agency. Generally, he will need the co-operation of a social worker in dealing with problems of placement, housing, financial relief and recreational facilities.

Full knowledge of community resources is essential for the clinical psychologist practicing in an old-age counseling center. Community resources for the help, care, recreation, education and employment of the aged are few relative to the resources for other age groups and vary considerably in type with the particular community, so that the most effective use possible must be made of what little is available. Although this point was mentioned previously, its importance to the clinical psychologist in effective old-age counseling cannot be overstressed. While, as with diagnosis, the same basic principles of psychological work with all age groups are the same, the consultative and therapeutic aspects of counseling the aged also have some features which differentiate them from these same aspects of counseling the younger adult or the child.

In the first place, the very fact of being old makes the patient unique— unique not only in himself and his social relationships but also in his therapeutic relationship. The psychologist is working with an individual older than himself—a patient with feelings and problems connected with aging which he will have difficulty understanding because he himself has never been old. It is a situation in which the therapist will tend to identify his client with his own parent and react to him accordingly. On the other hand, the patient may identify the therapist with his own off-spring around whom much of his conflict centers, or he may show his dependency needs and conflicts by reacting to the therapist as he did to his own parent during adolescence. To these things the psychologist must be especially alert.

Also, generally speaking, the old patient is a rejected person. He is rejected and discarded by society and industry in favor of younger per-sons, and often this rejection occurs long before his physical, emotional, social or intellectual decline warrants it. Frequently he is also rejected by his family and quite aware of their feeling that he is a burden and a nuisance to them. Looking at this problem realistically and recognizing the fact that rejection generally becomes intensified with the passing years and increasing infirmities, the old person actually does not have as bright a future to look forward to as the child or young adult. The psy-chologist must be ready to face these problems with his client without deception or flattery, and yet at the same time he must be able to visual-ize a real future for him. Helping his client to become socially acceptable and useful and thus combat rejection is one of the first tasks the psy-chologist has in working with the aged. Then too, the older patient has had a longer time than others to live with his personality quirks so that they have become crystallized and an integral part of him. Although they may be undesirable maladjustments and contributory to his present prob-lem, they are perhaps so ingrained that it is impossible to eradicate them, or their presence may serve as defenses against more serious emotional disturbance so that it is undesirable to try to change them. These things the psychologist must weigh carefully before initiating therapy, bearing in mind that change in the aged is slow with a tendency toward rigidity and inflexibility rather than growth and development as we know it in the young.

Finally, there is another aspect of the time element in working with the aged. With the young there is a lifetime ahead in which to grow, develop and change, and often time alone will effect an improved ad-justment even in the absence of therapeutic aid. With the young then we can afford to take our time in therapy because time is our ally. With the old this is not the case, for here time works against us. It works against us in two ways. First we have the known fact that the aged take a longer time to grasp, tire more readily, and are slower to change; and then we have the incontrovertible and discouraging fact that, in spite of this, there is actually little time left because this is the tail end of the life span and death cannot be far away. Obviously, the clinical psychologist in the field must weigh this point carefully and evaluate its implications along with the other considerations just discussed in formulating his counseling plans for his patient.

From this it can be inferred that, in most instances at least, the psychologist in an old-age counseling center should not plan on too prolonged therapy of his clients. This applies both to the individual sessions and to the total counseling time. The time of the individual sessions is mentioned because even though the interview times are usually more or less fixed in a counseling center, it is often quite difficult to limit the older person to this time. Because of his slower pace and the fact that he may have too much time on his hands anyway, he may seek to drag on the interview longer than the psychologist's time permits or his constitution and therapeutic gains warrant. However, if the psychologist makes clear in the beginning the amount of time allotted for the individual interviews, he should not have too much difficulty in this area.

The total counseling time will necessarily vary with the problem and the patient as it does in the counseling of individuals of all ages. Diagnostic or consultative work may be completed in as few as one or two interviews but the time for therapy must remain indeterminate, depending upon the therapeutic goals, the depth of therapy, and the rate of progress made by the patient.

Martin considered four or five visits to be usually sufficient for her rehabilitative work with the aged. While it would seem that in this short time her work must necessarily be on a somewhat superficial level and that deep underlying emotional disturbances could not be treated, yet she did get results and find justification for her belief that almost any old person could be salvaged if he were willing to put forth enough effort. Her method was essentially a directive one in which, during a series of four or five carefully planned visits, she made an appraisal of the patient's assets and liabilities by means of a study of his personal appearance, physical condition, health habits, life history and brief mental test; analyzed these with him; and encouraged him to banish resistance and adopt a more constructive attitude. She analyzed with him his daily program of living and helped him to develop a better one; gave him slogans and setting-up exercises for rehabilitation; worked on his money budget, income, employment problem and chances of advancement in his job if he were employed. She helped him to establish goals, aided him to gain a better and more realistic understanding of himself and his activity, and led him to want to go forward and to see how he could improve himself as an individual. Finally, she aimed to direct the client's thinking toward active participation in community and industrial life, stressing the fact that as a citizen he owed the community something in return for its services to him and also that participation must be earned. However, although she considered that gainful employment was extremely important for her aged clients, she did not find jobs for them as she felt that the experience of seeking his own job was important to the individual's rehabilitation.

While there are some counselors who still use Martin's counseling methods, either in essence with modifications or in entirety, there are others who, because of their own temperament, training and convictions, prefer a more nondirective technique which takes a longer time. Some also are making use of hypnosis and psychoanalysis, both of which were rejected by Martin. There are counselors who believe that hypnosis can frequently serve as an ego builder and initiator of activity, especially with those timid, shy, older persons who fear rejection and are bothered by feelings of inadequacy and inferiority. Some psychoanalytically trained psychologists are using psychoanalysis, particularly some of the briefer forms, in working with emotionally disturbed older persons and finding the results quite encouraging. A few, more physiologically minded psychologists are trying to incorporate some of the physiological methods of relaxation, posture control, etc., into their work with tense old patients in an effort to improve their physical tone and general sense of well-being. Some are also trying out group therapy with older persons. This is not to be confused with old-age clubs, recreational centers and adult education courses, of which there are many run by both trained and untrained leaders. Rather, reference is being made to those regular therapy sessions of six or eight old persons who, under the guidance of a trained therapist, meet for free discussion of their problems and resentments and, by means of this catharsis and the relationships they form with the therapist and other members of the group, strengthen their egos, develop insight, and thereby show improvement in their adjustment. Psychodrama is likewise a promising approach for those psychologists who are versed in this technique.

While it is not within the province of this chapter to discuss or advocate the most desirable therapeutic techniques to use in counseling the aged, the above approaches are mentioned for the purpose of illustrating what a clinical psychologist may do in working with patients in an old-age counseling center. Not all of the psychologist's work in such a center, however, will be with the aged client himself. There will be reports to be written for the center's files and to referring agencies, telephone calls and conferences concerning the patient, and referrals to be made to outside agencies. There will also be interviews with relatives of the patient, and sometimes this can account for a fairly large proportion of the psychologist's time.

Referral to an old-age counseling center is frequently made by relatives of the client, and more often than not a relative accompanies him to the center. Occasionally, relatives are concerned solely about the un-happiness, emotional disturbance or possible mental illness of the aging client, but it is more usual to find that referral to the center has been made because the relatives, and sometimes the patient himself, feel that matters have reached an impasse and that it is no longer possible to live together in the present condition of disharmony. These relatives may claim that papa's (or mama's) presence in their home places a great financial strain on them but that they would bear this burden gladly if only papa were easier to live with. They may say they have done every-thing in the world for him and expected nothing in return but that in-stead of being grateful, he constantly finds fault, criticizes the children and is irritable, cantankerous and difficult. On the other hand, the old person may claim that his children do not understand him, that his grandchildren are being trained badly and will come to no good end, that they take his things, and he has no privacy, no money and nothing to do; he may say they are only waiting for him to die so they can collect his insurance. Because of their greater rigidity, their slowness and re-sistance to change, and the relatively little time left to them, it is often necessary when working with old persons to manipulate the environment to a greater extent than one might in working with younger patients, so that in cases of conflict of this sort it is essential to work with the relatives as well as with the old person.

Because of the necessity of environmental contacts and environmental manipulation, part of the psychologist's time in an old-age counseling center may well be spent in the training of personnel and in community education. There are many ways in which volunteers may be used to advantage in community work and contacts which the staff of the center may find difficult because of the time element. These volunteers need some training in order that they may better understand the nature, problems and needs of the aged, and in this training the psychologist must be prepared to participate.

The psychologist should also take part in community education re-garding the nature, problems and needs of the aged. This involves meet-ings, conferences, and perhaps the giving of courses and lectures to interested lay persons, bearing in mind that such courses should be geared to an understandable and practical level.

Finally, there is the matter of research which should always have consideration as a part of a psychologist's work. Gerontology and geri-atrics are relatively new specialty fields, and there is much to be learned about them. We do not yet know enough about the psychosomatic aspects of aging, the differentiation between normal and abnormal aging, and what can be done to maintain efficiency and retard decline. We need to know much more about the normal aging process in general and what constitutes normal aging in the physical, mental, emotional and social areas. We want to know the most effective ways of maintaining health and happiness in the increasing number of years of old age. We also need research in the areas of medical care of the aged, housing, recreation and rehabilitation. The psychologist should be prepared to make his contribution to that area which interests him the most.

FUTURE TRENDS

As mentioned earlier in this chapter, most of the old-age counseling at the present time is carried on in setups other than in an independent old-age counseling center—that is, in old-age recreational centers or homes, in hospital geriatric clinics, in welfare agencies, etc. This slowness of independent old-age counseling centers to develop is probably due in part to a lack of funds and a lack of public interest in the old-age field. The majority of the aged who seek counseling seem to have a financial problem with which they want help either in the form of money or employment; therefore they cannot afford to pay fees. When they are living with relatives and there is family conflict and maladjustment, the relatives likewise are usually either unwilling or unable to pay fees. Public interest is growing, so that old-age recreational centers are being established and industrial preretirement clubs being formed, but it has not yet reached the point where municipalities or philanthropic individuals feel the need of spending the money to establish regular old-age counseling centers with trained personnel on the staff. However, there is reason to believe that in time this may come.

In the meantime, the most outstanding trend seems to be the establishment of geriatric clinics in general hospitals. In spite of the fact that these clinics are of relatively recent origin, many of them are rapidly changing and broadening their aims and outlook. Although first established for the study and treatment of diseases of the aged it was soon found that this was not enough. It was learned that not only does disease affect the life of a person but that the whole life pattern and living conditions of an individual affect the course of disease. Therefore, the trend now is to study the whole of the individual rather than just his disease. There is an attempt made to secure a complete life history of the individual. An appraisal is made of his intellectual and personality assets and liabilities. His general living conditions, his family relationships, his economic security, his occupation, and his recreational outlets are studied as well as his present physical symptoms. The interaction of these different facets is determined from the results of studies made by the various specialists, following which a course of treatment is decided upon. This treatment may include not only appropriate medical or surgical procedures, but also efforts to improve the general living situation. Many geriatric clinics co-operate closely with other departments of the hospital, such as the Occupational Therapy Department for vocational, avocational and rehabilitative procedures, the Physiotherapy Department especially for improvement in function with cases of crippling disabilities, and the Mental Hygiene Department for help with emotional problems. Some geriatric clinics accept, for study and treatment, younger persons in an effort to develop a preventive program which will enable more people to live longer at a higher rate of efficiency and health. Some include also community educational programs with special seminars for nurses, heads of old-age homes and others who spend their lives working with old people.

In addition, many geriatric clinics co-operate not only with other departments of their hospital but also with outside agencies which can offer them the help they need. These include, particularly, housing agencies and industrial or occupational agencies which can offer occupational training and/or jobs for the aging individual.

Obviously, the psychologist has a definite place in geriatric clinics of this sort. The nature of his work will be along the same lines as in an independent old-age counseling center, save that he will no doubt have closer contact and co-operation with medical specialists in the geriatric field. This would appear to be a healthy trend, for perhaps at no other time in life is close co-operation of the medical and social sciences quite so important as in the period of later maturity and old age.

REFERENCES

1. Donahue, W., & Tibbitts, C. (Eds.) *Planning the older years.* Ann Arbor, Mich.: Univer. of Mich. Press, 1950.
2. Donahue, W., & Tibbitts, C. (Eds.) *Growing in the older years.* Ann Arbor, Mich.: Univer. of Mich. Press, 1951.
3. Gilbert, J. G. *Understanding old age.* New York: Ronald Press, 1952.
4. Lawton, G. *New goals for old age.* New York: Columbia Univer. Press, 1943.
5. Lawton, G. *Aging successfully.* New York: Columbia Univer. Press, 1946.
6. Martin, L. J. *Salvaging old age.* New York: Macmillan, 1933.
7. Martin, L. J. *A handbook for old age counselors.* San Francisco: Geertz Printing Co., 1944.
8. Steiglitz, E. J. *The second forty years* Philadelphia: W. B. Saunders, 1946.
9. Tibbitts, C. (Ed.) *Living through the older years.* Ann Arbor, Mich.: Univer. of Mich. Press, 1949.

XVI.

THE CLINICAL PSYCHOLOGIST IN A
CLINIC FOR ALCOHOLICS

EDITH S. LISANSKY

In the United States at the present time, it is estimated that there may be as many as three million chronic problem drinkers. Many classifications of problem drinkers have been proposed, e.g., primary and secondary alcoholics, symptomatic drinkers, compulsive drinkers, etc., but it is likely that all problem drinkers have personal difficulties leading up to, related to, and caused by their drinking. Of these approximately three million individuals, about 750,000 are estimated to be alcohol addicts presenting severe emotional and social problems.

Individuals working in public clinics for alcoholics are impressed with the heterogeneity of the patient group. Men and women patients come from almost all social, economic and cultural backgrounds. The problem exists in all regions of the United States and occurs among professional people, business men, factory workers, housewives, writers, musicians, artists and white-collar workers.

HISTORICAL BACKGROUND

Since about 1930, research on the effects of alcohol on human beings has been under way in the Laboratory of Applied Physiology, Yale University. The emphasis of the Laboratory was originally on a research approach through physiology, medicine and biochemistry. In 1941, the Section of Alcohol Studies, later renamed the Center of Alcohol Studies, was set up to administer the expanding research program. The approach now became broader: studies in psychiatry, psychology, sociology, law, economics and education became part of the Center's program. Some of the research projects of the Center, completed and in progress, deal with drunken driving, industrial manpower loss through drinking, college drinking, alcoholism and occupational stability and the study of the diet, physiology, drinking habits and personality traits of various ethnic groups. In addition to research, the Laboratory has developed a classified archive and bibliography of all scientific literature on alcohol and a publication service.

In 1944, the Yale Center of Alcohol Studies established two public clinics, one in Hartford and one in New Haven. These were the Yale Plan Clinics, the first public clinics devoted to the treatment of alcoholism. These clinics, with modest staff and facilities, demonstrated the feasibility of treating the alcoholic effectively on a relatively inexpensive outpatient basis. In 1946, a part-time psychologist was added to the staff of psychiatrists, physicians and social workers, primarily for psychodiagnostic testing and to act as research consultant as well. There were several reasons why a psychologist's services were thought necessary. First, there were many patients maintaining contact with the clinic for prolonged periods through therapeutic interviews, and psychological tests would help in the understanding of patients. Second, tests would help evaluate the patient's assets, thus contributing toward screening. Third, there were the patients who came for a short-term but intensive diagnostic analysis, and the test report would in many cases be part of the diagnosis and recommendations. Finally, it was felt that the psychologist, with research training, had much to contribute in evaluating the effectiveness of the clinic program.

The public has become increasingly aware of the problems of mental illness in recent years and public attitudes are probably changing. This has been fostered to a large extent by the mass media of entertainment, by newspaper and magazine articles and by recent trends in literature. It has also been given impetus by the problems of the psychiatric casualties of World War II. It is recognized, for example, that it may be possible to rehabilitate and restore to useful citizenship the "town drunk." While many myths about alcoholism remain, people begin to know that alcoholism touches upon many respectable lives.

It is only in the last decade that the new public health approach toward the problems of alcoholism has developed. Traditionally, only the prisons and hospitals have dealt with the alcoholic, but new government-sponsored programs of education and treatment have begun. In 1945, the Connecticut Commission on Alcoholism was established. In setting up this Commission, the Connecticut State legislature acknowledged alcoholism as an illness and a public health problem. It was the first time a major government agency approached the problem of alcoholism with a broad rehabilitation program.

The funds of the Connecticut Commission on Alcoholism are derived from a percentage of the revenue which the State Liquor Control Commission receives as fees for permits. The Commission's responsibilities include the following:

. . . . to study the problem of alcoholism, including methods and facilities available for the care, custody, detention, treatment, employment and rehabilitation of persons addicted to the intemperate use of spirituous or intoxicating liquors.

. . . . to promote meetings for the discussion of problems confronting clinics and agencies engaged in the treatment and rehabilitation of alcoholics.

. . . . to disseminate information on the subject of alcoholism for the assistance and guidance of residents and courts of the state . . . [12, p. 1061].

With outpatient clinics of the Connecticut Commission on Alcoholism operating in New Haven and Hartford, the Yale Plan Clinic continued as a research and treatment unit of the Yale Center of Alcohol Studies. The Connecticut Commission now operates five full-time outpatient clinics (Hartford, New Haven, Bridgeport, Waterbury and Stamford), one part-time outpatient clinic (Niantic State Farm for Women) and a 50-bed specialized hospital for alcoholics, the Blue Hills Hospital in Hartford, the first of its kind in the United States. The services of part-time clinical psychologists are utilized in all Connecticut Commission on Alcoholism facilities, such services being sought for largely the same reasons as were true with the Yale Plan Clinics. Psychologists have been employed full time at the hospital, but budget considerations at the moment allow only part-time employment.

Since 1945, forty states and the District of Columbia have passed laws dealing with alcoholism as a public health problem. In twenty-two of these states, an agency, either newly and independently established or organized within an existing department, has been set up to deal with the problems of rehabilitation, research and programs of public education. In many of these states, outpatient clinics have already been established. Seven of the states include a clinical psychologist as part of the clinic team. In addition, many cities have organized local programs of their own and many of these include psychological services.

A brief survey was conducted by the writer of psychologists' services in clinics for alcoholics. Four state clinics and four city clinics participated in this survey. Although this is a small number of clinics from which to draw any conclusions, there are still so few agencies of this kind in the country, one may assume that these are typical enough. The results of the survey are included in the next section.

PRESENT STATUS AND USE OF CLINICAL PSYCHOLOGY

The Connecticut Commission on Alcoholism employs, at the moment, three psychologists and one of them, the writer, will describe her work in the typical New Haven outpatient clinic. The clinic team varies somewhat from clinic to clinic in Connecticut. At the New Haven clinic, there are two psychiatric social workers (full time), a psychiatrist (part time), an internist (part time), a psychologist (part time), and two secretaries. Patients attend the clinic on a voluntary basis. A social history is taken, a medical examination administered, and a psychiatric evaluation made. The patient may be referred to the psychologist for testing. The duration of contact with the clinic is extremely variable. There are those patients who come only once or twice and those who have maintained contact with the clinic for several years.

Of the eight government-sponsored outpatient clinics included in the survey, all include psychiatrists on their staffs although psychiatrists are full time in only one clinic. Three clinics employ part-time psychologists, and five clinics employ full-time psychologists. Social workers are employed in six of the eight clinics, an internist in four, and public health nurses, a recreation director, and a chaplain in one clinic each.

DIAGNOSTIC TESTING

Connecticut Commission on Alcoholism. The agreement between psychologist and the Connecticut Commission involves a specified diagnostic testing load, i.e., a certain number of patients to be tested monthly. With the limited financial resources involved and the employment of part-time psychologists, it is primarily the research and therapy role of the psychologist which is sacrificed. The history of clinical psychology and the training of clinical psychologists has placed major emphasis on testing, and psychologists are undoubtedly sought by clinics primarily as professional specialists in diagnostic testing.

About 10 per cent of all patients who contact the New Haven clinic are tested. Patients are usually referred by the psychiatrist or psychiatric social worker for differential diagnosis and personality diagnosis, although they are also referred occasionally for establishment of intellectual level or vocational guidance suggestions. *Differential diagnosis* is here taken to include problems such as the presence or absence of psychotic trends, organic deterioration, neurotic symptoms, etc. *Personality diagnosis* involves a description of the traits and attitudes of the patient as seen through test performance and interview and an attempt to present a dynamic exposition of the etiology and interrelationships of the personality traits. The written psychological report often contains recommendations about psychotherapy and about planning for the alcoholic patient's future. Inevitably involved in personality diagnosis is an evaluation of the patient's major assets and liabilities and his accessibility to treatment. Patients previously tested are sometimes retested after a period of therapeutic interviews and evaluations of progress or lack of progress are made.

The procedure of the clinic with new patients is a very flexible one which is adjusted to his needs. Except under unusual circumstances, e.g., the involvement of a court or another social agency, the patient is referred to the psychologist only after several weeks or even several months of contact. This serves two purposes: the patient has demonstrated interest in maintaining contact with the clinic, and he has also had the opportunity to become familiar with the clinic and its personnel. Patients are always prepared for the test appointment by the psychiatrist or psychiatric social workers so that they come, in most instances, without undue anxiety. The test session is usually held to a two-hour maximum: the time limit is imposed because of the limited stress tolerance observed so frequently among alcoholics. The patient is often seen more than once by the psychologist.

Tests most often utilized in the order of frequency of use are: the Rorschach test, a Sentence Completion test (worked out from Rotter's test by the writer specifically for alcoholism clinics), Thematic Apperception Test (a short form which includes ten pictures and which may be given in a single session), drawings of a man and woman and the Wechsler-Bellevue Intelligence Scale. The Bender Visual Motor Gestalt Test, the Wechsler Memory Scale, and an occupational interest inventory are also occasionally used.

Although not strictly a test technique, the interview is frequently a very considerable source of information. In establishing rapport with the patient, a few questions may be asked about the patient's schooling, occupation and marital status, and the patient's replies frequently lead to further discussion. In their search for the hidden, psychologists need not lose sight of the obvious.

The psychologist submits written reports and participates actively in case conferences. The recommendations of the psychologist carry weight in planning for the patient. The maximum use of psychological reports is usually made when the other members of the clinic team are fully aware of the methods and purposes of the psychologist.

Survey. In the three clinics which utilize only the part-time services of a psychologist, from three to six patients are seen each month for testing. There is tremendous variability in the other five clinics which employ full-time psychologists, depending on the proportion of time devoted to psychotherapy, the amount of time allocated to testing other patients besides alcoholics, etc. In only two instances are all clinic alcoholic patients seen for testing. Where patients are referred to the psychologist by the clinic staff, the major reason for referral is diagnostic, in most instances involving dynamic description to be utilized in therapy. Evaluation of prognosis is another important reason for referral. "Clues to deterioration and/or organicity" is specifically mentioned by one clinic and "research" by another clinic as reason for referral.

The basic test battery, i.e., the tests in use at all clinics in the survey, is: the Rorschach test, drawings, Thematic Apperception Test, and Wechsler-Bellevue Intelligence Scale. A majority of clinics also use the Bender Visual Motor Gestalt Test and a Sentence Completion test.

All psychologists in the survey submit written reports, many giving oral reports as well. All participate in case conferences. Seven agreed that test results were utilized in planning for the patient and one added a wry note, "Sometimes."

THERAPY

Connecticut Commission on Alcoholism. At outpatient clinics and at the Connecticut Commission's Blue Hills Hospital for alcoholics, psychologists have done psychotherapy, both group and individual. The psychologists who have worked on a full-time basis for the Commission have included therapy in their services. Clinical psychologists on the Commission staff who wish to undertake therapy are encouraged to do so by the medical and administrative personnel. However, psychologists are employed primarily for the services they render in diagnostic testing and for those psychologists employed on a part-time basis (at the moment, all three working for the Connecticut Commission), there is rarely enough time for work in therapy.

Survey. As one might expect, it is in the five clinics where psychologists are employed full time that the psychologist's services include therapy. In these five clinics, psychologists are engaged in individual interview therapy, and in most cases they participate in group therapy projects as well. All report supervision by the clinic psychiatrist; the nature and extent of this supervision is not specified, although one psychologist mentioned "occasional conferences."

The variability from one clinic to the next as to the amount of time devoted to therapy is very marked. One psychologist reports that he is devoting one hour a week to a patient. A clinic employing two psychologists reports that they spend 75 per cent of their time in therapy.

None of these reports is final because the clinics are so new and the psychologists so recently employed. There is still a good deal of trial and error about the psychologist's service. As one psychologist put it in describing his agency, "[It] . . . is going through some growing pains."

TEACHING

Since 1943, the Yale Center of Alcohol Studies has conducted the Yale Summer School of Alcohol Studies. Approximately one hundred sixty students attend each year, drawn from such fields as social work, medicine, law, psychology, the clergy, and education. The Summer School teaching staff consists of personnel from the Yale Center of Alcohol Studies, the

Connecticut Commission on Alcoholism, and specialists from other agencies and institutions. It focuses its teaching on the role of alcohol in our society and the problems related to its use and abuse. The writer participates in seminars dealing with the clinical approach, the personality problems and treatment of the alcoholic patient, research problems, case presentations, etc.

Survey. In the eight clinics surveyed, three report that the psychologist employed has university affiliation. In one instance, this comes with the clinic appointment; in the other two instances, such affiliation is independent of the clinical appointment. All but one of the psychologists report occasional lectures to medical students, welfare conferences, student nurses, and Parent Teachers Association groups.

RESEARCH

Psychologists' interest in alcohol research in the past has been primarily in problems like reaction time and work efficiency. The development of two relatively new lines of research is only recent: the experimental study of the relationship of alcohol to more complex behavior such as conflict (3, 8) and clinical studies of alcoholics' personalities (2, 5). Considering how recent is the growth of interest in the problem of alcoholism, the lack of psychological research to date is hardly surprising. One may expect that with the expansion of clinical centers for treatment will come further study.

At the Connecticut Commission on Alcoholism, research projects in progress and planned for the future by staff psychologists include: a comparison of projective test performance of alcoholics and a matched group of normal drinkers, a study of alcoholic women in outpatient clinics and state farms, a content analysis of Rorschach records, and a study of the integration of Rorschach and Thematic Apperception Test data.

Survey. Research projects completed to date are few. Some drug studies, e.g., evaluations of antabuse treatment, are reported. There are a few reports of psychological test results with alcoholics and a few evaluations of therapy techniques, e.g., one study on psychodrama. Research in progress is primarily of a practical sort, including: reviews of cases, evaluation of treatment, drug studies, psychological test investigations, studies of prison patients, and studies of voluntary and committed patients. A few psychologists expressed interest in basic problems of human behavior and personality, but this survey included only service clinics and their research necessarily is related to the practical problems at hand. If these results are typical of clinics in general, it speaks well for the training of psychologists. Seven of the eight clinics in the survey reported research projects completed, in progress or planned. There is no question but that psychologists are trained to ask questions and seek answers.

FUTURE OUTLOOK

It is questionable whether one can evaluate the trends of alcoholism clinics served by psychologists at this time because clinics for alcoholics are a new and recent development. With a few exceptions in the eight clinics surveyed, psychologists were sought primarily to do diagnostic testing.

The problems of testing in clinics for alcoholics are probably similar to what they are in other clinics. There are many tests and it seems at times as though some psychologists are using a barrage rather than a battery. The tests used by all or most clinics include the Rorschach test, Thematic Apperception Test, the Wechsler-Bellevue Intelligence Scale, drawings, the Bender Visual Motor Gestalt Test, and Sentence Completion tests. The trend seems, therefore, toward using tests which have demonstrated their clinical usefulness and toward using, in addition, newer techniques which are brief and relatively simple to administer and yet yield valuable information about the patient. There are many other helpful tests available, and one may assume that the selection of tests appropriate for a given patient is made with discrimination.

Where psychologists work in clinics for alcoholics on a full-time basis, they do therapy. Regardless of how little or large a proportion of time is spent in therapy, the principle is established and therapy is part of the psychologist's work. Research, too, is something psychologists undertake as part of their job. The value of the research done will vary, of course, but it seems to be true that psychologists consider research part of their responsibility in a clinic.

Clinics for alcoholics have developed only in the last decade. With growing interest in this problem we may expect a growing number of such clinics in the future. As testers, therapists, and research investigators, psychologists will be needed in these clinics.

REFERENCES

1. Bacon, S. D. *The administration of alcoholism rehabilitation programs.* New Haven: Hillhouse Press, 1949.
2. Billig, O. and Sullivan, D. J. Personality structure and prognosis of alcohol addiction: a Rorschach study. *Quart. J. Stud. Alc.,* 1943, 3, 554-573.
3. Conger, J. J. The effects of alcohol on conflict behavior in the albino rat. *Quart. J. Stud. Alc.,* 1951, 12, 1-29.
4. Haggard, H. W. and Jellinek, E. M. *Alcohol explored.* New York: Doubleday Doran, 1942.
5. Halpern, F. Studies of compulsive drinkers: psychological test results. *Quart. J. Stud. Alc.,* 1946, 6, 468-479.
6. Jellinek, E. M. (Ed.) *Alcohol addiction and chronic alcoholism.* New Haven: Yale Univer. Press, 1942.

7. Lolli, G. On "therapeutic" success in alcoholism. *Quart. J. Stud. Alc.*, 1953, 14, 238-246.
8. Masserman, J. H. and Yum, K. S. An analysis of the influence of alcohol on experimental neuroses in cats. *Psychosom. Med.*, 1946, 8, 36-52.
9. McCarthy, R. G. and Douglass, E. M. *Alcohol and social responsibility*. New York: Crowell, 1949.
10. Rotter, J. B. and Willerman, B. The incomplete sentences test as a method of studying personality. *J. consult. Psychol.*, 1947, 11, 43-48.
11. Alcoholism, 1941-1951: A survey of activities in research, education and therapy. *Quart. J. Stud. Alc.*, 1952, 13, 421-511.
12. *General Statutes of Connecticut* (1949 Rev., Vol. I). Hartford, Conn.: State of Connecticut, 1949.
13. *The Yale Center of Alcohol Studies*. Laboratory of Applied Physiology. Yale University, New Haven, Connecticut.

XVII.

THE CLINICAL PSYCHOLOGIST IN A
STUDENT COUNSELING BUREAU

WILLIAM M. GILBERT

There are three trends which seem to have converged to produce the ever-increasing use of clinical psychologists in student counseling agencies. (The distinction which, for some purposes, is now made between clinical and counseling psychologists is not pertinent, either for the work which psychologists do in a student counseling service such as that which will be described, or for the historical development of the use of psychologists in such services. Consequently the terms clinical psychologist and counseling psychologist will be used interchangeably with no distinction implied.) One of these is represented by the whole testing movement and the concomitant professionalization in providing testing and counseling services for persons with educational and vocational problems. The second trend is concerned with a change in general educational philosophy and methodology itself, away from the almost complete emphasis on the intellectualistic approach to education, which was common in the nineteenth century, to a broader personalistic approach. This approach took into account not simply traditional academic subject matter, but also included some acceptance on the part of colleges and universities of the responsibility for producing not simply scholars, but well-adjusted scholars who would also contribute effectively to society as citizens. The third trend relates to an increasing tendency for more psychologists to become interested in and devote more time to both research and treatment of motivational and emotional problems. This, of course, was accompanied by a still growing recognition on the part of psychologists of the practical and theoretical contributions of Freud and his followers and in fact the whole psychiatric movement as it related to psychologically, rather than organically caused emotional and behavior disorders.

The actual history of student counseling is part of the larger story: the development and expansion of student personnel programs. Williamson et al. (2) give a panoramic account of the growth and development in student personnel work. The vitality and the complexity of this whole movement make it ill-advised to offer any brief historical summary.

According to Cowley (1), the first student counselor came into being in 1889 at Johns Hopkins when Professor E. H. Griffin was appointed "chief of advisers," and soon became known as dean. Personnel deans were appointed at other universities in the 1890's, and in 1899 President Harper of Chicago gave further impetus to the trend. He emphasized the need for studying the student himself as an aid to assisting him in his educational training. This early form of counseling by faculty advisors or deans was the beginning of today's student counseling programs. However, there is a very considerable evolution from the first informal services of these counselors to the present specialized and organized services of student counseling bureaus. Rather than attempt to trace this evolution here it would be more pertinent to describe the functioning of one such student counseling bureau.

STUDENT COUNSELING AT THE UNIVERSITY OF ILLINOIS

Student counseling began in 1938 at the University of Illinois in the organization of a student counseling service, which at that time was called the Personnel Bureau. It is noteworthy and interesting that the stimulus for the organization of such a service came not from psychologists, as one might expect, but from a professor of English, Harris F. Fletcher, a Milton scholar, who had been charged with the responsibility of serving as advisor to a group of low scholarship students. It was at his suggestion that a committee was appointed to study the general problem, and that E. G. Williamson of Minnesota was invited to serve as a consultant to the committee and to recommend the kind of program which seemed best suited to the needs of this particular university. The structure of the bureau he suggested was partly centralized, partly decentralized. Reflecting this suggestion, the first budget of the counseling service included a director with responsibility for the general administration of the bureau, an assistant director who was a psychologist and responsible for the technical direction of the bureau's activities, a psychometrist, a personnel assistant, a receptionist-stenographer, and ten part-time faculty counselors. It is noteworthy that the original director of the bureau was not himself a professionally trained psychologist or counselor. The first director, H. W. Bailey, was a mathematician who had served successfully on a number of university committees, and who was well known and well respected by the faculty at large.

In addition to his supervision of the technical aspects of the bureau's services one of the prescribed functions of the assistant director was that of supplying counseling services for students with emotional and personality problems. Thus, this function of the bureau was recognized from the very outset. In 1940, an additional person, the present writer, was employed by the bureau to carry on what were designated as clinical counseling functions. The year prior to this the assistant director of the bureau had been aided in his work by the one-day-a-week services of a psychiatrist who came down to the campus from our medical college in Chicago. It apparently was recognized that this service could be little more than diagnostic in nature, and that additional personnel would be required to carry on the counseling needed by the emotionally disturbed students who came to the bureau for help.

Originally the student counseling service was organized as an agency of the college of Liberal Arts and Sciences. The batteries of tests, the results of which were intended for use in counseling, were administered at first to Liberal Arts and Sciences students alone. However, the counseling services of the bureau were available to students from other colleges. It soon became evident that students from other colleges were making a great deal of use of bureau services. Consequently, in 1942, the counseling bureau was made an all-university agency serving all colleges, and responsible to the Provost of the University, who functions essentially as a vice-president in charge of the academic faculty and the academic program generally.

It is believed that this alliance with the faculty of the university rather than with the university officers in charge of housing, social, and extracurricular functions of the university, has contributed both to a greater acceptance of the bureau's services by the faculty at large, and to a closer liaison with the department of psychology.

A rough indication of the growth of the bureau's psychological services is shown by figures representing the number of new clients who had never before made use of bureau services, for a few representative years. Naturally this number fluctuated to some extent with student enrollment, and during the past five years the total number of clients has exceeded the number of new clients by some four to seven hundred. In 1938-1939, the year the bureau was first put into operation, there were 910 students who made use of its services. It must be remembered that at this time the bureau was simply an agency within the college of Liberal Arts and Sciences. By 1940-1941, the number of new clients had increased to 1164. In 1942-1943, the year the bureau became an all-university service, this number was 1247. By 1945-1946, it had increased to 2092. In 1949-1950, the number was 2604, and during the past year, it was 2760 new clients. The total number of students and staff members who made use of bureau services this past year was 3422.

As indicated previously, the student counseling bureau is directly responsible to the office of the Provost, and is an all-university agency which serves both students and staff members. The bureau has an advisory committee consisting of representatives from all of the schools and colleges in the university. The relationship of the student counseling bureau to other offices and agencies of the university, including other student personnel agencies, is a purely co-operative one.

The staff of the bureau may be considered as being divided into six groups: the central administrative and clinical staff, the psychometric staff, faculty counselors, the interns, the graduate assistants, and the receptionist, stenographic, and clerical staff. In addition to the counselors who were provided for in the budget of the student counseling bureau, all of the advanced graduate students in the clinical and counseling curriculum of the psychology department fulfill part of their practicum requirement by doing counseling and psychotherapy in the student counseling bureau under close supervision. During the past year there were ten students in this course, each of whom counseled an average of two hours per week throughout the year, except for the first few months of the fall semester.

The central administrative and clinical staff is made up completely of clinical and counseling psychologists. The director and associate director are psychologists; in addition there are seven full-time, and three half-time clinical counselors. The psychometric staff consists of the chief psychometrist, who is also included in the number of clinical counselors listed above; two assistant psychometrists; and four full-time nonacademic clerical workers who carry titles as Jr. Personnel Assistants. The next group, the faculty counselors, consists of seven persons who devote one fourth of their time to bureau services. The fourth group of staff members consists of two half-time interns who are paid from the bureau budget, and one half-time intern who is serving on a United States Public Health Service fellowship. The next division of our staff consists of three half-time graduate assistants and one full-time graduate assistant. The sixth group of staff members consists of two full-time persons working in the reception office, and two full-time persons in the secretarial and stenographic office.

In this total staff there are nineteen different persons who could be classified as clinical and counseling psychologists. Six of these persons have their Ph.D.'s in Psychology. One of them, the director, is a diplomate in counseling, and the associate director, a diplomate in clinical. Two other counselors are also diplomates in counseling. The remainder of the nineteen persons we have designated as clinical psychologists have all obtained at least their Master's degrees, except for two of the half-time assistants.

The Work of the Clinical Psychologists

The primary responsibility of the student counseling bureau is to supply psychological testing, counseling, and psychotherapeutic services to the students and academic staff members of the university. Prospective students and recent graduates are also eligible for these services free of charge, except that extensive psychotherapeutic counseling cannot be extended to them. The services of the bureau are also available to private individuals, on request, for a designated fee. Except for the research assistants, all of the psychologists on the staff carry out counseling and psychotherapeutic services as a primary responsibility. This is as true of the director of the bureau, of the psychometrist, of the staff member in charge of research, and of the psychologist who supervises the study habits and developmental reading services as it is of other staff members with fewer but not less important responsibilities. In addition to the primary responsibilities of counseling and psychotherapeutic services, the senior members of the staff who have their Ph.D.'s hold rank in the psychology department and regularly teach one course per semester. As another secondary responsibility, the bureau as a whole and all of the staff members also recognize their research responsibilities. Finally, many of the psychologists carry a part of the necessary administrative work in the bureau. All members of the staff participate in major policy decisions, and in the execution of these policies.

The testing program, which the bureau conducts, is simply an adjunct to its general counseling services. All incoming freshmen are required by the executive committees of the various colleges to take a five- to six-hour battery of tests during freshman week, unless they have taken these tests and received counseling during the preceding summer. The bureau does specifically invite all students whose applications to the university are accepted sufficiently early to make use of this special summer counseling and testing program. About six to eight hundred students, or one fourth of the freshman class, regularly do make use of these special services. Similarly, after school has started in the fall, notice is given to transfer students of special testing services. The results of tests administered in these programs are put on IBM cards, norms are constructed, and reports of scores are made available to appropriate academic deans, and of course to the members of the bureau's counseling staff. The tests are administered and scored in this way as an efficiency measure. In addition to these tests which are administered in a group, counselors frequently assign other tests after counseling has been initiated in accordance with the needs of the individual student. In order to make this description of the testing functions of the bureau reasonably complete, it should be stated that the bureau also functions as a testing center for some ten regional, state, or national testing programs.

All of this testing is under the supervision of a psychologist. The individual tests such as Rorschach, T.A.T., Wechsler and the like are directly administered, scored and tentatively interpreted by a psychologist, one of the two assistant psychometrists. The common group tests are directly administered by the other assistant psychometrist or by one of the personnel assistants, all of whom are carefully trained and supervised by the psychometrist. For the scoring and processing of the large numbers of tests administered to all freshmen, additional temporary clerical help is obtained.

Counseling and psychotherapeutic services. From one half to two thirds of the counseling psychologist's time is devoted to actual counseling and psychotherapy with students and staff members. The proportion of time will vary somewhat from one psychologist to another, and from one time of year to another. As noted before, the bureau from its very inception accepted the responsibility of providing psychotherapeutic help for students with personality and emotional problems. The amount of work the psychologists in the bureau have done in this area has also undoubtedly been influenced by the fact that for the first eight years of its existence the bureau did not have easy access to psychiatric services. The medical school of the university is located 150 miles away from the university proper, and while the Illinois Neuropsychiatric Institute would in emergencies make its services available to students, it was only when extreme conditions presented themselves that the bureau felt justified in requesting their services, and in making the necessary arrangements. Even after psychiatry was represented by the appointment of one person in the Health Service, it was still necessary that the psychologists in the bureau carry on the majority of the work with emotionally disturbed individuals. The amount of psychotherapeutic work regularly done by bureau counselors has been not simply a function of the absence of or the smallness of the psychiatric staff; it has also been a function of the interest and conviction of the psychologists who have worked in the bureau.

This recognition of the motivational and emotional aspects of counseling has led to a comprehensive type of service which makes no distinction between counseling and psychotherapy, or between counseling psychologists and clinical psychologists. All of the psychologists on the Bureau staff work with students who have educational, vocational, or emotional problems. When no artificial fractionating of these problems is made, it has been found that most students have an interwoven combination of them. Significant educational and vocational difficulties usually involve strong motivational conflicts or conflicts in values which are of the same kind and order as those found in individuals whose symptoms are more conventionally clinical in nature. Thus it has become almost an operating principle that good "counseling" usually involves "psychotherapy" and good "psychotherapy" usually involves "counseling." The corollary, of course, is the desirability of some more comprehensive term to describe the work of these clinical-counseling psychologists such as psychotherapeutic or—if we wish to avoid the disputedly inherited medical terminology—psychological counseling.

In order to present a somewhat more concrete picture of the case load which the psychologists in the bureau handle, it may be informative to describe the range of cases briefly and to indicate the number of counseling interviews provided. The kinds of cases range from those of students who need simple reassurance that they have made a wise decision in deciding to come to college and in selecting the particular course of study they chose to pursue, for example, to students who nosologically could be classified as acute neurotics or prepsychotics, but who are sufficiently in contact with reality not to need hospitalization and who can do passing course work. When there is any indication of the need for medical consultation a liaison with a physician is established. This physician may be a general practitioner or a member of any of the medical specialties, including psychiatry. Where there seems to be a real suicidal risk, or homicidal risk, consultation with other professional persons is always invoked. With respect to the number of interviews provided for any given student there is no artificial administrative limitation.

For the year 1951-1952, a survey was made of the clients who made use of counseling services and the number of interviews devoted to each client. The range of number of interviews for the year was from one to eighty-five per student. Of the total number of clients, 91 per cent received from one to five interviews each, and 54 per cent of the total estimated hours spent in counseling were devoted to this group of clients. Seven per cent of the total group of clients received from six to thirty interviews which occupied 36 per cent of the total hours devoted to counseling. Two percent of the group received from thirty-one to eighty-two hours of counseling during the year, accounting for 10 per cent of the total time given to clients in counseling. Considering these totals together, we find that 9 per cent of the total number of clients had from six to eighty-five interviews each, and that 46 per cent of the total counseling time was devoted to this group. There are no accurate figures indicating the proportion of these clients with the greater number of interviews who were seen by the psychologists on the central staff. A rough estimate would be that from 75 per cent to 85 per cent of the clients with more than five interviews were seen by psychologists on the central staff.

There are two final characteristics of the counseling services provided by the psychologists in the bureau which seem to deserve special mention. One of these is that the counseling services are provided for staff members as well as for students, and—much more significantly—that staff members actually make use of the services. The records of the bureau show that during the past year, 150 of the bureau clients (and many of these would have been relatively long-term clients) were persons who had teaching or other staff appointments. It is not difficult to justify the expenditure of time with such individuals since they presumably influence large numbers of students, and since presumably their other research and service output would be hindered by a significant psychological problem.

The other characteristic of bureau services which may be of interest is that the psychologists on the staff are of many different theoretical and therapeutic orientations without any one of them being a disciple or emotional convert to his own preferred orientation. One staff member is definitely somewhere between the neo-Freudians and orthodox Freudians in his approach. Another is quite neo-Freudian in the Sullivan tradition. Several of the counselors are quite Rogerian in their approach. One of the counselors represents a modified Adlerian approach. Some of the advanced graduate students who counseled in the bureau have been Mowrerian in their orientation. A number of other members of the staff are frankly eclectic.

Psychodiagnostic services. While about 80 per cent of the bureau's clients are self-referred or come at the casual suggestion of a friend or instructor, the remaining 20 per cent of bureau clients are referred, either by the security officer, who in effect is the university's executive disciplinary officer operating under the direction of the subcommittee on student discipline, by the College of Education, which is interested that no teacher trainees who are psychologically unfit for teaching services are approved, by the various academic deans, by the deans of men or women, or by the speech clinic. Where a student is formally referred by one of these agencies, it is made clear to the student, both by the referring person and by the counselor, that a diagnostic report with recommendations will be sent back to the referring agencies if such has been requested. If psychologists are convinced, as they usually claim they are, that administrative action with respect to individuals should not be taken unless there is as complete a knowledge as possible of the psychological factors involved, then it becomes necessary either to supply such services through a separate agency, or through an agency like the Student Counseling Bureau. With ourselves, we have long debated the question as to whether a separate service such as that which exists at the University of Minnesota, or a service which is carried on by the counseling bureau is more preferable. Obviously our decision has been that, in our situation at least, it is preferable for the bureau itself to supply these services.

The bureau practice of making students aware that a report will be made and often of advising them in a general way of the nature of the report, seems to have prevented the development of any feeling among the student body that bureau services might not be confidential. The bureau, again, from its inception has carefully maintained complete confidentiality of its records, and this confidentiality has been respected by the higher university administration. Only in those instances where an individual can be considered as not being legally responsible for his actions or where there is clear and imminent danger of suicide or homicide, or where there is a clear and imminent threat to the security of the nation will the bureau take administrative action without permission of the client. In such instances there is a conviction that we are not really violating a confidence but are simply carrying out our general professional responsibilities. The publication of the American Psychological Association code of ethics has been a significant source of support and comfort since it has appeared and on at least one occasion a resort to this code was necessary.

Diagnosis of a clinical sort is also involved in individual counseling relationships. Generally speaking there is not a formal diagnostic workup before the student sees a counselor. However, after counseling has been initiated there is no hesitancy in then resorting to as much formal diagnosis as seems helpful. Almost always in cases of complex and serious emotional problems the Rorschach and T.A.T. are administered. Additional personality or other tests are also assigned. This material is considered in conjunction with that obtained in the early interviews. Often no formal report is ever made to the client, but account is taken of the total clinical picture in working with him.

Instructional and training services. It was mentioned previously that all the senior counselors on the staff of the bureau, that is those who have their Ph.D.'s, also hold rank in psychology and teach at least one course per semester in that department. This condition too, has existed since the early beginnings of the bureau. The first assistant director taught an advanced undergraduate and graduate course in student personnel work, one of the first clinical type courses offered by the department. Other psychologists as they were added to the staff later, taught courses in accordance with the needs of the psychology department.

For the past several years, the clinical and counseling programs of the psychology department have been unified. Persons who intend to function as clinical psychologists, and those who intend to function as counseling psychologists take exactly the same program, since careful consideration led to the conclusion that there was no basic difference in the fundamental knowledge or in the tools and techniques which both groups needed to know. The specific manner in which this integration works out at the advanced practicum level is of special interest. It is to this course that three of the psychologists on the staff of the bureau contribute their teaching services. The students in the course receive part of their practicum training and supervision in the psychological clinic, where their work is primarily with children. They receive part of it in the student counseling bureau where their work is, of course, with university students, and part of it through visits to a number of the mental hospitals throughout the state. Those students who are in the Veterans Administration clinical program need not participate in this last type of experience, since they receive it in the veterans' hospital.

Of the other two members of the counseling bureau's staff who teach, one has been teaching an introductory course in psychology in the general division of liberal arts, the other a course in the psychology of adjustment.

The psychologists on the bureau staff contribute actively to the regular staff meetings of the bureau which serve as a continued inservice training program for all staff members. In addition, the staff psychologists contribute to the training program for the graduate assistants in the men's and women's dormitories. Here too, a good working relationship with the persons in charge of these programs has been developed.

The various talks which the bureau's counselors are asked to give to many university and college groups, both student and faculty, can also be looked up as a type of teaching and training. Here, we are primarily concerned with giving these groups an understanding of the bureau's work, but also with helping contribute to their general understanding of the psychological aspects of teaching and of human nature in general. Similar discussions are often given over the university radio station. Here, the discussions are often directed to parents so that they may have a better understanding of the university generally, of the counseling services which are available, and of their own children who are, or who may become students of the university.

On the average these teaching and training services probably occupy from one fourth to one third of the time of the senior counselors on the staff of the counseling bureau.

Research. The clinical and counseling psychologists are encouraged to engage in research, but because of the primary service responsibilities of the bureau, there is not the same pressure for producing a large volume of research as there ordinarily is in a nonservice department. This fortunately is a situation that has been practically recognized both by the university administration generally, and by the Department of Psychology. Advancements in salary and in rank have been made regularly, primarily on the basis of the psychologist's contribution in the service and in the teaching areas.

A great deal of the research done in the bureau during the earlier years of its development, was of necessity devoted to problems that were directly related to the service program of the bureau. However, this has not always been the case, and various members of the bureau staff have from time to time engaged in research of a broader and more fundamental nature, and have made significant contributions. During the past several years, a number of individual research projects have been started, as have a number of co-operative group projects. One of these group projects has concerned itself with the prediction of success in the field of architecture. This program has included the development of a number of tests, at least one of which promises to be useful. In addition to this a number of more fundamental problems are involved in the design and in the handling of the data. This particular project is being done in co-operation with the bureau of educational research. Another project in which practically all members of the bureau staff have actively participated, in one way or another, has been concerned with an attempt to predict counselor effectiveness, and to measure the effect of training on such effectiveness. Plans are now underway for another joint project with the psychology department which will involve attempting to develop the methods for providing answers to a number of fundamental questions in therapy, with respect to diagnosis, the relationship between client and therapist, the effectiveness of different therapeutic approaches, and the outcomes of therapy with different types of clients.

In addition to these types of research which either are being done by individual members of the counseling bureau's psychological staff, or by groups of them, the bureau as an agency has co-operated with individuals from different departments and colleges within the university, by administering and scoring experimental tests of various sorts, by making its non-confidential files available to such persons, and by supplying general consulting services.

THE FUTURE OF CLINICAL PSYCHOLOGY IN STUDENT COUNSELING WORK

There does seem to be a general trend in counseling services throughout the country to offer more long-term counseling and psychotherapeutic services. This trend will probably continue. It is becoming increasingly evident that many problems which appear to be simple and superficial at first, including many educational and vocational problems, involve deeper and more complex motivational and emotional conditions which cannot be effectively altered in a few interviews. The time seems to be passing when psychologists and other counselors are satisfied with making a diagnostic assessment of an individual, informing him of the results of this assessment, and expecting him by some miraculous means to make the decisions, to make the personality changes, and to solve the conflicts which are implied by the assessment. One of the reasons for this is probably a very practical one. Unless longer-term counseling is supplied in accordance with any need for basic changes in personality reorganization, clients keep coming back with problems which seem to them new, but which basically are of the same order; that is, they keep coming back provided they have received even a little of what they needed in their earlier contacts.

Another equally important trend relates to a shift in viewpoint of psychologists whose orientation has been narrowly clinical in the sense of desiring to work only with persons with classical neurotic or psychotic symptoms often in a hospital setting. Many such clinical psychologists are beginning to find that counseling with students whose symptoms are educational or vocational in nature presents just as great a challenge and is often even more rewarding.

Along with the trend toward longer-term counseling there also seems to be an increasing recognition of both the possibility and need for more effective, efficient, and less time-consuming psychotherapeutic procedures than those used, for example, by classical analysts. If through the present great surge in experimentation and research concerning both diagnosis and therapy, this greater effectiveness and efficiency is attained, it seems probable that the demand for therapy will increase.

The present emphasis on both fundamental and applied research in diagnosis and therapy seems likely to continue for a long time. The need for improvements is so great and our present scientific knowledge so meager when we are dealing with individuals that today we are relying mainly on convictions and faith of a prescientific sort. Student counseling centers, associated as they are with colleges and universities, provide a natural setting for the necesary psychological research.

The large increase in university enrollment predicted for the late 50's and 60's will in itself require a considerable expansion of existing agencies simply in order to maintain the present availability and quality of service.

It thus appears that there are a number of trends and conditions which will increase the need for broadly trained psychologists who combine clinical and counseling functions. Whether university presidents and other responsible administrators recognize this need will depend to a large measure on psychologists themselves.

REFERENCES

1. Cowley, W. H. Some history and a venture in prophecy. In Williamson, E. G. (Ed.), *Trends in student personnel work*. Minneapolis, Minn.: Univer. of Minnesota Press, 1949, 12-27.
2. Williamson, E. G. (Ed.) *Trends in student personnel work*. Minneapolis, Minn.: Univer. of Minnesota Press, 1949.

XVIII.

INDUSTRIAL EMPLOYEE COUNSELING

M. E. STEINER

Counseling, conducted by the professionally trained psychologist, is a comparatively new activity in industry. The clinical psychologist, particularly well suited to the task of helping the employee to evaluate his mental and emotional assets, to plan realistic goals and to resolve his problems, must still bow to the industrial psychologist who is primarily concerned (and rightfully so) with the introduction of effective employee selection methods. While the industrialist may be enthusiastic about better selection procedures, he is not yet convinced that the maladjusted employee is his responsibility. The fact that psychologists, whether applied, clinical, or otherwise, are being brought into industry, however, if only in small numbers, is encouraging, for it indicates that industrialists believe psychologically trained persons can make worth-while contributions to complex industrial living.

HISTORICAL DEVELOPMENT

EARLY TRENDS

The giving of advice or imparting of information to an employee by his employer—now referred to as the "directive" method of counseling—is an old practice. In the small shop of early America where the relationship between employer and employee was a close one, the employee felt free to discuss even the most intimate problems with his employer. With the mechanization of industry, the speeding up of production, and the tremendous increase in the work force, however, the employee could at best maintain only a casual relationship with his employer. Industrialists concentrated on the accumulation of material resources. They were intrigued with the scientific achievements which spirited far ahead of the advances in industrial human relations. There was only dim awareness of the fact that human factors influenced production directly, that workers were more precious than even the most intricate machines which they operated, and that the success of an enterprise depended principally on the well-being of its employees.

While employee maladjustments were evident in industry during World War I, few plants set up counseling services to aid their problem employees. Psychologists introduced ability and aptitude tests, thus improving selection and placement, but were rarely called upon to counsel the emotionally disturbed employee. More observing employers noticed that employees did not check their personal problems at the gate but brought them to the work bench. Conversely, job problems were taken to the home and to the community. There were some who opposed the idea of establishing counseling services within their plants on the grounds that they smacked of paternalism. The emotionally disturbed worker, it was felt, should obtain help from specialists and agencies within the community.

After World War I, however, two well-known companies, The Metropolitan Life Insurance Company and R. H. Macy and Company, made psychiatric services available to their employees and were among the first organizations to do so. Counseling programs were instituted in other organizations with psychiatrists, psychologists, and trained interviewers all playing important roles in establishing such programs. With the enormous expansion of plants and personnel during World War II, employee problems multiplied, too, hence the noticeable increase in the number of industrial employee services available to employees at that time.

TYPICAL COUNSELING AND MENTAL HYGIENE PROGRAMS

The Metropolitan Life Insurance Company. The counseling program at this Company which employed a psychiatrist as early as 1922 was therapeutic in practice and was at first concentrated on employees with serious mental ills. Later, however, the employee clinic became an informal consultation service which all employees and supervisors were encouraged to use (2).

R. H. Macy and Company. At Macy's, a working team consisting of a psychiatrist, psychologist, and psychiatric social worker undertook to study and treat cases presenting emotional disorders. The intensive case studies collected during the years 1925 to 1929 brought to light the relationship of psychological factors to job performance. Swift and intelligent diagnosis salvaged a large percentage of workers who would otherwise have been too maladjusted to continue their jobs. It was generally agreed that both employee and employer benefited considerably from this service (1).

Western Electric Company. The most widely publicized industrial counseling program had its beginning at the Hawthorne Plant of the

Western Electric Company in 1928. A series of research studies which inquired into the effects of physical factors in the working environment on productivity, and the effects of employee attitudes toward colleagues and supervisors on work performance, demonstrated the importance of psychological factors. The indirect method of interviewing (analogous to Rogers' nondirective technique), introduced initially as a means of improving supervision by encouraging employees to talk freely about shop conditions, has become a valuable tool in counseling. The interviewing program not only led to a correction of poor working conditions, better supervision, improved training courses, but also fostered a better understanding of employees (3).

The personnel counseling program continues at Western Electric. Counselors are chosen from among employees, preference being given to college graduates who have majored in the social sciences. Inservice training is provided and each counselor is assigned to a specific department where he mingles freely with employees and supervisors, encouraging them to discuss their problems. Both on-the-job contacts and off-the-job interviews are conducted. The opportunity afforded the worker to air his grievances has led to an improved system of communication between management and the worker, more rapid job adjustment and, of course, increased production (6).

E. I. duPont de Nemours and Company. In an endeavor to expand its program of preventive medicine so as to assure the mental health as well as the physical well being of its employees, duPont instituted a mental hygiene service in 1943. The psychiatrist in charge assumed the duties of a regular industrial physician, at first, in order to familiarize himself with the plant setup and the employees. As a psychiatric practice developed, employees appeared for consultations voluntarily or were referred by supervisors. Short-term psychiatric treatment to alleviate the employees' immediate problems was attempted. In addition, a seminar on "emotions" was conducted for executives in order to familiarize the group with its own problems in human relations within the plant; prevent, detect and cure emotional disturbances which might otherwise develop into major ills, and promote the general health of all employees by encouraging group discussions and group consultations (12).

The Caterpillar Tractor Company. A clinical psychologist serving as personnel consultant played a significant role in introducing and conducting a comprehensive mental hygiene program at the Caterpillar Tractor Company. The program, initiated in 1944 and placed under the direction of the medical department, included training, testing, and counseling. In order to improve employee selection, the personnel staff responsible for hiring was given intensive interviewing training in supervised sessions. Lectures and group conferences were held to acquaint interviewers with the essentials of human psychology, and foremen received training in the management of human relations. The employee's assets and liabilities were evaluated by means of a battery of tests, including measures of intelligence, mechanical ability and emotional adjustment, and by a psychiatric interview. Those employees presenting problems were either referred to, or voluntarily called on, the personnel consultant who utilized the directive counseling method, since it was felt desirable to create in the employee an understanding of the true nature of his complaints. Psychological techniques, too, were employed to facilitate the readjustment of veterans to industry. With the cooperative efforts of all personnel involved in selecting, placing, and training these men, even those presenting noticeably severe personality disturbances were able to function satisfactorily on their jobs (10, 11).

Prudential Insurance Company. The counseling program at the Prudential Insurance Company supervised by a psychologist is, for the most part, limited to helping employees who are essentially "normal." The Counseling Center established as an organization apart from personnel administration is staffed by persons who have had previous specialized and professional training in interviewing and helping clients solve their problems. Both nondirective interviewing procedures and "interpretative statements or suggestions superimposed on a nondirective base" are employed in the counseling procedure. The staff is equipped to administer and interpret a variety of psychological tests, give vocational guidance and provide help in answering specific questions concerning financial aid, company policies, and services offered by the community. In reviewing the major details of the program, Bromer makes these comments: ". . . . we have tried to set up a comprehensive mental hygiene program, patterned after existing counseling and case work service, in a new setting—inside the walls of a business organization. Our service is not complete; we attempt no long term or intensive therapy. In the short time since the Counseling Center has been established we have succeeded in reaching a number of employees and providing help through individual counseling. In the future we hope to supplement our present service in several ways. The most important extension of this service, we feel, will be a venture in group counseling" (4).

General Electric Company. Employee counseling at the Bridgeport plant of the General Electric Company, which will be discussed in greater detail in the next section of this chapter, developed gradually with the expansion of the personnel testing program during World War II. Enlightened management, realizing that a psychologist trained in clinical and industrial psychology could be utilized to good advantage in helping employees solve their problems, supported counseling activities within the plant. Management's confidence in the value of such activities was enhanced by successful handling of a few experimental cases submitted by top executives.

The counseling activity was placed under the direction of the manager of personnel but existed as a function independent of Personnel. The fact that the counselor was not hampered by personnel procedures nor vested with authority to effect changes had special appeal to employees who preferred a confidential, objective approach to their problems. Counseling, however, did not exist as an isolated service but was integrated with other plant activities.

Though a few members of management may have felt that a formalized counseling program, offering mental hygiene service to employees within industry, tended to tread upon the sacred ground of the employee's private affairs or appeared to compete with services offered by the community, it was generally agreed that the logical place for employees to discuss problems involving their jobs was within the plant itself. Thus it was management's responsibility to make available skilled persons to help guide employees to a satisfactory solution of their problems if increased production and morale were to be maintained.

The writer, who will be referred to as the "counselor" was given offices on the ground floor of the new dispensary building which was centrally located. Employees could reach this area by two separate outside entrances and thus did not need to pass through production departments or business offices. Since there were no other offices in the immediate vicinity, employees could be assured of sufficient privacy when discussing their problems.

Armed with the interest and support of management, the counselor had to win the confidence of the medical department, the personnel department, the supervisors and the employees. Both the medical department and personnel department had for years been confronted with problem cases referred by supervision and had done a competent job in helping employees recognize their difficulties, referring them to agencies within the community better qualified or more adequately equipped to handle their problems when special treatment was indicated.

Supervisors either in groups or individually were informed of the counseling activities within the plant and assured that no attempt would be made to weaken the close relationship existing between supervisors and their employees. Supervisors were told that they would continue to play a major role in helping their employees resolve their job problems. They could consult with the counselor on procedures to follow when handling problem cases, if they wished, and could suggest the availability of the counseling service to their employees on a voluntary basis. It was especially important for them to stress the fact that no one was compelled to use the service. There was little feeling among supervisors, however, that the counselor would deprive them of their status, authority or privilege of assuming changes within their own departments. Most of them were anxious to "do right by" their employees and welcomed any assistance enabling them to do a more efficient job.

The employee, too, had to be convinced of the sincerity of purpose behind the counseling program. Suspicion had to be allayed, but this was accomplished only after the employees had had an opportunity to visit the counselor's office, express themselves freely without experiencing reprisals from their supervisors, and be assured that testing and other information revealed in the interview would be treated confidentially; the counselor divulging information to no one except at the request of employees to whom it pertained. No attempt was made to publicize the service since a gradual expansion of activities was intended.

The constructive relationship between the union and management was undoubtedly responsible for the union's co-operative attitude toward counseling activities. Only a few members voiced their objections to the program during the early stages of its development but a frank discussion with these men, in which management's sincerity in aiding the individual employee to achieve a satisfying adjustment to his job was pointed out, convinced even the most skeptical ones that they had no reason to be fearful. Those who had occasion to use the service were enthusiastic in their recommendations of it to fellow workers.

THE PRESENT STATUS: THE CLINICAL PSYCHOLOGIST IN AN INDUSTRIAL SETTING

The purpose for which employee counseling is set up, the organization of the service, and its operation within a specific plant varies from industry to industry. While counseling was not intended to eliminate all employee maladjustments, the program as conducted at a medium-sized General Electric plant during an eight-year period (1944-1952) did facilitate both interpersonal and intrapersonal adjustments, if follow-up reports of counselees and their supervisors can be accepted as confirmation of its effectiveness.

The scope of an employee counseling program can perhaps be shown best by a presentation of the counselor's duties. At General Electric, the writer serving as counselor, with the help of an assistant, participated in activities which will be described in this section. A large-scale counseling program such as that offered its employees by Western Electric would, of course, require the services of many more counselors.

Counseling Functions

Employee counseling was, for the most part, conducted on a short-term basis, with employees requiring intensive therapy being referred to specialists within the community. Thus it was necessary for the counselor to be equipped not only with clinical experience and an understanding of the plant organization, policies, and procedures, but also with a knowledge of the community facilities available.

Most employees utilizing the counseling service called voluntarily but some were referred by the medical department, the personnel department, or by their supervisors. Problems presented were closely related to the following employee needs recognized generally by managements of business and industrial organizations, psychologists, sociologists, and other professional personnel interested in the human relations field.

(1) Fair pay: adequate pay for work performed; pay equal to that received by workers on equivalent jobs within the plant or in other industries within the community; pay increases when merited.

(2) Chance of advancement: an assurance that jobs would be given to the best qualified workers; a chance to review job performance with supervisors, an opportunity to benefit from concrete suggestions offered by supervisors as to how work performance might be improved; a knowledge of lines of promotion.

(3) Job satisfaction: good physical surroundings; recognition and self-respect on the job, including praise for good performance, rewards for suggestions, opportunity to use skills; an understanding supervisor who gives workers a "square deal," handles grievances fairly, and does not resort to discrimination; good relationships with colleagues.

(4) Security (the most compelling need at all occupational levels): steady work; pensions, insurance, and other benefits; a sense of belonging to the organization, participation in formulating policies, keeping informed on changes; status as an individual.

Though both counselor-directed (directive) and counselee-directed (nondirective) methods of interviewing were utilized with employees, depending on which method was most applicable to the problem at hand, the latter was perhaps more frequently resorted to. The counseling procedure generally involved: (1) reviewing of available information on the individual; (2) providing a quiet, pleasant office for the interview; allowing for adequate time, eliminating interruptions; (3) stimulating the counselee to discuss his problems freely (nondirective interview); (4) testing the counselee, if tests were indicated; (5) reviewing test results; and (6) assisting the counselee in setting up a fruitful plan of action for solving his problem.

The problems presented related to the job, to the employee's health or to some home situation. It was not unusual to find an employee failing to function on the job, not only because he lacked requisite abilities but also because he had difficulty adjusting temperamentally. In such cases the employee was assisted in recognizing his emotional problem and advised to seek less demanding work within the plant or outside the Company.

Even when an employee did poorly on an assigned job but tests revealed good potentialities for performing satisfactorily on other assignments, he was given an opportunity to transfer to a more suitable job. Transfer was also arranged for an employee whose temperamental characteristics might be at variance with job requirements but whose abilities could be utilized on work demanding much less pressure. Where testing or counseling uncovered frank mental illness, the employee was referred to a psychiatrist for treatment or possible hospitalization. Home problems, too, were often part of the problem of poor job performance, but as an employee became more adept at handling his difficulties, job efficiency increased noticeably.

At the close of World War II the counselor interviewed a number of veterans who had seen considerable action. Some had been hospitalized for varying periods of time; others had been prisoners of war. All were invited to take advantage of vocational tests so that they might make the best possible use of their abilities. Though a few of the veterans appeared psychologically disturbed, they were able to adjust to their jobs satisfactorily because of the co-operative efforts of their supervisors, colleagues, and members of their families.

From time to time a few supervisors, pleased with changes observed in their employees as a result of counseling, were anxious to take stock of themselves. This counseling experience generally resulted in more successful relationships with their employees.

Not all counselees presenting problems chose to stay on with the Company, nor were they advised to do so. In the event that promising job openings occurred in other organizations, dissatisfied employees who had little chance for advancement within the Company were encouraged to consider such outside opportunities if their abilities, interests, and personality characteristics were in line with job demands. Hence, the friendly relationship between counselor and counselee continued long after the counselee severed his connections with the Company. It was, therefore, not unusual for the counselor to receive communications from former employees telling of their achievements on jobs with other firms or in business ventures of their own.

ADVISORY SERVICES

To employees. The counselor serving industry has to be sufficiently conversant with activities within the plant and within the community to direct employees to proper sources of help. Fortunately, at General Elec-

tric, a social worker was available for consultation on community services, while the personnel department staff provided information on loans,
housing, pensions, insurance, health, recreation and education. Frequently employees eager to continue their education called on the counselor to discuss educational and vocational plans. When time permitted
they were given a rather comprehensive battery of tests, results being
reviewed with them so that an evaluation of their abilities and interests
might aid them in choosing appropriate college, technical school or
business school courses.

To supervisors. Industry, realizing the importance of good supervision, has recently directed its attention to human relations training
programs for supervisors. Almost without exception supervisors want to
"do right by" their employees but, because they lack a knowledge of
effective procedures to follow in coping with problem employees, they are
likely to shy away from handling such problems themselves. To most
employees the supervisor symbolizes the Company; therefore, it is of the
utmost importance that only competent persons combining technical
know-how with skill in handling people be appointed to supervisory
positions if a high level of morale is to be maintained throughout the
plant. In this connection Lewin's work (7), demonstrating the effects of
specific patterns of leadership, is of interest.

Human relations courses have included, for the most part, lectures
on psychological differences and recognizable signs of maladjustment in
employees. Training has been provided in nondirective interviewing,
with case study and role-playing methods being employed. The counselor
has co-operated with the training director in setting up such courses, has
lectured to supervisory groups and has been available for consultation on
procedures to be followed by supervisors when handling specific problem cases.

To personnel. Perhaps the greatest assistance given the personnel
department by the counselor has been in the area of testing. Tests were
routinely administered at the plant to prospective office workers (secretaries, stenographers, typists, clerical workers, business machine opera-
tors), to training course candidates (manufacturing training, advertising
training, sales training, apprentice training) and to production workers
on certain jobs. Interviewers were instructed in the intelligent use of tests
when evaluating candidates for jobs. They were given background
information on measures used (their construction, reliability, effectiveness in predicting success on specific jobs) and were cautioned against
screening out candidates solely on the basis of tests.

Intensive interviewing training was made available to employment
interviewers and to training supervisors charged with the responsibility

of selecting promising young men for training courses. The counselor also assisted Personnel in setting up orientation courses for new employees and planning a preretirement counseling program. In addition, frequent informal discussions with interviewers enabled the counselor to pass along worth-while information on personnel practices.

To management. The counselor made information available to top management concerning employee reactions to Company policies and procedures if it appeared at all likely that changes could improve relationships between employers and their employees. Precautionary measures had to be taken, however, in transmitting such information lest individuals or groups involved be easily identified. It was pointed out that causes underlying employees' symptoms were frequently traceable to conditions within the plant and, hence, it was obvious that the removal of such causes would, naturally, result in the elimination of the problems themselves.

MISCELLANEOUS ACTIVITIES

Though there was generally little time for special studies, the counselor did have an opportunity to undertake such projects as measuring the effectiveness of the counseling program, checking the validity of tests, establishing norms for groups tested and determining the existence of occupational personalities (9). In addition, lectures on aptitude testing, personality measurement, industrial counseling and other psychological topics were given to club groups, Parent Teachers Associations, federal and state employee staffs, church groups and college classes. Visits were paid to community agencies, and staff members of the agencies were in turn invited to tour the plant. Thus the counselor gained first-hand knowledge of services offered by the community and had an opportunity to discuss problems of mutual interest with the agencies' personnel.

FUTURE OUTLOOK

NEED FOR COUNSELING

Psychologists and personnel workers in industry have expressed the belief that the need for a specialized service to aid employees in adjusting to their jobs satisfactorily will facilitate the acceptance of counseling as a permanent function of personnel management. Industry, generally, has been reluctant to assume responsibility for therapeutic counseling within its walls, but a growing awareness of the need for employees to discuss their job problems with an understanding person has prompted management to assign the task of interviewing maladjusted employees to a specific individual or group of individuals within the plant. The opportunity to talk over a grievance or a personal problem with an interested listener has perhaps been as conducive to a feeling of security as has a comprehensive benefit plan.

The expansion of personnel activities during the World War II emergency period introduced counseling, in one or more of its forms (informative, advisory, or therapeutic), into a great many war plants. At the conclusion of the war, however, some of these plants had no further need for counseling activities and discontinued them, while other plants, cognizant of the benefits derived from such activities, continued to support them. Because the war years had highlighted the importance of human relations in industry, management was anxious to make training in this area available to foremen and supervisors. A number of industries, especially the larger ones whose budgets permitted the undertaking of special projects, conducted attitude studies in an effort to ascertain what satisfactions employees derived from their jobs, what reasons were given for their complaints, and what kinds of relationships were experienced with co-workers and supervisors. The information revealed in such studies has promoted the growth of human relations courses, for it has become quite clear to management that favorable employer-employee relationships are dependent on a recognition of the human element involved.

Although it is difficult to measure the value of counseling in monetary terms, there are strong indications that it can contribute to the efficient operation of an industrial plant by assisting employees to become better adjusted to their jobs and thereby living happier lives, by increasing production, by raising the level of morale, and by decreasing turnover. Counseling should be a continuing function, not to be terminated during a recessional period when budgets are dwindling, for it is at such times that the level of morale is lowest and the need for counseling is greatest.

STATUS AND ORGANIZATION OF COUNSELING ACTIVITIES

What trends are counseling programs likely to follow in the future? Who will conduct such programs? These questions have stimulated considerable speculation amongst psychologists and experts in personnel administration. One investigator (2), for example, feels that factors determining whether counseling activities will be handled by the personnel department of a plant, by community agencies, or by a co-operative management-union arrangement will depend on the size of the plant and its location, the availability of community services, and, most important, the attitudes of the employee, management and the union. The investigator goes on to say that if counselors are to become a permanent part of the personnel staff, they will need to be sufficiently well qualified to render constructive assistance to both employees and management, foster good personal relations within the plant, keep management informed on employee and community developments and represent management in co-operative efforts within the community.

A psychologist (4), serving as director of counseling in a business organization, suggests that counseling might possibly be: (1) absorbed by personnel staffs, not necessarily adequately qualified to utilize procedures considered most fruitful in helping individuals; (2) undertaken by mental hygiene or psychiatric clinics sponsored by the company, or jointly by the company and the union; or (3) conducted by psychologically trained persons. He feels that "in most industrial situations, employees are reluctant to talk over personal problems with a personnel staff member who is constantly required to make judgments of their personal effectiveness on the job, to examine them and to evaluate them." In referring to counseling activities undertaken by psychiatric clinics, he points out that employees interested simply in talking over their ideas, feelings and plans with an understanding person, would hesitate to visit a mental hygiene clinic. He contends that counseling services, staffed by psychologically trained personnel, are perhaps best suited to the needs of employees, for counselors working on a confidential basis with clients can assist them, through the best possible means, to understand themselves, to evaluate their goals and to live more effectively.

Two psychologists (3) who are experts in counseling and guidance believe that the counseling field does not necessarily belong to psychiatry, clinical psychology, or to persons trained in interviewing techniques. They consider it very likely that industrial counseling may attract persons of diverse professional backgrounds who will utilize different techniques of therapy; the most valid techniques would eventually emerge as standard practice.

The writer is of the opinion that most industrial counseling programs will continue to be supported by industry itself. There appears to be an increasing interest in psychology among business and industrial leaders and a growing realization that personnel best qualified to perform counseling activities are those professionally well-trained (5). A psychologist serving in an industrial plant must possess the personal qualities and professional competence which will promote an interest in, and respect for, the psychological services which he renders. He must come equipped with training in clinical and industrial psychology, for he will be asked to conduct test validation studies along with counseling activities. A well-integrated personality that will win confidence, an objective attitude that will insure impartiality, and a sympathetic understanding of problems presented by both employees and management are attributes without which he cannot hope to function successfully (8). With a noticeable increase in counseling programs within industry, there is every indication that a greater number of well-trained psychologists will be needed to serve as industrial counselors in the future.

REFERENCES

1. Anderson, V. V. *Psychiatry in industry.* New York: Harper, 1929.
2. Baker, H. *Employee counseling.* Princeton: Princeton Univer. Press, 1944.
3. Blum, M. L. and Balinsky, B. *Counseling and psychology.* New York: Prentice-Hall, 1951.
4. Bromer, J. A. A new approach to employee counseling. Paper delivered at the graduate seminar in industrial engineering at Columbia University, March 1950.
5. Dennis, W. The background of industrial psychology. In Dennis, W. et al. *Current trends in industrial psychology.* Pittsburgh: Univer. of Pittsburgh Press, 1949. Pp. 1-13.
6. Homans, G. C. The Western Electric researches. In Hoslett, S. D. (Ed.), *Human factors in management.* New York: Harper, 1946. Pp. 152-185.
7. Lewin, K., Lippitt, R. and White, R. K. Patterns of aggressive behavior in experimentally created social climates. *J. soc. Psychol.,* 1939, 10, 271-299.
8. Steiner, M. E. *The psychologist in industry.* Oxford: Blackwell. 1949.
9. Steiner, M. E. The search for occupational personalities. *Personnel,* 1953, 29, 335-343.
10. Vonachen, H. A. et al. A comprehensive mental hygiene program at Caterpillar Tractor Company. *Industr. Med.,* 1946, 15, 179-184.
11. Weider, A. Some aspects of an industrial mental hygiene program. *J. appl. Psychol.,* 1951, 35, 383-385.
12. Psychiatrists in industry. *Business Week,* July 30, 1949, 25-26.

XIX.

THE CLINICAL PSYCHOLOGIST IN A
MUNICIPAL COURT

A. ARTHUR HARTMAN

The clinical psychologist is a latecomer to the court scene, but he has already assumed an important role. Here is an old battlefield, a Hundred Years War, in which verbal skirmishes and major legal battles have been fought by generations of medical men, lawyers, judges, and representatives of the general public. To note some of the more important issues: the definition of insanity, the legal aspects of expert psychiatric testimony, commitment of the insane, and the importance of the "uncontrollable impulse." In 1838, Isaac Ray, in his *Medical Jurisprudence of Insanity*, was already lamenting that legal and court practices were discrepant with medical knowledge of insanity.

Court psychologists, like many other present-day clinical psychologists, trace their more immediate paternity to Dr. William Healy. His establishment in 1909 of the first behavior clinic in America is well known. Not so often noted is the fact that this first psychiatric clinic team applied its talents initially to the study of delinquents in a juvenile court. It was not, therefore, a geographical coincidence that Chicago also initiated the first *adult* court clinic with the establishment in 1914 of the Municipal Court Psychiatric Institute.

Since that time the growth of psychological services in the adult courts has been sporadic. In the 1920's, Detroit, Baltimore and Cleveland set up psychiatric clinics; in the 1930's, New York, Pittsburgh and Seattle followed suit, and Chicago started its second clinic in the County Criminal Court. Recently New York City also opened an additional clinic for the magistrates courts. Thus the number of adult court psychiatric clinics totals less than ten, and these are all concentrated in the large cities.

Of course, this is not the entire picture of psychological participation in court work. Many less formal arrangements may be observed. For example, Philadelphia employs clinical psychologists as members of a more strictly medical unit. Psychologists are called in as consultants in many court contexts, particularly in connection with such problems as commitment of the feeble-minded. Many psychologists participate in court work as part of statewide ambulatory services by departments of public welfare or correction. As far back as 1928 the services of a psychologist were being utilized by seventy courts in twenty-seven states. In the writer's own experience with the Illinois Division of the Criminologist, in the 1930's psychologists were sent throughout Illinois to examine persons referred by county judges or states attorneys. A recent survey reports that 6 per cent of a sample group of clinical psychologists were doing all or part of their work in a penal or court setting, and 4 per cent of a similar sample of psychologists received all or part of their referrals from courts.

Clinical psychological techniques for appraising the personality of offenders have developed only within the past fifteen or twenty years. The courts have probably been more resistive to utilizing these developments than the schools, hospitals and other institutions. The strong trend toward individualized study and treatment of all human problems runs more directly counter, in the adult courts, to long-established rigid patterns which differentiate criminal responsibility on the basis of a philosophy of retribution, but here too changes may be observed. Twenty-five years ago the only basis for referral to a court clinic was to separate the psychotic and feeble-minded from other offenders; now, a judge may refer many types of cases for clinical study and psychiatric recommendations even where no question is raised as to gross disturbance.

It is premature to generalize about this newly developing field of clinical application, but a tentative description may be useful. The "typical" court clinical psychologist works closely with psychiatrists and psychiatric social workers, and less directly with probation officers or other court officials. He is responsible for a large number of examinations, usually under pressure of time. He works in an atmosphere which is more like that of a court room than a hospital. Referrals come from judges (95%), defense or states attorneys, police, probation departments and community agencies. The psychologist utilizes standard clinic tests, often in abbreviated form. Typically, his report is incorporated in the full psychiatric report and recommendations made to the judge. There is little opportunity for full staff conferences on all cases, or for treatment and follow-up, although this varies from one clinic to another. The psychologist is only rarely required to give personal testimony in court.

THE PSYCHIATRIC INSTITUTE

The clinical psychologist in the court setting has developed some unique functions. This can perhaps best be illustrated by describing the work of the clinic with which the writer is associated.

The Psychiatric Institute of the Chicago Municipal Court operates as an outpatient clinic which examines adults referred by the thirty-six judges of the court system. Included are cases of alcoholism, drug addiction, shop lifting, attempted suicide, all types of sex offenses, marital problems, peculiar behavior and arson. Persons representing the whole range of unusual or problematic misdemeanors are culled from the total of 500,000 cases which appear annually before the judges of the Municipal Court.

In structure the Psychiatric Institute conforms to the classic clinic team of psychiatrist, psychologist, psychiatric social worker. The professional staff totals twenty-two, with an additional twelve clerks and special bailiffs. Approximately 6000 patients are examined annually and an additional 10,000 relatives or complainants are interviewed.

The psychologist examines the patient first, often immediately after the preliminary court hearing. In the meantime the social worker obtains history data from any available relatives, and informational statements are taken from complainants, witnesses, or arresting officers. Reports from other agencies may also be obtained. All of this material converges at the time of the psychiatric examination. In most instances, all examinations, evaluations and recommendations are completed on the same day and reports are then made to the referring judge.

Of the total cases seen, about 30 per cent are considered to be mentally ill or in need of custodial hospital treatment; these are certified to the Psychopathic Hospital for further observation before commitment to a state hospital or return to the community. On the average one patient in a hundred is committed to the state hospital because of epilepsy or feeble-mindedness. About 15 per cent of the total are referred for private psychiatric treatment. Over one third of the patients are returned to court with no specific psychiatric recommendations; where the clinic finds them to be essentially normal, neurotic, reacting to temporary situational factors, or otherwise presenting no psychiatric condition affecting the particular offense for which they are under trial. Still another group of patients is already under the attention of outside social agencies to which the Psychiatric Institute reports its findings.

In some ways the court clinic corresponds to the emergency receiving room of a hospital, with the psychologist first on hand to evaluate the degree of urgency and need for specialized service. Patients are received in all stages of emotional disturbance; they may be showing continuing reactions to alcohol or toxic drugs; they may be in panic stage, violent, delusional, hallucinatory, amnesic, or just ordinarily tired, fearful or resentful.

This type of clinic is highly service-oriented. Daily it must meet in a realistic way the demands of courts, social agencies, police and other officials, and of the patients themselves and their families. There is little control over intake. Thirty-six judges send in their court problems, and the clinic, in a relatively short time, must examine each patient and report a decision to the court. On a single day as many as forty or fifty patients may be referred. Within a period of an hour, twenty or thirty patients may be brought into the waiting room; and with the patients come bailiffs, police officers, relatives, complainants, lawyers, witnesses.

This is the general setting to which the clinical psychologist has had to make some highly specialized professional adaptations. Each patient, as far as the psychologist knows up to the time he escorts him from the waiting room, may present any one of an extremely varied range of problems. Other sources of information are usually not available at the time of the initial psychological examination. This often means that the psychologist does not even know the reason for arrest.

The standard psychological examination which has evolved under these pressures is a relatively rapid procedure. It consists of three main sections: a structured-history interview, a series of brief psychological screening tests, and a summary report. The first section of the examination lists basic information and explores briefly the patient's adjustment in all the major life areas. The depth of inquiry varies with the case but the following data is obtained: identifying information, living arrangements, work record, military history, medical record, marital history, family background, school history, arrest and custodial record, and the present problem. This section is intended to yield a general picture of the patient in his present life setting and in relation to his past experiences. His record of past difficulties is also obtained along with his own story of the present arrest.

This type of structured interview can be interpreted, with experience and clinical skill, in much the same way as a projective procedure. Some patients reveal their main problem as soon as they give their name (or for that matter as soon as they walk into the examining room). The interview permits clinical observation of the patient's attitudes and reactions to many life situations in his past. It may also be necessary to evaluate from the internal evidence of the interview his reliability in giving information about himself and the current problem. Even the most rapid interview permits judgments about the patient's rapport, hostility, evasiveness, degree of reality contact, and other adjustment factors.

The second section of the psychological examination consists of the following series of items:

PSYCHOLOGICAL TESTS

Reading   Est. Level .... Special Factors ....

Writing

Speech   Methodist—Episcopal .... Artillery Brigade.....................

              Speech Variant ....

Arithmetic 20—1 test ...... 6 + 4 + 9 ...... 3 × 3 ...... 9 × 9 ...... 11 × 11 ......

Vocabulary muzzle—haste—(10) (Bord.) lecture—Mars—skill—(12)
Level   (Dull) juggler—brunette—(14) regard—disproportionate—
              (Ave.) lotus—incrustation—achromatic—(Sup.)

Three   1) ....
Wishes

              2) ....

              3) ....

Ink Blot   ....

T.A.T. Card   ....

Most Unpleasant..

Other Tests

We have been trying out these brief diagnostic behavior samples experimentally for the past year. They are not intended to supplant the full projective tests or usual personality study. They serve rather to detect the less obvious psychotics or mental defectives and to call attention to the more subtle personality deviations which might otherwise be missed in the usual examination. This ten-minute sampling of a wide range of behavior areas seems to constitute a very useful screening instrument, especially when its results are tied in with the examiner's knowledge of the interview data.

The way in which these short tests meet the court psychologist's need for a very broad-range initial examination may be illustrated with the

Writing item. The patient is asked to write a simple phrase, "This is a fine day," and then to write his name. What is yielded here is a sampling of motor and expressive behavior which might otherwise be missed in the usual interview. Tremor, heavy pressure, slowness, erasures, and other signs may point toward anxiety, organicity, toxic conditions or psychosis. For some patients, difficulty with this phrase may indicate lowered intelligence or limited education. Deterioration may be suggested by the patient's behavior in the familiar act of writing his own name. Paranoid individuals often refuse to write their names. An expansive or schizophrenic patient may elaborate on the writing phrase. Variations in rhythm, characteristics of the writing, and other deviations in response yield clues to personality.

Most of the other items on the brief test battery are self-explanatory. The *Reading* sample utilizes a series of one-line sentences approximately ordered in difficulty from first to eighth grade. The *Speech* item also includes an inquiry into past speech difficulty. The *Vocabulary Level* (from the Stanford-Binet) yields a very rough estimate of intellectual capacity which is useful mainly at the lower range in suggesting the possibility of gross retardation. On the *Ink Blot* test a single Harrower-Steiner card is given. The *T.A.T.* card we are currently using is Picture 2, The Farm Family, of the standard Murray series.

The psychologist in the court clinic is under the burden of arriving rapidly at the most difficult kinds of differential evaluation, even though these are tentative. The use of varied samples of motor, expressive, projective, intellectual and educational functions tends to reduce the possibility of gross errors in diagnosis. An incipient schizophrenic disturbance may not be suspected until the patient gives a clearly pathological response to the ink-blot item. A covered-over paranoid condition may be brought to focus when the T.A.T. card is described. A recent organic break may be revealed most clearly on the simple eight-year-level task of counting backwards from twenty to one.

The final section of the psychological report summarizes the findings. An attempt is made to present an integrated picture of the individual and an evaluation of his personality in terms of the immediate problems which brought him to the attention of the police. The court psychologist must, of necessity, be conversant with a very wide range of information. Psychological findings must be co-ordinated with a host of social and legal data. A single item, such as the patient's address, when considered against a knowledge of the different city neighborhoods yields immediate insights into his problems. Chronic alcoholics and simple schizophrenics concentrate in the Skid Row areas, on the fringes of the Loop; depressed and socially isolated schizophrenics gravitate to the cheap rooming-house sections; sex deviants cluster in some parts of the

Near North Side; other psychiatric syndromes are characteristically found in the suburbs, on the South Side, in the Loop hotels, or in other fairly circumscribed areas. The ecological patterns of the city practically spell out some personality diagnoses. Here the individual patient can be evaluated only through knowledge of the total "situational matrix."

In most of the cases this standard psychological examination, along with other clinic data, is all that is required by the psychiatrist in making his final examination and diagnosis. Where the problem is obscure or difficult the patient is referred back to the psychologist for further examination, with a statement of the diagnostic problem and a notation in one or more of the following: (1) intellectual level or functioning, (2) question of organicity, (3) general personality dynamics, (4) differential evaluation, (5) other problems.

From this point on, the test procedure of the court psychologist differs little from that of any clinical psychologist. Tests are selected in accordance with the needs of the case. Standard techniques are employed, with main reliance on the Wechsler-Bellevue for intelligence evaluations and on the Rorschach, T.A.T., MAPS Test, DAP and Bender-Gestalt for other areas. On occasion we have used the Rosenzweig Picture Frustration Test, the Blacky Test, the Halstead-Wepman Aphasia Battery, the MMPI, and other tests of intelligence, organicity, and personality.

There is, of course, constant pressure to limit the time of examining even for the complex cases. Where there is no question of commitment and the preliminary scores are obviously high, a Wechsler-Bellevue may be abbreviated or discontinued after the verbal section is completed. A Rorschach may go unscored to our files when the interpretation can be made by inspection. The omission of inquiries on the Rorschach and the rapid administration of T.A.T. cards is not infrequent. We attempt the maximum utilization of psychological techniques and clinical skills which the situation permits. Variations on usual test procedures may be advisable if the only alternative is a completely subjective judgment. There is a constant check on the accuracy and standards of these evaluations because of the immediate follow-up by other examinations such as those of the psychopathic hospital.

The court setting produces some other special variations in the work of the clinical psychologist. Most important is the wide range of problems to be studied. Our referring source is the court and the only selective factor is the committing of an offense, or behavior which calls the offender to the attention of the police. We are in no position to reject cases because of poor therapeutic possibilities, mental retardation, lack of social resources, or for any of the other reasons which determine the selection policies of most clinics. Here the police and the court processes act only as loose filters through which are screened cases of acute or incipient mental disease and all the psychiatric backwash of a complex metropolis. Where the patient is acutely disturbed, violent or withdrawn, a minimum screening examination is given. It is urgent under such circumstances to make these evaluations with dispatch so the patient can be removed from jail or court auspices to a hospital. Even when the patient is not disturbed there may be a question of accessibility. Few patients come to us of their own accord. They tend to identify the clinic with other court processes as potentially punitive. Since they know that the clinic examination directly affects their court disposition, they may be anxious, hostile, or motivated to disguise facts. These circumstances place high demands upon the clinician's skill in obtaining rapport and arriving at an evaluation. When a patient refuses to respond or gives minimal responses, the psychologist can rarely postpone examination. He must perforce come to some conclusion as to whether he is dealing with a malingerer, alcoholic, psychotic, mental defective, or aphasic, to list just a few possibilities.

The court psychologist's responsibility for diagnostic differentiations is greater than is characteristic in most psychiatric clinics. This is illustrated in another direction. In some cases examinations cannot be completed on a single day and it may be necessary to release the patient for a return appointment, or to hold him in custody in the jail. The psychologist's judgment is often critical in designating cases for emergency treatment: the possible suicide, the incipient psychotic, or the paranoid individual with good surface control who might, upon release, commit a serious assault. These and other important decisions about immediate disposition must often be made largely on the basis of the psychologist's examination.

The psychologists at the Psychiatric Institute are almost entirely occupied with the diagnostic function, although from time to time individual cases may be taken for treatment. Ordinarily, plans for psychiatric supervision of patients, or plans involving environmental changes are carried out by the psychiatric social worker. The psychologists, and the psychiatrists too for that matter, are involved mainly at the initial phases of recommendations for treatment.

The electroencephalographic examination is now a standard procedure in most court clinics. This technique up to a few years ago was mainly the psychologist's responsibility, at least at the Psychiatric Institute. The increased complexity of the instrument and the larger number of examinations now requires a special EEG technician, who works more directly with the psychiatrist. Conditions such as epilepsy, brain damage and arteriosclerosis are frequently seen in court work; anti-social acts may often be the first symptoms of these conditions. The question of organicity in the examination of patients is usually first raised by the psychologist. The usual clinical tests of organicity may then be given along with the EEG examination.

Research by the Municipal Court psychologists has been focused in recent years on the development of diagnostic procedures to meet the special needs of the court clinic. The main emphasis has been upon revisions of the interview and upon clinical validations of the brief diagnostic test samples. The ground work for much more extensive research is also being prepared. Since 1949 most of the psychological interview and test data have been coded and punched on IBM cards. All case records are microfilmed; the present total of these is fifty thousand. The EEG examinations, along with specialized inquiry data are recorded on a newly devised McBee Keysort card. A great repository of records is thus accumulating. The rich clinical material daily available affords an opportunity for research in psychopathology that awaits only space, time and inspiration.

THE ROLE OF THE PSYCHOLOGIST

The role of the psychologist in the court is ambiguous in some respects. He may define his own function as that of a scientist, an impartial observer; but he works in a complex atmosphere in which institutional practices, legal sanctions, and popular attitudes prevail. In the process of communication from clinic examining room to the court bench, psychological judgments become diluted, popularized or even distorted. The results of a Rorshach or Wechsler-Bellevue examination are viewed against a background of such concepts as that of free will, or of *mens rea,* the evil mind. Inasmuch as final reports to the judge are made by the psychiatrist, the strong court tradition of medicine carries weight, but even this may be ineffective in cases outside the specific areas of psychosis and feeble-mindedness which are protected by legal statutes.

The role of the psychologist in relation to the other professional disciplines presents some unusual departures from orthodox clinic practice. In general the lines of demarcation of function of psychiatrist, psychologist and social worker are less clearly drawn, and there is little competitivenes or rigidity. One reason for this may be the fact that the Psychiatric Institute mainly initiates but does not itself carry on extensive treatment functions. Another reason is the pressure of time and number of cases, as well as the fact that some of the psychiatrists are available only part time. The results of the psychological examination are therefore given considerable and often decisive weight by the psychiatrist.

At the Psychiatric Institute, the fact that the psychologist first sees the patient necessitates his obtaining certain basic information which ordinarily would be available in a social history. The social worker, who is occupied with the patient's relatives and with complainants, welcomes this information and in fact may rely on it closely. She may need to initiate important casework procedures such as obtaining petitions from relatives prior to the time the psychiatrist sees the patient. The preliminary psychological material on the case often indicates the social service needs. Thus we see considerable interaction between psychologist and social worker simply at the level of diagnosis and disposition of cases, while in most clinics a similar interaction takes place only at the treatment level.

In relation to the psychiatrist, the function of the psychologist is to prepare a diagnostic study of each patient which will permit a fairly rapid final diagnosis. There is little formal staffing of cases but brief conferences are frequent. If the patient is in an acute phase such as impending delirium tremens, or is potentially assaultive, direct referral will be made to the psychiatrist, and the social worker may be called in immediately to consider pertinent casework requirements.

Conferences between psychologist and psychiatrist are also held on the more complex cases. The extent of psychological examination required is often determined as the case study proceeds. For example, the psychologist does not ordinarily give a full Wechsler-Bellevue, even though he estimates from other data that the patient is mentally defective. If psychiatric examination and social history indicate that commitment is advisable, the patient is referred back for the full psychometric testing. A patient will be returned for projective tests where it appears from the accumulating information that he may be recommended for trial as a criminal sexual psychopath.

FUTURE DEVELOPMENT OF PSYCHOLOGICAL SERVICES

Historically, the time span of psychological services to the courts is brief, but two important developments can already be noted: (1) The psychologist's major function has changed from that of evaluating intelligence and specifically determining mental deficiency to the much broader task of evaluating the entire personality sphere. (2) The courts have shifted their emphasis from obviously disturbed or defective offenders to the much wider range of personality problems reflected in such behavior as fire setting, pathological stealing, marital disturbance and sex offenses.

In the early period of clinic growth, psychologists were preoccupied with intelligence testing. This reflected a prevailing belief in a close association between mental retardation and criminality. These facile unifactor theories have long been outgrown. The concept of the multiple approach to understanding human behavior now provides the working basis for the widest use of clinical psychological techniques.

The development of psychological services to the courts promises to be one of the new directions of growth for clinical psychology. A cultural lag in this area is evident. For example the U.S. government provides the most advanced psychiatric and psychological services to its prison departments but allots only meager consultation facilities to the Federal court system. Probation officers and others involved in presentence investigations of Federal offenders are keenly aware of this lack. It is likely, within the next decade, that the services of the usual clinic teams will be made routinely available to the U.S. courts.

Statewide systems of pretrial psychiatric and psychological examinations are also developing. A number of states have followed Massachusetts' precedent under the Briggs Law which requires pretrial professional examination of serious or repeated offenders. Similar legislation pertaining to sex offenders has been passed in one third of the states, including Illinois. Questions of psychopathy in sex cases are being increasingly referred by judges for clinical evaluation.

Pressures are also growing for development of clinic services for all the socialized court branches, such as the boys' courts, women's courts, and courts of domestic relations. In Illinois a new state law provides for a sixty-day "cooling off" period before divorce suits can be entered. One purpose of this law is to permit the judge to refer the couple for professional examination and counseling. The use of psychologists as counselors has been specifically proposed.

Bernard Glueck once predicted that the future court of criminal law will approach the character of a clinic in human maladjustment. We can envision the clinical psychologist and the clinic team of the future functioning, not as a court appendage for processing special cases, but as an integral part of a broad sociolegal program which would provide for:

(1) Psychodynamic studies of all serious offenders as well as all persons whose antisocial acts are symptomatic of disturbance.

(2) Treatment procedures in which professional findings will be coordinated with socioeconomic and legal facts to determine how the interests of both society and the individual can best be met.

(3) Training and research which will utilize the mass of dynamic material that passes through the court clinic, as a basis for improving our understanding and treatment of deviant behavior.

REFERENCES

1. Barnes, H. E., & Teeters, N. K. New horizons in criminology. New York: Prentice-Hall, 1943.

2. Bronner, A. F. Behavior clinics. In Branham, V. C., & Kutash, S. B. (Eds.) *Encyclopedia of criminology*. New York: Philosophical Library, 1949.
3. Guttmacher, M. S. Adult court psychiatric clinics. *Amer. J. Psychiat.*, 1950, 106, 881-888.
4. Sharp, A. A. (Ed.) *David B. Rotman, M.D., Addresses and papers, 1934-1948*. Chicago: Champlin-Shealy Co., 1948.
5. Shafer, R., Berg, I., & McCandless, B. Report on survey of current psychological testing practices. *Supplement to Newsletter, Division of Clin. & Abnorm. Psychol.*, June 1951, 4, 1-24.
6. Selling, L. S. Court clinics. In Branham, V. C., & Kutash, S. B. (Eds.) *Encyclopedia of criminology*. New York: Philosophical Library, 1949.
7. Zilboorg, G. Legal aspects of psychiatry. In *One hundred years of American psychiatry*. New York: Columbia Univer. Press, 1944.

XX.

THE CLINICAL PSYCHOLOGIST IN THE JUVENILE COURT AND YOUTH AUTHORITY PROGRAM

STANLEY B. ZUCKERMAN

An increasing awareness of the fact that young delinquents warrant handling and treatment separate from the older, hardened offender led to the gradual development of juvenile courts separate from the courts handling adult criminal cases. Since the adoption of a law in 1899 which established the first separate court for juvenile delinquents in Chicago, there has evolved a specialized juvenile court procedure. Under this procedure—which is by no means uniform from state to state but exists throughout the United States today—the offender is regarded less as a law violator and more as a youngster requiring care or custody by the state. In accord with this philosophy, these courts depart from the traditional procedures of criminal law which emphasize jury trial, rules of evidence and representation by counsel, and operate more informally. To assist the courts by furnishing information about the young delinquent's condition, clinics have been established. From a pioneer venture in Chicago in 1909, there have developed a number of court clinics, especially in larger urban centers, to aid juvenile courts in planning for their young charges.

Although the general public has had, and at times continues to have, a punitive attitude toward youngsters who violate laws, those who argue against "pampering" delinquents have seen the clinical study of the young offender become recognized as a part of the juvenile court process, at least in those areas where these services are available. Even though most of the large number of courts serving juveniles do not have their own clinical facilities, certain major cities maintain their own while others have reasonable access to community child guidance facilities and city- or state-operated psychiatric hospital clinics. Moreover, as authority to deal with problems other than delinquency has come to be vested in judges serving on the juvenile bench, these clinics have aided the courts in planning for dependent, neglected, handicapped, and other children.

It has been estimated that there are over 600 community clinics serving children in the United States of which the majority have staffs representing the disciplines of psychiatry, clinical psychology, and psychiatric social work. In contrast to the large network of community clinics, court-maintained psychiatric clinics numbered but 14 in 1952 (18), not counting several clinics with very small staffs, nor a hospital traveling team serving a juvenile court. (Clinics allied with but not supported by courts also have been excluded.) Thus, the total number of court clinics does not loom large compared with clinics of a more general nature. In addition to clinics maintained by juvenile courts, though, there are clinical teams serving in a closely parallel manner in the correctional process. These units are maintained by such detention-study centers as Youth House in New York and Juvenile Hall in Los Angeles, and operate also in facilities of the state and federal youth authorities.

THE OPERATION OF JUVENILE COURTS AND CLINICS

The manner in which the large urban juvenile court operates, and the role of the clinic, can be seen from the example which follows.

Johnny Jones, age fourteen, is picked up by the police while committing a burglary. Perhaps released over night in the custody of his parents, or held by the police juvenile officers while his family is notified, he is brought quickly to the juvenile court for a hearing. At this hearing, a legal determination is made—to establish whether, in fact, Johnny committed the offense alleged in the petition. The hearing is conducted in privacy, in a generally informal manner, and only infrequently is the youngster represented by an attorney.

If it is found that Johnny was not involved in the acts alleged in the petition, the court would dismiss the case. For minor infractions, the judge may decide to dismiss the youngster with a warning. In more serious law violations, if it is found that he committed such acts as claimed in the petition, he would be adjudicated delinquent. If Johnny is adjudged delinquent and had no lengthy prior record of offenses, he would be released in the custody of his parents for a month or so during which time a probation officer would conduct a field investigation. Also, if while at his first court hearing, Johnny seemed to present noticeable symptoms of emotional disorder, a clinical study might be ordered by the court. Unlike Johnny, if a youngster has appeared repeatedly in court, instead of being released he probably would be remanded to a juvenile detention center while a probation officer conducts the field study. In such cases, too, the judge is likely to make a clinical referral, although studies by the clinic staff may also be made at the initiative of the probation officer.

The nature of the clinical study would vary from agency to agency, but there is somewhat of a general pattern. In some settings the first contact would be with a psychiatric social worker who would explore details of the youth's family background, developmental history, child-parent attitudes, etc., and would prepare both the youngster and his parent for visits with the psychologist and psychiatrist. The next contact is often with the psychologist who would interview and test Johnny. With a probation or casework report for perspective, psychological findings would then be prepared in report form or discussed with the psychiatrist who might next see him. In some settings, the psychiatrist is obliged to make a physical examination and neurological check besides having one or more interviews. The material thus obtained by the team members might be submitted in separate reports, integrated at a staff conference, or simply embodied in the psychiatrist's report to the judge. Further contacts between the clinic and Johnny would depend on whether the clinic provides treatment, as well as on the action taken by the judge.

On the date of the second hearing, with the material from the field and from the clinic available for reference, the judge talks with Johnny and his family and makes a disposition. The data might suggest dismissal of the charges and no further official activity in the case. As an alternative, Johnny could be placed on probation for a period of time (often one year) during which he would be under the supervision of his probation officer to whom he might have to report at regular intervals. If psychotherapy has been recommended in the clinical report, an arrangement might be made for such treatment either with a private psychiatrist, with a community guidance clinic, or with the juvenile court clinic, depending on the family's ability to pay for treatment, the availability of such services, and other factors. If environmental changes have been recommended, the judge would be free to place Johnny with relatives other than the parents, in a foster or boarding home, or in a child-caring institution. Such other changes as those in school program, and transfer to a school for defectives or to a state hospital also can be arranged.

Youngsters involved in serious offenses, and those previously granted probation who have continued to get into trouble, are ordinarily committed for a period either to a private (frequently denominational) school, or to a county or state-supported correctional school. There, depending on the type of institution and the supply of trained staff, some further clinical work of a diagnostic and therapeutic nature might be done. In the best of private facilities, fairly intensive treatment under psychiatric direction is available. Opportunities for psychotherapeutic treatment in publicly supported institutions are variable. For the most part, the volume of cases is heavy and the professional staffs are greatly burdened. As a result, treatment is more often a product of the changed setting, restrictions on socially unacceptable impulses and the provision of outlets for more constructive drives, educational and vocational training, and possible identification with law-abiding staff members—professional or otherwise—to whom the youth may relate. After a period of time in the institution, especially if progress in the direction of greater maturity and socialization is made, the youngster is returned to the community on parole and under supervision.

The above outline of operation is reasonably representative of what might be found in the more progressive metropolitan juvenile courts which maintain their own clinics. Actually, most cities do not have such facilities and, in far too many smaller cities still, not only are clinic services unavailable, youngsters are detained till their court appearances in jails for older offenders. To obtain a cross-sectional view of current juvenile court practices in the United States, a survey was completed in 1950 embracing all cities with populations of over 100,000 (14). A high proportion of replies was received, but adequate details for a really graphic picture were obtained from a group of courts in twenty-three cities—serving a total population of almost 20 million. It was apparent that even in these courts which were in relatively large urban areas, only a small minority of the total juvenile court intake is exposed to study by an interdisciplinary team of psychiatrist, clinical psychologist and psychiatric social worker. Only 14 per cent of 43,222 cases seen at the intake of these courts as recently as 1947 were studied by a psychiatrist and a clinical psychologist. Presumably, even a smaller percentage were seen in collaboration with a psychiatric social worker. The percentage does not look quite as unfavorable, if instead of taking the total case load of the court, only those youngsters actually adjudicated delinquent are thought of as the group requiring attention. Approximately one third of the youngsters adjudicated delinquent were seen by a psychiatrist and a clinical psychologist in that sample.

Largely because of lack of personnel, in many of these courts the patient is seen either by a psychiatrist or by a psychologist. This type of study was afforded 29 per cent of the intake, or roughly two thirds of adjudicated cases.

These studies by one or more members of a clinical team are diagnostic in the typical juvenile court. Ordinarily the findings are summarized and presented to the juvenile court judge or to members of the probation department. The diagnostic impressions and suggestions of the clinical team members derived from their studies are not binding on court personnel, however. Their reports are purely advisory. The consensus of opinion of court officials replying to a question on this point is that recommendations of clinical staff members are generally followed.

It is well known, though, that instances occur in which these professional views are ignored.

From the viewpoint of the clinician, a serious problem in court clinic operation arises in connection with the related matter of clinical treatment. One fairly frequent finding in diagnostic studies submitted to judges of juvenile courts is that psychotherapy be made available to the youngster. If diagnostic services for the youthful offender seem relatively sparse, actual clinical treatment is much more so. Though court officials and others acknowledge the need for more treatment services, the provision of one hour or more per week of psychotherapy is extremely limited. Out of the total intake of 43,222 youngsters in the same twenty-three large cities, only 695 (1.6%) were being treated psychotherapeutically under court auspices. If only adjudicated cases were considered, the percentage would rise to a mere 3.8 per cent. It is apparent, then, that while juvenile court procedures and adjunctive diagnostic studies have come to be fairly well accepted by the middle of the twentieth century, clinical treatment services to youth after they have become social problems still have far to go to catch up with current needs. Brightening the picture somewhat is the fact that while localities have been hard pressed to provide these services directly through the courts, at least some of the states have stepped into the breach. Expanded services financed at the state level and more active participation by community guidance clinics are proving helpful. Similarly, the federal government now is reorganizing services for youthful offenders who violate federal statutes.

THE FUNCTIONING OF THE CLINICAL PSYCHOLOGIST

Delving into the role of the psychologist in fourteen court and court-allied clinics employing forty-three psychologists in all, it was found that the clinical psychologist in the juvenile court appeared to serve largely as a diagnostic tester and a consultant to the court personnel. Until recently, the psychologist's studies have centered on the establishment of the youngster's intelligence level, the relationship between his essential endowment and his functioning, "weak spots" in school achievement, subject disabilities, and personality problems evident upon interview— all of which may be contributory to delinquent behavior. Currently, increasing attention has come to be paid to more covert personality factors, and to a lesser extent, to interests and aptitudes. If the psychologist has not yet been utilized as an important person in the therapeutic process, the problem is partly an outgrowth of the fact that the court clinics have served largely in a advisory-diagnostic role. Within this framework, the psychologist has fallen heir to the job of answering questions of court personnel about the brightness or dullness of a youngster, about personality difficulties and other handicaps, and about school disabilities.

Clinical personnel working in such settings were asked for estimates of time devoted to different phases of work. Though the number of responses contributing to the tabulation of medians which follows is small, it should be borne in mind that the total number of court clinics is likewise small. The results seem to reflect reasonably accurately, though, how the "typical" court psychologist's time has been used in recent years.

Table 1

How the Court Psychologist Spends His Time

Function	Median Estimate
Intelligence testing	25%
Projective testing	15%
Interviewing	14%
Writing reports	10%
School achievement testing	5%
Staff conferences	5%
Other duties, miscellaneous, or unspecified	26%
Total	100%

Table I reflects the feeling of how court psychologists are being utilized rather than how it is felt that they should be spending their time. The figures indicate the still considerable emphasis on "I.Q. finding"—presumably in order to satisfy judges, probation workers and others desiring this information. While, in seeking explanations for delinquency, a growing interest in personality dynamics and a greater use of the projective techniques has resulted, there still remains somewhat of a lingering stress on the measurement of intelligence in court clinical settings.

In terms of specific instruments used, a youngster referred for study to a court clinic would usually be given, in addition to an interview, an individual intelligence test (usually the Terman-Merrill Revision of the Binet or Wechsler Intelligence Scale for Children if younger, or Wechsler-Bellevue if adolescent). This would ordinarily be supplemented by some measure of school achievement such as the Metropolitan, Stanford, Wide-Range, or Woody tests. The Rorschach and the Thematic Apperception tests seem to be used largely for "special cases." Other projective devices like the Human Figure Drawings, Bender-Gestalt, Sentence Completion,

Make-A-Picture-Story, and House-Tree-Person tests were mentioned by respondents, but appear to be used even less often. Significantly, individual performance tests, personality questionnaires, interest inventories, measures of aptitudes, and special tests, such as those for detecting brain damage, seem to be only infrequently employed.

To psychologists working in other settings in which a premium is placed on intensive work with a relatively small case load, this description of the work of the court psychologist may seem to reflect a low level of professional functioning. For this, psychologists in court service are only partly responsible since working in this manner is largely an outgrowth of court pressure for services. Demands are placed on small staffs leading to high-volume productivity and service that is less qualitative in nature. Thus, the diagnostic testing and reporting of the court psychologist seem to have been done at the expense of work in other areas which have come to be recognized as important. Collaboration with specialists of other disciplines has been curtailed, and conduct of individual and group psychotherapy has been quite limited. Court psychologists have been doing relatively little in the area of play therapy. Research and personal professional development have been greatly restricted. There has been little activity in such closely related areas as remedial reading and speech therapy. There remains a marked lag in organized training programs for psychologists in juvenile courts, and supervision of new staff is relatively sporadic. Work of an educational and public relations nature by the court psychologist is likewise markedly limited.

PROBLEMS ON THE JUVENILE COURT SCENE

While the above picture of the functioning of juvenile court psychologists is by no means the brightest, there probably has been some little improvement in the professional functioning, accompanied by some increase in the financial return for psychologists devoting themselves to juvenile court work in the few years since the study of court clinics was compiled. In at least one clinic even though the case load continues to be heavy, the special value of the psychologist as a researcher has been recognized. The staff has been expanded, and psychologists have been given a key role in highly constructive team research now being conducted with the help of a grant from a philanthropic organization.[1]

However, the direction of future developments in psychology in juvenile courts will hinge on resolving certain fundamental questions. In what type of setting can clinical psychologists and other allied specialists best serve the needs of delinquent youth? From a theoretical viewpoint, it seems reasonable to assert that youngsters should have access to

[1] Dr. Harris B. Peck. Personal communication. April 11, 1953.

clinical services before they become problems of the juvenile court. By developing an adequate network of clinical facilities serving preschool youngsters, by having optimally staffed school psychological services and adequate community child guidance facilities, the complex of emotional, physical and social pressures that produce delinquency can perhaps be modified before the individual "acts out" impulses which lead to involvement with law-enforcement agencies. While it is perhaps wishful to visualize, the best solution might be maximal educational and preventive work with an adequate supply of clinical personnel serving youngsters at a local level before patterns of delinquency fully crystallize.

Until such community resources become available, it would seem that an important transitional step would be the expansion of court clinics—fully staffed and operating at an optimal professional level. The need for expansion of such clinics arises partly from the present heavy pressures coupled with the fact that there is no slackening up of new cases in prospect. According to the U. S. Children's Bureau, an estimated one million boys and girls are picked up by the police each year. Of these, approximately 350,000 (in the ratio of four boys to one girl) are brought to juvenile courts. An additional 150,000 youngsters are involved in contacts with juvenile courts as dependent, neglected and handicapped. This large number of cases is partly an outgrowth of the substantial population growth in the country and the spurt in the number of youngsters arising from increased family formation in the 1940's. In addition, in 1952 the Children's Bureau reported a rising trend in juvenile delinquency in the ten-year to seventeen-year age group as compared with the three years preceding. By 1960 it has been estimated that law-enforcement agencies will be dealing with 50 per cent more cases in this age group than in 1950 (5). The expansion of clinical facilities in connection with juvenile courts seems indicated to help meet this need. However, even if additional clinical facilities are provided, their effectiveness would be closely linked with the professional level at which the sponsoring juvenile courts operate.

While in larger communities the problems presented by delinquent youngsters are aired before specially selected juvenile court judges, elsewhere—particularly in rural areas—the juvenile court is an offshoot of the county probate court. The judges on these benches are, despite excellent intentions, in many instances handicapped by lack of training in disciplines leading to a sensitive understanding of youngsters, their deep-rooted problems, and the rehabilitation process. This situation which has led to wide variations in the handling of delinquents in different counties within each state, and especially the general need for more adequate service to young offenders, contributed to the development of the youth authorities which represents an approach to the solution of some of these problems.

THE DEVELOPMENT OF THE YOUTH AUTHORITIES

Following considerable interdisciplinary collaboration, under the aegis of the American Law Institute, a "Model Act" was drafted in 1940 which was first implemented with the creation of the California Youth Authority in 1941. As outlined in the model Youth Correction Authority Act, the authority was not conceived as a program for juveniles: rather, it was designed to provide more effective rehabilitation for youthful offenders in the somewhat neglected sixteen- to twenty-one-year age group, many of whom had been handled routinely as adult criminals. Special circumstances led to the extension of the Youth Authority's jurisdiction over California's juvenile correctional institutions in 1942, and prompted the legislature to apply these principles to younger delinquents as well. As a result, the Authority was given responsibility for offenders from childhood up to twenty-one years of age. For a while, the development of the Youth Authority in California was handicapped by the inroads of World War II on budget, materials, and professional staff. Gradually, though, the Authority received more liberal appropriations and the program picked up speed. Meanwhile, by the end of 1950, the basic pattern of the youth authority was enacted in Wisconsin, Minnesota, Massachusetts, and Texas. The Federal Government, too, set up a roughly comparable youth correctional system for violators of federal laws, which is just now coming into operation. Since 1950, there have been moves to create similar programs in other states.

In essence, the youth authorities probably contribute most valuably in stressing rehabilitation as opposed to the older retributive approach, and in providing services which are beyond the reach of smaller local communities. Because professionally trained probation workers are scarce in some areas, because some of the judges serving on the juvenile court bench may be relatively ill-equipped for dealing with problems of youngsters, and because specialized clinical facilities are lacking, a statewide youth correctional program can contribute valuably by making trained personnel and resources available. Though there are differences in the basic laws and in the operation of the youth authorities in the different states, they have in common certain features. They are dedicated to the idea of individual study of the offender using up-to-date diagnostic methods. Beginning with the premise that delinquency is caused by a complex of interacting factors, they aim to provide appropriate treatment—not for a specified period of time (as in fixed sentences meted out by criminal courts) but as individually indicated. Such treatment is to be afforded either in the community through contacts with trained probation staff members, through guided utilization of community resources, or else in several types of institutions ranging from minimum to maximum security, staffed with clinically trained personnel. To the extent feasible, they attempt to provide a corrective program in the community rather than in the more rigid, artificial atmosphere of an institution. Finally, the youth authorities offer field services, besides those of an investigative or supervisory nature, aimed at effective community organization for delinquency prevention. With field and institutional services under single direction, a higher degree of co-ordination as well as harmony in basic philosophy can be achieved.

The operation of a typical youth authority program may be seen from the example which follows. When a youngster commits an offense, if the judge in the local court decides that the offense is of such a nature that the youth requires removal from the community, he is committed to the custody of the authority. Taken to a reception center, the youngster would be screened medically and then studied by a psychologist and usually a social worker. Other observations of him are made by nonprofessional, resident personnel during a study period, usually ranging from forty-five to ninety days. In selected cases, psychiatric referrals are made. Meanwhile, field data are gathered by a probation worker. Thereafter, at a hearing, a decision would be made as to whether the youngster can be returned to the community again—either to his own home or to some other placement under the supervision of a probation officer. If release seems inadvisable, he may be sent to one of the state institutions operated by the authority—perhaps a forestry camp, a correctional school, or a reformatory. If committed to one of the state institutions, the youngster would then have contact with professionally trained resident staff. When it is felt that he is seemingly ready to return to the community again, he would be released under the supervision of a parole officer.

Besides serving the individual offender in this manner, the youth authorities have been active in education and in mobilizing efforts at the community level to curb delinquency. These activities have centered on bringing together representatives of local health, welfare, recreational, religious, educational, and law-enforcement groups to promote better mutual understanding and more co-operative planning for services for young people. In general, in the states in which youth authorities have been established, there has been an improvement in the caliber of services provided for delinquent youngsters over that which existed previously. This improvement has been reflected in the reduction of the number of youngsters confined in correctional institutions, in better residential care, in more effective integration between field and institutional services, and in greater stress on preventive activities. However, recent constructive efforts in the treatment of the delinquent and in preventive community organization have not been limited to areas with youth authorities.

Actually, in some phases, the level and quality of services for the delinquent youth and his family are as far advanced in other states without the statewide organizational structure. In certain communities, work of a treatment nature is more intensive and some of the preventive activities are perhaps more highly developed. However, for lack of a statewide organization, there can be considerable variation in services afforded from one locality to the next. The youth authorities, though they are relatively new agencies and struggling with budgetary limitations and lack of professional staff, offer greater uniformity, a more consistent philosophy and services otherwise beyond the finances of smaller communities.

THE ROLE OF THE CLINICAL PSYCHOLOGIST IN YOUTH AUTHORITY PROGRAMS

As in the juvenile courts, psychologists have been called upon to contribute to an understanding of the whys and wherefores presented by the individual delinquent. They have been relied on heavily in the diagnostic centers and in the correctional institutions operated by the youth authorities. Although their work has been largely diagnostic, psychologists have come to play a fairly important part in the somewhat limited individual and group psychotherapeutic work which has been done in the correctional schools and institutions.

While there is no set pattern of operation, the work of the psychologist in the reception centers can be described in general terms. After admission, each youth is referred for diagnostic study. In preparation, the psychologist usually reviews the available case history material and observations which may have been made by other personnel of the center. Contacts with the youngster are often begun with questions about how he is getting along in his new locale, what difficulties led to his coming there, and his plans for the future. The interview is often followed by testing, but the approach is flexible.

Individual testing is relied upon heavily for psychological data. To quite an extent there is a need to supply results of intelligence measurement for which individual tests like the Terman-Merrill and Wechsler (children's and adult) scales are utilized. Personality appraisal by such projective methods as the Rorschach and the Thematic Apperception Test, being time-consuming, seem still largely in the "luxury" category. The extent of reliance on group tests varies considerably. All centers appear to employ group measures to obtain data on school achievement which are useful diagnostically and in program planning. In some settings, group intelligence tests (e.g., Civilian Revision of the Army General

Classification Test) are used to obtain information on intellectual level conveniently and to allow time for personality testing. For study of the personality, group methods are fairly often used both in administering such inventories as the Minnesota Multiphasic and the Bell, as well as experimentally with such projective tools as the group Rorschach and Sentence Completion tests. The group situation is utilized, too, for exploring interests and for aptitude testing with older youngsters for whom such paper-and-pencil tests are suitable. Finally, in one program it may be noted that the one test listed as most frequently administered was the "Audiometer Test." A color-vision test also figures prominently in the testing program in that state.

The results of the individual and group testing and interview impressions are incorporated in reports. Before or after these reports are prepared, the psychologist may confer on dynamics, disposition possibilities, and program with the caseworker, probation officer or psychiatric consultant (if one is available). Since reception centers are designed for a fairly short stay, psychologists serving in such units do little therapeutic work other than brief counseling. However, they may be active in planning the activities and program for their centers.

Psychologists employed in training institutions operated by the youth authorities have the advantage of the possibility of more extended contact with the young people in their care. Though not optimally trained for psychotherapeutic responsibilities, the pressing needs of youngsters in correctional institutions have led these psychologists to inaugurate some individual and a few group therapy programs. While meeting certain needs, these therapeutic efforts would probably be more effective if systematic supervision and training were available. Other responsibilities of the institutional psychologists include diagnostic testing, preparation of reports dealing with the question of the youth's readiness for release on parole, and consulting with other resident personnel. Also, at institutions and at reception centers, psychologists have contributed a significant share of such research as has been done.

In the youth authorities, the juvenile courts and the detention centers, as in almost all correctional settings, the work of the psychologist is made more demanding because of the nature of the essentially authoritarian framework within which he operates. Unlike clinics to which patients come for help because of concern about their symptoms, most young people come in contact with these agencies quite against their will. Just as they do not like being apprehended and tried, usually they do not welcome clinic referrals, but bring along considerable suspicion and resentment. Interviews are colored by the patient's realization that the psychologist prepares material and reports which relate to his "freedom." The psychologist is often regarded as someone to be fooled—as an obstacle to be overcome to avoid confinement or to gain release—instead of as a person who can afford help with underlying difficulties.

The psychologist serving in institutions must cope with an added handicap arising from the fact that his work is often only imperfectly understood by the other employees. This problem is especially real in institutions with a core of "old-timers" in custodial jobs, since constructive psychotherapeutic efforts can very readily be counteracted by contacts with guards or houseparents who have doubts about, or are opposed to, any but traditionally punitive methods. As a final burden, the psychologist doing therapeutic work in correctional settings at times has the problem of divided loyalties about the use of confidential material of an incriminating nature. While not an insuperable difficulty, he must reconcile his responsibility to the individual—who may be potentially dangerous—with his responsibility to society as a whole.

Psychologists working in these settings generally seem to have adapted to such problems and to have tried to work constructively within these and other limitations. Some effort, perhaps not consistently effective, has been exerted to interpret to nonprofessional personnel the role and possible contribution of psychology and its practitioners in the rehabilitation process. Perhaps partly as a reflection of the need for further interpretation is the fact that despite their special training in the dynamics of human behavior, psychologists are as yet to be utilized fully at the level of formulating policy and giving direction to youth authority programs. Leadership for these programs has come from other disciplines—law, probation and parole work, and social work. Reasonably well accepted at the operational level in the reception centers and in training facilities, psychologists have yet to play an important part in over-all program planning and in such other areas as field services and preventive work.

OUTLOOK

For proper perspective, it should be borne in mind that like juvenile court clinics, which are in a limited number of major cities, youth authorities are operating in a handful of larger states. Further, there is no strong indication of an impending landslide for the adoption of such statewide programs elsewhere through the country. While substantial progress has been made under the youth authorities, like the children's court clinics, neither represents a final solution to the problems of delinquency. Though there is little argument, in responsible quarters, about the fundamental approach and the operating principles of the authorities, there remains some division of opinion about the advantages of the organizational framework. Thus, some contend that it is more desirable to work with smaller units. Since a team of specially trained juvenile court judges collaborating with clinical psychologists, psychiatric social workers, psychiatrists, and casework-trained probation workers involves a large financial outlay, operation of courts thus equipped to handle problems of youngsters on a regional instead of a county basis—as in the manner of superior or district courts—has been advocated. Especially in areas where the demand for services might be limited and the costs prohibitive if supported by a county, such regional courts have been recommended as preferable to a combination of conventional juvenile courts linked with statewide central reception centers.

Other planners in the field of services for youth argue that it is a mistake to focus entirely on the behavior problems of youngsters and that youth correctional services are properly part of a total program of child welfare. This group advocates the integration of youth correctional services with other child welfare activities.

Just how the divergent trends in the youth correctional field will be resolved is hard to predict at the present time. It seems likely, however, that economic and other forces may well preclude unusually rapid headway in the next few years. Rather, such progress as may occur will probably take place at a moderate rate.

For psychologists, the field will offer much of the stimulation and many of the same problems which exist currently. One of their main compensations and probably a major motive will be the challenge that is present in their work. They will have to work against great odds. Large case loads are reasonably sure to persist, bolstered by the basic increasing population trend. It does not appear that there will be a very rapid raising of standards of professional operation as a result of an influx of trained workers in the field. Psychologists in correctional programs will have to contend with much pathology in the family backgrounds, contributing to the delinquency of their patients and making subsequent readjustment in the community so much more difficult. The youngsters referred to their clinics usually will lack insight and motivation for self-help, but will appear because it is required. They will be drawn heavily from economically and socially underprivileged families. Also, there will be only limited possibilities of environmental modification, and no great number of new treatment resources to help clinicians to enable their charges to lead more normal, socialized lives. Finally, there will remain a very great need for research to lay bare the fundamental factors contributing to delinquency on the one hand, and its eradication on the other.

REFERENCES

1. Beck, B. M. *Five states*. Philadelphia: American Law Institute, 1951.
2. Bennett, J. V. Blueprinting the new youth correction program. *Federal Probation*, 1951, 15, 3-8.

3. Castner, B. M. Clinical services of the youth authority. *California Youth Authority Quarterly*, 1948, 1, 26-30.

4. Cosulich, G. *Juvenile court laws of the United States*. New York: National Probation Association, 1939.

5. Eliot, M. M. We can do something about juvenile delinquency. *The Child*, 1952, 17, 2.

6. Ellingston, J. R. *Protecting our children from criminal careers*. New York: Prentice-Hall, 1948.

7. Ellingston, J. R. Is the youth authority idea really paying off? *Proceedings of the American Prison Association*. 1950, 197-204.

8. Gardner, G. E. The institution as therapist. *The Child*, 1952, 16, 70-72.

9. MacCormick, W. A. A new service to youth. *The Massachusetts Teacher*, 1949, 28, 5-6.

10. Reed, G. J. Minnesota's YCC program. *Focus*, 1953, 32, 49-51.

11. Rubin, S. Changing youth authority concepts. *Focus*, 1950, 29, 77-81.

12. Teeters, N. K., and Reinemann, J. O. *The challenge of delinquency*. New York: Prentice-Hall, 1950.

13. Turnbladh, W. C. More about youth authority concepts. *Focus*, 1951, 30, 23-25.

14. Zuckerman, S. B. *The clinical psychologist in the juvenile courts of the United States*. Unpublished doctor's dissertation, New York University, 1950.

15. *The community, the state and the delinquent child*. Texas State Youth Development Council, Austin, 1950.

16. *Prevention and treatment of delinquency*. California Youth Authority, Sacramento, 1952.

17. *Progress report*. State of Minnesota Youth Conservation Commission, St. Paul, 1952.

18. *The 1952 directory of psychiatric clinics and other resources in the United States*. The National Association for Mental Health, Inc., New York, 1952.

19. *Third annual report to the governor*. Texas State Youth Development Council, Austin, 1952.

XXI.

THE CLINICAL PSYCHOLOGIST IN A
TRAINING SCHOOL FOR DELINQUENTS

KIRK TORRANCE

Institutions dealing with delinquent children have a number of purposes, in which may be included physical care, education, punishment, removal from the community, security, and rehabilitation. Of these purposes, that of rehabilitation is considered to be the primary one, in the sense that it is the one which ultimately makes a difference to the child, and to the community after his release. The definition of rehabilitation involves a combination of all that is done within the institution to benefit a child, or to contribute in a positive way to his future welfare.

Training schools usually serve children between the ages of eight and eighteen approximately, with some variation at times in different institutions. The ideal goal of any training school is to combine the various influences on members of its population in such a manner as to increase the chances that they will live future lives more satisfying both to themselves and to others, and to reduce to the greatest degree the chances that they will again break the law after their release. A psychologist serves the institution to the degree that he is able to contribute to this purpose.

HISTORICAL DEVELOPMENT

Ten years or more ago there was a traditional regard for the psychologist as a specialized diagnostician or technician, whose specialty was the measurement of intellectual functioning or various abilities. In training schools at that time, it was customary for psychologists to administer individual or group measures of intelligence, and in some cases measures of academic achievement, reporting scores in terms of intelligence quotients, or other numerals, with perhaps some comments as to the type of examination to which these scores apply. These results were often combined with data obtained by other professional services, or placed on a sheet involving an outline only, with little explanation or further comment. Some training schools employed no psychologist at all, and in those which employed more than one, or in which training facilities were set up, the psychological function was frequently limited as described.

The development of psychology in training schools has been influenced to a large degree by the philosophy at work in the particular training school, which varies in different institutions. Such philosophies can be classified roughly as punitive, confining, legalistic, educational, and therapeutic. These approaches, and the resulting roles of psychologists, may be described to some degree as follows:

Punitive. In such an institution the concept is held that boys who break the law are deserving of punishment, and therefore should be subjected to discomforts and pain so that they will not be inclined to repeat their delinquent behavior, for fear of the consequences that it will bring. Although this approach has often been shown to have little or no lasting effect, some persons remain who agree with this point of view. Psychologists are seldom needed in such an institution, and are seldom satisfied in such an environment.

Confining. The primary purpose of this type of institution is to hold those who live there, so that they will be kept away from other members of society, and kept within the boundaries of the institution. This is often with the thought that society needs to be protected from them. The goal in this instance is safety, and custody, with perhaps the provision of minimal comforts during confinement. Other aspects of the institutional program are secondary to this consideration. In such an institution, psychologists may not be employed, or might perhaps work on a part-time basis, since the understanding of the individual boy is not of primary importance.

Legalistic. The purpose of such an institution is to fulfill the law regarding the care and training of delinquents, removing them from the community, and keeping them for a period of time equal to the expectations of the law and the community. As a goal, the law must be satisfied, and the persons sent to such an institutional program may justly feel that they have paid their debt to society. In this type of institution, psychological services are not especially needed, since it is the observance of the law more than the effect on the boy that is considered.

Educational. The philosophy of this orientation holds that boys need proper school and vocational training to improve themselves, as implied by the title "Industrial School" or "Training School." Since training is of considerable importance in such institutions, the capacities for training and the interests in training need to be determined, and the work of psychologists is usually concerned with such capacities and interests. This goes a step beyond the measurement of intellectual capacity, but does not necessarily include the understanding of personality characteristics.

Therapeutic. An institution with such an orientation attempts to utilize all of the forces which might work to the benefit of the individuals in its care. This requires both an understanding of the forces involved, and an understanding of the individuals who are subjected to these forces. In both respects, a variety of psychological functions in such an institution can contribute to its program, and a much more adequate functioning is possible. Diagnosis is applied as already described, but also includes evaluation of the personality factors of the persons sent to the institution. Therapy is applied in different ways to bring about personality changes, and research is applied to an understanding of the individuals in the institution, a better clarification of the techniques used, and a better understanding of the effects of the institution itself. All of these functions are needed in such an institution for the full development of its treatment goals and methods. Consequently, there is much work for psychologists in training schools where this type of approach prevails.

It is recognized readily that no training school contains any one of these points of view consistently, and that persons can be found in nearly any training school who represent each of them. However, the functioning of psychologists within a training school setting, especially one which represents a therapeutic orientation, is greatly affected by the attitudes of other persons in the situation, and sometimes the functioning of psychologists is limited by these attitudes. Such attitudes are probably more significant in training schools or other correctional institutions than in mental hospitals, clinics, or other organizations which are more directly of a therapeutic type.

The historical development of psychology in training schools may be described as the increase of psychological services which becomes possible with the growth of the total training school program, following the progression indicated by the different approaches described. It may be seen that as the program of a training school advances in its degree of constructive effect on boys committed to it, the significance and usefulness of psychological services becomes greater.

ILLINOIS STATE TRAINING SCHOOL FOR BOYS

The Illinois State Training School for Boys receives boys from the entire state, mostly ranging in age from nine to seventeen years at the time of arrival. Their period of stay averages about seven to nine months, and usually ranges from about three months to two years. The capacity of the institution is about 500 boys for a suitable treatment program, and the population has varied from 350 to 600 at various times. Assignment within the institution and duration of stay has been decided by a staff composed of representatives of various units of the institution, such as social, religious, educational, vocational, and psychological services. Boys are housed in eighteen cottages, which range in capacity from thirteen to forty-two boys. Approximately two thirds of the population attend the Academic School, and the other third is assigned to various work activities, utilized in treatment primarily to provide favorable working relationships with adults.

The Psychology Unit, consisting of four psychologists and one stenographer, is in the Clinic Section of the institution, which consists of Social Work, Psychiatry, Religion, Medicine, Dentistry, and Records, in addition to Psychology. The Clinic Section in turn is part of the Program Service of the training school, and this includes Recreation, Education, and Cottage Life, in addition to the Clinic. The Program Service and Administrative Service constitute the two primary divisions of the institution.

As a result, the professional relationships of psychologists are primarily with other units of the Clinic, but they carry on contacts with other parts of the institution as well. Psychologists frequently serve on institutional committees and on the staff which considers placement of boys within the institution, goals of planning and treatment, and suitable time for release. They have at various times assisted in the recreational program, helped in the planning of inservice training for employees, and in planning treatment policies for the institution. They serve as consultants for employees on psychological matters, and sometimes provide assistance in research projects carried on by other services in the training school. The policy of maintaining familiarity with the total program, and with persons involved in it, is often more important than more specialized activities.

It must also be observed that the foregoing description of organizational structure applies to the Illinois State Training School for Boys during the years 1952 and 1953. Beginning with 1954, a rearrangement of the procedures for handling delinquents in the State of Illinois may produce changes in the former structure, and these changes are not completely defined at the time this is written.

The positions for psychologists which exist at present include three full-time psychologists, one student worker, one psychologist who specializes in speech and hearing, and one clerk-stenographer. The speech and hearing specialist falls at a Psychologist I level in the State of Illinois, which requires graduation with major courses in psychology, one year of graduate work, and one year of actual experience in clinical psychology, preferably with at least one course in speech and hearing, and an interest in this field. There are two positions as Psychologist II, which require a master's degree with specialization in psychology, and two years of actual experience. There is one position as Supervising Psychologist I, which requires a masters degree and three years of actual experience.

The Student Worker position has no stated requirements, but is usually filled by a person having a bachelor's degree who is interested in getting practical experience in psychology. This position is usually used as an internship.

Standards of employment vary from state to state, and are apparently determined to some degree by the training facilities and availability of psychologists in the state where a training school is located. In Illinois, positions are obtained through civil service, and usually require the completion of an examination for qualification. In addition to the stated requirements for the positions in the Psychology Unit, it has been found desirable to select persons who show an active interest in the work of the training school, and in the type of program which it represents.

FUNCTIONS OF THE PSYCHOLOGY UNIT

Each member of the institutional staff is regarded as a member of a team, contributing both specialized and generalized services to the organization as a whole. Co-ordination of function is considered of primary importance in accomplishing the institutional goal of more satisfactory adjustment after release. The characteristic specialized function of the psychologist is considered to be the study and treatment of the behavior and personality of the individual boy within the institution. This is related to the function of the social worker, who approaches the boy from the standpoint of family, community, and institutional relationships; the psychiatrist, who frequently deals with psychopathological conditions from a medical standpoint; the chaplain, who is concerned with religious belief and practice; and the physician and dentist, who deal with physical and dental health. Many functions, such as staff participation and treatment by individual interviews are shared by a number of different professions, including psychology. The Psychology Unit seeks to integrate its services with those of other areas in such a way as to provide the most benefit to boys in the training school population, with a view toward a more effective accomplishment of the more general purpose of the total organization. Some of its functions may be described in further detail.

PSYCHOTHERAPY

The most direct role which the psychologist plays in the treatment program is through psychotherapy, here used in the sense of direct contacts with boys, having the deliberate purpose of producing personality changes which accompany a fuller understanding of themselves and more satisfactory adjustments with other people. This requires experience in interviewing methods, and understanding of personality. It may be in the form of individual interviews or group therapy. No particular orientation is specified as a therapeutic approach, since each psychologist has had different training, and uses the approach which he finds best adapted for him as a result of his experience. In this respect, the psychologist is one of a number of persons offering this service, the others being the psychiatrist, social worker, chaplain, speech therapist, school administrator, disciplinarian, vocational director, and others who have occasion for individual contacts with boys on a regular basis.

Referral to Psychology for individual therapy is usually made in meetings of the institutional staff, and is occasionally suggested by a social worker, psychologist, or boy in the institution. Each psychologist on the staff usually has from one to three cases at a time for individual therapy, and at the time this is written one psychologist has a therapy group consisting of six boys who meet once a week. Individual interviews are held from two per week to one every two weeks, depending on the nature of the problem and the time available. Usually boys are referred to psychology when regular individual contacts are felt to be desirable, and when it is felt by the staff that the boy has the capacity to profit from such contacts.

Although all employees of a training school are engaged in therapy directly or indirectly, the psychologist appears particularly suited for this function because of his training in the scientific understanding of personality and behavior, and in the study of therapeutic principles. In considering the therapeutic conditions of the training school, it becomes evident that the requirements for successful psychotherapy are somewhat different from those in the community. One of the chief differences is that persons coming for therapy in the community usually act on their own choice and volition, making contact with a therapist because of a need for help that is both felt and expressed. In a training school, on the other hand, the child is sent by the court, against his own choice and volition, and in most cases takes the point of view that he needs no help, that the only effective treatment for him is release. When psychotherapy is offered in the form of help in understanding the boy's problems, it is unwelcome, because the boy often sees his confinement as his only problem, and regards the interest of other people in his affairs as a meddlesome imposition. Consequently, other methods than the usual ones often need to be utilized in order to produce a change in the personality of the boy. Psychologists contribute to psychotherapeutic effectiveness by assisting in the development of such methods.

DIAGNOSIS

A less direct, but more specialized function of the psychologist is diagnosis, which includes the determination of various characteristics of a boy which are useful in planning for that boy. This usually includes the use of diagnostic devices such as measures of intelligence, interests, aptitudes, and skills; and projective methods to assist in the understanding of personality. These devices usually require specialized skills and training for both administration and interpretation, and usually consume a large proportion of the psychologist's time. The techniques regularly used at St. Charles include the Machover Figure Drawing, the Revised Beta Examination, a sentence completion test devised at this institution, and a brief scale for determining level of literacy, also constructed at this training school. These are followed by interviews with each boy, and other brief examinations, which vary with the examiner, and the characteristics of the boy. For referrals and other special problems, more commonly used measures are employed, such as the Wechsler-Bellevue scales, the Rorschach Test, the Thematic Apperception Test, and the Bender-Gestalt. For examining boys with vocational problems, a wide variety of interest and aptitude scales are available.

For diagnostic study, every new boy as he arrives is seen routinely for the group examinations, followed by an individual interview and individual examination by one of the psychologists on the staff. Referrals can be made by the staff, or by a social worker, teacher, work supervisor, or other employee, and are usually requested when the boy offers a personality problem which seems to require more thorough personality study than would be feasible at the time the boy arrived. Other referrals are to find further evidence of organic damage, for vocational study and guidance, for follow-up of original examination to show the nature and degree of personality change that has occurred, to decide on further treatment, or to decide on possible transfer to other institutions. Written reports of all examinations are made, and placed with the other clinical records of the boy, for consideration by staff or by other professional employees. A copy of each report is sent to the Academic School, to be available in the file there. Findings from psychology reports are used to assist in placement of the boy within the institution, planning of individual treatment, comparison with other diagnostic findings, determination of nature and degree of emotional disturbance, consideration for release, and many other specialized considerations.

CONSULTATION

Another indirect role in which psychologists contribute to treatment is through consultation with other employees who deal with boys in assisting them to gain a better understanding of the boy from their own standpoint. Such employees may include cottage parents, school teachers, social workers, work supervisors, or others who influence boys in any way. In this respect, the psychologist's understanding of personality and behavior may be of assistance to other persons in the form of comparing different approaches to the same problem for a clearer understanding of it. For the most part, contacts of this sort are of an informal nature, although in recent months time has been scheduled for psychologists to be present in the Academic School for observation, and consultation with school employees at certain specified times. In other areas, psychologists usually contact employees when there is occasion to discuss a particular boy or a particular situation.

RESEARCH

The role of research is even less direct, but perhaps most important. In any situation, the meaning of actions in regard to that particular situation needs to be known, and in order to be known, studies must be made to determine it. Through training and experience in research techniques, the psychologist is also somewhat more specialized than other employees. By the use of research, there is continual checking and re-checking of methods and results, with a view to an ultimate understanding and improvement of them.

Studies by psychologists at St. Charles so far have concerned themselves with comparison of projective evaluation with behavior, patterns of vocational interests characteristic of delinquents, patterns on the Wechsler-Bellevue test which are characteristic of the training school population, and the relationship of psychological findings at the time the boy arrives with his adjustment later during his stay in the institution. Some research is done by persons not actually employed at the training school, but using the training school facilities as a means of collecting data. This policy has been encouraged whenever such a study appears to make a worth-while contribution to the understanding of delinquency or related subjects, and is usually done by persons who are attempting to meet requirements for advanced degrees.

TRAINING

Another highly important, though less direct role of a psychologist is training, which in an institutional situation must be distinguished from training of a more general nature. A psychologist qualified for employment in the institution has had a general training covering many of his activities, but invariably needs more training in the methods, procedures, and applications in use at the particular place where he is employed. Training also applies in a more general way, since any employee should become more proficient in his function, and training is necessary for this purpose. Without a training function, the development of a psychology program is slower, and its usefulness to the institution eventually tends to decrease rather than increase.

At St. Charles, training is for the most part incidental to the work experience involved, and is primarily oriented around this experience. It includes such activities as discussion of diagnostic findings, recording and later evaluation of contacts with boys, attendance at professional conferences, presenting information about topics or techniques of interest, conferences to discuss therapeutic techniques, and other similar means of increasing the information and experience of psychologists. Seminars are usually held by psychologists once a week, and by the Clinic Section every two weeks for discussions with institutional personnel, and with outside speakers at times. Only part of this training is formalized, but much of it is planned with a view to offering a variety of clinical experience.

COMPARISON WITH OTHER TRAINING SCHOOLS

In preparation of this article, requests for information were sent to a number of other training schools throughout the country, and of these, replies were received from five.[1] These represent a comparison with the program at St. Charles, and help to illustrate general and particular possibilities in the work of training school psychologists.

Generally, these institutions reported diagnostic work as the most time-consuming feature of their programs, with therapy next in order of frequency. The next greatest amount of time was reported as being spent in meetings and conferences, and the psychologist was reported as being a member of, or chairman of, the guidance committee, classification board, or other administrative group that decides such matters as placement and length of stay. Research, training, and other administrative duties were reported as being part of the functions of psychologists, but much less time apparently is spent in these activities.

The questions asked of these institutions included what they considered the most important contributions of psychology, both in relation to the present program, and potential future contributions. Diagnostic and therapeutic contributions were fairly well described in the replies, and constituted the most prominent contributions that were considered important. Others mentioned were assistance in planning the institutional policy and program as to training and therapy, helping to maintain a more beneficial institutional climate, inservice training for employees,

[1] Those institutions providing information, in addition to the Illinois State Training School for Boys, were as follows:
> Boys' Industrial School, Lancaster, Ohio
> State Industrial School for Boys, Topeka, Kansas
> Fred C. Nelles School for Boys, Whittier, California
> Maryland Training School for Boys, Lock Raven, Maryland
> Iowa Training School for Boys, Eldora, Iowa

Profound appreciation is expressed to these institutions for their willingness to provide information concerning their psychological services.

assistance in adequate classification and assignment of boys, and the use of psychologists in helping to understand the nature of disciplinary problems. There was particular emphasis on the therapeutic contributions of psychologists, both in direct effect on children within the institution, and in the general program.

Potential contributions to the program of the respective institutions were described in quite distinct ways by the different replies. One was concerned about communication of psychological results in terms of making reports intelligible to the rest of the staff, one was concerned about more adequate development of the number of therapists and therapeutic skills of psychologists, one was concerned about increasing staff and gaining more administrative acceptance, and one was concerned about the function of psychologists in training other employees so that the total program could be oriented more therapeutically through this training. The fifth institution did not reply specifically to this point. There was considerable agreement among all those who replied as to the need for professional development of psychologists, and the role that they can play in employee education and the development of institutional policy.

Because of the small number of training schools represented in these results, the findings should not be considered typical of training schools in general, but only as a report of points of view in a few schools that were willing to express some characteristics of their psychological services. They illustrate the variety of values that are placed on psychological functions in different institutions.

GENERAL COMMENTS AND FUTURE GOALS

The foregoing discussion of psychological functions in training schools gives several directions as to present trends and possible future developments. The function of any profession in a specialized field such as the institutional treatment of delinquents is to some degree related to the nature of the population to which the services of the profession are directed. Some institutions, such as those for psychotics and mental defectives, have a somewhat more clearly defined population than those for delinquents. Where psychotics have a common characteristic, mental illness, and defectives have a common characteristic, inadequate intellectual functioning, there is no single characteristic of personality that delinquents are found to have in common which is not also a characteristic of some persons not considered delinquent. The psychologist who deals with delinquents must therefore have an understanding of a wide variety of behavior conditions in persons with whom he deals. However, since the age group of training schools is primarily within the adolescent years, the personality and behavior of adolescents is one of his primary concerns.

Of the many potential contributions of psychology, one which would seem to be particularly important is a more adequate development of research, with a view to a better understanding of what is being accomplished in an institutional population, and what effect such experiences are actually having on institutionalized persons. In considering the present programs of training schools, it becomes very evident that there is much more to be learned about these conditions. Other applications of research are practically unlimited as far as personality, delinquency, and behavior in general are concerned.

Psychological services to employees as well as to the institutional population represent another opportunity for future development, since the changes in the employee population are often significant in the changes which occur in institutionalized persons. Such work can include the development of better methods of employee selection, and the use of methods with persons already employed that would assist them in improving their functions within the institution. This is seen in the role reported by many psychologists in employee training, and the increasing recognition of the value of such training.

Another area for future progress in psychology which is now being developed is a more systematic understanding of the personality characteristics which seem to be related to delinquent behavior at different times, and the manner in which these personality characteristics can be utilized in treatment. If something is done within the institution to change the boy's attitudes, feelings, convictions, or concepts during his confinement, he is in a better position to contend with the influences that led him to break the law, even though he is returned to the same environment from which he originally came. Although personality and therapy of delinquents have been widely studied, much more needs to be known to show a real difference in treatment effectiveness.

There is opportunity for future development of psychology in training schools in every direction in which psychologists already function in such institutions, and all that has been described as present function has its future implications. The direction of future developments would appear to depend upon further research discoveries, more experience and understanding of present methods, the use of new methods, and the opportunities provided by the particular situations in which psychologists function.

XXII.

THE CLINICAL PSYCHOLOGIST IN THE
PRISON

NORMAN FENTON

The history of clinical psychology in the prisons needs to be written. The author is well aware that his account will have limitations because the historical data have not, as yet, been assembled critically in an authentic publication. The first recorded use of clinical psychology in a prison, albeit as an experiment there, was in 1910 at the New York State Reformatory for Women at Bedford Hills (18). One of the first research laboratories for the study of adult offenders was established at Bedford Hills with Dr. Mabel Fernald in charge. Subsequent studies prior to 1916 were made in various state institutions by the Fernalds, von Kleinsmid, Knollin, the Ordahls, Renz, and others. Lewis M. Terman (19) has summarized the findings of these early studies of prison and reformatory inmates. According to Jackson (12), the first organized psychological service in penal institutions in this country was initiated by Edgar Doll in the State of New Jersey in 1919. In subsequent years, a number of other states, initially New York and Massachusetts and later Indiana, Texas and Pennsylvania, to mention a few, inaugurated psychological studies of prison inmates. Early in 1930, the Federal Bureau of Prisons organized its classification services under the United States Public Health Service, and thereafter employed a number of clinical psychologists in its institutions.

In 1926, Overholser (17) found, in a study in which replies were obtained from fifty-six penal institutions, that four had full-time and eight part-time psychologists. Of thirty-one reformatories answering his inquiry, six had full-time and nine part-time psychologists. In 1933, the Handbook of American Prisons and Reformatories reported, as quoted by Jackson (12), that twenty-three penal institutions were employing psychologists. Marquis (16) reported the total number of correctional psychologists in juvenile and adult institutions in 1941 to have been ninety-six. This number, he indicated, had dropped to eighty by 1944 as a result of war conditions. Developments during the past decade have probably increased this total to well over one hundred.

In the past, the clinical psychologist in the adult penal institutions has been concerned largely with routine testing and classification. The role which may in the future be played by psychologists in the prisons may best be understood if we consider not only their functions in administering the customary clinical instruments, but also their usefulness in connection with individual and group psychotherapy. In the more advanced adult penal institutions of the United States and Europe, the psychologist has now become part of a therapeutic team, each of whose members is expected to make specialized diagnostic contributions, but all of whom are responsible for the treatment of the disturbances of personality which bring adult offenders to prison.

THE PREVENTION OF RECIDIVISM

The basic problem before the adult penal institutions in the solution of which the clinical psychologist of the present and the future may play a major part is the discovery of specific methods of treating successfully the men and women who are committed to prison. While all types of criminals present problems which should be of interest to the psychologist, one of the most interesting and challenging, perhaps, is the forger. Those who fall into this category have a compulsion to write checks either as a means of meeting real or fancied financial emergencies or sometimes seemingly from the mere impulse to do so. This problem behavior may be expressed either when sober or when under the influence of alcohol. As a group, forgers are superior intellectually to other criminals and also have had better educational advantages. These men and women have usually rather pleasant and agreeable personalities. They are good prisoners and perform useful work in the institutions. In most cases, they are released from prison upon initial commitment after a relatively short stay. From the standpoint of society, the prisons merely provide custody. What is attempted by way of treatment does not usually result in cure of the causal conditions in the personality of the forger. Sooner or later many of these men and women are wont to repeat the behavior which brought them into prison in the first place and to be returned there as recidivists.

What is true for the forger is also true of the imprisoned robber, the burglar, the sexually deviant, and those guilty of other common types of criminality. A large percentage of these prisoners under ordinary circumstances, especially the younger group, are likely to go to prison, spend varying lengths of time there, return to society, and thereafter commit additional offenses for which, should they be apprehended, they are brought back to prison. In the better penal institutions of today men and women are retained under adequate and humane custodial auspices. While there, many types of treatment are provided including medical, psychological, and psychiatric observation and care; academic education; vocational training; recreation; opportunities for religious instruction and practice; and general social welfare assistance. Although these methods, when used as a general therapeutic battery, may seemingly be fruitful for better adjustment in prison and perhaps on parole, none, however, have been demonstrated as yet to be specifically effective for particular types of offenders in so far as the prevention of recidivism is concerned.

Figuratively speaking, psychologists, especially in the more advanced prison systems, may be considered at the present time as members of a team of social scientists which is struggling on the side of society against the unsolved problems of criminality. Other members of the group are the psychiatrist, the physician, the psychiatric social worker (sometimes called the sociologist), the educational or vocational counselor, the academic and vocational teacher, the chaplain, and other professional personnel. In addition, of course, in the good institution, these specially trained individuals work with the professional prison administrators, wardens or superintendents, correctional captains, sergeants or officers, stewards, tradesmen, classification and parole personnel, and those with other designations who are charged with the responsibilities for the custodial services, maintenance and other aspects of institutions for adult offenders. This team of prison workers should be concerned not merely with the immediate problem of taking care of the adult criminals. They should have as a fundamental purpose, which would be especially prominent in the minds of the clinical psychologists, the necessity for understanding the causal backgrounds for criminality in the lives of individual offenders and the development of specific methods of training and treatment for the types of criminality which bring men to prison. In a still more fundamental sense, the prevention and control of criminality in society and the avoidance of imprisonment are the essential problems before social scientists in the prisons and elsewhere.

THE PSYCHOLOGIST IN THE PRISON SYSTEM

The activities of the psychologist in the prison program[1] may best

[1] In an unpublished report in 1951, Raymond Corsini and Wilson Newman summarized data from a questionnaire sent out to eighty-eight prison psychologists. Of those queried, thirty-nine or 44 per cent replied. They found that the master's degree was the academic level of the greater number of those who replied, thirty-one in all. Of the others, seven had the doctor's degree and nine the bachelor's degree. The master's degree is the civil service requirement for senior clinical psychologist in several jurisdictions. The median salary for prison psychologists was reported to be about $4,500. The upper range of these salaries was above $8,000. The psychologists who replied indicated on the average that the desirable ratio of inmates to psychologists was about one psychologist to 250 inmates, with a range from 50 to 500. It is apparent that this ratio would be influenced by the number of allied technicians employed, such as psychiatric social workers, psychiatrists, vocational counselors, and educational or guidance counselors.

be understood by the development of the diagnostic and treatment program in a concrete prison situation. A reorganization in the prison system of California offered an opportunity for the writer to participate in organized efforts to meet the challenge described in the previous pages, namely, to assist in the transition of a prison system from a custodial emphasis to one concerned with the diagnosis, guidance and treatment of its inmates. Although some forerunners of desirable emphases upon the understanding and treatment of inmates had been present in the program of the California prison system prior to that time, the summer of 1944 saw the beginning of organized efforts to accomplish the above-mentioned transition to a professional program.

After almost ten years, the accomplishments in California are still far short of the ultimate objectives. Probably another decade or two of professional leadership and continued and additional legislative support of the program will be required to accomplish the desirable objectives. It may be interesting and informative, however, while recognizing the limitations of present achievements, for the reader to follow the course of the activities and developments in the prison system in California during this period of time.

THE ESTABLISHMENT OF THE RECEPTION-GUIDANCE CENTER AT SAN QUENTIN

The first development in California of interest to clinical psychologists was the establishment at San Quentin in the fall of 1944 of a reception center, or as it was legally designated, a diagnostic and psychiatric clinic. This agency was subsequently named the Reception-Guidance Center of the California Department of Corrections, to lend emphasis to its constructive purposes. This initial project faced the problem of examining adult male offenders received in 1944 at San Quentin for the entire prison system and planning a program of guidance and treatment for each one of them during his incarceration.

Among the historical forerunners of the special reception center at San Quentin for an entire prison system, may be mentioned the Diagnostic Depot at Joliet and the receiving section at Menard, established in Illinois in 1933; the reception unit at St. Cloud in 1935 for the Minnesota prison system; and the development of reception facilities at Jackson, Michigan in 1937 for that state. In Wisconsin, a statewide traveling field service first established in 1925 has examined new admissions in the institution to which assigned. The most interesting reception unit, opened recently at Menlo Park in New Jersey, has a broader social purpose than mere prison classification, in that children as well as adults are examined with a view to presentence study of offenders as well as for institutional classification.

The first Reception-Guidance Center of the California Department of Corrections was located within the outer walls of San Quentin Prison, upon which it is dependent for its maintenance and custodial services. Since its clinical services are departmental in character, these are not under the Warden of San Quentin, but under an Associate Warden, especially chosen for his background in correctional casework, responsible directly in this area to the central office staff in Sacramento. The clinical staff of the Reception-Guidance Center has included psychiatrists, clinical psychologists, social workers, chaplains, educational counselors, teachers, physicians and recreational workers. The first head of the Center was a clinical psychologist (7).

A primary purpose of the Department of Corrections in the establishment of the Reception-Guidance Center was, in so far as possible, to segregate the newly arrived inmates from the regular prison population during the two-month period of initial study. Because of limitations of housing, this has never been fully accomplished at San Quentin. However, the construction of two new facilities especially planned as reception-guidance centers has been undertaken. The first, which was opened in 1951 at Chino in Southern California, offers complete segregation of the newly received inmates. After their study has been completed and administrative details for transfer arranged, the men are transferred from the reception-guidance centers to one of the six prisons in California.

The problem before the staff of the reception-guidance centers may be recognized by a brief statement of their case loads. During the current year, over 5,000 prisoners will be received in the reception-guidance centers; including about 850 parole violators and 750 Youth Authority wards. Those who enter may range in age from fifteen years to over eighty. Vocational backgrounds are equally varied, as are the health and physical status of the men. Prison inmates as a group tend to come from the ranks of unskilled labor in about twice the proportion of laborers in the population as a whole. Represented among them will be the various major religious and racial backgrounds. The cultural and economic levels are much lower than for an unselected group in the community.

The Major Areas of Clinical Study

The staff of the Reception-Guidance Center attempts to compile a case study of each inmate. The following areas are included in such studies: (1) the social background, (2) criminal history, (3) medical examination, (4) vocational study, (5) educational history and analysis, (6) religious history and attitudes, (7) initial adjustment to prison, (8) personality summary (psychological and psychiatric studies). Because of limited space, we will describe only the work of the psychologist in this clinical team. Not only will the customary work of the clinical psychologist be considered but also vocational and educational studies which may be the responsibility of the clinical psychologist in the smaller penal institution, where the professional staff is limited. In such institutions, the psychologist may be expected to utilize services of interns and inmates in carrying out necessary routine activities.

Whatever other assignments the psychologist may have, he will need to co-ordinate the group testing program. It has been customary in California to begin the test survey by a brief orientation talk to give the inmates an idea of what is expected of them. This is usually conducted by one of the professional staff. Prior to the orientation talk, it is the practice in the California reception-guidance centers to give the Wide Range Vocabulary Test, Form A or B, to separate out such groups as the non-English speaking, nonreaders, and illiterates. These groups may be given nonverbal tests, such as the Revised Beta or the Otis Alpha and the Cornell Selectee Index; the latter is read aloud by the examiner. The non-English speaking groups are handled when possible by means of interpreters. Inmates who are literate are given the regular group test battery during a period of sixteen or more hours. Additional tests may be given as time permits and the case warrants. The above tests are also included in those listed by prison psychologists who replied to the questionnaire sent out by Corsini and Newman.

VOCATIONAL ANALYSIS AND GUIDANCE

In the reception-guidance centers of California, the vocational study is carried out by specialists called vocational counselors. A vocational interest test and various aptitude and performance measures in the vocational field are administered by these specialists or by the clinical psychologists. The tests which have been used routinely include the Kuder Preference Record, the Revised Minnesota Paper Form Board Test for Mechanical Aptitude, the MacQuarrie Test for Mechanical Ability, and the Differential Aptitude Test (forms for clerical and mechanical ability). A variety of tests may be used to supplement these, if time permits, in accordance with individual need.

The interview, which includes the use of oral trade questions and other means for estimating the man's vocational competence as well as his occupational interests, is utilized to integrate the data from the tests and other sources. A good measure of his actual competence and willingness as a worker and also a report of his attitudes and personal qualities has been obtained from the observations of the man by the supervisors of the work projects where in the past Reception-Guidance Center men have been employed. The definition of tentative vocational plans within the man's capacity while in the institution or later on parole are arrived at, therefore, with his own co-operation, supplemented by considerable data from tests, behavioristic observations and the vocational interview.

THE STUDY OF EDUCATIONAL BACKGROUND

The educational status of the man is determined by group tests such as the California Progressive Achievement Test Battery or the Stanford Achievement Tests. Other measures of scholastic background are used in individual cases. As previously noted, the Wide Range Vocabulary Test, Form A or B, is used routinely to differentiate the groups for various purposes, especially in group testing. Usually this information is supplemented by communications from educational authorities or relatives and, of course, by the personal interview. The inmate's learning process has been noted in an actual school situation during the day. Plans for educational work during his stay in prison may be defined specifically in terms of the man's interests and ambitions and the offerings of the institutions. On parole, the program may be planned for the releasee in terms of adult educational programs and other opportunities for education in the communities to which they are released.

THE PSYCHOLOGICAL STUDY

The clinical psychologist carries on his study of the men by means of group and individual mental tests and tests of personality. Group tests of mental ability or personality which have at various times been used routinely are: the Army General Classification Tests, Revised Beta Examination, the California Test of Mental Maturity (short form), the Cornell Selectee Index, and the Otis Alpha (nonverbal). The individual tests which have been used are the Stanford Revision of the Binet-Simon Test and the Wechsler-Bellevue. The personality test most widely utilized has been the Minnesota Multiphasic Personality Inventory. Projective methods for the study of personality have been employed with a minority of cases. These have included the Rorschach, the Draw-a-Person Test, and the Murray Thematic Apperception Test. Because of heavy case load these and other of the projective techniques are, unfortunately, not used nearly as often as desirable. Test results and other data of the case history are evaluated by the psychologist and supplemented by his personal interview with the inmate. The clinical psychologist is free to use other devices, as time permits, in his study of the inmate. For example, in the appraisal of intellectual impairment in older inmates, the Goldstein-Scheerer, the Lowenfeld Mosaic and the Bender-Gestalt have been employed.[2]

2 In the Corsini-Newman study referred to previously, the findings were similar regarding the use of projective tests, although not all prison psychologists were in agreement as to their value.

THE STAFF CONFERENCE

An important feature of the Reception-Guidance Center program has been the staffing of the cases at a friendly, democratic session at which all reported their findings. This takes place toward the end of the man's stay. It has varied in length and thoroughness with the size of the staff and the case load. Data from all eight areas of inquiry are reported in the order indicated above. The staff tries to evaluate these observations. The attempt is made, thereafter, to interpret each history in terms of the causal factors in the cases. When time permits, they discuss the unmet needs in the lives of these prisoners during childhood or later which may have brought about conflict or frustration and prepared the soil in which their personality disturbances grew.

After the data of the case have been contributed by members of the staff, each from his own point of vantage, and the group as a whole has formulated some tentative explanations of causal factors, the conference has usually turned to the important questions, first of determining the degree of treatability of the man, and then of formulating recommendations for his treatment in prison. In those cases where custodial precautions are not indicated by the seriousness of the man's case, the willingness of the man to change has been important in determining the type of institution to which he may be sent. Whether he may be recommended for transfer to a prison with very close custody and supervision or to one in which the restraint is minimal and the program designed for men capable of taking some responsibility themselves, is dependent in part upon his attitudes as noted by the clinical psychologist and other members of the staff. Generally, the recommendations for treatment have been determined by the man's needs and attitudes, and have been considered in the order of the major areas of clinical study presented above. An effort has been made to formulate definite and practical recommendations which take full cognizance of the peculiar problems of prison management.

Another major responsibility of the clinical psychologist in the Reception-Guidance Center as in other clinical agencies has been the study of inmates with a view to the diagnosis of mental deficiency. This has been carried out when possible by means of individual mental tests in relationship with the total history. In these cases, the psychiatrist has usually collaborated with the psychologist. At the staff conference, the diagnosis of mental deficiency may be confirmed by the clinical group. Evidences of serious personality maladjustment have also been referred by the psychiatrist to the psychologist for supplementary study and later clinical discussion, usually at the staff conference. Cases of overt mental disorder have been hospitalized immediately upon recognition with the

approval of the psychiatrist in the psychiatric ward of the San Quentin
hospital or at the California Medical Facility at Terminal Island.

The staff conference has served not only the purpose of integrating
the data about each man and planning for his career in prison and on
parole, but also has been an excellent occasion for the study of the
functions and procedures of the Reception-Guidance Center itself. As
a medium for inservice training of prison personnel, it has also been
very valuable; correctional officers, trade supervisors and administrative
officials have been invited to attend. It will be valuable also for purposes
of training if electrical transcriptions or possibly sound motion pictures
may some day be made of the actual case conferences.

GROUP GUIDANCE AND TREATMENT

The work of the psychiatrists, clinical psychologists and educators
has also included in addition to individual counseling, some efforts in
group guidance or therapy. Space permits only a brief statement of this
work which is still in the process of development. It will clarify the
situation if we recognize three levels of group work. The first, which is
rather superficial, has been called group counseling or guidance. The
second is a limited group therapy restricted in length of time to one or
a few months. The third is group psychotherapy on a deeper or more
intensive level.

The major objectives of group guidance are to help the men, especially
those willing to co-operate in treatment, to gain some insight into their
problems, and to guide them toward understanding and acceptance of
themselves and toward the development of constructive interests and life
plans. In the Reception-Guidance Center, this program of guidance has
been preceded by other methods of orientation. Thus, the men are
reached initially in the county jail by a practical bulletin of information
about prison life, concerned with such things as mail, visits, clothing and
the like. This is designed to allay certain fears and to correct common
misconceptions found among incoming prisoners, which formerly tended
to add to their initial emotional upset and to delay adjustment to prison.
This publication is supplemented by a longer bulletin given to the men
upon arrival in the Reception-Guidance Center. These two publications
were prepared by the staff and in collaboration with inmates; the latter
contributed questions and problems. A pamphlet illustrated by a talented
inmate describing the Reception-Guidance Center program was prepared
with the assistance of the staff and inmates for distribution to the
families of prisoners to improve their understanding of the guidance
and treatment program on behalf of the inmates and to elicit their helpful co-operation.

This group guidance for orientation is associated with a series of lectures given by members of the staff and by visiting lecturers to orient the men in regard to the program of the prisons and the conditions of parole. A period for questions follows each lecture. The heads of the several prisons have been invited to tell the men about their specific institutional programs. Legal problems such as the length of sentence are discussed by members of the paroling authority called, in California, the Adult Authority. The members of the Adult Authority and the Chief State Parole Officer also describe the conditions under which men are supervised on parole. Since the men who fail on parole are encountered by new prisoners in the county jails or at San Quentin and since these parole violators are likely to be very outspoken in their criticism of the parole system, in addition to the above group guidance, it is hoped that arrangements may sometimes be made to bring successful parolees to the Reception-Guidance Center to discuss their experiences and treatment after leaving the institution. This is by way of antidote to the pessimistic accounts of those who have failed on parole.

The educational experience of the men in the group guidance program of the Reception-Guidance Center includes developmental reading, arithmetic and studies of different occupations. The latter discussions are enriched by assigned reading materials and by the use of visual aids such as sound motion pictures. The offerings of the various institutions and the general labor situation in California and elsewhere are used as the basis for much of this study and discussion of occupations. The importance of academic work is also stressed, including the value of the high school diploma in placement on parole. Reception-Guidance Center inmates are told that many men in the California prisons have been able to complete the requirements for the diploma from the secondary school. Many have also graduated from the elementary school while in prison. Their diplomas, signed by the State Director of Education, contain no mention of the prison itself.

The classrooms are also the setting for group discussions of social and economic problems in general, and especially those relating to crime and its causation. The guidance counselors in charge of these classes have been employed by the local school districts and usually have had some background in psychology or social casework. In the freedom of these classes inmates have been permitted to release hostilities toward many aspects of life in prison and society. The counselors have been successful in getting the men to express their feelings and so be relieved of some of the tensions and hatreds and misunderstandings which beset them. This program of group guidance inaugurated under the leadership of a clinical psychologist has been a most interesting phase of the program.

Another important aid for inmate orientation and adjustment related to the group guidance program has been the activity of the inmate council, originally developed and conducted by a clinical psychologist. Each class in the educational department elects a representative. Meetings are held weekly, at which time the topics considered may issue from earlier discussions in each of the classrooms or from observations of the council members. The actual problems of the men are considered. Many helpful suggestions for the conduct of the Reception-Guidance Center have been obtained from this source. It has also served as a safety valve, since the major frustrations have been discussed at the council and reports of the outcomes of these discussions have been taken back to the class groups. The participation of the group in their own government serves as a therapeutic experience in the understanding of law and its observance.

THE PARTICIPATION BY CLINICAL PSYCHOLOGISTS IN GROUP PSYCHOTHERAPY

In the prison system the psychologist has, in the writer's opinion, much more to give to the program than mere participation in the clinical program at reception. This would be especially true for the psychologist with a background of psychotherapy.

In what has gone before, we have considered the clinical psychologist primarily as diagnostician and also incidentally as a leader in group counseling or guidance and in prison management. In most reception centers for adult offenders, as in the states of Illinois or New York, the clinical psychologist, primarily by virtue of the large case load, has had to confine most of his activities to diagnosis. In the reception-guidance centers of California, with a yearly intake of 5,000 and with only five clinical psychologists on the staff, there is little time left for therapy after the test results have been evaluated, most of the inmates interviewed and reports dictated.[3] The use of psychological interns and inmate assistants has freed the clinical psychologists from some of the routine testing, especially group tests, and from the machine scoring thereof. Otherwise, the five psychologists would not be able to handle the large case load. In a few individual cases, the psychologists may extend their studies to include longer individual interviews, with perhaps some superficial therapeutic accompaniments. In exceptional circumstances, when the interest of the psychologist is strong enough, he may conduct some short-term individual or group therapy.

In the California prison system, the routine activities of the clinical psychologist were restricted for a number of years largely to the admission diagnostic study and the other activities discussed above. With the addi-

3 Additional adjunctive staff during the past year were five vocational counselors, five psychiatrists, twelve sociologists and, for a time, twelve teachers operating as educational or guidance counselors.

tion of clinical psychologists to the staff at San Quentin who participated in therapy, and especially later with the opening of the Medical Facility of the Department of Corrections in 1951, a new development took place in the psychological work. The program at Terminal Island was developed under very able and understanding psychiatric leadership. At this institution at present, there are two clinical psychologists. Both are part of the clinical and therapeutic team of the institution. More than half of their time is devoted to individual or group psychotherapy.[4] Each psychologist has about ten groups meeting twice a week. Some of the groups handled at the Medical Facility by the clinical psychologists are planned for the orientation of inmates with only superficial therapeutic values. Other groups consisting of improved psychotics may be given supportive therapy. Most of their groups are scheduled for regular group therapy of a deep and intensive character.

The clinical psychologists find themselves in a democratic climate. They are accepted on an equal professional status with other therapists, medical or social-psychiatric. Their reports are signed by themselves and are considered officially by the paroling authority. Consultation with the chief of staff, an able and dynamic psychiatrist, and others of the therapeutic team occurs individually or in the staff conferences on cases. There is a mutual give and take on these occasions. In addition, the weekly conference with a psychoanalytically oriented consultant from the outside is another means of evaluating their psychotherapeutic work and of inservice growth.

GROUP THERAPY IN THE PRISON

There can be no uniform prescription regarding group therapy in the prison or elsewhere. The size of the group may vary with the purposes, the depth of the treatment, and other factors, including the point of view of the institutional administration. Corsini and Newman, cited previously, found that twenty of the thirty-three psychologists who replied to their inquiry reported thirteen types of group therapeutic methods being used by them. In California, in the psychiatric department at San

---

[4] The use of testing instruments at the California Medical Facility, as reported in a personal letter by Marvin R. Schafer, supplements those already given in the reception-guidance centers. At admission, interns and inmate assistants administer the Shipley-Hartford, the Grayson Perceptual, the Machover Draw-a-Person, and the Saxe Sentence Completion tests. These measures are used in determining the individual's treatability and in the formation of homogeneous therapy groups as regards mental ability and emotional disturbances. At various times supplementary testing is conducted which includes the Minnesota Multiphasic Personality Inventory, the Wechsler-Bellevue, the Picture Frustration, the Draw-a-Person and occasionally the Rorschach and the Thematic Apperception tests. For experimental purposes, the Szondi and the Kahn Symbol Arrangement tests may be given. The staff intend later to analyze these results to determine whether they afford possible aid in the prediction of adjustment on parole.

Quentin and at the Medical Facility of the Department of Corrections, groups are brought together for deeper therapeutic purposes. The size of the group, consisting of volunteers, may range from six to twenty; the optimal range would be six to fifteen. These groups may be homogeneous as to crime or emotional problems. For administrative reasons at San Quentin, the length of attendance has been limited to three months for most, but not all, of the groups. At the Medical Facility, the length of continuance is not limited.

The point of view of the program at the Medical Facility is a modified psychoanalytic approach. After initial discussion of procedures, the therapist permits the inmates considerable freedom in the conduct or movement of the sessions. An inmate leader may be used to direct discussion. The therapist comes in only upon inquiry or when the situation warrants his intercession because of confusions or conflicts. "The participation of the therapist," Marvin R. Schafer reported in a personal communication in 1953, "is held to the minimum but he remains responsible for the session and its 'control' at all times. His presence helps to keep the inmates conscious of the necessity for 'working through' the experiences and feelings that have been significant factors in the development of their personality and its criminal activities. When it is necessary for the therapist to be absent, the men meet on their own, choose their leader for the day and proceed with the session."

As the material is brought out, discussions may include the analysis of defenses, the interpretation of dream material, the discussion of how socially acceptable symptoms may replace what is disapproved, the nature and origin of attitudes toward authority, the nature of transference, the various mechanisms of adjustment, and other matters of psychological interest and importance. The techniques of the psychodrama have been used to supplement more formal therapy with some groups. The program of group psychotherapy in the prison is still so relatively new that it would be unfortunate if it were crystallized into routine methodology. The individuality of the therapist is more important than any technical structure of the process. The whole program is dependent for effectiveness upon the general atmosphere of adjustment in the institution, which must be founded upon secure administrative support of psychotherapeutic objectives.

FUTURE NEEDS

Enough has been said in this chapter to indicate the importance of the clinical psychologist in the treatment of the personality problems of prisoners. Individual psychotherapy is greatly needed; the clinical psychologist should be trained to render this type of service. The more economically administered group therapy is now becoming a recognized feature of the institutional treatment program for adult offenders. In the future, prisons must develop more extensive use of group therapy conducted by the therapists trained in social psychiatry and psychology as well as in psychiatry. At the present time, the beginning of the transition from diagnosis to therapy in the prisons has begun. Group therapy carried on by clinical psychologists and other specialists must as rapidly as possible be expanded in the adult correctional institutions.

By training and interest, the clinical psychologist should be able to contribute also to penal administration, to the development of new methods of treatment and better preparation for parole. Their part in the inservice training of prison personnel is important. The nature and treatment of the adult offender may be presented to the ordinary prison officers with interest and effectiveness by the psychologist. In the absence of specific cures, an important therapeutic agency is the general prison environment. Too much emphasis cannot be given to the influence upon the inmates of adult correctional institutions of the total prison environment of which the human relationships are the heart. The treatment program can best influence inmates in relation to a general supportive background of acceptance and helpfulness in the attitudes of the entire personnel of the prison. The sympathetic and understanding attitudes of the rank and file of personnel is a necessary accompaniment of effective treatment. The clinical psychologist through his part in the inservice training program, his discussions of individual prisoners with the prison employees, and his preparation of materials of psychological interest for their reading should have an important part in this instruction of the staff.

The ordinary layman has many prejudices and misconceptions in regard to the adult offender. The psychologist may help to overcome this adverse public opinion. The education of the public in regard to the nature and treatment of criminality is another project in which the psychologist must collaborate.

A final value of the psychologist to the prison system and to society is found in the possibilities for the inauguration and conduct of studies into the causes and the treatment of delinquency and criminality. A rich field for research concerning the maladjustments of human nature to society is offered by adult criminality. In a more fundamental sense, these studies should have the positive goal of acquiring knowledge that may help to prevent delinquency and criminality. Thereby they may contribute immeasurably to the advancement of human life.

REFERENCES

1. American Prison Association. *Handbook on classification in correctional institutions.* New York: Amer. Prison Assoc., 1947.
2. Bixby, F. L., & McCorkle, L. W. Guided group interaction in correctional work. *Amer. Sociol. Rev.,* 1951, 16, 455-461.
3. Burton, A. Directory of clinical psychologists engaged in correctional psychology. *J. Psychol.,* 1948, 19-23.
4. Burton A. The status of correctional psychology. *J. Psychol.,* 1950, 28, 215-222.
5. Corsini, R. Functions of the prison psychologist. *J. consult. Psychol.,* 1945, 9, 101-104.
6. Corsini, R. Psychological sources in prison. In Branham, V. C., & Kutash, S. B. (Eds.), *Encyclopedia of criminology.* New York: Philosophical Library, 1949, 405-413.
7. Fenton, N. The process of reception in the California prison system. *The Prison World,* 1945, 7, No. 5, 10-11, 22-24.
8. Fenton, N. Lay and professional collaboration for the advancement of classification. *Proc. Amer. Prison Assoc.,* 1946, 161-169.
9. Fenton, N. *An introduction to classification and treatment in State Correctional Service.* Sacramento, Calif.: Department of Corrections, State of California, 1953.
10. Giardini, G. I. The place of psychology in penal and correctional institutions. *Federal Probation,* 1942, 6, 29-33.
11. Greco, M. C. Clinical psychology and penal discipline. *J. clin. Psychol.,* 1945, 1, 206-213.
12. Jackson, J. D. Prisons and penitentiaries. In Fryer, D. H., & Henry, E. R. (Eds.), *Handbook of applied psychology.* New York: Rinehart, 1950, 573-581.
13. Jolles, I. An experiment in group guidance. *J. soc. Psychol.,* 1946, 23, 55-60.
14. Kennedy, M. L. The organization and administration of a group treatment program. *J. correct. Educ.,* 1951, 3, 14-19.
15. Knowles, J. A. The role of the prison psychologist. *Proc. Okla. Acad. Sci.,* 1949, 30, 172-175.
16. Marquis, D. C. The mobilization of psychologists for war services. *Psychol. Bull.,* 1944, 469-473.
17. Overholser, W. Psychiatric service in penal and reformatory institutions and criminal courts in the United States. *Ment. Hygiene,* 1928, 12, 801-838.
18. Rowland, E. Report of experiments at the State Reformatory for Women at Bedford, New York. *Psychol. Rev.,* 1913, 20, 245-249.
19. Terman, L. M. *The measurement of intelligence.* Boston: Houghton Mifflin, 1916.
20. *Biennial reports.* Sacramento, Calif.: Department of Corrections, State of California, from 1944 to 1952.
21. *The Guidance Center of the Adult Authority.* San Quentin, Calif.: The Guidance Center, 1945.
22. *Reports of the Bureau of Statistics.* Sacramento, Calif.: Department of Corrections, State of California, published at intervals since 1945.

XXIII.

CLINICAL PSYCHOLOGY IN A
REHABILITATION CENTER

SALVATORE G. DIMICHAEL
and JAMES F. GARRETT

Any effort to define a rehabilitation center is subject to criticism since common agreement among workers in the field has not been achieved. One group has defined it as "a facility operated for the primary purpose of assisting in the vocational rehabilitation of disabled persons and in which a co-ordinated approach by many professions is made to the physical, mental and vocational evaluation of such persons and to the furnishing of such services as are required" (17, p. 1). A somewhat more comprehensive definition, and one subscribed to by the authors, has been proposed by Redkey: "A Rehabilitation Center is a facility in which there is a concentration of services including at least one each from the medical, psychosocial and vocational areas, which are furnished according to need, are intensive and substantial in nature, and which are integrated with each other and with other services in the community to provide a unified evaluation and rehabilitation service to disabled people."[1]

Obviously, such centers may be designed to serve a variety of clientele. When the centers are established primarily for the blind, they are usually known as an *adjustment center* but these conform generally to the definition stated above. Such centers might also be geared to the needs of the aurally impaired, the mentally retarded or the improved mental patient, although progress in these areas has been exceedingly slow. To most rehabilitation workers, the term "rehabilitation center" usually connotes one serving clients with severe orthopedic disabilities. Both historically and numerically, this group has been the focus of the "center" movement.

As in any developing program, there is no one pattern of rehabilitation center. Centers vary considerably from one locality to another and are related to community needs. Thus, in one center, strong emphasis will be placed on the medical aspects of rehabilitation, with little on the psychosocial or vocational. Such centers are sometimes called *medical*

---

[1] Redkey, Henry R., Personal Communication, August 26, 1953.

rehabilitation centers. On the other hand, many centers consider their primary service to be vocational, with less emphasis on the medical or psychosocial. These centers are often called *vocational rehabilitation centers.*

One may also expect from one center to another a variation in aims, in methods, in staff and in physical equipment. Thus, the medical rehabilitation center will stress physical restoration goals and services, be controlled by medical practitioners, be staffed largely by physicians in the various medical specialties and by allied personnel such as physical and occupational therapists, and will contain a good deal of equipment along the lines of the physical modalities (heat, light, water, etc.). On the other hand, the vocational rehabilitation center will stress vocational training and placement, be controlled by vocational education or guidance workers, be staffed by a variety of vocational teachers, counselors and placement specialists, and will contain trade training facilities.

PSYCHOSOCIAL SERVICES IN A REHABILITATION CENTER

That the rehabilitation center unconsciously provides some psychosocial service no one could deny. The center provides for most of its clients an environment that minimizes unwholesome stresses of previous patterns of living, removes the client from some of his former responsibilities, gives him security by an interested staff, and permits the development of adjustment skills through interpersonal relationships with other disabled and nondisabled persons. This, in reality, is "milieu therapy" and all centers do this to greater or lesser degree.

Rehabilitation workers accept the principle that rehabilitation always must consider the emotional factors, even though at different stages of the rehabilitation process the medical or vocational phases may predominate. This follows when it is realized that most people take pride in physical growth and achievement, and that these attitudes are culturally associated with physical well-being as well as economic factors. When a disability comes, what are its affects on the individual? What emotional defenses does he use? Experience will attest to the great variety used by even one handicapped group.

This diversity of problems means that many psychological services are required in any center purporting to offer a comprehensive program. Hence a wide variety of competencies are in demand. Moreover, one psychologist may not be able to furnish all of the skills required, and this factor alone has led to some interesting relationships of centers with other community resources such as the State divisions of vocational rehabilitation and the State employment services.

The use of psychologists in rehabilitation centers has had a sporadic history which is difficult to pin-point. To the best of our knowledge, the Institute for the Crippled and Disabled in New York City employed the first full-time psychologist around 1940. Most earlier efforts, so far as we know, were on a part-time or consultative basis. The function of this psychologist, at the beginning, seemed to be largely the administration of intelligence tests, which quickly expanded to a more comprehensive service as the psychological skills were more appreciated. Since the Institute furnished a pattern for the operation of similar services due to its training activities during and after World War II, the contributions of psychologists to rehabilitation centers were fairly well accepted.

In the area of adjustment centers for the blind, the retraining center set up by the Army at Avon, Connecticut during World War II had the greatest effect on the use of psychologists in that specialty. On the other hand, the long history of work by Samuel P. Hayes in institutions for the blind and that of Mary Bauman at the Trainee Acceptance Center in Philadelphia had considerable influence on the beneficial development of psychology in personal adjustment centers. All these efforts promoted the growth of adjustment centers for the blind and in turn the use of psychologists in them.

From these modest beginnings, the use of psychologists in rehabilitation centers has grown. Since most centers emphasize the "team" approach, and the psychological needs of the client have come to be regarded as a cornerstone of rehabilitation, the value of the psychologist's contribution in diagnosis, planning, counseling and treatment has been recognized. With the postwar expansion of rehabilitation centers, the demands for the services of psychologists in them has increased.

The pattern of psychological services in a rehabilitation center today is not fixed. Much depends on the organization of the center, its budget, and understanding of the psychologist's role. Generally speaking it is more usual to find psychologists functioning in centers offering comprehensive rehabilitation programs than in those heavily emphasizing either the vocational or medical aspects. Most centers are small and do not seem to find it feasible to hire psychologists full-time because of apparent budget limitations, although this trend has changed somewhat in the last few years. While some centers do not employ a psychologist, they have made arrangements to secure such services from other community agencies (8). There is mounting evidence of increased understanding of the contribution of the psychologist to rehabilitation, but there is still much room for development in this area not only among center administrators but also among psychologists themselves.

To indicate the variety of organization of psychological services, it may be well to mention typical rehabilitation centers. At the Institute of Physical Medicine and Rehabilitation, which is part of the New

York University Bellevue Medical Center in New York City, the services are furnished in the Division of Psychosocial and Vocational Services through a staff of psychologists who handle the gamut of problems from evaluation of learning ability to vocational diagnosis and counseling (11). On the other hand, at the Institute for the Crippled and Disabled in New York City, which is affiliated with Columbia University, psychological services are provided through a Division of Social Adjustment Services by several psychologists whose chief functions are those of evaluation and retraining (therapy), with vocational guidance a function of another service (Vocational Rehabilitation Service). In contrast with these large centers, the Crossroads Rehabilitation Center in Indianapolis has a psychologist "on call," while at the Hartford County Rehabilitation Workshop in Hartford, Connecticut, psychological services are provided by the State Division of Vocational Rehabilitation. It is apparent that there is, as yet, no uniform pattern for the provision of psychological services in rehabilitation centers. What is presented in the following section is a generalized picture rather than the actual service and function of the clinical psychologist in any one rehabilitation center.

FUNCTIONS OF THE PSYCHOLOGIST IN A REHABILITATION CENTER

1. To Administer and Interpret Tests with Appropriate Adaptations to the Physically and Mentally Handicapped

The psychologist in the vocational rehabilitation center must be adept in the administration and interpretation of a wide variety of tests and testing techniques. This requirement of broad competency is due to the fact that the rehabilitation center is conducted with such broad aims and emphasizes the concerted efforts of many disciplines to provide services to the client at one time. Each discipline wants the psychologist to furnish some assistance in its phase of the total evaluation of the individual. To be of maximum professional assistance, the psychologist must be well versed in many types of tests: mental, personality, interests, dexterities, aptitudes, skills, and achievement. These will help to evaluate the client in terms of personal, social, educational, and vocational phases of adjustment not only with respect to present status but also in terms of future prospects.

The psychological evaluation of the handicapped calls for considerable flexibility in approach, experience with the various handicapped groups and primary dependence upon clinical judgment. For example, the administration of a mental test requiring sensorimotor control under narrow time limits would not indicate the true mental ability of a cerebral palsied client. Strother (16), in a detailed discussion on the evaluation of the cerebral palsied, states the need to make a preliminary evaluation of sensory and motor defects and a method of communication with the child. To do this, the psychologist should know the implications of the medical findings to his selection of suitable psychological tools.

If standard tests cannot be applied, the examiner must depend on his ingenuity and experience in selecting materials and procedures. Sometimes it is a matter of modifying standard test materials so that they may be easier to see or to manipulate. Sometimes the procedure must be changed, perhaps to a multiple choice situation, so that the child can respond with a simple sign. In such cases, of course, there are no applicable norms but a subjective estimate of the child's ability may be made.

Another discussion of the special adaptations necessary with a certain handicapped group, the blind, is that of Bauman and Hayes (2). They describe the special tests which have been developed for the blind and also take the point of view that a flexible approach is required. In some cases, the psychologist may read a printed test to a blind client who may then respond orally or record his answer by typing or some other mechanical method. If such a test has close time limits as administered to the sighted, one cannot use the norms established for the sighted without allowances for the different procedure. For some tests, the time allowances for the blind have been worked out on the basis of special studies.

The interpretation of test results must take into account the special features of the influences of the disability. With all handicapped groups, it is necessary to consider the age at onset of the impairment. Usually, a period of some instability is found immediately after the disability is incurred. It takes time before the person readjusts himself emotionally, and before the activities of living are executed as expeditiously as possible through retraining of the many remaining abilities. Moreover, improvements in mechanical aids and prostheses will enable the handicapped to attain vocational and other goals which were previously not open to him.

Persons with congenital disabilities frequently are deeply influenced by parental attitudes toward the impairment; on the other hand, handicaps acquired in adulthood are influenced much more by the personal attitudes antedating the disability. Interest-inventory scores have to be carefully considered in terms of special experiences accompanying the handicap. For example, it is commonly held that high scores in social service activities are found among the handicapped who have been hospitalized for long periods of time. If the environment has been limited for the individual, it is occasionally possible that interests may show marked changes when the person is introduced into new areas of occupational and social experiences.

The factors mentioned above, and many others, indicate the need for skillful clinical interpretation. A test-centered approach is fallaciously scientific (although it may be justified in some kinds of research). The evaluation of test results are as good as the experience, skill, technical background and sound understanding of the psychologist who interprets them.

2. To Evaluate the Individual from the Vocational Standpoint

One of the main purposes of the comprehensive rehabilitation center is to develop the maximum capabilities of the individual to become as self-sufficient as possible in earning his own living. Some rehabilitation centers also attempt to help the very severely disabled to attain a life of increased self-care, when vocational adequacy is not deemed to be possible in terms of current knowledge of rehabilitation methods. However, the vocational goal is deemed to be extremely important, with equal recognition of the fact that personal, social, physical and educational adequacy go hand in hand with the vocational.

The psychologist always has an essential role in the determination of the person's vocational potentialities and skills by the whole rehabilitation team. The psychologist's data for his evaluation should be obtained from a comprehensive study of the client. The data includes past history, observations of the person in different settings at the center, in diagnostic and counseling interviews, perhaps in group guidance or therapy sessions, in ratings made by other staff members, in reports from the family members, and many other possible sources, in addition to the more formal testing. These data may be viewed from several points of view, but the vocational picture takes a prominent part.

The plan, conduct and success of a rehabilitation program depend to a great extent upon the motivations of the client. It is a trite truism among rehabilitation workers that the degree of disability is not the paramount factor governing incapacity. The level and direction of the motivational patterns will guide every staff member in his phase of the diagnosis, treatment and plans for the client. The psychologist will be expected to contribute his understanding of the client's drives, frustrations, and the specific elaborations of derived motives. These evaluations will have to be made in practical terms which may be recognized and applied by members of the staff. The psychiatric consultant also plays an essential role in the determination of motivational patterns. However, the viewpoints and observations of all staff members are included in the total evaluation.

The interview is often a very illuminating source of data in the evaluation of motivations. The psychologist should be proficient in interviewing techniques, appreciate the values and limitations of data so derived, and be able to distinguish the more basic characteristics of the client from the transient manifestations of his behavior.

On the basis of his evaluation, the psychologist will be expected to make suggestions on suitable occupations for the client to consider in his rehabilitation program. This specific function may present a pitfall to the psychologist. On the one hand, he may refrain entirely from making such suggestions; in such instances, the other staff members are confronted with the problem of deciding the practical significance of psychological data. On the other, the psychologist may become too categorical in his vocational recommendations and probably will be vulnerable if his knowledge of occupations is unduly limited. DiMichael (5) discusses this matter in some detail in an article dealing with psychological reporting. He states that psychologists should meet this problem, without incurring the criticism of vocational counselors, by making guarded suggestions. It is also pointed out in the article that the usual training of most psychologists has prepared them to analyze the individual, but their knowledge of the realities of occupations is deficient. In many instances, their understanding of the complete demands of the job has to be picked up by incidental experience. This deficiency in training has been acknowledged by the Education and Training Board of the American Psychological Association. Graduate courses in occupational information are now required for approval of curricula for the training of Counseling Psychologists (Vocational) who will be working with the handicapped in Veterans Administration hospitals and clinic centers.

3. To Counsel with Clients in Personal, Social, and Vocational Areas

In the smaller rehabilitation centers where there is less specialization of function by staff members, the psychologist may be responsible for vocational counseling, and also for personal and social counseling. This may apply to the larger centers in the near future if the training of psychologists better prepares them to assume these functions. The pivotal phase of the rehabilitation program is the counseling process. Through it, the client takes the responsibility for using the services available to him. Since the rehabilitation services are adapted to the special needs and problems of the individual, counseling serves as the medium whereby the client sees the unity of the total program and the contributions of each part to the whole. Strictly speaking, the rehabilitation center may provide only those services which the individual is willing to accept. Counseling, then, is the medium whereby the rehabilitation program is conceived, planned, and carried through by the client and the counselor in a confidential relationship.

The counselor works almost entirely with normal individuals in the setting of a vocational rehabilitation center. The psychologist-counselor will be much better prepared for this function if his training is oriented primarily to the normal individual. Typical current training in clinical psychology stresses work in a mental hospital with abnormally disturbed persons, and is not well suited to the work of the psychologist in a rehabilitation center. Difficult problems of adjustment may beset the client referred to rehabilitation centers but they seldom are pathologically serious. If deep-seated emotional disturbances are present, arrangements usually are made to provide treatment in other community facilities.

A current and detailed knowledge of the occupational world is needed by the vocational counselor. He must have a broad understanding of occupational demands, an appreciation of the psychosocial pressures in various job settings, a knowledge of the physical demands of different jobs, and the economic trends in the communities to which his clients will return. The vocational objective for his client will have to be worked out in very close collaboration with the counselor in the client's own community. The continuing counseling and placement will be the ultimate responsibility of the counselor in the community. In fact, the counselor in the rehabilitation center must dovetail his work into the broader community rehabilitation program.

The broad aspects of rehabilitation require that the counselor in the center be well versed in making use of community facilities and agencies that may contribute to the total restoration of the client in his ultimate social setting. There is the constant necessity of working closely with community agencies, not only those close at hand but others with whom contact is almost entirely by correspondence.

The need for personal adjustment counseling with the handicapped is great. The newly disabled must work through his feelings such as shock and depression, reorganize his values to accept the psychological realities of the disability, gradually modify the self-concept of his physical and psychological self. The individual's personality patterns prior to the occurrence of the disability have a very significant effect upon the readjustment process, both its quality and duration. Some of the emotional patterns are normal phases of adjustment to disability. The psychologist has to differentiate between the intense but normal reactions and the pathological. It is becoming better recognized that certain intense reactions actually may accelerate the readjustment process and that the attempt to lighten these affects by kindly distractions may not be therapeutic.

The cornerstone of rehabilitation is positive motivation because the client must make active use of the service in preparing for and eventually finding suitable employment. Naturally, motivation cannot be created but may be stimulated by the counseling psychologist. If the latter does not have the counseling responsibility, he should indicate the desirable approaches for the counselor to apply in each case.

4. To Screen Patients for Referral to the Psychiatrist and to Co-operate in the Therapeutic Program

Practically all clients accepted by rehabilitation centers may be expected to have disturbing personal-social problems. However, some individuals may show symptoms bordering on abnormality, while some may also be neurotic or psychotic but may or may not have been so recognized before admission. Even if certain clients previously had been known to have abnormal emotional conditions, it is sometimes possible to rehabilitate them vocationally within the limits of their psychiatric as well as physical disabilities. An increasing number of rehabilitation centers are engaging psychiatrists on a part-time or consultant basis. In the larger centers, a special division within the staff may consist of a clinical psychologist, psychiatric social worker and psychiatrist.

Since one of the essential characteristics of a rehabilitation center is its utilization of the "total approach," one may expect to uncover borderline and full-blown emotional disturbances during the diagnostic process. The psychologist usually is involved in screening patients for a thorough psychiatric evaluation, and also in contributing his findings to the total diagnosis.

There has been a greater appreciation of the need for psychiatric services in a rehabilitation center, and increasing use of them. A report on the functions of a psychiatrist, clinical psychologist and psychiatric social worker, and some findings on a special study are described by Grayson et al. (12). In centers staffed by such a mental hygiene team, the larger part of psychotherapeutic counseling is done by the psychologist and social worker in close co-operation with the psychiatrist. The psychotherapy is symptomatic; if psychiatric problems dominate the rehabilitation program, the psychiatrist will refer the client to other resources for intensive therapy (14).

Some form of therapeutic group work always has been utilized by rehabilitation centers, especially adjustment centers for the blind, to help the clients understand their personal and social problems more objectively. These may be termed "group guidance." Recently some of these sessions have been modified, sometimes fairly drastically, to become "group therapy." Different forms of the latter are being used with no clear preferences emerging. In fact, descriptive accounts of all the different approaches are not yet available. Some therapists question the value of group therapy in a rehabilitation center, although there has been wide acceptance of the value of group guidance. In view of the promise of group therapy as a time-saver and useful adjunct to individual therapy, research is needed to appraise effects of group therapy with the physically handicapped in a rehabilitation center.

5. To Interpret Findings and Recommendations to
   Different Members of the Staff

In view of the abiding principle that a rehabilitation center provides the client with a unified series of different services at one time, the concept and practice of teamwork is given great emphasis (20). Both professional and non-professional workers must collaborate frequently. This approach requires the use of regularly scheduled case conferences attended by representatives of various disciplines, outside agencies, and occasionally by nonprofessional volunteer workers. More important by far are the daily informal intercommunications by which teamwork is accomplished and focused on the needs of each client.

The psychologist and other members of the staff constantly are discussing their respective findings and adapting methods and techniques in the light of changes in the client. This setting requires that the psychologist be adept at explaining his professional insights and points of view. He must be equally alert in sensing the theory and practice of other disciplines so as to grasp their special contributions and viewpoints. Out of this mutual give-and-take process there accrues mutual benefit to all staff members but the main purpose is the maximum good to the client.

Many examples may be given to show specific ways in which psychologist and staff members of other disciplines continually collaborate. With the supervisor and shop teachers in the vocational department, the psychologist may discuss more efficient principles of learning, may recommend the kinds of activities in which the client will be profitably interested, and may discuss preferred teaching methods for a certain handicapped person. The vocational counselor is interested in the client's motivational patterns, counseling approaches and specific techniques; perhaps prevocational job tryouts are needed because of the incompleteness or the uncertainties of psychological diagnosis in very difficult cases. With the physiatrist, there may be discussions on the client's ability to make intelligent use of a prosthesis, as well as his motivation to undergo the training required in its use; there also may be a question as to whether the client is willing to accept a prosthesis psychologically or whether it may be discarded as a sign of nonacceptance of the disability. The close relationships with psychiatrists already have been mentioned. Perhaps a neurologist would like assistance in assessing a brain-damaged case and in outlining a suggested program of treatment to the entire staff.

Frequent contacts are made with the occupational therapist regarding the individual client's abilities, preferences, work habits, suspected talents or known learning blocks; and the psychologist in return will obtain reports on progress which will enrich and modify his evaluations of the clients. The physical therapist must know how to motivate the particular client so that he will expend maximum efforts in training unused or underdeveloped muscles. The speech pathologist may work in or outside the center with certain clients, and will need to know the details of the psychologist's evaluations so as to plan for the ideational, learning and motivational aspects of treatment. Placement specialists with the handicapped appreciate the importance of the personality and social demands of the work environment and look for suggestions that will enable them to make suitable long-term job placements; it is hardly ever possible to obtain an ideal work environment but the compromises should be as wholesome as possible. Then, too, there will be occasions to speak to members of the client's family about the psychological factors in the rehabilitation program inside and outside the center. Finally, there are the recreational directors, the attendants, and the nurses, with whom some aspects of the findings are discussed.

6. To Participate in the Public-Relations Functions of the Rehabilitation Center

There are three main reasons why the psychologist must spend some of his efforts in public relations. First, the purposes of a rehabilitation center are not well known either to professional groups or the general public; it is a very recent development. Secondly, the center is established in terms of the needs of the community and its work should be highly integrated with the other community agencies which it is intended to complement and supplement. Third, the psychologist must be concerned with relationships to his own profession.

Rehabilitation centers are highly dependent upon community support, both financially and in the referral of clients. A full utilization of facilities is dependent upon an informed professional and lay public. Each professional worker of the staff is expected to interpret the general nature and aims of the center, as well as to explain the special contributions of his discipline.

There is another aspect of rehabilitation which in the long run is very important; the wholesome acceptance of the physically and mentally disabled by society. The personal and social problems of the disabled are intensified or created by the negative attitudes of the family, friends, employers and people in general. Every public appearance by a rehabilitation worker serves to educate a social group in adopting a better pattern of attitudes based upon an understanding of the difficult adjustment problems of the disabled and the obstacles set up by society to rehabilitation.

The center also must integrate its activities with related social agencies and private practitioners. Perhaps a physician or psychologist in private practice or on the staff of another agency may refer his report to the center. It will be necessary to consider the ethical problems involved in working with "outside" members of one's own or other professions.

Moreover, the very short supply of well-trained psychologists for rehabilitation work must necessarily concern those engaged in the field. Universities must be made aware of the acute professional needs, and graduate schools of psychology must be interested and assisted to set up pertinent training.

7. To Supervise Psychological Trainees

The point made immediately above makes it necessary for the conscientious psychologist in rehabilitation centers to welcome the supervision of promising trainees. Few universities offer specific training to prepare the candidate for specific work in vocational rehabilitation (8). The trainees should acquire the body of knowledge and skills that should form the common core for all psychologists. In addition it is suggested that candidates have suitable training on the psychological aspects of physical disability; that they attain a high degree of competency in total psychological evaluation of the physically and mentally handicapped including the use of vocational, educational and personality tests; that they be well informed on the general nature of physical disabilities and the effects of the latter upon the physical demands of different occupations; that they have a general knowledge of the world of work, and on the requirements of different occupations, and a knowledge of the literature on the placement of the handicapped; that they attain competency in vocational and personal-adjustment counseling.

The university training may include a period of internship in the setting of a rehabilitation center. Otherwise, the student may seek employment as an assistant to an experienced psychologist in the center. In the past, most psychologists in rehabilitation settings have had to learn to "swim on their own." The difficulty of the work indicates that it is far better for the student to obtain experience and additional training under supervised clinical practice.

8. To Conduct Research in the Psychological Aspects of Rehabilitation

The civilian and the veteran rehabilitation programs have been under pressure to provide practical services to the handicapped, but there is a great need for research in order to place the work on a more scientific foundation. The relative youthfulness of the program probably accounts in large measure for the dearth of research in the many aspects of rehabilitation. Since the somewhat recent incorporation of a total rehabilitation approach, psychology has been widely accepted as one of the essential disciplines. Leaders in rehabilitation have fostered and encouraged research in spite of the pressures for practical services.

There are a vast number of major research problems in the psychological aspects of rehabilitation. For example, a small publication in 1951 listed about 300 topics in "Research Suggestions on Psychological Problems Associated with Blindness" (18). One might very well cross out the word "blind" in many of the stated research problems and insert the name of any other handicapped group and the problem might be pertinent. Recommendations on research topics will also be found in almost every article dealing with a psychological research report made in the journals devoted to special handicapped groups (such as *American Annals of the Deaf, American Review of Tuberculosis, Journal of Exceptional Children, New Outlook for the Blind*), or in any of the regular psychological periodicals. Occasionally an article deals specifically with research needs, such as the one by DiMichael (6). Three of the most recent and comprehensive treatments on the psychology and rehabilitation of the handicapped are the books listed in the bibliography under Barker (1), and DiMichael (7), and Garrett (10).

It may be well to make explicit an important point which has been assumed throughout this chapter. There is no special psychology of handicapped people which makes them qualitatively different from the nondisabled. The problems and physiological reactions of the handicapped may be accentuated by the greater "load" placed upon them and the difficulties of adjustment due to personal and social pressures. The psychological mechanisms are basically the same as for all people and the differences between disabled and nondisabled are matters of degree. Nevertheless, special experience, knowledge and skills are required to deal with them effectively.

REFERENCES

1. Barker, R. G., Wright, Beatrice A., Meyerson, L., & Gonick, Mollie R. *Adjustment to physical handicap and illness: A survey of the social psychology of physique and disability.* (Rev.) New York: Social Science Research Council, 1953.
2. Bauman, Mary K., & Hayes, S. P. *A manual for the psychological examination of the adult blind.* New York: The Psychological Corporation, 1951.
3. Cholden, L. S. Group therapy with the blind. Paper read at American Psychiatric Association, Los Angeles, May, 1953.
4. Cholden, L. S. Some psychiatric problems in the rehabilitation of the blind. Paper read at American Psychiatric Association, Los Angeles, May, 1953.
5. DiMichael, S. G. Characteristics of a desirable psychological report to the vocational counselor. *J. consult. Psychol.*, 1948, 12, 432-437.

6. DiMichael, S. G. Report on unsolved technical problems in vocational preparation and placement. Proceedings 8th Governor's Conference on Exceptional Children, State of Illinois. Springfield, Illinois. Commission for Handicapped Children, 1951, 21-38.
7. DiMichael, S. G. (Ed.) Vocational rehabilitation of the mentally retarded. Reprinted in *Amer. J. ment. def.*, 1952, 57, 167-337.
8. DiMichael, S. G. & Dabelstein, D. H. The psychologist in vocational rehabilitation. *J. consult. Psychol.*, 1946, 10, 237-245.
9. Garrett, J. F. Applications of clinical psychology to rehabilitation. In D. Brower and L. Abt (Eds.), *Progress in clinical psychology*. New York: Grune & Stratton, 1952. Pp. 443-449.
10. Garrett, J. F. (Ed.) *Psychological aspects of physical disability*. Federal Security Agency. Office of Vocational Rehabilitation. Washington: U. S. Government Printing Office, 1952.
11. Garrett, J. F., & Myers, J. S. Clinical psychology in the rehabilitation process. *J. Rehabilit.*, 1951, 17, 3-7.
12. Grayson, M., Powers, Ann, & Levi, J. *Psychiatric aspects of rehabilitation*. New York: The Institute of Physical Medicine and Rehabilitation, Bellevue Medical Center, 1952.
13. Hamilton, K. W. *Counseling the handicapped in the rehabilitation process*. New York: Ronald Press, 1950.
14. Rennie, T. A. C., Burling, T., & Woodward, L. E. *Vocational rehabilitation of psychiatric patients*. New York: The Commonwealth Fund, 1950.
15. Switzer, Mary E., & Rusk, H. A. *Doing something for the disabled*. New York: Public Affairs Pamphlet No. 197, 1953.
16. Strother, C. R. The psychological appraisal of children with cerebral palsy. In *Psychological problems of cerebral palsy*. Chicago: The National Society for Crippled Children and Adults, 1952. Pp. 5-19.
17. U. S. Office of Vocational Rehabilitation. *Rehabilitation Centers*. Federal Security Agency. Office of Vocational Rehabilitation. Washington: U. S. Government Printing Office, 1950.
18. U. S. Office of Vocational Rehabilitation. *Research suggestions on psychological problems associated with blindness*. Federal Security Agency. Office of Vocational Rehabilitation. Washington: U. S. Government Printing Office, 1951.
19. U. S. Office of Vocational Rehabilitation, *Directory rehabilitation centers*. Dept. of Health, Education and Welfare. Office of Vocational Rehabilitation. Washington: U. S. Government Printing Office, 1953.
20. U. S. Office of Defense Mobilization. *Report of the task force on the handicapped*. Washington: U. S. Government Printing Office, 1952.

XXIV

THE CLINICAL PSYCHOLOGIST IN A SCHOOL SYSTEM

MILTON A. SAFFIR

The school system is a very logical and widely utilized setting for the clinical practice of psychology, although the titles by which psychologists and psychological departments in public schools are known do not often include the term "clinical." Bureaus or departments of child study, child guidance, special education, or pupil personnel are the most widely used names for the school agency which provides clinical psychological service.

The practitioners of clinical psychology in a school or school system are identified by a long and varied list of titles, differing from state to state among the dozen or so which have statewide certification for such specialists, and from school unit to school unit in other parts of the country. A survey by Dr. Wilda Rosebrook and a committee of the Division of School Psychologists of the American Psychological Association, in 1949, found some thirty-eight different titles in use, the most frequent being "school psychologist," "director of special education or handicapped children," and "psychologist." Other frequently used designations are "psychological examiner," "child study assistant," "mental tester," and "school counselor." The label "clinical psychologist" is used infrequently for members of a school staff.

That the school psychologist is indeed engaged in the clinical practice of psychology will be clear from the description of his functions in this chapter. It is true that his services border on and overlap those of the guidance and counseling specialist at one end, and those of the educational psychologist at the other, but that he is essentially a clinical psychologist is evident from the definition of school psychologist in the bylaws of the Division of School Psychologists; "A school psychologist is a psychologist a major portion of whose work is the application of clinical psychological techniques to children and adolescents presenting problems in school, or the psychological supervision of psychologists doing such work" (1, Art. 2, Sect. a).

The reasons for the diversity of titles used by practitioners of clinical psychology in the schools lie in the historical background for the development of this field of service. School psychological services had their beginnings long before the term "clinical psychology" was widely known. Their development was part of the earliest history of this field of psychology, yet they were also the result of trends and developments in the field of education. Influenced thus by two separate disciplines, and to different degrees in different communities, the school psychologist has represented under his various titles a specialty both in education and in psychology. In some school systems he has been primarily an educator who had acquired special techniques from psychology; in others he has been a psychologist who had moved into a school setting.

The first clinical psychological agency in a public school system in the United States was organized almost as early as the first American psychological clinic. The Bureau of Child Study and Pedagogical Research, in the Chicago Public Schools, with Dr. Fred W. Smedley as its first director, was established in 1899, only three years later than Witmer's clinic at the University of Pennsylvania.

As with the other very early work in clinical psychology, the Bureau concerned itself with anthropometric tests and measurements. Thousands of individual examinations gave data concerning strength, endurance, lung capacity, sensory discrimination, and other such items which were believed to be indicators of mental capacity. Although Dr. Smedley became ill and died only a few years later, the Bureau has operated continuously since 1899 as an important representative of clinical psychology in the school setting.

With the establishment of classes for the mentally retarded in more and more cities, and with the availability of American revisions of the Binet scale, the role of the school psychologist became more and more definitely set. He was responsible for examining the candidates for the special classes to determine their IQ and thus their eligibility in accordance with state laws or other standards.

Although some psychologists in schools even today do no more than administer Binets and calculate the IQ's, the larger number broadened and deepened their functioning as education and clinical psychology developed. For one, the services of school psychologists have been extended to children other than those suspected of mental retardation. These have come to include the blind and the deaf, the crippled, the disabled readers, the gifted, the truant and delinquent, and the normal child with problems involving learning, behavior, or personality difficulties. The age groups served have been extended to include the nursery school, high schools and even colleges. The diagnostic services have been broadened from calculating a Binet IQ, through the stage of using a wider repertoire of tests and techniques to determine IQ's more validly, to the point where they now conduct thorough psychological evaluations of the individual referred to them. School psychologists have become more concerned with what happens to the child after their examination; their recommendations have developed beyond merely placement in an appropriate special class, to include referrals to other professional resources, and treatment programs ranging all the way from environmental manipulations to play therapy and other forms of individual and group psychotherapy. Their role within many of the schools rather early came to include responsibilities for group testing programs, later for remedial education, and still more recently for guidance and mental hygiene activities, work with teachers and parents, public relations, curriculum development, etc. Since local autonomy in education is a basic American principle, the ways in which the school psychologist developed in his widespread local settings have led to wide divergences in role and function. There has remained, however, a sufficient similarity to define clinical psychology in the school setting, the work of the school psychologist, as a specific, unitary professional field.

THE MAJOR FUNCTION OF THE SCHOOL PSYCHOLOGIST

The major function of the school psychologist, as of clinical psychologists in other settings, is the study of and assistance to individuals who present some problem in order to help them make an improved adjustment.

The following description of the major work of the school psychologist will therefore focus primarily on the features of his functioning which differentiate him from clinicians in other settings. Though the description will be in terms of the over-all American picture, it is only fair to point out that the details will be influenced more by the pattern in the Bureau of Child Study of the Chicago Public Schools, with which the author has had his most prolonged contacts, than by that of any other single specific school or school system.

SOURCE AND KIND OF REFERRALS

The first distinctive feature about school psychological services is the source of referrals. In the vast majority of cases, children are referred to the school psychologist by school personnel, mainly teachers and principals. Other school officials who make referrals are school nurses and physicians, visiting teachers or school social workers, supervisors, and administrators. In most school systems parents represent the next most frequent source of referral. In some schools—mainly high schools, but occasionally also elementary schools—a sizable number of self-referrals take place. Except in a small minority of school systems, the number of referrals from sources completely outside the school—such as courts, social agencies, or private physicians—represent only a small fraction of the total referrals; many school psychologists never or only rarely get such referrals.

An obvious consequence of the facts about the sources of referral is that the reasons for referral are predominantly poor adjustments to the school situation. Problems at home, in the community, or in the child's personal make-up, are, of course, often associated with problems in the school setting and are in many cases included as reasons for referral. In very many instances, too, the school psychologist studying a child who presents a problem at school, deals with his outside-of-school adjustment because it is tied up with his school problems or because it is an important part of the child's total need. Broad and varied as the actual problems with which the school psychologist deals may be, the sources of his referrals determine that he must always include major attention to adjustment in the school setting and that he will have a significant responsibility to school personnel.

Another important feature of the school psychologist's work is tied up with the population from which his referrals are drawn. While they are always children in the role of school pupils, they include all the children of school age in the community except the few whom compulsory school attendance laws do not reach. With a much larger population than other clinicians to serve, and with the legal necessity for practically every child being in school every day, it is not surprising that the school psychologist encounters a broader variety of problems than do other psychologists, and that he must expect a very high volume of referrals.

A third distinctive feature of the referrals to school psychologists consists of the reasons for referral, and related to, but not identical with them, the kinds of problems which are referred.

Since the school's function is to educate children, it is obvious that difficulties in learning would be a primary reason for referral to the psychologist. Whatever other problems the school psychologist might handle, he is sure to have a large number of cases in which poor school progress is the major symptom. As clinical psychology has developed it has become clear that the real problems of poor learners may often lie in emotional rather than intellectual areas, but the psychologist in the school setting, more than in any other one, must be prepared to handle a large volume of children who have difficulty with their school subjects.

Maladjustments reflected in socially unacceptable or undesirable behavior are the concern of clinicians in many settings. The school psychologist has referred to him the whole range of behavior problems seen by others working with children, but he finds a much larger proportion of them to be those in which the behavior is disturbing in the school situation. Among the behavior deviations which are referred to him, a high proportion will consist of nonconformity in the classroom situation, aggressive conduct at school, lying and petty stealing, clashes with school authorities, and truancy. There is a very common misconception—even among psychologists—that punitive, disciplinary action is the only approach which school personnel use with children whose behavior patterns are disturbed. While the number of teachers and principals who fit such a stereotype is still too large, it is a fact that a very large proportion of them appreciate the clinical approach to behavior difficulties. Hence, the number of referrals of such cases to school psychologists is quite large— and would be larger if more school psychological services were available.

Early studies of the differences in attitude between teachers, psychologists, and psychiatrists, toward the seriousness of various problems in children, indicated that the teachers were likely to minimize withdrawal symptoms and other manifestations of personality problems that were not overtly aggressive. As more recent repetitions of these same studies have shown, the picture has changed as a result of the development of the mental hygiene point of view in education, and in society at large. It seems probable that the work of the school psychologist has also had much impact on the psychological sophistication of school personnel. At any rate, the number of referrals for personality problems is a constantly increasing one. Again, the insufficiency of school psychological services, and the urgency of cases of learning and behavior difficulties, have tended to hold down the number of such referrals.

A fourth category of referrals to school psychologists are those cases in which there is no maladjustment, but where a whole classification of children needs clinical psychological study to further their educational interests. These include the physically handicapped, the gifted, and entering first graders for whom the question of reading readiness is quite important. The ultimate in this category of referrals is found in those very few schools which are so well to do that it is possible to make an individual psychological study of every pupil as a guide for the teacher's work with him.

WHERE THE PSYCHOLOGIST WORKS

A second distinctive feature of clinical psychological services in the school setting is the places where such services are rendered. In most clinical settings the client comes to the psychologist's office or headquarters; a large proportion of school psychological services are carried on not at a central office but at the school which the pupil attends.

The vast majority of school psychologists serve not a single school, but a group of schools ranging in number from a few to fifty or more. Many serve the schools of an entire county, as in Pennsylvania, or an even larger geographical area, as in Illinois (under the auspices of the Superintendent of Public Instruction). Where the psychologist serves a number of schools, he frequently conducts his examinations by visiting each of the schools in turn, or on call, although in some places the practice is to conduct the studies at his central office or in a district or regional office.

Providing clinical services at the pupil's school has both its advantages and its disadvantages. On the positive side are the opportunities to observe the child in his day-to-day setting, to consult with his present and former teachers, to study more of the school's records and the child's productions, and to observe the characteristics of the school itself and the community. The child is often less apprehensive when he remains in a familiar place. From the standpoint of economy there is the advantage of eliminating lost time through failed appointments, since the absent pupils can be readily replaced by someone else on the waiting list. Remedial or treatment techniques can be demonstrated, even within the class setting. Contacts can be more easily established with parents who are too unconcerned or unco-operative to make a trip to a central office.

Disadvantages inherent in the psychologist's going to the client include the inconvenience of travel, unavailability of examination or treatment equipment or materials that are too bulky or infrequently used to be carried around, and having to work with children in unsuitable surroundings (particularly during the present period when so many school plants are ancient and badly overcrowded). Often the psychologist visiting the home school is identified by the child with the elements in the school toward which he has hostile, indifferent, or otherwise negative attitudes. Children, and their parents, may feel less free to discuss confidential matters or material hostile to the school when they are in their local school instead of at a more neutral locale. The absence of the prestige value of a specialist and a clinic setting is in some cases quite a significant factor. And finally, the traveling psychologist may suffer from the less frequent contacts with central office facilities such as case records, professional library, and consultation with colleagues and supervisors.

One way in which school psychological departments have handled this matter is through provision of both visiting psychologists and central office clinics. The latter are used for specialized services, such as diagnostic reading or speech examinations, behavior studies, or in situations requiring performance tests or other special equipment. These services usually supplement the studies made by the psychologist at the school. In any case, however, the traveling psychologist does spend a portion of his time at his central office for preparing reports, consultations with supervisors, staff meetings, and other such functions.

INTERPROFESSIONAL COLLABORATION

A third major feature of clinical psychological services in the school setting is in the matter of collaboration with other professions. In only a minority of instances does the school psychologist operate as part of the traditional team of physician-psychiatrist, clinical psychologist, and social worker.

Many school psychologists—probably far more than the majority—work independently of all professions other than educators. In such instances the psychologist must take on some of the functions of specialists in the other fields. He may test vision and hearing, inspect teeth and tonsils, judge nutritional status, and be alert for indications of physical disorders or significant elements in health histories. In doing these things he does not substitute for a physician, but does search for evidence that will merit referral for medical examination.

Similarly the school psychologist who operates alone will need to take social histories, interview parents, make home visits, and carry on other functions which belong in the field of social service. In personality evaluations he conducts interviews and interprets evidence which in other settings are the function of the psychiatrist. He utilizes, through referrals to and reports from outside agencies, private and public, what is available in his community. When, as often happens in the smaller communities, there are few or none, he is the nearest one to being a specialist in these other areas and functions as well as he can within the limits set by the law and by his own competence.

The picture given above is by no means the situation under which all school psychologists operate. Many school systems do have other professional specialists on their staffs, regularly or as consultants, and in some there are special collaborative arrangements with such outside agencies as health departments, child guidance clinics, social casework agencies, or university departments. There are even some school settings which have as full a set of professional collaborators as is to be found in any other setting for clinical psychological services. .

What is characteristic even of these school settings, however, is the difference in the pattern of the team, or interrelationships within the team, that is to be found from one school system to another. Among the school specialists with whom the school psychologists may be found to be working, in a closely or a loosely integrated relationship, are one or a combination of the following: school physicians, psychiatrists, nurses, social workers, visiting teachers, truant officers, speech pathologists, speech therapists, physiotherapists, and a whole array of specialists in various fields of education. Because one of the professional skills of the psychologist is the integration of findings by other professions who work with children, the school psychologist has sometimes been the one responsible for persuading the superintendent or the school board to add other specialists to the school staff.

THE CLINICAL STUDY

The actual process of making a clinical study of a school pupil varies much from case to case, from psychologist to psychologist, and from school system to school system. On the one hand, the variation tends to be greater than for studies of children in other settings where the psychologist operates less independently of other professional practitioners; on the other hand, the basic similarities of all schools tends to produce greater similarities in clinical practice. Since similarities in procedure among school psychologists are easier to describe and compare with that of other clinical settings, it will be those features which the following discussion will emphasize.

The general pattern of a clinical study is to assemble from all possible sources—records, histories, tests, interviews, and direct observations—the data which will throw light on the causative factors for the problem. From his analysis of these data, the clinician seeks ways to eliminate, modify, rechannel, or counteract the forces leading to maladjustment and to set up a pattern of influences toward a more desirable adjustment.

The sources of data available to the school psychologist are in some ways richer than for other clinicians, but in others less full. School records, including scholastic ratings, standardized group tests of capacity and achievement, and other such materials accumulated over a period of years, give more objective information than is usually available. The experience of a number of teachers who have worked intensively with a child in a relationship that approaches the closeness of that of the parent, yet can be more objectively described, are a rich source of data that is often unavailable to psychologists working outside the school setting.

On the other hand, the school psychologist is often more limited than other clinicians in utilizing the parent as an informant. Because he must be less selective in the cases he accepts, he is much more often confronted with situations where the parent is unco-operative or unavailable. The pressure of the number of cases he must examine may force him to limit his contacts with the family to only a small proportion of his case load. Conventions and taboos concerning such areas as sex, religion, and intimate elements in the intrafamilial picture tend to operate more restrictively for him than for psychologists in other settings. More psychologists in school than in other situations are denied access to data in private social agency files, for only some of the school psychological departments have been admitted to social service exchanges. To the extent to which the school setting has fewer specialists from other professions, the school psychologist will lack data which are available to other clinical psychologists.

The school psychologist relies on an individual intelligence test—usually the Revised Stanford Binet, but to an increasing extent the

Wechsler Intelligence Scale for Children—as a major part of his clinical techniques much more than do psychologists in most other settings. There are many reasons for this: the large proportion of cases in which the learning difficulty is the principal problem; the fact that mental capacity is a more crucial factor in the child's adjustment to school than to any other area of his functioning; the centrality of learning as the school's concern, so that the impact of other problems on the ability to learn and the influence of the learning process on other elements in the pupil's behavior and personality is of great importance; the fact that this technique is one which no other member of the school staff has been trained to employ; tradition dating back to the period when the psychologist's only function in the schools was the diagnosis of mental deficiency; and, finally, the fact that until recently many school psychologists had such limited training that individual mental testing techniques represented a very large proportion of their total clinical psychological skill.

Still another characteristic of the school psychologist's diagnostic technique which differentiates him from other clinicians is his emphasis on the inclusion of a more comprehensive school history and the administration of academic achievement tests. The latter may be administered by other school personnel, or by the psychologist himself; they may include tests of a few basic tool subjects such as reading mechanics, reading comprehension, spelling, and arithmetic computation, or may be much more extensive in range, including diagnostic tests in reading or other areas. The reasons for these emphases are similar to those given above to explain the role of the individual intelligence test. In addition to them, however, is the school psychologist's keen awareness of the frequency with which academic problems may cause or intensify or complicate other problems in the child's adjustment, and, conversely, the ways in which academic successes and satisfactions can compensate for less easily handled or completely unmodifiable factors that contribute to his problems.

Although the picture is changing, it is still true that the school psychologist uses projective techniques rather infrequently. Lack of training in such techniques has been one factor to explain this, but this is not the sole reason. Less contact with psychiatrists and much more with educators influences his orientation. The pressure of case loads operates against the use of methods which are time-consuming. The demand for what is immediately practical and of service is very evident in a school setting, and the psychologist there can move only slowly in teaching the value of thoroughness and depth studies for their long-range benefits.

In reporting findings, the school psychologist's responsibility is almost always to the teacher and principal. Much less often than other clinical psychologists does he report for professional psychological or psychiatric staffs, hence his terminology, etc., must be geared to lay rather than professional understanding. Although case conference techniques, in which the school psychologist discusses his findings informally with teachers and other school personnel, are recognized as most desirable, the pressures of case loads and waiting lists often limit the opportunities for such reporting. The majority of psychologists in the school setting prepare formal written reports, brief or thorough, which go into the child's records at his school.

TREATMENT

Turning now to the treatment aspects of the school psychologist's clinical service, it should be pointed out that a comprehensive definition of treatment includes much more than psychotherapy. Though many psychologists in school systems carry on extensive and intensive programs of psychotherapy, including the many forms and varieties that have been developed in recent years, the bulk of the treatment with which the school psychologist is concerned is not of this type.

The school psychologist's treatment programs generally function through recommendations for activity by others. He makes many referrals to agencies outside of the school—medical, psychiatric, social service, recreational, etc. He sees appropriate school placement as a part of a treatment program, whether it involves a special class or school, an opportunity or adjustment class, or a change in grade. Remedial teaching, private tutoring, changes in teaching methods, levels, or goals, and handling the child at school in a different way are all forms of psychological as well as educational treatment. Suggestions and recommendations to the teachers, parents, other adults who are in contact with the pupil, and the child himself involve programs of action which are designed to set off psychological changes within the child. Very often the school psychologist will use more subtle forms of psychological treatment with the child, the parents, or the teachers—efforts to change attitudes indirectly and in casual contacts, through the right sort of listening, understanding, supportive actions, or manner. Follow-up contacts, formal or incidental, may be part of the psychologist's treatment program. It is thus evident that the school psychologist does have a very important role in treatment as well as diagnosis even in those situations where he does not schedule a series of psychotherapeutic interviews or play-therapy sessions. It should be emphasized, though, that more and more school psychologists are developing their skills and finding the time to carry on even these time-consuming forms of therapy.

RESEARCH AND TRAINING

With respect to two other functions which are quite commonly the concern of the clinical psychologist—research and training of interns or externs—the role of the school psychologist has unfortunately been minimal, though he recognizes their importance. The demands for service in the schools are so much greater than the amount of clinical psychological man-hours that are available, that research time is seldom available. The situation has not been helped by the fact that school salaries have always been lower than in other professional fields, so that a larger proportion of clinicians in schools than in other settings are at a lower training level and hence less research-minded. The relative infrequency of research activities by the school psychologist is particularly unfortunate because the size of the school population, the possibilities of various kinds of controls, the availability of follow-up opportunities, and other factors make the school setting an unusually well-endowed place for research.

The lack of as close ties between the universities and the public schools as between the former and medical institutions has been a significant factor in limiting the number of school systems which serve as internship training facilities. The lack of organized training programs for school psychologists in all but a very few universities—and even in those, only very recently established or still in the beginning stages—has been another reason for the scarcity of internship programs under supervision of school psychologists.

OTHER ACTIVITIES

If there are relatively few school psychologists engaged in some of the foregoing activities which are important functions of other clinical psychologists, there are a host of functions which the school setting provides for the clinician much more often than do other settings. Because they are not primarily clinical, this does not seem the appropriate place to describe them, though they are activities to which the school psychologist makes a unique contribution because of his clinical experience and insights. They include responsibilities for: setting up, administering, and utilizing group testing programs; carrying on or supervising remedial teaching; statistical analyses; consultation on educational problems in the areas of special education, school organization, curriculum, teaching methods, personnel, and guidance; broad programs of mental hygiene for both pupils and teachers; parent education; inservice training of teachers; public relations; and many other duties which school superintendents and other administrators assign to the school psychologist because of his unique training and experience.

Finally, there should be mentioned the frequency with which school psychologists are called on for outside-of-school clinical work—volunteer or on a fee basis. Because there are so many smaller communities in which the school psychologist is the only available psychological resource, he may be called on to handle the problems of children or adults which are referred to him by doctors, parents, private schools, courts, social agencies, etc. These occasional cases, and part-time teaching of psychology courses, result for many school psychologists in a much longer work week than one would expect from the fact that the school day is usually shorter than the work day in other settings.

CURRENT PROBLEMS OF SCHOOL PSYCHOLOGISTS

Because the school psychologist represents a specialized area in both clinical psychology and education, he is concerned not only with the problems in each of these professions, but with special problems which contribute toward making his field a separate subprofession. Hence he not only joins both psychological and educational organizations, but has a separate one of his own, the Division of School Psychologists of the American Psychological Association. He has no professional journal of his own, though there are the beginnings of one in the Division's Newsletter which is circulated to nonmembers as well as members. Foremost among the professional concerns of school psychologists is the matter of standards of training, and related to it, certification.

The training of school psychologists involves a most anomalous situation. Ideally, the psychologist working in the school setting needs all the understandings, techniques, skills, and experience of the most highly trained clinical psychologist. This is because of the variety of problems of children, teachers, and parents which he must handle and because he so often must function without the benefit of other professional collaborators. He should also be very highly trained in many areas of education, including experience in classroom teaching such as is required by many of the state certification laws and many of the school systems which employ psychologists. Diplomate status in clinical psychology, a Ph.D. in education, and considerable classroom teaching experience would scarcely be too high a standard for one who is expected to do well what a school psychologist is supposed to do.

The current situation represents the opposite extreme. School psychologists in the American Psychological Association include a higher proportion of minimally trained persons than almost any other group of psychologists—and there are a very large number of school psychologists who do not belong to the American Psychological Association because they do not have the lowest membership qualifications.

It is true that the many very competent school psychologists are being joined by well-qualified clinical psychologists who are entering school service in larger and larger numbers even though they find it difficult to meet teaching qualifications and other detailed course requirements that differ markedly from state to state. But the attractiveness of the opportunities and the challenge of clinical psychological service in a school setting is offset by the low salaries that are traditional in education.

Concern about these and other problems of school psychologists is growing not only among school psychologists, but among psychologists in general and among educational administrators and agencies concerned with mental health. The most recent development, at the time this chapter is being written, is the calling of a Work Conference on the Qualifications and Training of School Psychologists by the Education and Training Board of the American Psychological Association. This conference has been requested by the Division of School Psychologists and financed by United States Public Health Service funds.

FUTURE OUTLOOK FOR CLINICAL PSYCHOLOGY IN THE SCHOOLS

Anyone concerned with the value and role of clinical psychology in society must be impressed with the tremendous opportunities represented by the school setting. No other locale provides the possibility of reaching every person in the country, and at age levels when it is easiest to prevent maladjustment or effect readjustment. No other field offers nearly so much of an opportunity to make clinical psychological services available to all who need or can benefit from such services. Few settings offer such rich possibilities for research in clinical psychology, and few offer such freedom to explore and experiment with new techniques and new avenues of service. It appears that no other neighboring profession is as ready and eager to accept what clinical psychology has to offer as is the field of education.

With such great possibilities, it is encouraging to note the recent increase in the rate of development of clinical psychology in the school setting. Public and private school systems are becoming among the largest employers of psychologists. Agencies which promote mental health programs are seeing the opportunities in education. Increased popular interest and support of the schools, as exemplified by the numerous citizen's commissions on public schools throughout the country, are opening up new resources, moral and material, from which the schools can draw in improving and expanding their services to children. These movements seem likely to increase the utilization of clinical services in the school setting to the point where these services will become a most important aspect of clinical practice in psychology.

REFERENCES

1. American Psychological Association, Division of School Psychologists. *Newsletter.* Complete file, 1946-1954.
2. Hall, M. E. Current employment requirements for school psychologists. *Amer. Psychologist,* 1949, 4, 519-525.
3. Bureau of Child Study and the Chicago adjustment service plan. Annual report of the Superintendent of Schools. Chicago: Board of Education, City of Chicago, 1940. Pp. 391-430.

XXV

THE CLINICAL PSYCHOLOGIST IN THE READING CLINIC

KATHERINE KENEALLY STEFIC

The fields of clinical psychology and remedial instruction have become allied through their common interest in the development and growth of the individual child. Historically, as Louttit reports (10), the interest of the clinical psychologist in the problems of children was his first focus of activity. In 1896 Witmer presented a series of proposals concerning the practical investigation of problems of school children using methods available from psychological laboratories. In 1909 Healy began his work with juvenile delinquents, with Fernald functioning as the psychologist. At the same time, changes were being made in the teaching procedure in public schools. The trend at the beginning of the century was away from mass education to a return to an interest in providing for individual differences as practiced in the one-room school house. Several plans were started in the early part of the twentieth century to put into practice the theory of individualization of instruction. All of these plans were based on the individual's needs and provided in several ways for allowing children to proceed at their own rates of learning.

At present we find both clinical psychologists and educators working together more and more frequently. Since reading is a major tool in all pursuits of higher education and recreation, it is natural that emphasis is being placed in that area. For many years teachers have been trying to help children who fail to learn to read. In the past, emphasis was placed on drill and the teaching of subject matter rather than teaching the individual child. Lack of understanding of the psychological and emotional causes of reading failure often hindered a corrective program.

In the late 1920's many schools, mainly at the secondary level, became interested in correcting these learning difficulties. Strang (14) describes remedial classes that were started in various high schools. Remedial clinics and laboratories were established in several universities in the latter part of the 1930's, among which were the Psycho-Educational Clinic at Harvard University, the Boston University Clinic, the University of Chicago Reading Clinic, and many others in various parts of the country.

The awareness of the problem of reading difficulty and the desire to correct the problem became a major aim of educators. The reading clinics were interested in prevention as well as correction of reading difficulties and placed the emphasis of their efforts in working with elementary school children. The clinics, at the same time, offered training to teachers through fellowships and courses designed to teach the understanding of the causes of failure and the methods and techniques of correction.

In order to correct a reading disability a diagnostic study of each child became a necessity. Each child was given a nonverbal test of intelligence, in most cases the Stanford revision of the Binet test, as well as various achievement tests to discover the child's grade level in various school subjects.

The majority of the group tests of achievement were almost entirely tests of reading and were of little help in diagnosing the difficulties of nonreaders. Children who were retarded a year or more in reading could use group tests but the test results usually indicated only grade level in vocabulary and paragraph comprehension with no indication of specific difficulties. At present, however, there are at least two well-known diagnostic tests of reading ability. Gates (9) and Durrell (6) have published individual tests that analyze the reading difficulty and aid the clinician in planning individual corrective programs. These tests indicate specific difficulties in the areas of oral and silent reading, word recognition and word analysis.

Although these tests were a big step in understanding reading difficulties, other factors that blocked learning had to be considered. Lack of motivation, short attention spans, and behavior and emotional difficulties were considered as possible causes of lack of success in reading.

In this area, the clinical psychologist has been a source of help in locating the causes of many behavior and emotional disturbances that interfere with or block learning. Many remedial clinics have clinical psychologists on the staff. Other reading clinics send their reading cases to the research departments in public school systems, to child guidance clinics, or to mental hygiene clinics in their areas for a complete psychological examination. The influence of emotional and behavior disturbances as the primary cause of many reading failures has been reported by Blanchard (4), McCullough, Strang and Traxler (11), Gates (8), Odenwald and Shea (13), Betts (3), and Ellis (7). Aguilera and Keneally (1), in a survey of remedial cases in an eleven-year period, found that the majority of children referred to a child center for remedial instruction also had emotional or behavior difficulties. One of the problems at the time of the diagnostic study is to determine whether the emotional disturbance is the cause or the result of school failure. With the child who is emotionally disturbed solely because of school failure the emotional block usually disappears with success in the remedial learning situation. Psychotherapy is not usually necessary in such cases. The child whose emotional difficulty stems from poor parent-child relationship, sibling rivalry and other difficulties usually receives psychotherapy and remedial instruction simultaneously. Children who are too disturbed to profit by remedial instruction do not enter the reading clinic until their emotional difficulties have been resolved.

THE SCHOOL CLINIC

Some cities and towns appoint a remedial teacher for each school. This teacher cares for the retarded readers during the school day. Although this is an excellent solution to the problem, it is unusual because most school budgets are limited and do not provide for the hiring of special remedial teachers.

Some large cities have set up central reading clinics to which teachers may refer their retarded readers. This type of clinic usually has a staff of trained remedial teachers. Each teacher has his classroom experience and special training in remedial work. The school psychologist who is a member of the research department is responsible for the administration of intelligence and achievement tests. The psychologist also makes recommendations for further personality testing if the child has an emotional or behavior problem. Usually the head of the reading clinic has had training in psychology and often administers personality and projective tests or may supervise those who do.

The psychologist not only works with the children in the clinic but offers services and advice to classroom teachers in the form of test interpretations and in suggesting appropriate methods of teaching retarded readers.

THE UNIVERSITY READING CLINIC

In 1949 a survey of reading clinics by Myer and Keyser (13) listed a total of sixty-four college and university clinics, thirteen public school clinics and eight private clinics. A later survey by Boyd and Schwiering (5) revealed a total of seventy-six reading centers, sixty of which were in colleges and universities, twelve associated with public school systems, and four with independent child guidance clinics. However, neither of these was a complete or exhaustive study and it is undoubtedly true that the amount and kinds of remedial help are on the increase.

Many of the reading clinics in the colleges and universities were set up as part of the education department for the purpose of providing an opportunity for the training of teachers. Under the supervision of the directors of the clinics, teachers are trained to administer tests of intelligence and educational achievement tests in order to diagnose the specific reading difficulties of each individual. Remedial techniques for the correction of reading difficulties are emphasized.

Such clinics, in increasing numbers, are adding clinical psychologists to their staffs in order to supplement their testing programs and to evaluate emotional and behavior difficulties which may be present. In some cases, university clinics may also avail themselves of the services of affiliated medical schools which have a psychiatric training program. In these clinics the clinical psychologists are responsible for the complete psychological study and educational evaluation of each child. Thus the psychologist may consult with individual teachers and aid them in setting up remedial programs to meet the specific needs of each child.

THE REMEDIAL CLINIC OF THE CATHOLIC UNIVERSITY CHILD CENTER

The Child Center of the Catholic University of America began in 1916 when Dr. Thomas Verner Moore, O.S.B., M.D., Ph.D., established the Clinic for Nervous and Mental Diseases at Providence Hospital in Washington, D. C. This clinic was established as part of the Psychology Department of Catholic University and its chief function was the study of mentally retarded children. The clinic was also used to train students of the National Catholic School of Social Service. In 1937, when the Catholic University School of Social Work was founded, the clinic was moved from Providence Hospital to St. Thomas Hall on the university campus and was named "Child Center."

The purposes of the Child Center are threefold: (1) service to the community, (2) training of students, and (3) research. The Child Center accepts children from infancy to eighteen years; in addition, a few adults are seen. The main function of the Child Center is the diagnosis and treatment of emotional and behavior disorders. The aim of therapy is to allow the child to regain his self-confidence so that he can modify his behavior toward a more profitable adjustment. No treatment is undertaken without the active participation of a parent or a parent substitute.

Graduate students in four disciplines: child psychiatry, clinical psychology, social work, and remedial teaching are accepted for training and supervision in their respective fields. These students are considered a part of the staff of the Child Center and attend staff, diagnostic, and treatment conferences. All students are given the opportunity to work as a member of a therapeutic team consisting of representatives from each discipline.

Staff of the Child Center. The present staff of the Child Center includes two full-time child psychiatrists and three psychiatric consultants. Psychiatric consultants supervise members of the staff who are carrying treatment cases and also offer consultative service to the various therapeutic teams to evaluate progress and treatment of specific cases. Weekly staff meetings are held, in which the treatment of cases is reviewed. The director of medical services carries treatment cases and also devotes part of his time to supervision, teaching and administrative duties.

The chief clinical psychologist has a full-time assistant and three graduate students who are externs in psychology. The psychology staff is responsible for the testing program in the Child Center. The clinical psychologists, including the externs, all carry cases in therapy under the supervision of the staff psychiatrists.

Parents or parent substitutes are seen by one of the four psychiatric social workers on the staff. Every child who is seen for treatment at the Child Center is accompanied by one or both parents or a parent substitute. The parent substitute may be a caseworker from one of the several social agencies or a foster parent. The social workers are responsible for intake, initial interviews, and conduct weekly interviews with parents of children who are in treatment.

The Remedial Clinic. The Remedial Clinic became a part of the Child Center in 1939 when Dr. Moore, as a result of his experience with children at Providence Hospital, found that many of the emotional and behavior problems were related to school failure. The Remedial Clinic is directed by a psychologist and is staffed with a clinical psychology extern as well as graduate students who have had some teaching experience. Some of these students intend to enter the remedial field and others are working toward a doctoral degree in clinical psychology.

Children accepted for remedial and reading instruction are of average or superior intelligence whose reading age level is one year or more below their mental age. The majority of the children accepted for the remedial clinic are emotionally disturbed or have behavior problems in addition to their reading difficulty. All children in the Remedial Clinic have a complete diagnostic study prior to their entrance in the remedial class. During the diagnostic study each child is tested by the clinical psychologist. Intelligence tests and several projective personality tests comprise the usual battery administered to the child. The child is also given educational achievement tests and a diagnostic reading test by a member of the Remedial Clinic staff to find his reading grade level and his specific reading difficulties in order to plan a remedial program for him. A staff psychiatrist also interviews the child to determine whether there are emotional problems which may require psychotherapeutic treatment. During the period of study, the child's problem is discussed by the parent and the psychiatric social worker and, at this time, the clinic functions are explained and the fees determined.

An evaluation of each child's mental level is of major importance in order to plan a specific remedial program. The results of various verbal and nonverbal tests should indicate a child's vocabulary level, his ability to discriminate between similarities and differences, memory ability, reasoning ability, and evidence of reversals, all of which are of importance in the task of teaching a child to read. An objective evaluation of mental age makes it possible to determine the exact amount of reading retardation. In some cases referred for school failure the results of intelligence tests indicate that the child is reading up to his mental level and, although he is below his chronological age in reading ability, he is not a retarded reader and remedial work is not recommended.

After the completion of the study a diagnostic conference is held in which a member from each discipline participates; reports of findings are presented and future plans for service discussed. An interpretation of the findings of the diagnostic study is made to the parent in a subsequent interview with the social worker. If a child has been found to be extremely disturbed it is usually recommended that he receive psychotherapy prior to entering the remedial clinic. In other cases, remedial instruction and a program of psychotherapy may be carried on concurrently. Occasionally, only remedial help may be given if it is felt that the child's emotional problems are the result of school failure.

Children attend the Remedial Clinic from 9 to 11 A.M. daily. They are taught individually or in small groups of two or three. These small groups are composed of children reading on the same grade level or those having the same specific reading difficulties. The groups are flexible so that a pupil may move from one group to another as his needs require. Remedial instruction is carried on in a permissive atmosphere with a few limitations set up by teachers and pupils together. All lessons are based on each child's specific difficulties. Detailed lesson plans are necessary for a successful remedial program. Thus each pupil's mental ability, rate of learning, and interests are carefully considered. The short attention and interest spans of these children who lack security and confidence often require a frequent change of activity. Exercises, drills, and games are graded in difficulty and constant reviews are provided to help the pupils master new reading skills. Records of progress are kept for each individual. In this way, each child is kept aware of his rate of progress. Achievement tests are administered every four to six weeks to determine what gains the child has made. When a child is up to his grade level he returns to his regular classroom. The amount of time spent in the clinic varies with the individual. The child's mental ability, his attitude toward school, and his desire to learn to read are all factors which, in some measure, determine the length of attendance in the Remedial Clinic.

Changes in attitude and behavior, in school and at home, often result from the child's experience in a reading clinic. Although the emphasis is placed on remedial instruction, these changes in attitude and behavior become apparent in the clinic as the child succeeds in reading. Extremely aggressive and hyperactive children may tend to become less aggressive, while the shy, withdrawn child tends to become more outgoing. Thus, remedial instruction offers a kind of psychotherapeutic program in itself. Another important factor in this change seems to be the child's desire for social acceptance in the group and the wish for his teacher's approval. Individual tutoring also affords each child an opportunity to form a relationship with an adult who is permissive and accepting toward the child despite his school failure. It is interesting to note that when these children return to school the director of the reading clinic is apt to receive more reports of changes in behavior and attitude, from teachers and school principals, than comments on their gains in reading ability.

FUTURE OUTLOOK

The psychologist has the opportunity to render invaluable service in the field of remedial instruction. Our knowledge of techniques and methods of teaching reading, types of motivation suitable to school-age children, and ways and means of preventing school failure need to be explored. The psychologist can help in this area by stimulating and continuing research. The clinical psychologist can do much more than administer tests of various kinds, important as they are. Certainly the need for psychotherapy with these children with school problems is great and, presently, clinical psychologists are being trained to render such service.

In the field of training and teaching, the psychologist can offer future remedial teachers a dynamic orientation to the problem of reading failure. Nor must his teaching be limited to the academic realm, for there is an opportunity for public education. Here the psychologist can help the layman to overcome many of his prejudices and can clarify the erroneous conceptions which surround his concern with academic failure.

REFERENCES

1. Aguilera, A., & Keneally, K. G. *School failure—psychiatric implications* (in press). New York: Child Care Publications.
2. Anderson, I. H., & Dearborn, W. F. *The psychology of teaching reading*. New York: Ronald Press, 1952.
3. Betts, E. A. *Foundations of reading instruction*. New York: American Book Co., 1946.

4. Blanchard, P. Psychogenic factors in some cases of reading disability. *Amer. J. Orthopsychiat.*, 1935, 5, 361-371.
5. Boyd, G., & Schwiering, O. C. Remedial instruction and case records: a survey of reading clinic practices. *J. educ. Res.*, 1950, 44, 494-506.
6. Durrell, D. D. *Analysis of reading difficulty.* New York: World Book Co., 1940.
7. Ellis, A. Results of a mental hygiene approach to reading disability problems. *J. consult. Psychol.*, 1949, 13, 56-62.
8. Gates, A. I. *The improvement of reading.* (3rd Ed.) New York: Macmillan, 1947.
9. Gates, A. I. *Gates Reading Diagnosis Tests.* New York: Bureau of Publications, Teachers College, Columbia University, 1933.
10. Louttit, C. M. The nature of clinical psychology. *Psychol. Bull.*, 1939, 36, 361-389.
11. McCullough, C. M., Strang, R., & Traxler, A. E. *Problems in the improvement of reading.* New York: McGraw-Hill, 1946.
12. Myer, T. R., & Keyser, M. L. *Survey of reading clinics.* Ames, Iowa: Dept. of Publications, State University of Iowa, 1949.
13. Odenwald, R. P., & Shea, J. A. Emotional problems of maladjustment in children with reading difficulties. *Amer. J. Psychiat.*, 1951, 107, 890-893.
14. Strang, R. *Problems in the improvement of reading in high school and college.* (2nd Ed.) Lancaster, Pa.: The Science Press Printing Co., 1940.

XXVI.

THE CLINICAL PSYCHOLOGIST IN THE HEARING CLINIC

HELMER R. MYKLEBUST

Clinical psychological services in the area of auditory disorders have been slow in developing. Historically, experimental psychologists have made noteworthy contributions to the field of audition. Hearing has been scientifically studied for a number of years, but it is only during recent years that the individuals with hearing disorders have been studied seriously. It has been assumed by psychologists and other specialists such as otolaryngologists, that lack of response to sound was an invariable indication of reduced auditory acuity. This assumption has led to over-simplification of the problems of auditory functioning. The area of auditory disorders and the psychopathology of hearing involves many factors and many disorders other than impairment of acuity. This area is broad and is more beneficially thought of as *auditory behavior*. The concept of auditory behavior and not the concept of simply reduced auditory acuity is an essential aspect of the work of the clinical psychologist in the hearing clinic.

In view of the fact that auditory disorders can occur from central nervous system damage, from impairment of the hearing mechanism itself, or from emotional disturbance, it becomes the clinical psychologist's task to assist in the evaluation of the nature of the auditory problems presented by the individuals with whom he works. This entails the psychology of sensory behavior from the point of view of the total functioning of the organism. It is important to operate from a concept of auditory behavior rather than simply a concept of hearing impairment. If an individual has impaired auditory acuity, making it impossible for him to keep in contact with his environment through hearing, it seems that this individual's behavior must be organismically different. For example, when the deaf individual is using his eyes for foreground activity he has no sense modality for exploration of the surrounding environment from the point of view of a distance sense. Instead, he must use other sense modalities in a compensatory manner. This is typical of the individuals with marked impairment of hearing acuity. While vision is being used in the foreground, kinesthesis becomes the supplementary, or signaling sense. Therefore, such an individual *feels* footsteps and then looks up to use his vision further to explore the disturbance, or change, in the environmental field.

It is apparent, on the basis of research and clinical experience, that the work of the clinical psychologist in the hearing clinic is complex and directly related to total behavior. The emphasis must be placed on the individual with the auditory disorder and not on the auditory disorder itself if the interrelatedness of auditory disturbances with general behavior is to be adequately recognized.

ROLE OF THE CLINICAL PSYCHOLOGIST

Scientific psychological study of individuals with deafness dates mainly from the early work of Pintner. He and his co-worker, Paterson, published their first important work in 1915. Pintner continued his interest in the psychology of deafness throughout his professional career and together with his students demonstrated the significance of this area for the clinical psychologists who were to follow. One of the important consequences of Pintner's work was that the administrators of a few public and private schools for the deaf added psychologists to their staffs. These psychologists were the forerunners of the clinical psychologists who are now in hearing clinics.

A considerable impetus was given to the use of clinical psychologists in hearing clinics during World War II. This was an outgrowth of pressing clinical problems associated with deafened veterans and psychogenic deafness. However, despite these problems and earlier developments there continues to be an exceedingly limited number of clinical psychologists engaged in work with the auditorially handicapped.

The early work of psychologists who became interested in persons with deafness was chiefly in ascertaining the effect of deafness on mental and emotional development. This continues to be a challenging problem but the clinical psychologist's role now is more specific. He must assist in making a complete clinical appraisal, including intelligence, emotional factors, language disorders, motor capacities, and the degree and type of auditory disorder. Moreover, he has direct responsibilities for counseling, psychotherapy and research. He frequently works collaboratively with an otolaryngologist, an audiologist, a speech pathologist, a psychiatrist, a teacher, and a rehabilitation worker. His various functions are discussed briefly below.

DIAGNOSIS

The functions of the clinical psychologist in the hearing clinic vary according to the setting of the clinic. Many hearing clinics are operated in conjunction with speech clinics in what have come to be named "Speech and Hearing Centers" in universities. Hearing clinics also are operated in departments of otolaryngology in medical schools. Irrespective of the setting of the clinic, the clinical psychologist's work includes responsibilities of diagnosis. This is similar to the clinical psychologist's responsibilities in other types of clinics. He assists other specialists in the objective evaluation of the individual's problem. In general, the diagnostic responsibilities follow the nature of the problem presented by the individual. In preschool children the major responsibility is that of making a differential diagnosis. Many children are referred to the clinic on the basis of presumed impairment of hearing acuity. It becomes the clinical psychologist's task to determine whether the problem is impaired hearing acuity or whether the problem is mental deficiency, aphasia, or psychic deafness, because these are the conditions which are most often found in these children. This is a complex task, because most of these children are nonverbal children; the diagnostic techniques and procedures must be selected and applied accordingly. The younger the child the greater is the need for such differential diagnosis. Often the clinical psychologist works closely with the pediatrician, child psychiatrist and otolaryngologist in making such a diagnosis.

MENTAL CAPACITY

A careful evaluation of mental level is essential. This is especially true of the young children. If deafness is sustained at school age or later, including during adulthood, the problem of diagnosis of mental capacity becomes less critical. However, the clinical psychologist makes an appraisal of the mental capacity of all of the individuals who present problems of auditory disorder. In general, the use of nonverbal tests is routine. Even with those school-age children or adults who sustained deafness or hearing impairment after language has been acquired, the use of verbal tests presents difficulties. Such tests as the Wechsler-Bellevue and the Grace Arthur are highly useful in evaluating the mental capacity of adolescents and adults. Appraisal of the mental capacity in the preschool child with auditory disorder is a more complex problem. Tests which have been found useful include the Hiskey Test of Learning Aptitude for Young Deaf Children, the Cattell Infant Scale and the performance part of the Wechsler Intelligence Scale for Children. Many of the items on the Cattell do not involve extensive verbal communication and for children below three years these items are especially useful. The primary purpose of the appraisal of mental capacity is to ascertain whether the child falls within normal limits of mental ability. This appraisal should ascertain whether the child's lack of speech and presumed deafness can be attributed to mental deficiency. If the child is four years of age but his mental age is one year or less, then the presumption of deafness may be erroneous. However, if this child has a mental age of three or more, then his lack of speech cannot be attributed directly to factors of mental inferiority. The normal average child of two years uses short sentences, therefore the child whose mental age is three years or more should be considered mentally capable of comprehending what he hears and developing speech unless other factors, such as deafness or aphasia, are superimposed. Another purpose of the evaluation of mental capacity is that of securing clinical evidence relative to the possible existence of brain injury. Performance on mental tests with evaluation of perceptual and conceptual factors is an important source of clinical information regarding the integrity of the central nervous system. The mental examination also provides evidence for possible emotional involvements. If the child rejects the situation and finds it impossible to relate to the examiner, his behavior must be evaluated in terms of the behavioral symptomatology which usually is associated with the various types of auditory disorders.

MOTOR CAPACITY

The clinical psychological examination routinely includes appraisal of motor capacity. This evaluation assists in determining the relative importance of peripheral versus central and organic versus functional factors. For example, it is apparent that individuals who sustain deafness from meningitis frequently have gross disturbance of balance because of a concomitant destruction of the semicircular canals. Furthermore, it is apparent clinically that individuals who have sustained central damage causing an auditory disorder frequently present problems of motor incoordination. The motor tests assist in eliciting this type of diagnostic information. If the problem is functional, usually the motor behavior is intact or presents a different type of deviation than that which derives from damage to the semi-circular canals, or impairment of the central nervous system. Tests which have been found useful in appraising the motor capacities of individuals seen in the hearing clinic include the Heath Rail-walking Test, the Oseretsky Tests of Motor Proficiency, and the Van Der Lugt Psychomotor Scale for Children.

SOCIAL MATURITY

Appraisal of social maturity has been found especially helpful in the diagnosis of problems presented by individuals having auditory disorders. The Vineland Social Maturity Scale is the instrument which has been used most successfully. This Scale can be administered when many other objective procedures cannot be applied. It is administered through an informant, which circumvents the marked language incapacity of so many of these persons. Evaluation of social maturity provides evidence regarding the genetic and functional level. This information provides a basis for further diagnosis and for remedial procedures.

LANGUAGE EVALUATION

Evaluation of the symbolic or language behavior is a critical aspect of the total diagnosis. The primary disability of individuals seen in a hearing clinic is in the area of language behavior. Children with marked deafness from early life do not acquire verbal language normally. Children with congenital aphasia are deficient in symbolic behavior in general. Mentally deficient children with presumed deafness usually are highly deficient in the acquisition of language. Children having severe emotional disorders, such as infantile autism or childhood schizophrenia, frequently have no overt verbal language receptively or expressively. The clinical psychologist is confronted with the urgent need to establish the type of language disorder which is present. In doing so it is useful to differentiate between inner, receptive, and expressive language. Deaf children usually have highly developed inner language and therefore can express themselves in gesture, facial expression, etc. Aphasic children frequently are highly deficient in symbolic behavior in general and find it impossible to use gesticulation or any other form of symbolic functioning. Children with severe emotional disturbances frequently manifest a complex symbolic functioning, but this symbolic functioning relates to their inner life only. It is disassociated from realistic contact with other people and with the environment in general. One of the most challenging and intriguing aspects of the clinical psychologist's work in the hearing clinic entails this study and appraisal of individuals with deviate types and deviate degrees of ability to function symbolically. Inasmuch as there are no tests of symbolic behavior for young children it is necessary for the psychologist to devise techniques which are useful clinically. This can be done by using various types of toys and other familiar objects and to engage the child in activities of a play nature. The extent to which the child can relate himself perceptually, conceptually and realistically to such situations is a primary source of clinical information regarding his use of symbols. With some school-age children and with adults the Halstead-Wepman and the Eisenson Tests are useful. Clinical appraisal of language functioning frequently includes tests of inner language, ability to comprehend spoken language, ability to speak, ability to read and to write.

SPECIAL APTITUDES

Evaluation of special aptitudes often is included in the clinical psychological appraisal. There are a number of tests which can be used for this purpose. Interest inventories, however, can be used only with those individuals whose reading ability is adequate. The Kuder Interest

Inventory has been found useful in the study of the interest patterns of deaf college students. Frequently adolescents and adults are referred to the hearing clinic by vocational rehabilitation agencies. The appraisal of interest pattern and special aptitudes is especially important in such instances. Vocational pursuits are somewhat more critical to individuals with special handicaps and, therefore, this question is encountered frequently. Determination of educational achievement is related to the evaluation of aptitudes and to vocational guidance. The use of standard achievement tests is helpful but such tests cannot be accepted at face validity when applied to individuals with language disability concomitant to auditory impairment. The clinical psychologist finds it necessary to evaluate and to validate the responses of the individual. Frequently it is possible for a deaf person with marked retardation in educational achievement to earn a relatively normal score on an achievement test. This perhaps is due to his being able to pick the right word from several words and to complete sentences accordingly, but to be much more handicapped in the use of spontaneous spoken or written language. Appraisal of educational achievement is a significant aspect of the total evaluation of individuals with auditory impairments.

PERSONALITY

Appraisal of personality adjustment is an important aspect of the total diagnosis. Again the use of standard tests is questionable and invalid in many instances. In general, projective techniques assume normal language facility and fluency. Such language facility is a primary incapacity of individuals seen in the hearing clinic. However, these techniques frequently can be used with the hard-of-hearing and with the deafened. With those persons whose deafness was sustained at birth or in the prespeech age, frequently it is not possible to apply either projective tests or tests of the inventory type. If these tests are used, clinical validation of them is necessary. It is becoming increasingly apparent that emotional problems are associated with problems of deafness. Various studies are in agreement that individuals with impaired hearing acuity find it more difficult to make normal adjustments to their environment. Psychologists in the past frequently have assumed that people with deafness were especially prone to paranoia. Recent studies have not entirely supported this observation. Rather, the greater problem has been found to be that of general withdrawal and poor contact with the environment. Individuals having marked deafness from early life are more likely to have undue fantasy and to be more unrealistic about the world in which they live. Their problem is not limited to that of paranoia. Furthermore, there is a difference between individuals deaf from early life and those who sustained deafness in later life. The pattern of general withdrawal is present in both groups, but those who have had hearing until early adulthood apparently are not prone to concomitant paranoia. Those who have marked deafness from early life tend to be unrealistic and withdrawn and also to be somewhat paranoid. This generalization, however, must be cautiously applied because great variations are present and the age of onset and the extent of the deafness seems to be directly related to the problem of maladjustment. In general, the greater the deafness and the earlier it is sustained the greater is the difficulty of adjusting to the world.

AUDITORY CAPACITY

Perhaps one of the most consequential functions of the clinical psychologist in the hearing clinic is the administration of different types of auditory tests. Inasmuch as lack of response to sound can be due to different factors it is not possible simply to apply an auditory test and then to conclude that the individual has a certain degree of deafness. Rather, it is necessary to use various types of tests and to evaluate the responses on the basis of the total symptomatology which the individual presents.

One of the basic procedures for determining the degree of hearing acuity is to administer an audiometric test. This is a pure tone test. Routinely, seven frequencies of sound are used. This includes one frequency above and one frequency below the speech range. Considerable clinical experience has been gained from the use of the audiometric test over a period of time. However, only recently have some of the limitations of this test been recognized. It is apparent that the pure tone audiometric test is invalid below three years of age and can be used only occasionally with children between the ages of three and six years. It is becoming rather apparent that on the average a six- to seven-year general maturational level is required for valid threshold responses to the pure tone test. This test can be used, however, for certain clinical purposes below this age level.

In addition to pure tone audiometry the clinical psychologist in the hearing clinic must be familiar with and have facility in the use of various other types of auditory tests. For example, he should have facility in the use of speech reception tests such as the Harvard Spondee List and the Harvard P-B List. These tests are widely used for purposes of evaluating auditory capacity and integrity. The literature on the use of these tests is relatively extensive. They are useful not only for purposes of determining speech reception thresholds, but they are useful in ascertaining the integrity of an individual's general comprehension through audition. These tests are administered either in recorded form or with live voices. Certain standard equipment is necessary for obtaining maximum usefulness from these tests.

In work with children frequently it is necessary to use free field techniques. Free field procedures are those which are not delivered directly through ear phones into the ear, but rather, the sounds are generated through an amplifier and loud speaker directly into the testing room. Free field techniques include the use of pure tones, recordings of sounds which the average child encounters in his environment, musical recordings, and the use of speech sounds. These tests are done in a standardized manner and through calibrated equipment, so that relatively accurate threshold measurements usually can be derived. In addition to such free field tests it is common to use various types of toys and other instruments to produce sounds in a clinical manner. For example, the examiner might have a set of bells and various types of toys which when manipulated will produce sounds. These are informal free field tests, but the value derived from them clinically in work with children is considerable. There are many young children who do not find it possible to listen, although they can hear. This is especially true of some brain-injured and emotionally disturbed children. For such children informal techniques sometimes provide validating information to supplement the more formal type of auditory test. The ingenuity of the clinical psychologist in using these tests is highly important. There are a number of children who, because of their inability to listen, cannot respond to formal auditory testing but can respond successfully to auditory tests of a relatively informal type.

A number of tests have been devised for determining psychogenic deafness in school-age children and adults. One such test is the Doerfler-Stewart, commonly referred to as the D-S Test. This test consists of giving an auditory stimulus which usually consists of spoken words. Simultaneously a noise level is introduced. This can be done either through standard ear phones or through a speaker in a free field situation. Individuals with true organic deafness do not show undue variability in their thresholds for speech when the noise is introduced. Usually individuals with psychogenic deafness find the introduction of noise highly disturbing. This causes their thresholds for speech to shift greatly. The conclusion is that the psychogenically deafened individual can subjectively control the level of intensity to which he will respond. However, when noise is introduced his subjective standard is interfered with and he no longer can adhere to his usual criterion. As a result he finds it difficult, if not impossible, to control the level at which he feels he can respond to the amplified speech sounds. This test is helpful in many situations. It assumes normal auditory perceptual behavior. Furthermore, on the basis of clinical experience it seems to be less useful for individuals with psychotic problems as compared to those with problems of neurosis. It does not differ from other tests in the need for careful administration and interpretation. This becomes a primary task for the clinical psychologist when problems of psychogenic deafness are presumed.

During recent years the psychogalvanometer has been used in an attempt to ascertain the presence of deafness in early life. Many speech and hearing centers now include equipment for the administration of the psychogalvanic skin resistance hearing test. Most psychologists are familiar with this type of testing, therefore it will not be described in detail here. Authorities differ relative to its validity and general clinical usefulness. On the basis of clinical experience and research it is becoming increasingly evident that face validity cannot be assumed in this test. For example, until further research evidence is available it must be stated that clinical experience suggests that the psychogalvanic skin resistance response varies in brain-injured, in psychotic, and deaf children. Furthermore, before validity is assumed it will be necessary to have considerably more data on normal children. At the present time it seems that even children who have no handicaps do not uniformly respond successfully to this test.

COUNSELING, GUIDANCE AND PSYCHOTHERAPY

The clinical psychologist in the hearing clinic, like many clinical psychologists in other settings, carries substantial responsibility for counseling, guidance and psychotherapy. These responsibilities fall primarily into three areas. He must counsel the parents of children with auditory disorders. The importance of this work cannot be questioned. Many of the parents who find themselves in the position of rearing a child with a handicap of this type are greatly confused and bewildered. Their problem of anxiety often is considerable. In some instances the experience of learning about their handicapped child is truly traumatic. This means that the parents frequently are in need not only of counseling and guidance, but of more formalized psychotherapy. It is not possible to deal adequately with the child without dealing with his parents. In certain instances the parents' problems are greater than those of the child in spite of his disabilities. The clinical psychologist assists in appraising these problems and carries major responsibility for the inauguration of a satisfactory program for the parents. In doing so he avails himself of the help of psychiatrists and psychiatric caseworkers. Often he is in a position in this connection to assist in developing a parents' group type of program which is now common in all areas of handicapped children. These parents' groups become an opportunity for group therapy. Therefore they require skillful, professional direction and assistance.

Another area in which the clinical psychologist carries responsibility for counseling, guidance and psychotherapy is with the individuals who have auditory disorders. Many people with deafness are in need of special guidance. These special needs are present throughout the life span of the individual. Special guidance is necessary during the preschool period, during school age, while assuming responsibilities in connection with employment, and when family obligations are assumed. One of the inherent aspects of a handicap is that it increases the dependency needs of the individual. Often it becomes the primary task of the clinical psychologist to help the person to accept these greater dependency needs rather than to rebel against them. In general, the counseling and psychotherapeutic aspects of the work with individuals having auditory disorders is of considerable consequence and importance.

The third aspect of the work in counseling, guidance and psychotherapy is that of assisting teachers and schools with the various types of problems which arise. These problems include a wide range, from peculiar learning and language disorders to superimposed problems of psychological maladjustment. It is common for the clinical psychologist in a hearing clinic to devote a certain amount of time to reports and to conferences dealing with the problems which arise in connection with the children with whom he has had previous contact and who are now in special schools.

There is a real need for further development in the area of counseling, guidance and psychotherapy of individuals with deafness and other types of auditory disorders. At the present time it is difficult to secure psychiatric assistance for deaf children and adults because most psychiatric procedures assume verbal facility and easy communication. The clinical psychologist in the hearing clinic therefore has an obligation to stimulate the development of nonverbal procedures for psychotherapy. Such procedures would include, especially, various types of play techniques for the lower age levels. When a child is severely limited in expressive and receptive language capacity it is necessary for him to express his attitudes and feelings through what he does. Likewise, it is necessary for him to respond to his needs through the use of toys and through other motor and visual means.

RESEARCH FUNCTIONS AND NEEDS

There are many opportunities for research in connection with the work of the clinical psychologist in the hearing clinic. This includes study of the psychology of sensory behavior and the psychology of language. In fact, the area of auditory behavior in general has been explored only casually. Its relationship to adjustment and maladjustment is not well understood. That audition plays a significant role in adjustment seems apparent. It is interesting to recall that hallucinations apparently are more auditory than they are visual. This problem might be understood more readily through further research on the nature of hearing and nonhearing. Furthermore, in the future it will be necessary to establish the developmental, maturational aspects of audition. This is a major need. More is known about the maturational aspects of vision than of hearing at this time. When the various maturational aspects of audition have been more rigorously established it will be possible to describe atypicalities in hearing more adequately.

Another area which warrants the research efforts of psychologists is that of auditory perception. Visual perception has been studied rather extensively over a long period of time. Auditory perception has been studied only meagerly. It can be expected that one of the primary progressive achievements during the ensuing years will be that of careful evaluation of auditory perceptual behavior and its relationship to human behavior in general. The psychopathology of auditory perception is clearly present and apparent to the clinical psychologist in the hearing clinic. Work in the hearing clinic also provides an opportunity to study the process of intersensory perception. Recently a study of the visual perception of deaf children revealed that the deaf child seems to perceive visually in a different manner than the child with normal hearing. This suggests that when sensory deprivation is present the sensory perceptual processes are shifted organismically. Perhaps this is one of the most challenging aspects of the problem presented by individuals with sensory deprivation.

While the clinical psychologist does not have responsibility for teaching of speech and speech reading, he does have responsibility for the study of these problems. It is apparent that individuals vary greatly with respect to the ease with which they can learn speech and learn to read the lips. A significant factor in this connection is the degree of hearing impairment. However, a certain number of individuals, with no residual capacity to hear, acquire speech and ability to read speech with much success while others do not. The study of speech and speech reading becomes a significant aspect of the total language and symbolic process related to the problems of deafness and other types of auditory disorders. Therefore, the clinical psychologist has an opportunity to conduct research also on these problems.

TRAINING FOR THE PSYCHOLOGIST IN THE HEARING CLINIC

The clinical psychologist in the hearing clinic has some specialized needs in regard to his background and training. An essential need is extensive training in child development and in the clinical psychology of children. In addition he needs training in the area of language development and in the psychopathology of language. He needs a background of training relative to the ear and its function. In general, this means that he needs a working knowledge of the field of otology. Some audiological training also is beneficial because this provides him with a background in the use of essential electronic equipment. It is reasonable to assume that clinical psychologists will increasingly become engaged in work with the auditorially handicapped. Clinics are being established routinely and various states are adding clinical psychologists to the staff of their schools for the deaf. It is apparent that this is an area of expansion of the clinical psychologist.

REFERENCES

1. Barker, R. G., Wright, B. A., Gonick, M. R., & Meyerson, L. Adjustments to physical handicap and illness. *Soc. Science Res. Council Bull.* (Rev. Ed.), 1953, 55, 1-440.
2. Davis, H. (Ed.) *Hearing and deafness.* New York: Murray Hill, 1947.
3. Doerfler, L., & Stewart, K. Malingering and psychogenic deafness. *J. Speech & Hearing Disorders*, 1946, 11, 181-186.
4. Eisenson, J. *Examining for aphasia.* New York: Psychological Corp., 1946.
5. Hardy, W. G., & Pauls, M. D. The test situation in PGSR audiometry. *J. Speech & Hearing Disorders*, 1952, 17, 13-24.
6. Hirsh, I. J. *The measurement of hearing.* New York: McGraw-Hill, 1952.
7. Hiskey, M. *Nebraska test of learning aptitude for young deaf children.* New York: Psychological Corp., 1941.
8. Myklebust, H. R. Differential diagnosis of deafness in young children. *J. excep. Child.,* 1951, 17, 97-101, 117.
9. Myklebust, H. R. Aphasia in children. *J. excep. Child.,* 1952, 19, 9-14.
10. Myklebust, H. R. Significance of etiology in motor performance of deaf children with special reference to meningitis. *Amer. J. Psychol.,* 1946, 59, 249-258.
11. Myklebust, H. R. & Burchard, E. M. L. A study of the effects of congenital and adventitious deafness on the intelligence, personality, and social maturity of school children. *J. educ. Psychol.,* 1945, 36, 321-343.
12. Myklebust, H. R. *Your deaf child, a guide for parents.* Springfield, Ill.: C. C. Thomas, 1950.
13. Myklebust, H. R. Research in the education and psychology of the deaf and hard-of-hearing. *J. educ. Res.,* 1947, 40, 598-607.
14. Myklebust, H. R. & Brutten, M. A study of the visual perception of deaf children. *Acta-Otolaryngologica, Supplementum,* 1953, 105, 1-126.
15. Pintner, R., Eisenson, J., & Stanton, M. *The psychology of the physically handicapped.* New York: F. S. Crofts, 1946.
16. Stevens, S. S., & Davis, H. *Hearing: its psychology and physiology.* New York: Wiley, 1938.
17. Strauss, A. A., & Lehtinen, L. E. *The brain-injured child.* Grune & Stratton, 1947.

XXVII.

THE CLINICAL PSYCHOLOGIST IN THE
SPEECH CLINIC

JOSEPH M. WEPMAN

The role of the clinical psychologist in the speech clinic can best be understood in terms of the relationship that exists between the two fields of clinical psychology and clinical speech correction. Speech clinics have been one of the newer areas of interest to clinical psychologists. The two fields have had roughly parallel development as clinical disciplines. The relationship between them, until very recently, was almost completely temporal, however. It is true that there are areas in which the two have had mutual interests, such as human behavior, growth and development in the child, and in specific interdisciplinary referrals for service. The speech clinics have, however, in their clinical activities, more often than not, expressed a philosophy based upon symptom reduction and motor-pattern training, while clinical psychologists have recognized and developed a more holistic viewpoint toward man and his problems. This difference in basic philosophy has, until quite recently, produced barriers to collaboration at the clinical level and to inevitable distinctions at the training level. Within the past decade, however, there has been a narrowing of the gap between the two, as speech clinicians have accepted a broader psychological orientation in their work.

Speech correction has grown from its major origin in the speech arts into a corrective, educational discipline; one designed to bring an individual's presenting pattern of communication closer to the standards of an exacting society. Growing from this expressed need, it has become a field devoted to one type of educational correction of recognized speech defects. It had devoted little or no time or effort to the individual as such, but considerable skill and research to his communicative efforts. As long as this predominant philosophy was held, the relationship between speech correction and psychology was tenuous, at best, and seen only in a limited number of clinics.

In more recent years, however, as clinical psychology has grown and as more holistic philosophies have been more widely accepted, the effect upon the field of speech correction has become notable. The two fields now seem to be striving for the same or similar goals. Note, in this respect, the following statement taken from the summary of the American Speech and Hearing Association's representatives at the Midcentury White House Conference in 1950. They held in part that:

1) Effective speech correction involves meaningful exploration of the specific needs of each child. . . .
2) It involves group instruction so far as possible, because speech is social behavior. . . .
3) It incorporates fully the time-tested laboratory findings of experimental psychology that we learn best to do that which we are most rewarded for doing. . . .
4) It is based on an appreciation of the close relationship between speech and personality, and so everything possible is done by the qualified speech correctionist to improve the personal adjustment of the child . . . [1, p. 137].

Thus, according to authorities in the field, speech correction has accepted a more definite psychological orientation. With this growing tendency to recognize that functioning individuals have many needs, the tendency to establish closer relationships between the two fields is growing. With this shift in point of view has come an expanding interest in and use of clinical psychology in each of its three traditional dimensions; diagnosis, research and therapy.

THE DIAGNOSTIC RELATIONSHIP

It is in the first of these areas, differential diagnosis, that some relationship between these two clinical areas has always existed. As the speech clinician searched for a wider knowledge of his patients, he most often called upon the psychologist's diagnostic skill to assist him. This was first most evident in the area of evaluation of the intellectual capacity of patients. That this remains as a continuing interest is attested by the number of referrals made to psychologists for this information, as well as the number of speech correctionists who have added the study of intelligence testing to their own training. With the passage of time and the development of projective tests, concomitant with the changing philosophy noted earlier, has come a growing demand for a broader knowledge of the patient under treatment. The tendency has been for speech clinics to expand their referral requests by asking for personality evaluations in addition to estimates of intelligence. The well-known complications of personality evaluation have usually limited this relationship to a referral one, since, in most cases it has been impossible for speech clinicians to secure sufficient training to make their own projective analyses.

These numerous referrals have led to the development of a much closer relationship between the two fields. An extension of this area of differential diagnosis as a meeting place of common interest and co-operation has led to the not infrequent use of clinical psychologists as part of the diagnostic team in many speech clinics. The psychologist is playing an increasingly important role, especially in large hospital and university speech clinics, where many professional disciplines consider each case on its merits as determined by extensive diagnostic procedures.

In some such clinics, the psychologist is often seen as a member of the speech clinic staff. In others, he functions through a separate service contributing his diagnostic skills on individuals with speech problems, just as he does on individuals with other problems, as they occur throughout the over-all clinical program. More specifically, clinical psychologists are now taking an increasing part in the differential diagnosis of speech problems in those clinics operated separately from other clinics. This is especially true where the speech clinic is autonomous and physically apart from other clinics as in some of our major universities.[1]

Through his diagnostic skill, therefore, the psychologist is in growing demand in speech clinics. As the result of these contacts he has brought to them an ever-broadening concept of the individual and has assisted in bringing about a changing philosophy toward differential diagnosis of speech defects. It will be seen later that psychology has had a similar effect upon both research and therapy in speech clinics.

THE RESEARCH RELATIONSHIP

Research is the second of the major contributions of clinical psychology and is one of increasing importance to such professional services as speech clinics. The psychologist's training in research design, in statistics and in scientific method generally, is rapidly becoming of immediate interest to speed therapists. The history of research in speech and speech correction is replete with descriptive discussions of presenting speech problems. Coincident to the acceptance of a more psychologically oriented viewpoint in the general philosophy of these clinics has come the recognition that research, like diagnosis, requires specialized training and understanding of more than the presenting problem.

As the concept of therapy for the whole person has gained wider acceptance, the need to study the individual in relation to his communication difficulty has been recognized. The speech clinician has more and more turned to research reported by psychologists. In addition to a broader reading of psychological literature there has been a decided trend

[1] An example of such a clinic is to be seen at Northwestern University in Evanston, Illinois.

toward accepting the increased relationship by the publication of articles by psychologists in the professional journal of the American Speech & Hearing Association. A brief survey of the speech therapist's quarterly, the *Journal of Speech & Hearing Disorders,* shows that in the 1948 volume only six of forty-eight articles were authored in whole or in part by psychologists. In the 1952 volume, however, twelve of thirty-nine articles had such authorship. This increase from 12 per cent to 31 per cent seems indicative of the increased relationship commented upon earlier. Typical of this psychological emphasis are articles on various methods of psychological measurement in speech correction (2, 13, 16, 20) and consideration of various aspects of personality and personality disturbance in persons with speech defects (3, 5, 6, 18).

The research contribution of the psychologist in the field of speech correction is a much needed one. From the stated increase of articles by psychologists related to speech clinics and speech correction in the professional journals, it appears that that interest is now being displayed on a growing scale. Naturally, as the fields show this increasing interest in each other's work, the tendency for them to interact will become a more common one.

THE THERAPY RELATIONSHIP

The psychologist can and should play an important role in the therapy offered in speech clinics. Naturally, as the holistic concept of man is more widely accepted, the therapist most sought after is one whose training prepares him to deal with the basic needs of patients. As the problems seen in speech clinics are more frequently diagnosed in terms of the total personality of the patients, the presence of psychogenic disorders underlying the communication efforts are more often recognized. That they produce the observable symptoms called speech defects has gained more widespread acceptance. The clinical psychologist, equipped as he is to deal with this phase of a problem, finds himself well able to function in a speech clinic. This therapeutic effort takes many forms at the present and may best be seen in certain types of problems commonly seen in such clinics.

First, the presenting speech problem may be determined, through differential diagnosis, to be primarily psychogenic, as in the problem of aphonia for example. Here, the presenting problem is a loss of voice. The differential diagnosis usually determines the causality. If organic or physical reasons for the loss of voice have been eliminated by the physician, the psychological character of the problem remains as a necessary probability. However, voice problems, non-organic in etiology, may result from misuse of the mechanism due to occupational misuse (as in singer's nodes) or may be a conversion symptom. Following the differential diagnosis, the treatment determined by it may well fall into the category of psychotherapy or, as has proven to be the case so many times, may require a collaborative therapy. The speech pathologist may well be needed to assist the patient in producing a normal voice by training procedures, while the psychotherapist may be needed to assist the patient in gaining an understanding of the forces which have made the misuse of the larynx and consequent loss of voice essential to him. Where the therapist is both clinical psychologist and speech pathologist this problem may result in a single therapeutic effort. However, where the two disciplines are separately practiced, two collaborating therapists may produce the better approach.

The need for such collaborative therapy is equally well demonstrated in other problems. For many years, for example, stuttering has been a treatment problem for the speech pathologist. While no statistical results are available as to the best form of therapy, educative or psychotherapeutic, there seems to be a marked tendency today to recognize that the approach of choice may be dual in nature. Certain motor aspects of stuttering seem to respond well to speech therapy. Anxiety and tension concerning the inability to produce rhythmical speech may respond best to psychotherapy. The combination of good speech therapy and good psychotherapy seems, to this writer, to be the most acceptable method to be employed. Again, a therapist possessing both skills would seem to be the one best suited to treat stutterers. Yet, in actual practice this may be more difficult than it appears by the very nature of the relationship necessary between the patient and the therapist. Collaborative therapy using the skills and techniques of both the psychologist and the speech pathologist often appears to be most satisfactory. Stuttering as a type of communication problem still presents one of the more difficult of all individual symptoms and the combined efforts of psychologists and speech pathologists in diagnosis, in research, and in therapy are still very much needed.

One more example demonstrates still another facet of the use of psychologists in a speech clinic. The child developing speech frequently passes through a period of what appears to be delay in acceptable articulation. While this is recognized by most people as a passing problem dependent upon the maturation of the child, the general tendency to accept statistical norms as presented in such studies as Gesell's (9) makes anxious parents even more concerned about their children. When these children fall into the slower-developing part of the distribution of all children, parents tend to become over anxious and to transmit this anxiety to their children. Thus, therapy with the parents of children who are slow in developing speech or slow in developing good articulation of speech is a constant need in a speech clinic. The role of the psychologist becomes apparent. In one clinic known to the present writer, children are not accepted for speech therapy unless the parents enter a group for parent therapy.[2] This combination of events, with the psychologist handling the parent group, and the speech pathologist, the children's group (or the children individually), has resulted in what is believed to be a most successful approach to the problem.

Thus, in therapy the psychologist can play a very real and significant role in the speech clinic using his skill as a therapist without needing to be a speech pathologist. His skill and training in assisting patients in gaining insights into their own, as well as into the problems of others, is not only a necessary part of good clinical procedure, but a vital part in over-all speech therapy. As this role gains wider recognition, the opportunity for clinical psychologists in speech clinics increases as does the demand for psychologists.

APHASIA CLINICS

A special case in point for the clinical psychologist in the speech clinic setting is the problem presented by the patient suffering from language defects consequent to brain injury. This is a comparatively new area which has had its greatest impetus in the past ten years. During World War II the need to assist in the rehabilitation of brain-injured soldiers was faced by the speech pathologists brought into service by the medical department of the U. S. Army. In some centers the work went forward on a speech re-education basis. Speech therapists and others using direct training techniques were responsible for the language therapy. Usually, in these centers, aphasia was diagnosed as a speech problem exclusively. In other centers, however, the over-all need for readjustment was recognized, and clinical psychologists became an integral part of the diagnostic and therapeutic team.

Thus, in one aphasia center the following description of the use of clinical psychologists was reported:

The psychologists were used in two capacities. As psychometricians they administered three types of examinations: (a) tests of intelligence designed at the onset of training to give information concerning the areas in which the patients could function at their highest level and areas in which the patients showed their greatest disability; (b) tests of personality which indicated the areas of psychological adjustment and maladjustment of the individual patients; (c) tests of educational achievement which indicated the levels of the patients in the various areas in which they needed re-education. Added to these objective tests were screening meas-

2 The University of Chicago Speech Clinic.

urements of the patient's language involvement given by the writer. These tests were used both diagnostically and for planning the individual re-education programs.

The second function of the psychological staff was in the area of individual and group therapy. The psychological well-being of each patient was considered of primary importance. In only one case where an organic psychosis existed was it necessary to call upon the psychiatric staff for assistance. In the beginning, the therapy was supervised by the chief psychiatrist; as experience was gained by the psychological staff, this supervision was limited to voluntary conferences between the psychologists and the chief psychiatrist [21, p. 407].

Psychologists have taken a more and more essential part in some of the aphasia programs instituted since the war. For many years psychologists have been interested in attempting to understand and define the effects of brain damage (7, 8, 14). Others interested in the function of the cortex have done much work with the brain-injured patient as well as with related animal research (10, 11). As language loss became recognized as just one of the after effects of brain injury and that the aphasic patients suffered from all of the common psychological ills subsequent to cortical trauma, the overlap between the research contribution of the psychologist and the therapeutic efforts of the speech pathologists became evident.

Psychologists have contributed in a major way, also, to diagnostic procedures with the brain-injured patient. They have devised aphasia tests and developed research bearing on the therapeutic problem presented by the aphasic patient (12). In therapy as well, the psychologist's grasp of the over-all problem of personal readjustment has been appreciated, and today treatment for aphasia has become a problem recognized as being best handled by a therapeutic team rather than a single therapist (22).

Thus, in a recent book on aphasia therapy the point is stressed that psychological considerations must have a prominent place in the care of such patients. It is held by the author, that "it is often necessary to work through a patient's behavior pattern with him. A recognition on his part of his problem and an opportunity to ventilate his feelings concerning it often assist him in resolving it" (22, p. 107).

Direct research into such areas as: (1) the aphasic patient's ability to learn new material, (2) the relationship between social readjustment and language recovery, (3) the value of group psychotherapy with aphasic patients, and (4) the additional values of group therapy with the families of aphasic patients, are among a host of problems now being studied. Most of the questions arising in the field of aphasia therapy are the product of psychologists and speech therapists working empirically with

aphasic patients in speech clinics. Their solution lies in the research
programs established in different centers by teams of speech therapists
and clinical psychologists.

In this area, aphasia diagnosis and treatment, probably more than in
any other single facet of the existing speech clinic, is the role of the
clinical psychologist best defined. Here the need for both psychologists
and speech therapists was often widely recognized from the onset and
where that was true the two fields have gone forward more or less
together.

THE TRAINING RELATIONSHIP

A final indication of the growing trend toward interrelation between
the two fields, which should eventually dissipate most of the early barriers
against full co-operation, is to be seen in the curricula offered in universities and colleges where both speech and psychology are taught. In some
schools,[3] psychology courses are required for every speech pathologist.[4]
In many other schools, minors in speech correction are available for
psychology students, and minors in psychology can be elected by students
in speech correction.[5] In still other schools, basic instruction in speech
correction is a part of the required training for every clinical psychologist.[6]

Textbooks frequently used in psychology courses have likewise recognized the interdisciplinary rapport that is necessary. Thus, to mention
only a few, Louttit (17) in his general text on clinical psychology, and
Landis and Bolles (15) in their book on abnormal psychology, both
include full chapters on disorders of speech. While in books of reference
such as Burton & Harris (4), *Case Histories in Clinical and Abnormal
Psychology,* one of the cases discussed is that of a speech problem.

The interaction at the training level as well as in the common literature produces a growing mutual recognition of needs in the two fields.
Clinical psychologists with their broad training relative to man's problems are becoming indoctrinated in the importance of communication.
Certainly, the psychologist with an orientation to speech and to speech
defects will find the warmest welcome in the speech clinics discussed here.
At the training level, then, there is a noted tendency for a closer relationship both in the courses offered and in the textbooks used.

CONCLUSION

Speech correction as a specialized field dealing with one part, albeit
an important one, of human behavior, is slowly, but definitely, recog-

---

3 The following are intended as examples, only.
4 Purdue University.
5 University of Iowa.
6 University of Chicago.

nizing the need for the skills and training of the clinical psychologist. As time goes on an ideal rapprochement can be visualized where every speech pathologist functioning independently in a speech clinic will have the background and training of a clinical psychologist. Oppositely, the very importance of verbal communication and the ills that can befall a person when this ability is less than adequate, points to the need for an understanding of speech and language by every clinical psychologist.

The role of the clinical psychologist in the speech clinic extends from differential diagnosis through research and therapy. His ability to function collaboratively with other clinicians, contributing his psychological insights as well as his skills to the problems inherent in such a field as speech correction, are becoming more apparent. The day is approaching when speech-oriented clinical psychologists will be as numerous as psychologically oriented speech pathologists are now becoming. When this day comes, every speech clinic will utilize clinical psychologists, since both fields will have a single common goal—the understanding of man's behavior in his ability to communicate.

REFERENCES

1. American Speech and Hearing Association, Committee on the Midcentury White House Conference. Speech disorders and speech correction. *J. Speech & Hearing Disorders*, 1952, 17, 129-137.
2. Berlinsky, S. Measurement of the intelligence and personality of the deaf. *J. Speech & Hearing Disorders*, 1952, 17, 39-54.
3. Bryngelson, B. Personnel counseling and the speech clinic. *J. Speech & Hearing Disorders*, 1948, 13, 107-113.
4. Burton, A., & Harris, R. E. (Eds.) *Case histories in clinical and abnormal psychology.* New York: Harpers, 1947.
5. Dub, A. Great psychological effects of a minor speech defect. *J. Speech & Hearing Disorders*, 1948, 13, 251-255.
6. Fiedler, F., & Wepman, J. An exploratory investigation of the self-concept of stutterers. *J. Speech & Hearing Disorders*, 1951, 16, 110-114.
7. Fulton, J. F. *Frontal lobotomy and affective behavior.* New York: Norton, 1951.
8. Garfield, S., & Fey, W. F. A comparison of the Wechsler-Bellevue and Shipley Hartford Scales as measures of mental impairment. *J. consult. Psychol.*, 1948, 12, 259-264.
9. Gesell, A. et al. *The first five years of life.* New York: Harpers, 1940.
10. Goldstein, K. *After effects of brain injuries in war.* New York: Grune & Stratton, 1942.
11. Halstead, W. *Brain and intelligence.* Chicago: University of Chicago Press, 1947.
12. Halstead, W., & Wepman, J. The Halstead-Wepman Aphasia Test. *J. Speech & Hearing Disorders*, 1949, 14, 9-15.
13. Hawk, S. S. Personality measurement in speech correction. *J. Speech & Hearing Disorders*, 1948, 13, 307-312.
14. Hunt, H. Testing for psychological deficit. In Brower, D., & Abt, L. (Eds.). *Progress in clinical psychology.* New York: Grune & Stratton, 1952, 91-107.
15. Landis, C., & Bolles, M. M. *Textbook of abnormal psychology.* New York: Macmillan, 1946.
16. Lewis, D., & Sherman, D. Measuring the severity of stuttering. *J. Speech & Hearing Disorders*, 1951, 16, 320-326.

17. Louttit, C. M. *Cinical psychology.* New York: Harpers, 1936.
18. Mowrer, O. H. Speech development in the young child: I. The autism theory of speech development and some clinical applications. *J. Speech & Hearing Disorders,* 1952, 17, 263-269.
19. Myklebust, H. The relationship between clinical psychology and audiology. *J. Speech & Hearing Disorders,* 1949, 14, 98-103.
20. Myklebust, H. The use of clinical psychological screening techniques by audiologists and speech pathologists. *J. Speech & Hearing Disorders,* 1950, 15, 129-134.
21. Wepman, J. The organization of therapy for aphasia. *J. Speech & Hearing Disorders,* 1947, 12, 405-409.
22. Wepman, J. *Recovery from aphasia.* New York: Ronald Press, 1951.

INDEX